Imperial Revenue, Expenditure and Monetary Policy in the Fourth Century A.D.

The Fifth Oxford Symposium on Coinage and Monetary History

edited by

C. E. King

B A R International Series 76
1980

B.A.R.

B.A.R., 122 Banbury Road, Oxford OX2 7BP, England

B. A. R. International Series 76, 1980: "Imperial Revenue, Expenditure and Monetary Policy in the Fourth Century A. D.".

ISBN 9780860540847 paperback
ISBN 9781407350943 e-book
DOI https://doi.org/10.30861/9780860540847
A catalogue record for this book is available from the British Library
This book is available at www.barpublishing.com

CONTENTS

Preface

The fifth Oxford symposium on coinage and monetary history, the first to concern itself with the ancient world, was held at Wolfson College on 28-30 September 1979. A small group of historians, archaeologists, and numismatists met to reconsider some of the problems concerning the economic history of the fourth century A.D. We hoped that by pooling our various skills and interests we might reach a clearer notion of the functioning and management of the economy in those years. Although many of the major issues still resist an easy solution, by the end of the symposium the participants found that their understanding of most of the subjects discussed had been deepened. Given the controversy that bedevils so many areas of fourth century economic history we felt this was no mean achievement and more than compensated for the time and effort needed to prepare our papers.

The studies in this volume represent the authors' conclusions reached after independent research and mutual discussion. The debt each of the contributors owes to the others and the symposium as a whole is self evident. Not all of the views expressed are "orthodox" but perhaps it is orthodoxy which is in need of redefinition in some instances.

All of the participants felt they had benefited greatly from the multi-disciplinary approach to the study of the economic history of the later Roman empire. Too often historians, archaeologists and numismatists have concentrated on specialized research within their own area and have made little or no attempt to interpret their findings in a broader context. Since the expressed purpose of all of the Oxford symposia has been to encourage an interdisciplinary approach to economic and monetary history in specific periods, it was satisfying to discover how valuable insights from students in other fields could be.

C. E. K.

ABBREVIATIONS

A Ant Hung	- Acta Antiqua Academiae Scientiarum Hungaricae
Acta Arch Hung	- Acta Archeologica Academiae Scientiarum Hungaricae
Administration	- J. Lallemand, <u>L'Administration civile de l'Egypte de l'avènement de Dioclétien à la création du diocèse 284-382</u>, Brussels, 1964.
Amer Journ Anc Hist	- American Journal of Ancient History
Ann Soc Arch Namur	- Annales de la Société Archéologique de Namur
Annales (ESC)	- Annales (Economie, Sociétés, Civilisations)
Annali Ist Ital di Numismatica	- Annali Istituto Italiano di Numismatica
ANRW	- Aufstieg und Niedergang der Römischen Welt
Arch Ert	- Archaeológiai Értesitö
Arch J	- The Archaeological Journal
Armées et fiscalité	- Armées et Fiscalité dans le monde antique, CNRS, Paris, 1977
Atti Acc Naz Lincei	= NSA
BAR	- British Archaeological Reports
BASP	- Bulletin of the American Society of Papyrologists
Bayer Vorgeschichtsblätter	- Bayerische Vorgeschichtsblätter
BIAB	- Bulletin de l'Institut Archéologique Bulgare
BJ	- Bonner Jahrbücher
BlätterfurMünzfr	- Blätter fur Münzfreunde
BMCRE	- British Museum, Coins of the Roman Empire in the British Museum
BollNum	- Bollettino Numismatico
BSFN	- Bulletin de la Société Française de Numistique
BSoc Arch Varna	- Bulletin de la Société Archéologique à Varna
Bull Cercle d'Et Num	= CENB
Byzantinobulg	- Byzantinobulgarica

Cah Alsaciens d'Arch d'Art et d'Hist	- Cahiers Alsaciens d'Archéologie, d'Art et d'Histoire
Capitation	- A. Déléage La Capitation du Bas-Empire, Macon, 1945
CE	- Chronique d'Egypte
CENB	- Cercle des Etudes Numismatiques, Bulletin
CSL	- J. P. C. Kent, The Office of Comes Sacrarum Largitionum (Ph D thesis, unpub.) London 1951
DAI	- Deutsches Archäologisches Institut
D'ARCH	- Dialoghi di Archeologia
Devaluations	- Les dévaluations à Rome, Collection de l'école française de Rome, 37, 1978
ERW	- F. Millar, The Emperor in the Roman World, 1977
Essays H. Mattingly	- R. A. G. Carson, C. H. V. Sutherland (eds.) Essays in Roman Coinage presented to Harold Mattingly, Oxford, 1956, 190ff.
FMRO	- Die Fundmünzen der römischen Zeit in Osterreich
FMRD	- Die Fundmünzen der römischen Zeit in Deutschland
Folia Arch	- Folia Archeologica
GRBS	- Greek Roman and Byzantine Studies
HA Colloq	- Historia Augusta Colloquium
HSCP	- Harvard Studies in Classical Philology
Jb Num	- Jahrbuch für Numismatik und Geldgeschichte
JEA	- Journal of Egyptian Archeology
J Ec Hist	- Journal of Economic History
JJP	- Journal of Juristic Papyrology
JNG	- Jahrbuch für Numismatik und Geldgeschichte
JRS	- Journal of Roman Studies
LRE	- A. H. M. Jones, The Later Roman Empire
Met Script Rel	- F. Jultsch, Metrologicorum Scriptorum Reliquae, Leipzig, 1864
Mitt Num Gesell in Wien	- Mitteilungen der Osterrichischen Numismatischen Gesellschaft

MM	- Münzen und Medaillen
NC	- Numismatic Chronicle
NK	- Numismatikai Közlöny
NSA	- Notizie degli Scavi di Antichità
NZ	- Numismatische Zeitschrift
PCPhS	- Proceedings of the Cambridge Philological Society
PLRE	- A. H. M. Jones, J. R. Martindale, J. Morris, The Prosopography of the Later Roman Empire, Cambridge, 1971
Politique Monétaire	- J. P. Callu, La politique monétaire des empereurs romains de 238 à 311, Bib. Ec. Fr. Rome, 214, 1969
PSAS	- Proceedings of the Society of Antiquaries of Scotland
PWRE	- Pauly Wissowa Real Encyclopädie der Classischen Altertumswissenschaft
Quaderni Ticinesi	- Quaderni Ticinesi Numismatica e Antichità
RA Est	- Revue archéologique de l'Est et du Centre-Est
RBN	- Revue Belge de Numismatique et de Sigillographie
RE	- A. H. M. Jones, The Roman Economy, Blackwell, 1974
Reps Res Com Soc Ants 31	- D. S. Neal, The Excavations of the Roman Villa in Gadebridge Park, Hemel Hempstead 1963-8 (Reports of the Research Committee of the Society of Antiquaries of London, 31, 1974)
Rev Phil	- Revue Philologique
RFC	- Rivista de Filologia e di Istruzione Classica
RH	- Revue Historique
RhMus	- Rheinisches Museum für Philologie
RIC	- The Roman Imperial Coinage
RIN	- Rivista Italiana di Numismatica
RN	- Revue Numismatique
RSN	- SNR
SCMB	- Seaby's Coin and Medal Bulletin

SCN	Studii şi Cercetări de Numismatică
SMB	Schweizer Münzblätter
SNR	Schweizerische Numismatische Rundschau
Staat und Manufaktur	A. Persson, Staat und Manufaktur im römischen Reiche, Lund, 1925
Studia Arch Valladolid	Valladolid Univ. Dep. de prehistoria-Estudia Romana
Studii şi Cercetări	Studii şi Cercatări Istorie veche şi Arheologie
Taxation in Egypt	S. L. Wallace, Taxation in Egypt from Augustus to Diocletian, Princeton, 1938
VHAD	Vjesnik Hrvatskoga Arheóloškoga Društva
YAJ	Yorkshire Archaeological Journal
ZPE	Zeitschrift für Papyrologie und Epigraphik

INFLATION AND THE ECONOMY IN THE FOURTH CENTURY A.D.

C. R. Whittaker

In a brief reference in A treatise on money (II.151) J. M. Keynes remarked on "the coincidence that the decline and fall of Rome was contemporaneous with the most prolonged and drastic deflation (my ital.) yet recorded"; but in a footnote he observed that the scarcity of precious metals, which he himself adjudged to be the source of deflation, was currently disputed by leading scholars. "The subject" he added tantalisingly, "may deserve re-examination".[1]

This seems to me typical of the contradictions, paradoxes and confusion which surround almost every facet of the economic and monetary history of the later Roman empire. Just what is it we are talking about? Inflation or deflation? Straightaway therefore I may make my first point that, regardless of whether Keynes was right or wrong about the shortage of gold, the context in which he was writing makes it clear that he was referring here primarily to profit and commodity deflation, whereas my concern in this paper is mainly with an income inflation in the fourth century A.D.

This paper is constructed in two parts, perhaps artificially, some may think, since the subject of economic decline in the Roman empire of the fourth century can be, and often is, discussed without reference to any monetary aspect at all. On the other hand, in this day and age, when inflation is always central to any economic analysis, to have ignored it would have been perverse, particularly when the subject is so much a part of every numismatic history of the period. The general aim therefore here is to enquire whether inflation does indeed have any importance for a comprehension of the economy of the late empire; and if not, then why not.

The conclusions I have come to, after grappling with the refinements and paradoxes of monetary history, while at the same time trying to fit them into the matrix of the general economic scene—which itself is less than clear-cut—are not, I confess, dramatic. They are:

(i) that inflation, if it can be called such, deserved its neglect by economic historians. That was more or less the response given by A. H. M. Jones to Rudi Thomsen at the 3rd International Economic History Conference at Stockholm in 1965;[2] and fourteen years on I believe he was right;

(ii) that there is nevertheless a sense in which it is important to understand why inflation was unimportant. In so doing one gains an insight into the economic relationship between gold and commodities;

(iii) that inflation was not the cause of decline in productivity; and indeed there was not an obvious decline, despite the pressures of imperial fiscal policy: but I do concede some decline in the commodity market;

(iv) that the cost of the army and the bureaucracy were not the economic millstone which sank the Roman empire; or at least the argument will not stand tout court like that. What I have tried to clarify is why the economic resources of the empire which were there could not be mobilised in times of military crisis.

INFLATION, GOLD AND THE ECONOMY

There is a fundamental problem at the outset in discussing monetary history and inflation. Contrary, I think, to the assumptions of some numismatists that monetary changes which took place in the third and fourth centuries were bound to have had a radical and disasterous effect upon prices, wages and (to quote one recent writer) "the whole fabric throughout the empire",[3] the work of Lopez, Corbier and others has demonstrated that debasements in coinage were not necessarily economic events at all, and certainly not economic disasters.[4] In discussing whether what he calls picturesquely the "debauchment of the currency" caused the fall of Rome, J. K. Galbraith notes that the theory partakes of a long historiographic tendency "to attach vast adverse consequences to monetary behaviour of which the observer happens to disapprove"... a tendency which, he says, "should, needless to say, be regarded with the utmost suspicion,"[5]

(a) Let me start with fiduciary coinage. Bruun in RIC VII states unequivocally that "the fourth-century bronze coinage was non-fiduciary,"[6] for otherwise, he says, we could not understand why the price of gold against the bronze coinage should rise in the course of the century. Some numismatists seem to agree,[7] others to disagree[8] with equal fervour in what one might call purely numismatic arguments about the relative weights, metallic standards and face values of coins concerning which very little is actually known.

The debate should be ended. If, as we now know from Diocletian's Currency Reform of 301, the potentia of a coin could be set by imperial fiat and even doubled overnight;[9] and if, as we knew long ago from Licinius' actions in the 320s, the face value of a nummus could be halved,[10] then it is surely indisputable that the main subsidiary coinage of the fourth century, whatever it had once been, and however close the intrinsic value of the billon and bronze was to its face value, was by the fourth century fully accepted in principle as token money. This did not reduce its role as what is called "commodity money"—that is, it still functioned as if it were intrinsically valued as long as it was guaranteed against commodities (usually gold), but the intrinsic value was irrelevant to its activity as a medium of circulation.

How such an absolute separation between intrinsic and commodity money came about in the third century is not my concern. A gradual debasement by the use of metal alloys rather than a sudden diminution in the size of the coins probably indicates the conservatism of a market which had always tended to measure coins by their intrinsic metal weight. I do not suppose emperors knew what they were about.[11] But the point about commodity money is that, once the separation has taken place, its value thereafter depends on its scarcity and the amount of precious metal it represents. Roman emperors constantly and vainly believed that if they reformed the subsidiary circulating pieces by making bigger and better coins they could halt the market tendency to reject their tokens. But since the face value of the coins was always more than their cost of production, and since the state made little or no attempt to restrict their issue, the circulating value constantly moved towards a dependency on the quantity in current use, regardless of any intrinsic value coins may have possessed. In explaining this characteristic of monetary behaviour Marx and Keynes were in complete agreement.[12]

(b) In this respect the subsidiary coinage behaved quite different from gold, regardless of what emperors may have hoped.[13] For, gold is itself a commodity with its own value.[14] Clipped or over-valued coins would have simply forced the market price of the metal above the face value of the coins, taking with it all other prices. That is what happened to the silver coinage in the reign of William III in England, provoking the wrath of John Locke who exclaimed, "But 'tis silver and not names that pay debts and purchase commodities".[15]

From the relative stability of gold commodity prices in the fourth century, I conclude that even if there were some attempts to overvalue gold coin for short term fiscal gain, such as a controversial text of a Constantinian law might suggest, they were bound to be short-lived and in the end emperors were forced to restore public confidence by stamping the guarantee of purity and weight on the coins.[16]

(c) What follows from this is that the so-called inflation of the fourth century was a straightforward example of the over-issue of token money, which only reduced the value of the token and changed nothing but the name of the coin (denarius, antoninianus, maiorina, centenionalis, etc.). That, on the whole, seems to me to be the lesson to be learnt from Callu's recent study of the search for an acceptable bronze nummus in the fourth century. Despite the fact that there was "a certain equilibrium of coinage", the value of successive copper pieces would not remain stable.[17] Clearly it is difficult to be certain that price rises were not sometimes triggered by official over-valuing of gold in the manner just described. But they were not permanent. If the general trend of Egyptian old denarii prices is anything to go by—and they are to some extent confirmed by Syrian, Palestinian and Italian prices—the period of fastest change was from 324 to the 360s, with a sharp jump after the 350s. Thereafter there was a slowing down, especially in the 380s and 390s,[18] with some evidence that after 395 bronze values almost stabilized.[19] It is no coincidence that this equilibrium occurred after bronze coinage had been restricted for some time since the reign of Valentinian I, when one of the main bronze series was withdrawn (whether the maiorina or not) and soon after a gold fractional coinage had been introduced.[20] The reason for the equilibrium, in other words, was not because "there was sufficient gold"[21] to meet the economic needs of the empire but because the subsidiary circulating medium had been reduced more nearly to the quantity of gold in circulation.

Why there should have been such fluctuations earlier is a matter of speculation and I am inclined to think it was mostly a matter of chance. The most obvious answer would be that, just as in the third century, so in the first half of the fourth, emperors and pretenders financed their large and numerous armies throughout the wars of succession by unplanned debasement and issue of the subsidiary coinage from a plethora of mints.[22] By contrast, after the emergence of Constantius II and Julian as undisputed rulers of a united empire in the 360s, troops were more centrally controlled, mints were closed down and the quantity of copper fell in relation to gold.[23]

(d) On the question of the quantity of gold, there seem to me to be very real problems about interpretation of the evidence and hence what economic conclusions are to be drawn. According to Jones, for instance, rising prices caused by inflation and the overissue of debased coins, must have driven gold out of circulation; until that is, it was prised out of hoards by fiscal measures in the fourth century—and clearly that is a persuasive possibility. Yet, as Jones himself notes, third century hoards are conspicuously lacking in gold, and it has recently been suggested by Veyne that enough old gold of previous epochs was circulating to satisfy exchange if one adds the few third century issues which were struck but subsequently recalled and restruck in the fourth century.[24] In other words, the absence of coins in hoards and the paucity of strikes is no guide to the circulation of gold.

If that is true, as I believe possible, then it raises the cognate question of the circulation of gold in the course of the fourth century. From the prices in Seaby's catalogue for 1964, for instance, it appears that after the vota xxx issue of Constantius II (i.e. post 354) until the reign of Theodosius gold in hoards is about three times as common as in the earlier half of the century.[25] Again two possibilities present themselves: either gold was actually circulating more freely from the 360s onwards—"an age of gold", as it is sometimes called; or gold was going out of circulation into reserves, as I think more likely. The point of importance, of course, is, What was the mass of gold in circulation? It is the same question one asks about the so-called "haemorrhage" of gold beyond the frontiers or the current production of the mines, which respectively take gold out of circulation or put gold back in. For it is only with this information that one can really make calculations about commodities and markets, if we are to follow the celebrated equation of Irving Fisher which says that P(rices) x Q(uantity of commodities) = M(ass of gold) x V(elocity of circulation).

In this connection therefore, it is naturally of some importance that, despite the enormous unreliability of the figures we possess, there seems to be general agreement among historians, since the publication of the Aezani fragment of Diocletian's Price Edict, that the price of commodities against gold maintained an astonishing—not to say suspicious—stability throughout the fourth century, and indeed from the early empire.[26] Since in our period it is unlikely that velocity of exchange differed greatly (although one must obviously expect some variation) this ought logically to mean that the quantity of gold and commodities, as the two remaining variables of the equation, roughly reflected each other in the fourth century. Any decline in one should be an indicator of the other.

(e) If I am correct about the equilibrium of fourth century gold prices and the apparent increasing thesaurisation of gold of the second half of the century, how are we then to interpret the evidence which says that Constantine suddenly liberated gold in significant quantities from confiscated temple treasures or that there was a massive haemorrhage of gold beyond the frontiers throughout the period?

The most frequently quoted evidence about Constantine comes from the anonymous writer of the de rebus bellicis who accused the emperor of issuing gold in such lavish quantities as to make it like copper in commercial transactions—profusa largitio aurum pro aere ... vilibus commerciis assignavit (2.1). Obviously this is an exaggeration and may in fact be no more than the author's prejudiced and simplistic account of Constantine's act of introducing the smaller, light-weight solidus.[27] Raiding the treasures of temples was a stereotyped charge against bad emperors (cf. Hdn. VII 3.5, against Maximinus), doubtless also often true, since temples provided a tempting store of public and private resources. But it is worth noting that Julian, in his encomium of Constantius II (Or. 1.8b) contradicted what he later alleged about Constantine's temple raids by attributing some of the gold not to temples but to the reserves in the imperial treasury of Maxentius. Obviously therefore the event needs to be treated with some prudence. For our purposes however it does not particularly matter what the source of the gold was, and in the end it seems impossible to resist the united chorus of Eusebius, Libanius and later Christian historians that there really was an increase in the circulation of gold. On the other hand, as I have said, gold prices did not drop; nor, as far as one can judge, did gold go directly back into hoards. Ammianus and Zosimus, who never lost a chance to attack Constantine's avarice or his lavish gifts to his friends, made no comment at all about his making prices rise.[28] I therefore draw the conclusion that the increased quantity of gold in circulation reflects an increase in commodity exchange and a period of some prosperity in the earlier half of the fourth century, as a number of our sources claim—fortunatus caeli temperie, fructuum proventu (Epit. de Caes. 41.24).

As to the "haemorrhage", there is a moral fervour that attaches to the distaste ancient writers felt about paying gold to barbarians, which recurs throughout Roman history. Accumulation of texts therefore will not quantify the phenomenon but simply prove that it happened in the third and fourth centuries as before.[29] There was a historiographic tendency in earlier epochs to describe as a scandal what turn out to be non-events[30] and the chances of the same being true in this period must be taken into account. No economic conclusion can therefore be drawn from ritual legislation c. 374 to prohibit the export of gold (CJ IV.63.2). If there was difficulty about the mines in Armenia and the Balkans in meeting the needs of the eastern empire alone, the Spanish mines, particularly those of Gallaecia and Lusitania, appear to have done well in the fourth century in producing metal and emperors—pretiosa metallis, principibus fecunda piis (Claud. laus Serenae 54.5). How well, is impossible to say, since we know nothing about the balance of production against export.[31] Payment of gold to barbarian gentiles and federates in the latter part of the century would not, of course, have necessarily affected circulation; though this may have been partly responsible for a preference by the state for the aurarius canon in the 380s and 390s to the annona levy.[32] We can however presume that barbarians frequently made purchases as well as sales. Very little gold has turned up on Persian or trans-Danubian archaeological sites and Goths, it seems, had an irresistible taste for Roman wine.[33]

* * * *

That concludes what might be called an historian's eye-view of the tangled world of monetarism. My main conclusion is to confirm Mazzarino's dictum that, "Monetary phenomena are not enough to determine a crisis".[34] So far, I would add, it is not entirely obvious that there even was a crisis, although I have hinted that the thesaurisation of gold in the latter half of the fourth century does provide some clue to what was taking place—a decline in commodity exchange after a period of some activity. The rest of the paper therefore is devoted to a brief examination of three aspects of the economy in the fourth century, which rightly or wrongly have been associated with inflation: that is the "natural" economy, taxation and the effect of copper price changes. Can we in these three areas determine some sort of crisis?

THE "NATURAL" ECONOMY

Classical theory has it that economic catastrophe and debasement of the denarius in the third century drove gold out of circulation, thus reducing its price and forcing the government to abandon the use of money. Constantine's massive confiscations of gold are then supposed to have led a return to a cash economy, which, reinforced by fiscal measures and monetary reform, ensured that a substantial part of the public and private sectors became extensively monetised by the latter half of the century, albeit at the expense of increasing centralisation, and bureaucratic controls.[35]

There is no need here to go into the refinements of the supposed conflict between the public and private sectors nor which was in favour and which against a natural or monetised economy.[36] The debate however serves to highlight the contradictory positions taken up on the matter and shows that the transition from money to kind and back again is anything but clear cut.

The real question to be asked about the natural economy and the monetised economy in the fourth century, is how far this is a "pseudo-dilemma", to use Marc Bloch's word. His celebrated attack on the rigidity of the distinction in mediaeval economics, although published as long ago as 1933, contains conclusions which are not always read by ancient historians.[37] Exchange in kind, he pointed out, does not necessarily reflect a shortage of precious metals so much as a mistrust of the state. Payments, though recorded in money, were frequently made in services of goods, and, even when paid in money, treated money as a metal of value not a medium of circulation.. But equally, if money was a measure of value, one can hardly talk about a natural economy, particularly when some payments in kind (dues for instance) required market transactions to procure the commodity.

In sum, a non-monetised economy does not betoken a return to simple barter and abandonment of all media of exchange, while in a monetised market there could still be a great deal of exchange in kind. We must beware of exaggerating the differences between the two.

Everything in the fourth century goes to illustrate the validity of these conclusions. adaeratio and coemptiones were a standard part of the state's fiscal system for ensuring that tax in either cash of kind could be levied at the convenience of the authorities in any period. Although tax in kind did in fact offset the effect of price inflation of the denarius, it looks increasingly probable that there never was a "system" of annona militaris as such and that tax levies in kind for troops became fairly regular well before the decline of the denarius. Tribute in kind had always existed, more widely in my view than is usually admitted. Compulsory purchase and stoppages in military pay were probably often simply bookkeeping operations, to judge by Pliny's praise of Trajan for actually permitting the fiscus to pay for what it "purchased" by supplementary "indictions" (Paneg. 29.4).[38] I am not, I hasten to say, trying to suggest that tax in kind did not increase in the third century and I agree that there was some return to commutations of annona for cash in the course of the fourth century. What I wish to stress is that the important factor in such an evolution and reflux was not monetary but military:[39] the increasing mobility of troops and the development and dispersal of regional field armies in addition to static frontier garrisons.

The difference therefore between a "system" of annona and a "system" of monetary tax was perhaps not so great and the so-called natural economy must be regarded as only a marginal factor in the decline of the commodity market. We must remember that in 299/300, when the inflation of the denarius was rampant, the soldiers of Diocletian recorded on the Beatty Papyri were paid in cash for their "annona". Whereas in Africa the imperial horrea at towns such as Utica, Maxula, Hippo Regius, dating from the early empire indicate probably but not with certainty that in this province at least much of the tax had always been levied in corn and continued to be despite adaeratio in the later fourth century.[40]

It is difficult to see how debasement of the denarius could have driven gold out of circulation in the third century[41] and it would be more logical to suppose that gold, but gold with other commodities, declined in production and exchange, but did not cease, due to the upheavals of the military and political crisis. The loss of Dacia in 257/8, for instance, and the breakthrough of the Francs and Mauri into Spain in the 260s must have drastically reduced the several tons of gold produced annually. This, in my view, would explain the absence of gold hoards in the third century while also justifying the hypothesis that old gold continued to circulate in the reduced commodity markets of the period. With the restoration of order under the tetrarchy, as we have seen in Spain, the mines began to function again. I have already suggested that the reappearance of gold in the economy under Constantine was less a result of imperial confiscations than of a genuine revival of the commodity market. By contrast, in the second half of the century, I believe, we must not be misledby legislative and fiscal demands for gold into assuming that this commodity demand was sustained,

TAXATION

We are fortunate in recent years in having not only Jones' celebrated article on "Overtaxation and decline of the Roman empire" republished together with a hitherto unpublished article on "Taxation in antiquity" in the posthumous collection of The Roman Economy but also a commentary by the editor P. A. Brunt, which seems to me to make my task fairly easy in proposing some modification of Jones' view.[42] By and large Jones argued that, quite apart from abuses in collection, official levels of taxation rose in the fourth century to unprecedented levels, resulting in "progressive abandonment of land" and a decline in productivity which had already been aggravated by the scarcity of gold. "Rarely in recorded Roman history", he concluded, "has there been a louder and more persistent chorus of complaint against the taxes than under the later Roman empire". We have seen in recent years, however, that bitter complaints about taxation may occur also in periods of unparalleled prosperity. And as we known, opposition to taxes, chronic arrears and tax amnesties had a long history in Rome.[43]

The question is therefore whether on this evidence we can assume taxes in the later empire really were increasing and removing from the land a greater proportion of the surplus produce. Taxes, as every ancient writer knew, were for the most part salaries for the soldiers. "He fed his army with riches on a scale not done before by a Roman leader", says Themistius (Or. 18.222a) explaining tax rises under Theodosius. But if wars were indeed the "fathers of taxes", as Gregory of Nazianzus said (Or. 19.14 = PG 35.1061), it is probably more accurate in all periods of Roman history to say that it was the employment of extra soldiers in times of crisis, perhaps simply bringing units up to strength, that always put pressure on tax payers.[44]

Apart from this kind of crisis pressure, however, I have some doubts as to whether the basic costs of the standing army in the fourth cnntury did in fact increase over previous epochs. The nominal size of the army in the fourth century, although far from certain, is generally, since Mommsen, accepted as being around 600,000 men.[45] This is roughly the figure given by Agathias—probably derived from a record of the "old" army as it had existed when the empire was last unified under Theodosius I—and it can be justified by the sort of calculations Jones made from the Notitia Dignitatum. Mommsen may also have been right in thinking that before Theodosius the numbers were rather less, perhaps by one sixth. That would mean that from the army of Septimius Severus of approximately 350-400,000 soldiers the numbers did not even double, despite gloomy exaggerations by Lactantius (de mort. pers. 7). So even if we add in the much enlarged body of civil servants and state functionaries, who were the other main item of state expenditure, the total numbers on the state pay roll in the fourth century could hardly have exceeded twice the number of a century before.

The other side of the military salary equation is less easy to determine with such a dearth of information. It seems probable that despite Jones' underestimation of the pay scales recorded in the Beatty Papyri from Panopolis, he was generally right that salaries in Diocletian's time did not keep pace with contemporary denarius prices in Egypt.[46] In the later half of the fourth century, when the annual stipendium et donativum in bronze had probably become nominal, and when celebratory donatives were often paid in gold or silver, an ordinary legionary could expect to earn with commutations no more than, and probably much less than 1/6th of a pound of gold.[47] If then we accept that the stipendium plus donativa of a Severan soldier averaged out at between 400-600 denarii per annum, his real purchasing power was between 1/3 nnd 1/2 pound of gold at official rates of exchange; or approximately double that of his equal in the fourth century. The same is true of civil functionaries, to judge by a comparison of the salaries of spectabiles with that of their approximate equivalents, the ducenarii of the early empire. The dux of Libya in the sixth century, for instance earned about nineteen pounds of gold a year (including legalised appropriations) which is rather underhalf the 44½ pounds of gold given to the ducenarius.[48]

The conclusions are obvious. The debasement and devaluation of the denarius were a means not of increasing taxation but of increasing the size of the army. Unless therefore there was a serious decline in the productivity or fiscality of the empire, there is no reason to suppose the larger army of the fourth century could not have been paid for by the surpluses off the land. Ammianus' famous account of Julian's tax reductions in Gaul in 356 seem to show that, in Julian's view at least, the indictio sollemnis, the standard tax, was sufficient to meet the diocesan needs, including the wars on the Rhine frontier. There was no need of the incrementa or conquisita (Amm. Marc. 17.3.4-6; cf. 3.2). From Cérati's calculations of the value of capitula, it would appear that after the "crippling" superindictions levied by the praetorian prefect of Gaul (Amm. Marc. 16.5.14) the tax total was reduced from about 20% to only 5% of average yields.[49] The final figure of the indiction therefore was about half of what we usually assume to have been the normal tithe tax in the high empire. According to the figures produced by Camille Jullian, there was ample surplus to pay the 70-75,000 soldiers he calculated to be stationed between the Rhine and Pyrenees.[50] In Africa in our period the standard gold-grain indiction was 6 2/3 solidi, or just over 1/12 of a pound of gold per century. Asuuming average yields and prices for Africa in the high empire, the theoretical tithe at that time works out at around 1/6 of a pound of gold.[51] So again the standard indiction in the fourth century seems to have been about half that of the previous epoch. The case of Egypt is less clear, although Bowman's study in this symposium provides important confirmation of the low taxation level suggested by Johnson and West, which has in the past been frequently challenged.[52] Even the high scales of 48-50 per cent, which some experts have suggested, would not be without precedent in the earlier history of Egypt and there is no special reason to believe that pressures on Egyptian peasants were greater than usual.

The impression one gains—and it can be no more—is that the basic balance sheet of the later empire, that is, the standard taxes to pay the salaries of public servants, had not altered greatly from that of the high empire and attempts to impose frequent superindictions in times of emergency were generally counterproductive, since they only created uncollected arrears. I shall return to that point at the end. My concern here is simply to establish the hypothesis that the larger army and bureaucracy of the later empire was not in itself a factor of decline; provided, that is, productivity was maintained.

And that brings me to agri deserti, I wrote several years ago (a) that I could detect no general decline in agrarian productivity, despite a certain amount of shifting centres of productivity; and (b) that there was a danger in taking the preoccupations of a bureaucracy with what was essentially a fiscal problem as evidence that land was being progressively abandoned. Since these conclusions have been considered in some quarters too negative, I may perhaps be permitted to review and nuance what I then said.[53]

Although the archaeology of towns needs cautious interpretation, since size and building activity are not sufficient guides to levels of rural prosperity, the conclusions of Patlagean, after a recent careful study of both town and country in the eastern half of the empire is that " a monumental building revival is clearly marked in the fourth century" (this includes large and small towns); and that "the vicissitudes of war and peace are not marked by any permanent desertion of the countryside."[54]

In northern Italy Ruggini long ago demonstrated the agrarian prosperity of the region of "Italia Annonaria" in the fourth century and, although she found some reason to agree with Mazzarino that it was mainly large towns which did well, the much quoted evidence of Ambrose (e.g. Ep. 39.3 = PL 16.1099) concerning the semi-ruined condition of towns in the later fourth century can be shown to be both localised to the district of Aemilia and not necessarily permanent. The decay of cities in the fourth century, in sum, was often a special Roman perception of cities as civic institutions—civitas in parietibus—and not as economic units. As to the countryside, Ambrose's sermons are filled with references to the rich man's unquenchable thirst for more land—villarum quotidie terminos proferentem (Exp. Ps. CXVIII.6.32 = PL 15.1278; cf. 8.5 = PL 15.1295, etc.). It is irrelevant here that there were special reasons for this affluence due to the presence of the court and praesental troops, since the rise and fall of regional prosperity and production is precisely the phenomenon that would account for the fiscal concern with agri deserti.[55]

In Africa the very recent book by Lepelley on cities in the later empire illustrates why the African provinces, even in 411, could be called regni nostri maxima pars by Honorius (Act. Conf. Cathag. 411 I.4, (ed. Lancel)), just ten years or so, it should be noted, before the legislation of massive remission on the land (CTh XI.28.13(422)), which I have previously argued was a political not an economic gesture. Judging by about 230 inscriptions over a period of 150 years, Lepelley proposes to see a building boom between 361-395 after a period of almost total inactivity from 305-312 and little better from 312-361, reflecting in his view the drain of disposable surpluses from the provinces in the wars of succession.[56] Certainly this is a possibility, and the urban activity can quite properly be coupled with the flourishing export of African table-ware, oil and garum, including reorganisation of the production of lamps in the early fourth century and, what was once denied, export of oil from Tripolitania in this period.[57] But I suggest below an alternative interpretation of the building activity less directly tied to commodity exchange.

In the western empire conditions were much less stable militarily and the overall picture much more difficult to assess. The rich prosperity of villas like Arnesp, Chiragan and Montmaurin in the century from about 325/30 is an indication that rural production did not cease after the transformation of many towns into military centres.[58] Despite repeated attacks across the frontiers, Britain is described in one standard work as having villas in their "hey-day" in the first half of the century and possessing prospects in 370 that "had never been brighter" in another.[59] Discussion about Spain at a recent symposium insisted that there was high rural prosperity on the massive estates and that urban life, especially in the period between the Council of Elvira and 408/9, flourished.[60]

In Gaul and along the Rhine it is clear that the frontier zones suffered badly; but not all.[61] Some parts of the Rhineland look better off and, as we know, a good deal of the northern Gallic lands, which were badly damaged after the invasions from 352 onwards, nevertheless received many German settlers with whom a kind of symbiotic existence grew up that was not lacking in prosperity.[62] While there may in general have been a decline in the overall number of villas occupied, those left seem to have grown richer and larger.

The towns certainly suffered, many of them irreparably and particularly in the period after the mid-fourth century—vastationes atque excidia civitatium (Salvian, de. gub. dei, V.9.45). An imperial order to the praetorian prefect of the Gauls in 400 speaks of skilled workmen leaving the city for the countryside in hidden, out-of-the-way regions (CTh XII. 19 (400)). Julian found Besançon a "tiny town" (πολίχνη) when he visited it, a mere shadow of its ancient size (Ep. 8. 414C).[63] Lyon never recovered once the troops' supply centre had moved to Trier.[64] I am therefore persuaded that in the provinces of the north-western empire in the second half of the century there must have been some loss of prosperity due to the undoubted decline of the urban markets and loss of urban commodity demand.

Nevertheless, we must not exaggerate. In the countryside, villagers who deserted their ruined houses for the safety of the walled fortresses could be persuaded in times of peace to return to farming, as Themistius proposed in 383/4 (Or. 34. 62). Disorganization, says Velkov about Thrace, must not be confused with depopulation.[65] Despite the decline of the Pannonias after Adrianople (exitium et clades, Amm. Marc. 31.2.1, Claud. in Ruf. 2.45) and the well documented ruin of some places like Carnuntum (Amm. Marc. 30.5.1), it is better, says Mócsy "to speak of...displacement of the centres of influence than of a gradual decline of the towns; this displacement caused the decay of some regions, but not of the whole area".[66] Again it is the large and prosperous estates away from the frontiers that are striking. In rural districts, far from the 'Untergang' once believed, an inscription published in 1967 proves that a Roman official was sent to Pannonia Secunda to revise the land cadasters.[67]

The only point I wish to add has nothing to do with productivity as such but with its relationship to market activity. A recent study of oil production in Tripolitania demonstrates how emperors in the third and fourth century came through confiscation and appropriation to have direct control over the distribution of African oil all over the Mediterranean. The importance of the study is not only, as the author intended, that it makes comprehensible how provisions were made for annona supplies to Rome and the frontiers, but also that it constructs a framework within which we can picture the non-commercial distribution of commodities from imperial and other wealthy estates to various parts of the empire.[68] Obviously a good deal of such produce continued to be commercial and to provide the massive gold incomes of rich magnates which are known in the later empire (Olymp. FHG IV.67). But what Ruggini has shown is how the distribution of rural surpluses fell increasingly within the orbit of the rich estate owners (I include the emperor and the church in this category), who despatched goods in kind between private estates.[69]

In theory this closed circuit would have reduced the circulation of commodities in the normal operation of the market and fits in well with the view expressed earlier that gold hoards in the later fourth century illustrate a decline not a rise in the commodity market. That is to say, we have a demonstration of the general law that "the total price of commodities in circulation (my italics) determines the mass of the circulating medium."[70] This later half of the century is also the point at which emperors began to express concern at the growing power of the principales and, as we can see now, it coincides with Lepelley's dates for building activity in Africa. The very men who were undermining the urban centres were also adorning them. Thirteen out of sixteen of the buildings put up in Numidia between 364-367 were by one man, P. Caesonius Caecina Albinus, a member of a family with massive property in Africa and typical of this class of potentes.[71] It is worth noting that coin hoards which are fairly common in mining regions are hardly found in Baetica, the richest agricultural region, and are perhaps another indicator of the non-commercial activity of the great estates.

I do not therefore believe, either on a priori grounds of general tax levels or as a result of the circumstantial evidence, one is entitled to deduce from the perpetual bureaucratic thirst for fiscal profit that the land itself was everywhere parched and dry. If there was a significant decline in urban life along the frontiers of the northern provinces, the main effect of this was upon the market activity and secondary produce of the towns not upon rural prosperity.

WHO WAS AFFECTED BY PRICE CHANGES?

If we now ask who in the end was affected by the debasement and issue of the subsidiary coinage, the simple answer must be state servants, whose real pay was roughly halved. But simple answers will rarely suffice and what we really want to know is to what extent, if at all, the inflation of copper prices hit the general public, thereby provoking a social chain reaction. "Deflation" in Keynsian terms "involves a transferance of wealth from the rest of the community to the rentier class...just as inflation involves the opposite".[72] Borrowers gain and lenders lose when prices rise and a wise man invests his spare cash in commodities. Is that what we witness in the fourth century?

The ancient world was never short of profiteers who speculated on local or seasonal shortages and price fluctuations, particularly of basic foodstuffs. But that is the form the accusation against this type of person usually takes. Julian's attempt in 362 to peg prices at Antioch was coupled, in his words at any rate, with putting extra corn onto the market in time of famine (Jul. Misop. 357D, 369B), not with contemporary reforms of the nummus.[73] And Gallus' attempts at price control in Antioch eight years earlier were explicitly against seasonal fluctuations (celerari vilitatem intempestivam urgens, Amm. Marc. 14.7.2) not steadily rising prices. It seems to me probable that the well known preamble to Diocletian's Price Edict attacking extortionate prices by profiteers who strip the soldiers of their pay really is a commentary on the effect of the debased and devalued coinage with which the soldiers were paid. The implication however is not so much that there was speculation against the effects of inflation, but that the market simply refused to accept the soldiers' pieces at their face value. The same process is described by Themistius c. 348 (Or 33.367. b-c) when he speaks of currency being "driven out of the market" (ἅ ἔναγχος ἐξελήλαται τῆς ἀγορᾶς) because it did not have the same accounting value (οὐδ' ἰσαρίθμως) as it once had.[74]

What matters in this gap between the market and official valuation of the subsidiary coinage is who, apart from the salaried state employees, lost. I confess I do not understand the reply that it was "the small creditor class and the urban professional".[75] The latter, if it means businessmen, ought to have been the ones to profit and if they did suffer it was for reasons other than inflation; for it is well known that entrepreneurs did not flourish in the later empire. The former, even if logically the ones who would have felt inflation, were able to devise perfectly satisfactory means to counter devaluation and ensure loan repayment in real equivalents.[76] And, in fact, creditors did very well despite inflation.

The main objections to any general theory of a redistribution of wealth from rentiers into the hands of entrepreneurs and the debtor class are two-fold; first, there is the obvious fact that such a movement runs entirely contrary to all the evidence in the fourth century of decline of the entrepreneurs and the growth of massive estates.[77] But secondly, and more important, is the absence of credit money or negotiable instruments of credit and therefore the relative rarity of long-term loans and mortgages.[78] The volume of loans did not, by and large, much exceed the stock of money, despite a lot of credit activity. The united Christian condemnation of usury and interest-bearing loans is the fourth century expression of the low level of this type of economic activity in all periods of ancient history.[79] Rentiers therefore were protected against the effects of currency manipulation and borrowers did not suddenly strike it rich. Banks of exchange, when forced into activity by the state, lost some profits (P.Oxy.1411). There may have been some lucky debtors. But we may be sure that in general large scale loans were computed in precious metals or share-cropping schemes and petty debtors of bronze currency were not likely to evade their more powerful creditors in the unequal world of the fourth century.[80]

Even the main loss through inflation, which Jones conceded, the disappearance of municipal charity trust funds, needs to be explained with rather more refinement than that, since in Italy the decline of such schemes anticipated the effects of debased coinage by a full generation and must therefore be attributed to a decline in local patriotism.[81] Inflation may, of course, have killed off existing trust funds, although it is difficult to see quite why this should have happened if the trusts were mainly invested in land. We can also say that there seems to have been no inhibitions about massive charitable endowments in cash to the church in the fourth century, made by the same local élites who formerly displayed their philanthropia in a civic context.[82] Once again therefore the change, although real in social terms, was minimal in economic terms.

Despite an extremely hostile sketch by the anonymous de rebus bellicis in the middle of the fourth century dealing with the monetary and economic ills of the period—tax burdens, military expenditure, lack of treasury reserves, extravagence and poverty—there is never a word about rising prices. Nor in Ammianus. In all the cries about the destitution of the poor and the exploitation of the rich coming from the vitriolic pens of church leaders like John Chrysostom, Gregory of Nyssa, Basil of Caesarea or Ambrose, I cannot find a single one who attributes the poverty to the manipulation and decline of the coinage and no more than a handful who refer even to high prices, in spite of the chronic problem of local fluctuation in rural produce.[83] Nor are such references quoted by authors better versed in the sources than I.

But the one subject on which the sources are unanimous is taxes. Yet, as I have tried to show, the tax expenditure burden was not particularly oppressive; it was the local incidence that was the problem. It was the conquisita which Julian forbad in Gaul. It was *exquisiti tituli* which wrecked the Illyrian province, says Ammianus (19.11.3), because of overpayments criminally levied by those who had the support of the *potestates*. The cost of the soldiery was only a pretext in Valentinian's reign, according to Zosimus. What oppressed was "profiteering by officers" or "greed of officials" (τὴν τῶν ἀρχόντων πλεονεξίαν) "going beyond the norm of the allotted tax" (ὑπὸ τῶν ἐπιτεθέντων εἰσφορῶν ὑπερβαινόντων τὸ μέτρον) (Zos.4.29). The unfair, uneven and often corrupt application of special taxes was what concerned writers, and against which imperial legislation apparently had little or no control. The history of the fourth century is strewn with records of imperial interventions to effect tax reductions, local and general, and attempts to prevent by legislation the levy of *extraordinaria* without direct imperial authority.[84] This is not to say superindictions were never legitimate for the military emergencies—which I assume meant bringing units up to strength and hiring foreign mercenaries. A law of 416 makes it clear that superindictions had by then become regarded as a regular tax (*CTh* XI.5.2). But the same law also makes clear that the *possessores* did not have the same enthusiastic view of this necessity. And therein lay the rub.

The title *de patrociniis vicorum* in the Theodosian Code (XI.24) is dated entirely after the 360s. The evidence of Libanius on the activities of the *epiphaneis*, the *principales*, dates to the 380s; Salvian's evidence is still later. What they all show is that from the later part of the fourth century a small privileged class were able to resist fiscal demands by the command of private armies, force maieur and superior influence in high places. In so doing they shifted the burden of both municipal *munera* and state *extraordinaria* onto the backs of the smaller, independent, landowner of curial class and to the poor peasant. The trend which began but was officially resisted in the first half of the century finally in the 360s received the seal of imperial approval.[85] Significantly this was at exactly the point when there was most probably a commodity decline. It was just because the state transferred the formal responsibility to the *principales* for the collection of the taxes of their tenants, while finally conceding the rights of these same *principales* to distribute the local fiscal burdens—both measures, I do not doubt, in an effort to improve the efficiency of tax collection—that the state cut its own throat. For it provided the rich with the instruments of increasing their own independent power by the protection they could offer to small landowners in return for loss of independence; and it provided the poor with a very real means of surviving the economic effects of the arbitrary and often corrupt fiscal demands.

The fact that many of these rich magnates were imperial officials and powers at court, meant, as Weber saw, that provincial officials had become like tax farmers. They handed over to the ruler a fixed sum and kept the surpluses for themselves. In effect, in both the imperial and the private domain emperors had lost control of taxation and it was the local magnates who exploited the surplus capacity. This was not yet feudalism as long as the rich *possessores* continued to hold political positions in the centralised court and state; but it laid the groundwork of mediaeval "seigneurie".[86]

Many have discussed the full effects of this form of contract involved in *patrocinium*. Here I stress only two points. First, this is why taxation did not in general drive land out of production; and secondly, it was the spiral of fiscality not inflation which transformed the empire by preventing the state from raising the level of taxation to meet the emergency on the frontiers.

NOTES

1. It is of some interest that Keynes did make a start on a history of ancient monetary standards, producing eventually seven chapters of which unfortunately only five can now be traced. The chapters will be published in vol. XXVIII of Keynes' Collected Writings under the general editorship of Professor Sir Austin Robinson, to whom I am grateful for permission to examine the manuscripts. The chapters are confined to primitive, oriental and Greek weights and coins.

2. A. H. M. Jones, The Roman Economy, ed. P. A. Brunt, Oxford, 1974, 138ff.

3. D. Sperber, Roman Palestine, A.D. 200-400 : money and prices, Ramat-Gan, 1974, 178.

4. R. S. Lopez, "The dollar of the Middle Ages," JEcHist, 1951, 209ff.; M. Corbier, "Fiscalité et monnaie: problèmes et méthode" DArch, 9-10, 1976/7, 504ff., which is substantially repeated in her contribution to the seminar, Les "Dévaluations" à Rome (Coll. Ec. Fr. Rome, no. 37, 1978), 273ff.

5. J. K. Galbraith, Money, Penguin, London, 1976, 19ff.

6. Roman Imperial Coinage, (ed. C. H. V. Sutherland and R. A. G. Carson), VII, London, 1966, 8.

7. E.g. J. Lefaurie, "Réformes d'Aurélien et de Dioclétian" RN 17, 1973, 73ff.; at 117-8, re. the misnamed billon "follis".

8. E.g. J.-P. Callu, "Problèmes monétaires du IVe siècle" in Transformation et conflits au IVe siècle (Antiquitas, Reihe 1 no. 29, Bonn, 1978), 103ff.; at 110, re. the silver siliqua in the mid-fourth century; M. Crawford, "Finance, coinage and money" ANRW II.2, 1975, 565, 569, etc.

9. geminata p[ote]ntia : see K. Erim, J. Reynolds, M. Crawford, JRS, 61 1971, 171-7.

10. RIC VII (n. 6), 12 with refs. and discussion of the papyri.

11. For the third century, see Crawford, "Finance" (n. 8) 563, 568-71 and "Ancient devaluations : a general theory" in Dévaluations (n.4); 147-158; Corbier, ibid, 511-2 suggests the denarius of the third century was always "founded on a certain weight of metal" though fiduciary.

12. K. Marx, A contribution to the critique of political economy (trans. N. I. Stone), Chicago, 1904, 160; Keynes, A treatise on money I. 14.

13. J.-P. Callu, La politique monétaire des empereurs de 238 à 311 a.C. (Bib. Ec. Fr. Rome, 214, 1969), 445.

14. Recently stressed by P. Veyne, "Rome devant la prétendue fuite d'or. etc.", Annales (ESC), 34, 1979, 211ff. at 221, though going back to Marx.

15. This example is quoted by Marx, Contribution (n.12), 92-4.

16. CTh XII. 7.1; the septem solidos of the text was amended by Mommsen to sex solidos to argue against a fluctuation in gold; but this is not accepted by Callu or Kent; see in general, Callu, "Problèmes" (n.8), 106-8, J. P. C. Kent, "Gold coinage in the Late Roman Empire", Essays...H. Mattingly, ed. R. A. G. Carson, (London, 1958), 190ff. at 199-204. CJ XI.11.2 (367) appears to be ordering that commidity prices should move with gold, which may mean there were minor fluctuations in gold of the sort which troubled the collectarii (Symm. Rel. 29), since their margin of profitability was only about $2\frac{1}{2}\%$.

17. J. -P. Callu, "Denier et nummus (300-354)" in Dévaluations (n.4), 107ff.

18. In A. H. M. Jones, "Inflation under the Roman Empire" in Roman Economy , (n.2), 212-3; R. S. Bagnall and P. J. Sijpesteijn, "Currency in the fourth century and the date of CPR V 26", ZPE 24 1977 , 111ff., esp. 116-120.

19. Callu, "Denier" (n.17), 119, E. Patlagean, Pauvreté économique et pauvreté sociale à Byzance, Paris, 1977, 411.

20. CTh IX. 23.2 (395); see J. W. E. Pearce, Roman Imperial Coinage IX London, 1951 xxvi, 205 for gold fractions and ibid. xviii, xxix, xxxi for the restricted quantities of bronze, although P. himself gives no estimation of the matter. Callu, "Denier" (n.17), 121, is criticised by Chastagnol for equating centenionalis and maiorina.

21. A. H. M. Jones, The Later Roman Empire, Oklahama, 1964 , 207.

22. In general, see Jones, LRE (n.21), 442, and in the third century, Crawford. 'Finance' (n.8), 568-9. Bronze continued to be the principle medium for military payment in the fourth century and is found in large quantities in various 'Kriegskasse' hoards; e.g. 10,000 pieces (up to A.D. 333) at Campona, A. Alföldi, RIN, 24, 1921, 1ff.; 12,000 pieces (up to A.D. 327) nr. Vindobona, K. Pink, Jahrb. f. Landeskunde v. Niederöster. 20 (1932), 60, etc.

23. On mints in general, M. Hendy, "Mint and fiscal administration under Diocletian, his colleagues and his successors, A.D. 305-24", JRS, 62, 1972, 75ff. at 77, 81. The mint at Sirmium, for instance, closed c. 325/6 after Licinius' defeat, reopened after 351 during the wars of succession and closed after 364, except for occasional strikes of gold; details kindly provided by C. E. V. Nixon, The Roman coins from Sirmium (forthcoming as a volume in E. Ochsenschlager, V. Popovic (edd.), Sirmium).

24. Veyne (n.14), 216.

25. The English price drops from c. £45 to c. £15 for a gold solidus; D. R. Sear, Roman coins and their values, B. A. Seaby Ltd., London, 1964. I am grateful to Professor Philip Grierson for this information and for other help in discussion.

26. E.g. L. Ruggini, Economia e Società nell' "Italia Annonaria" Milan, 1961, 385; Callu, "Problèmes" (n.8), 121; Patlagean (n.19), 408-9. Sperber (n.3), 150-2, traces the prices back to the Augustan age but I confess I am sceptical. The gold-wheat prices quoted by Jones, "Inflation" (n.18) 200-1, 206-8, while confirming a return to early empire prices in the later fourth century, are based on an incorrect valuation of gold in 301. The Aezani fragment is republished by J. Reynolds and M. Crawford, ZPE, 34, 1979, 197 with earlier refs. Temporary or minor fluctuations of the sort noted above (n.16) would not necessarily show up on the scattered price information we possess.

27. The general unreliability of the Anonymous' evidence about monetary events is demonstrated by L. Tondo, "Il de rebus bellicis e la politica monetaria" RIN 78, 1976, 201ff.

28. For refs. to Constantine's confiscations of temple treasures and gold, see Jones, LRE (n.21) 1083 n.33; and for the evidence of Zosimus, Ammianus, etc. see E. A. Thompson, A Roman reformer and inventor, Oxford, 1952, 32-3.

29. The texts are collected by Callu, Politique monétaire (n.13), 313.

30. Veyne (n.14), passim.

31. Also mining in Cantabria and Asturia, Claud. laus Serenae 75-77; for Gallaecia, cf. Pan. Lat. II (XII) 4.4, 28.2. In general, J. M. Blásquez, "Conflicto y cambio en Hispania durante e siglo IV" in Transformation et conflits (n.8), 53ff. at 69, 91; by contrast, the rich mines at Cartagena had stopped, ibid. 70.

32. A. Cérati, Caractère annonaire et assiette de l'impôt foncier au Bas-Empire, Paris, 1975, 85ff.

33. For markets with the Goths, see Themistius, Or. 10. 135c and ILS 775 (A.D. 371) for a fort called Commercium. In general, see V. Velkov, Cities in Thrace and Dacia in late antiquity Amsterdam, 1977 , 178ff., Patlagean (n.19), 375-6.

34. S. Mazzarino, The end of the ancient world (trans. G. Holmes), London, 1966, 152.

35. This is essentially the position taken by A. H. M. Jones in his many contributions; see, e.g. LRE (n. 21) 29-31, 439-40, 445, 460, etc.

36. In effect the debate between G. Mickwitz, Geld und Wirtschaft im röm. Reich des vierten Jahrh. n. Chr., Helsingfors, 1932, and S. Mazzarino, Aspetti sociali del quarto secolo, Rome, 1951; compared by A. Cérati (n. 32), 154-6.

37. M. Bloch, "Natural economy or money economy: a pseudo-dilemma" in Land and Work in Mediaeval Europe (trans. J. E. Anderson, 1967 = Annales (ESC) 1933), 230-243.

38. The real question is when what began as ad hoc practice of supplying troops with tax in kind became general and normal. Corbier, "Fiscalité" (n. 4), 536, argues it was so in Egypt by 144/5, based on P. Mil. Vogliano 75.

But the practice was already widespread elsewhere much earlier and I see no way of deciding when, if ever, the practice became a "system". R. Étienne, Bordeaux antique, Bordeaux, 1962, 91-2, gives evidence of Gallic supplies for the Roman army which he believes (but cannot prove) were taxation in kind continuously from Pompey to Julian. Other refs. from the early empire to supplies in kind as tax are given by Jones and Brunt in Roman Economy (n. 2), 169-70—e.g. Tac A. IV. 6.4; IV. 72.11; Agr. 19, probably Dio 62.3.3. The administration for the collection and transport of this kind of direct tribute is discussed by H. Pavis D'Esurac, Le préfecture de l'annone; service administratif imperial d'Auguste à Constantin, Rome, 1976, 160-4, 176-86, esp. 185-6. For early empire military collections, see P. Le Roux, "L'armée de la péninsule iberique économique dans le haut-empire romain", in Armées et fiscalité dans le monde antique, CNRS, Paris, 1977, 341ff. at 350ff. In the same work, D. Van Berchem, "L'annone militaire est-elle un mythe?", 331-6, defends a Diocletianic date for the systematisation of annona taxes, but his main argument is directed to when the transportation of supplies became liturgic not whether the tax was levied in kind or cash.

39. See the comments by M. Carrié in Armées et fiscalité (n. 38), 338-9. How far was the increase in imperial estates and confiscations by the res privata (discussed in this symposium by F. Millar) directed towards provisioning the soldiers? This was the thesis put forward by E. Gren, Kleinasien und der Ostbalkan in der wirtschaftlichen Entwicklung der röm. Kaiserzeit (Uppsala/Leipzig, 1941), esp. 140-6.

40. For the refs., see G. Rickman, Roman granaries and store buildings, Cambridge, 1971 , 181-2; cf. the evidence quoted for Sardinia, Egypt, Spain and Asia, some of it well before the third century A.D. African annona was apparently not commuted in the later fourth century—CTh XI.1.11 (365), 1.33 (366).

41. Jones, "Inflation" (n. 18), 224.

42. N. 2 above.

43. The quotations are from Jones' article, "Inflation" (n. 18), 82, 84, 179 etc. For tax complaints and arrears, Corbier, Dévaluations (n. 4), 290, R. MacMullen, The Roman Government's response to crisis A.D. 235-337, New Haven, 1976, 149, 281 n. 88.

44. Briefly, with refs., Crawford, "Finance" (n. 8), 591-2, Corbier, 'Fiscalité' (n. 4), 529-31; contra, MacMullen, (n. 43), 104-6, who argues for transport as the main extra expense. In fairness to MacM., it is no answer to say that transport came directly from extra corvée of the taxpayers, since that meant lost working days—unless one explains that the majority of peasants were economically underemployed. cf. Julian, Or. 1.21B for lighter liturgies in peace time. Payments to gentiles and foederati in latter part of the fourth century was the usual method of expanding the army in emergencies; cf. Cérati (n. 32), 182.

45. Jones, LRE (n. 21), 679-84, following Th. Mommsen, Gesammelte Schriften, (repr. Berlin/Dublin/Zurich), 1965, VI, 263-4. E. Gabba, Per la storia dell' esercito romano in età imperiale, Bologna, 1974, 72-3,

accepts that the army was doubled by Diocletian and thereafter did not exceed this figure, despite evidence of great recruiting drives.

46. Jones, LRE (n. 21), 623; corrected by R. P. Duncan-Jones, "Pay and numbers in Diocletian's army" Chiron 8, 1978, 541ff., esp. 550. J.-M. Carrié, "Les finances militaires et le fait monétaire dans l'empire romain tardif" in Dévaluations (n. 4), 227ff., was written before Duncan-Jones' article and is less acceptable. The maximum possible figure for annual donativa (given by D-J) is c. 10,000 denarii, but this is highly con-jectural and reached only by projecting the monthly figures we possess which may include special once-off celebratory payments, even if not quinquennial. A figure nearer 50,000 denarii therefore seems preferable (also suggested by D-J).

47. Jones, "Inflation" (n. 18), 208 gives this high figure; but in fact there is no evidence that the accession and quinquennial donations of all Augusti and Caesares were paid in all parts of the empire. Assuming that they were (as Jones does), they would have averaged out at maximum at about 4 solidi p.a. cf. Szilagyi, "Prices and wages in the western provinces of the Roman empire" AAntHung, 1963, 327. Together with the values of annona (c. 4-5 solidi p.a.) and clothing (c. I solidus p.a.) the total would be c. 1/7 lb. of gold. One can only guess at special donatives, like that given by Julian, Amm. Marc. 20.4.18.

48. Jones, "Inflation" (n. 18), 210.

49. Cérati (n. 32), 350.

50. C. Jullian, Histoire de la Gaule, VIII, Paris, 1926, 47-48, 102.

51. For earlier African prices and yields, see R. P. Duncan-Jones, The economy of the Roman empire Cambridge, 1974 , 50-51; assuming lowish average yields of c. 4,000 modii per century p.a., at highish prices of 4 HS per modius (= 16,000 HS p.a.) and after deducting 50% for fallow, this would produce a tax of c. 200 denarii p.a. = 8/45 lb. of gold. The later African land tax is recorded in Nov. Val. III 34.2(451) which says that before this date the tax was 160 siliquae per century = 6 2/3 solidi = c. 1/12 lb. of gold.

52. A. C. Johnson and L. C. West, Byzantine Egypt: economic studies, (reimp. Amsterdam), 1967, 240. For the higher rate in Egypt, see the evidence in Jones, LRE (n. 21), 464, which works out at 48% of net crop after seed (according to figures kindly provided by R. P. Duncan-Jones). J.-M. Carrié, "Le role economique de l'armée dans l'Egypt romain" in Armées et fiscalité (n. 38), 373ff. at 386, calculates between 33-50% tax level but seems to agree that Egyptian peasants were not pressed harder than in the second century A.D. For earlier Egyptian taxes, see Brunt in Jones, Roman Economy (n. 2), 183-4.

53. C. R. Whittaker, "Agri deserti" in M. I. Finley (ed.), Studies in Roman property, Cambridge, 1975, 137ff.: review by J. Andreau, Annales (ESC), 33, 1978, 343ff.

54. Patlagean (n. 19), 232, 307.

55. Ruggini (n. 26), esp. 33-35, 52-65, 77-80, 99, repeated breifly in L. Cracco Ruggini and G. Cracco, "Changing fortunes of Italian cities from late antiquity to the early middle ages" RFC, 105, 1977, 448ff.

56. Cl. Lepelley, Les cités de l'Afrique romaine au Bas-Empire (Thèse d'etat, Sorbonne, 1977, typescript) esp. 1012-1038; cf. A. Carandini, "Produzione agricola e produzione ceramica nell' Africa di età imperiale" in Ommagio R. Bianchi Bandinelli, Studi Miscellanei 15, Rome, 1969/70, 102-3.

57. Ostia III, Studi Miscellanei 21, Rome, 1973, 337, 571, 590: the archaeological evidence of produce itself runs dramatically contrary to the conclusions reached from the legal evidence—see C. Dupont, La réglementation économique dans les constitutions de Constantin, Lille, 1963, 93 who says "indisputably" there was a "disquieting situation in certain regions and poverty of cultivators, especially in rural Africa" (my italics).

58. For refs. to Gallic villas, see M. Labrousse, Toulouse antique des origines à l'établissement des Wisigoths Paris, 1968, 571-2. For towns as military centres, see A. L. F. Rivet, Town and Country in Roman Britain (2nd edit.), London, 1964, 84-6. W. Rodwell and T. Rowley (eds.), The "Small towns" of Roman Britain", BAR 15, Oxford, 1975, contains no evidence of widespread destruction of "small towns", but undoubtedly some were abandoned (e.g. Gatcombe, p. 181) and many kept going only by the redistribution of the field armies to the towns (e.g. remarks on pp. 59-64, 93, etc.).

59. S. Frere, Britannia, London, 1967, 360: G. Webster, in A. L. F. Rivet (ed.), The Roman villa in Britain, London, 1969, 222, though the number of villas certainly declined after about 360 and much damage was suffered from invasions in the mid-century (ibid., 227).

60. Blásquez (n. 31), passim, esp. 91; re towns, see p. 93 for the remarks of Chastagnol and Étienne; L. Ruggini, "Struttore socio-economiche della Spagna tardo-romana" Athenaeum 53, 1965, 438, however notes that the coin hoards indicate lack of economic activity.

61. E. M. Wightman, "Peasants and potentates: an investigation of social structures and land tenure in Roman Gaul" (forthcoming in Amer. Journ. Anc. Hist.): I am grateful to EMW for an advance view of her article.

62. E. Demougeot, 'La Gaule nord-orientale à la veille de la grande invasion germanique de 407' RH, 236, 1966, 17ff., esp. 40-41, for the new civilization of the frontiers. J. J. Hatt, Histoire de la Gaule romaine, Paris, 1959, 317, points out that the evangelisation of the countryside by Martin depended on a certain state of peace in the later fourth century.

63. Jullian (n. 50), VII. 26-28, VIII. 214-5.

64. L. Cracco Ruggini, "Les structures de la société et l'économie lyonnaise au IIe siecle "in Les martyrs de Lyon CNRS, Paris, 1978 , 65ff. I am grateful to M. I. Finley for this reference and for an advance view of his remarks concerning declining urban commodity demand contained in his forthcoming book, Ancient slavery and modern ideology (forthcoming, London, 1980). Rivet in "Small towns" (n. 58), 113, notes the absence

of monumental buildings in towns of fourth century Gaul and the reduced size of places like Périgeux, Tours, Amiens. Paris never recovered from the third century, P.-M. Duval, Paris antique, Paris, 1961, 277, 280.

65. V. Velkov, "Les campagnes et la population rurale en Thrace au IVe-VIe siècle", Byzantinobulg, 1, 1962, 31ff.; and in Cities (n. 33), —recovery after Adrianople (36-37), no major towns abandoned, although some reduced in size (133), also new towns grew (136); rural life continued at the same economic level (197); cf. Patlagean (n. 19), 304-7.

66. A. Mocšy, Pannonia and Upper Moesia, London, 1974, 297ff.

67. J. Harmatta in Transformation et conflits (n. 8), 95-6.

68. D. Manachorda, "Testimonianze sulla produzione e il consumo dell' olio tripolitano nel III secolo". DArch 9-10, 1976/77, 542ff.

69. Ruggini (n. 26), 128-151. E.g. the activity of Symmachus bringing produce from his Apulian estates (Ep. 6.12), or later a similar use of church and state property in Sicily (Greg. Ep. I, 42 & 70, IX. 124-7; P. Ital. 1 + 3).

70. K. Marx, Grundrisse, Pelican, 1973, 810.

71. J. Matthews, Western aristocracies and imperial court, A.D. 364-425, Oxford, 1975, 27-8.

72. J. M. Keynes, Essays in persuasion, (repr. London), 1951, 189.

73. Cf. G. Elmer, 'Die Kupfergeldreform unter Julianus Philosophus' NZ 70, 1937, 25-42: J. H. W. Liebeschuetz, Antioch: city and imperial administration in the later Roman empire, Oxford, 1972, 126.

74. Callu, 'Denier' (n. 17), 117, links this to a coinage reform of 338.

75. E.g. MacMullen (n. 43), 118-9; cf. Lafaurie (n. 7), 130.

76. See e.g. Diocletian's currency reform of 301, JRS 61, 1971, 173, lines 5-10—ut eandem pecuniam ita numerent ut valuisse cognoscitur antequam . . . . facta fuerit adcessio. Patlagean (n. 19), 263, discusses the system of land debt—contracts in the eastern empire (what is called in Arabic mgharsa) which I have also suggested was widespread in Africa; C. R. Whittaker, "Land and labour in North Africa", Klio 60, 1978, 831ff. esp. 360. Repayment was usually demanded in produce and corvée service.

77. It is hardly necessary to cite evidence; see, e.g. Basil of Caesarea, Homil. in divit. 53C, 57A, 58A, etc. (= PG 31. 284, 293, 296) with his portrait of the grasping rich 'enslaving' their neighbours and taking their land; Ambrose gives the same view (p. 11 above); so also Libanius, Or. 48.37 etc.

78. M. I. Finley, The ancient economy, London, 1973, 141-2, Patlagean (n. 19), 177-8.

79. E.g. Basil, Homil. dict. temp. famis et siccitatis 66B (= PG 31.313), the attack on usury "in time of starvation and drought". John Chrysostom, Homil. in Matth. 56.5-6 (= PG 58.555-8), condemns all usury, even that of normal 12% interest rates.

80. For the tyranny of such share-cropping schemes, which virtually tied the indebted peasants to the land, see the attack by John Chrysostom, Homil, in Matth. 61.3 (= PG 58.591-2), where landlords demanded 50% of the produce. I have discussed this system in my article "Rural labour in three Roman provinces" (forthcoming in PCPhS, Supplement), but see also the refs. in n. 76 above.

81. Jones, "Overtaxation" (n. 42), 138-9; Italian schemes discussed by Crawford, "Finance" (n. 8), 568.

82. Patlagean (n. 19), 181-203 discusses with sources gifts as an agency for redistributing wealth.

83. E.g. the index rerum et sententiarum of Ambrose in PL 15, under the headings dives, divitia, etc., pauper, paupertas etc., pecunia, nummus, etc., makes not a single ref. to prices. John Chrysostom's Homil. in Matth. 20.2-3, under the rubric "Lay not up for yourselves treasures upon earth", stresses moths, rust, thieves, but never once devaluation or inflation as deterrents to saving and hoarding. Theodoret, Ep. 37 (Source Chrét. 40), notes an extreme lack of gold to pay taxes because no one is purchasing rural produce but oddly does not say (even if it was true) that prices had collapsed. Exp. tot. mund. 58, says propter maioris † praesentiam omnia in multitudine abundat, sed plurimi pretii, which (though corrupt) seems to mean that commodity prices rose when the emperor's court was present. Sperber (n. 3), 142, quotes two passages from rabbinic texts, which he claims to mean that over-expansion of the money supply put prices up; but the texts do not actually say this and seem to me to indicate only that a poor harvest puts up prices and that taxes take all surplus cash.

84. E.g. Euseb. v. Const. 4.2 - 25% tax cuts; Them. Or. VIII 113C - Valens' 50% reductions; CTh XIII 11.2 (386) - cuts in capita evaluations; CTh XI 16.11 (365), 6.1 (382) - no unauthorized superindictions cf. Jones, LRE (n. 21), 1188-9, n. 99, for a list, plus MacMullen (n. 43), 149, 281, n. 88.

85. Compare CTh XI 16.4 (328) restraining principales' rights to allot municipal burdens with CTh VIII 15.5.3 (366) which concedes the right—principales a quibus distributionum omnium forma procedit. In general, see the summary by A. F. Norman, Libanius Selected Works II, Loeb, London, 1977, 411ff. and I. Hahn, "Das bäuerliche Patrocinium in Ost u. West", Klio 69, 1967, 261ff. The power exercised by aristocracies outside formal office is one of the major themes which runs through Matthews's study of the later fourth century (n. 71).

86. See the excellent analysis by Patlagean (n. 19), 278ff.: contra, Wightman (n. 61). The endless and vain legislation about returning coloni to their origo from 322 onwards was the state's attempt to protect the medium landowner against the potentes, as well as assisting its own fiscal interests. Weber's remarks are made in his study of bureaucracy in Wirtschaft und Gesellschaft, part III, cf. 6, esp. p. 656.

THE ECONOMY OF EGYPT IN THE EARLIER FOURTH CENTURY*

Alan K. Bowman

1. The contribution of the papyri

The economic history of the fourth century has recently received a good deal of attention. Apart from works which deal with Egypt specifically, more general discussions of the empire draw, more or less heavily, on the evidence of the papyri.[1] Understandably, since there is a considerable amount of detailed papyrological evidence for this period. Many of the documents are, however, difficult to interpret and still imperfectly understood. It is perhaps not surprising, then, that the reader who searches for some consensus of scholarly opinion on the state of the economy in this period will find a broad range of views.[2] It is hardly necessary to emphasise the need for a thorough re-examination of the evidence of the papyri. A synthesis of this evidence might then provide us with the means to compare Egypt with the rest of the empire in this period. For obvious reasons, I cannot attempt to do this here. I hope it may nevertheless be useful to point out some of the difficulties presented by the papyrological evidence and to indicate the major areas in which the papyri might be expected to yield information, with the caveat that any conclusions which emerge at this stage are merely tentative. Given the relative abundance of evidence, it seems sensible to limit the scope of this enquiry to the earlier part of the fourth century, in particular to the first four decades. At the outset, some observations about the methodological problems inherent in interpreting the evidence and in placing Egypt in the context of the empire as a whole.

I have elsewhere[3] criticised the tendency of Roman historians to point to the supposed atypicality of Egypt and thus absolve themselves from the need to determine its ability to illuminate conditions in the empire as a whole. Historians of the later empire are, in fact, not especially culpable in this

---

* The following standard works appear as short titles or abbreviations in the footnotes:

A. H. M. Jones, The Later Roman Empire, 284-602 (1964) (LRE)
A. H. M. Jones, The Roman Economy (1974) (RE)
A. C. Johnson, L. C. West, Byzantine Egypt, Economic Studies (1949, reprint 1967)
L. C. West, A. C. Johnson, Currency in Roman and Byzantine Egypt (1944, reprint 1967)
T. Frank, Economic Survey of Ancient Rome II, A. C. Johnson, Roman Egypt to the Reign of Diocletian (1936)
Armées et fiscalité dans le monde antique (CNRS, colloques no. 936, 1977)
Les "Dévaluations" à Rome (Collection de l'école francaise de Rome 37, 1978)
J.-P. Callu, La Politique monétaire des Empéreurs romains de 238 à 311 (1969)

respect. If we accept the view that one of the major effects of the Diocletianic reforms was to assimilate Egypt to the rest of the Empire, it might seem reasonable to 'mix and match' our evidence, to draw upon the papyri in formulating general views, as several important works of scholarship have done.[4] It is very easy, of course, to insist on the need to understand Egypt on the basis of a secure interpretation of the papyrological evidence before attempting to extend that understanding more widely. But such perfection of method _is_ merely an ideal and we are frequently faced with the difficulty of effecting a _rapprochement_ between two (or more) different sets of data which are themselves imperfectly understood. These rather abstract remarks can be neatly illustrated by pointing out some of the difficulties which are involved in attempting to synthesise the evidence for economic and monetary reform in the early fourth century.

The inscriptional evidence for the coinage reform of A.D. 301 and the Maximum Price Edict present, in themselves, various difficulties of interpretation which need to be considered in relation to the evidence of the coinage and of the papyri.[5] Take the price of gold. The papyri are fairly clear: in A.D. 300 the price of a pound of gold was 60,000 _denarii_, _c_. A.D. 304-6 it was 100,000 _denarii_.[6] The Aezani copy of the Maximum Price Edict gives a price of 72000 _denarii_ for December, 301.[7] So far, so clear. But an attempt to relate these data to the price of silver and to the coinage reform complicates matters. After September 301 the _argenteus_, struck at 96 to the pound, was worth 100 _denarii_, therefore 9,600 _denarii_ for a pound of silver. At the ratio of 12:1 applied to silver and gold in the Price Edict, a pound of gold would be worth 115,000 _denarii_ in September 301.[8] Two explanations are possible. Either the Price Edict brought this high price down to 72,000 or, alternatively, the coinage reform and Price Edict allowed for overvaluation of silver coinage in relation to bullion whilst expressly denying it in the case of gold.[9] In other words, the 12:1 ratio of gold to silver bullion was real whilst the 12:1 ratio of the _aureus_ to the _argenteus_ was artificial.[10]

The application of papyrological evidence to problems of this sort may cause difficulties genuine or spurious. The case of _P. Ant_. 38 exemplifies the latter. An obscure text which may, or may not, provide evidence for the price of bronze in A.D. 301, according to the editor, and thus perhaps bear upon the details of the monetary reform. When the date is corrected to A.D. 300 it becomes less relevant.[11] Genuine difficulties are raised by the evidence for the value of the so-called _follis_. A value of 12½ denarii, raised to 25 by the reform of 301, is supported by papyrological evidence.[12] Three rather obscure texts refer to an apparent revaluation of coinage mentioning values of 12½ and 25 _denarii_. They might be made to fit into the scheme of A.D. 301 or, alternatively, they might be connected with the coins issued by Licinius and marked XIIS (at a date once thought to be _c_. A.D. 308 but now put about a decade later than this).[13] Whatever one makes of this, it does not seem to cast any light on the XX.1 or KA markings on post 301 _folles_. Scholars who accept a follis of 25 _denarii_ in September, 301, postulate a reduction to 20 _denarii_ in conjunction with the issue of the Price Edict in December.[14]

In short, it seems abundantly clear that problems still exist and a papyrologist might be forgiven for hoping that the experts in coinage will reach numismatically secure conclusions against which the papyrological data may be tested. Unfortunately, Egypt itself has not yielded a very rich harvest of fourth century coinage and it appears difficult to gauge the relationship between rising prices and the amount and type of coinage in circulation. The papyri themselves continue to reckon in drachmas and talents long after the Alexandrian tetradrachm went out of production.[15] On the whole, given the extraordinary volume of agricultural productivity in Egypt, I doubt whether we are justified in applying to it conclusions about the circulation of coinage which are based on numismatic data from other provinces.

A related question is the nature and effect of inflation in the fourth century. Jones remarked that if we are to understand the ancient economy we have to divest ourselves of modern notions of how the economy works and what means might be employed to deal with problems.[16] Not only is this impossible, it is far from clear that it is desirable if it means that modern concepts are in principle not useful in analysing ancient society. Let us oversimplify and sketch out what might be regarded as a communis opinio. The third and fourth centuries were periods of massive inflation. Prices expressed in denarii or drachmas rose enormously in a relatively short space of time. Diocletian's reforms attempted to curb this inflation but they clearly failed and by the middle of the fourth century, with the increased use of gold coinage, the basis of the monetary economy had changed. But scholars do not agree on the nature of the inflation in the fourth century. It has been said that the price increases expressed in copper coinage do not represent "real" inflation because there were no such massive rises in terms of the purchasing power of gold.[17] The question of whether the cost of living rose for most people depends on the extent of which they were able to use gold in making monetary transactions. If, as I believe, gold was only available in very limited quantities in the early fourth century, then most people would have experienced a fall in their standard of living unless salaries kept pace with price increases. A thorough investigation needs to take account of the availability and use of gold, payments in depreciating copper currency and the extent to which these were supplemented by payments in kind. The nature of imperial monetary policy is also crucial. If we suppose that the government enabled people to cope with higher prices by simply putting more currency into circulation, then we must ask whether there were any limits to its ability to "print" money and when they might be reached.[18] In other words, inflation cannot be viewed only from the point of view of a cost-of-living index or of the health of a national economy in relation to an international system, as in the modern world. For the Roman empire we must ask, primarily, whether the government's ability to extract revenue was impaired and what was the economic condition of the taxpaying population after the revenue had been extracted.

These are very complex questions and the general tone of pessimism which has so far been dominant may suggest that I have no very great hope of being able to answer them satisfactorily at this stage. A contribution might be made, however, by emphasising the peculiar virtue of the papyri—the fact that they do tell us a very great deal about the economic behaviour of individuals both in private transactions and in their relationship with the government. They tell us about the burdens imposed on taxpayers and the extent to which they could be met (or avoided), about the nature and pattern of landholding (the basis of most of the wealth produced in Egypt) and about the way in which people actually used the money that was available to them. The remainder of this paper is devoted to an examination of these three crucial areas of the economy in the light of what the papyri actually tell us. I cannot pretend either to be aiming at completeness or to be immune from reliance upon readings and interpretations of documents made by editors which may later turn out to be crucially misleading. The practice of merely plucking a few of the choicer fruits might at least indicate what seem to me to be some of the more profitable lines along which further enquiry might proceed.

2. Taxation

Under Diocletian the tax-system in the empire was radically reorganised and we must ask how this reorganisation affected Egypt. I do not propose to discuss the details of *capitatio* and *iugatio*. The *iugum* as a unit of taxation does not appear in Egypt in the early fourth century but the principle of assessment, a rate of tax which might vary from year to year and which was applied differentially to land of differing quality and yield, rests on the *aroura* unit.[19] Personal taxation was also imposed. The tax-schedule (or, at least, its existence) is well-enough attested as are the new census procedures.[20] Several features of the new system are of great interest and lead us naturally to the question of how it differed from the previous procedure.

The land-tax yielded large quantities of foodstuffs and now subsumed the *annona militaris* which had been raised in the third century by irregular impositions. The machinery of collection and distribution of *annona* to the soldiers was systematised. I believe that *P. Beatty Panop*. 2 (A.D. 300) provides early evidence for the system which operated, in its essential features, for the whole of our period. Its great virtue lay in the centralisation of the points of collection and the directness of the distribution to the soldiers, a major part of the burden being imposed on local officials, appointed as liturgists by the councils.[21] As far as consumption was concerned, it seems clear that there was a significant increase in the number of military personnel in the province receiving rations in this form, but there is no doubt that the land-tax continued to supply more than simply the required *annona militaris*.[22]

Several points can be made concerning the burden of taxation. The great virtue of the new tax rates was that they tied taxability to productivity and did not exempt land of poor quality.[23] But taxpayers still had difficulty meeting their obligations. Farmers in small towns or rural villages were still liable to be abused by the tax-collectors and find themselves paying more than their due. A papyrus of A.D. 314 from the archive of Aurelius Isidorus (*P. Cair. Isid*. 73) contains a long list of complaints about illegal exactions by the komarchs of Karanis. Taxpayers commonly fell into arrears with their payments and were allowed to make up deficits in cash. An arrears list for the chaff collection drawn up in A.D. 314 shows deficits going back three years and involving almost half of the payers listed elsewhere (*P. Cair. Isid*. 17, A.D. 314). The procedure of commutation into cash is commonly attested for arrears (*adaeratio*); one might assume that the government would be unwilling to take bad currency instead of good produce and we must assume that it did so only because it had no alternative if the produce was simply not available.[24] Scholars have attempted to explain the incidence of *adaeratio*, though it is actually not clear whether it increased or decreased during this period, with reference to the state of the currency but I suspect that it was treated by tax-collectors and ultimately by the government as an acceptable method of fulfilling obligations if all else failed. If a commodity were commuted into gold, the loss was presumably minimal, as for instance with provision of recruits (P. Abinn. 35). Copper currency could be returned without loss to the government either in the form of payment for the soldiers instead of annona or in payment for requisitions at a rate below market prices.[25] In any case, collectors themselves would be keen to collect their quotas in some form in order to avoid having to underwrite deficits themselves.[26] It is difficult to be sure that this system had an immediately ruinous effect on the prosperity of the taxpaying population. We know that farmers formed themselves into groups with corporate responsibility for the payment of taxes. Flight from the land is attested although the evidence is not sufficient to suggest abandonment on a massive scale. Petitions in which taxpayers complain of their inability to pay and threaten or refer to desertion sometimes suggest an element of exaggeration and people who did flee were sometimes known to be farming elsewhere.[27]

Apart from taxes in kind, the government continued to extract revenues in cash. It is natural to suppose that it did not wish to suffer the effects of depreciating currency and some scholars have supposed that the copper currency now largely functioned as a means of exchange between private individuals whilst the government resorted to operating largely in commodities.[28] But there is good evidence for the continued collection of personal taxes in cash in the first half of the fourth century; several documents refer to payments which are somehow based on κεφαλαί; and many tax accounts show payments in copper currency which are not obviously made as a result of adaeratio.[29] P. Rylands 616 (c. A.D. 312) records, inter alia, the assessment of money taxes for a number of nomes in the Delta; the total appears to be in excess of 17 million denarii, which is not an insignificant amount even at this date (it would buy over 154 lbs of gold at the official government rate).[30] Transportation taxes were collected in copper currency, though there is evidence from the early years of the century of taxes on trades being assessed in gold.[31] It is worth noting the practice of exacting cash in order to pay for government requisitions and the evidence of P. Cair. Isid. 73 that this led to abuses. Apparently, governmental purchases of bullion were financed in this way for we have evidence of payments in copper currency εἰς λόγον ἀσήμου or some similar phrase.[32] This seems a more plausible interpretation than to suppose that taxpayers were allowed to commute their obligations in bullion into copper currency since this would negate the whole point of the imposition.

The exaction of gold and silver bullion demands some attention. The government conducted compulsory purchases of bullion (it is not clear how regularly) which landholders were compelled to acquire for sale to the government at fixed rates. The assessment was probably based on landholding; Aurelius Isidorus appears to have provided bullion at the rate of 12 oz. silver and 1 oz. gold per hundred artabs of wheat paid in taxes.[33] The rates which the government paid for this may well have been below the market price and the copper currency paid out for it may have been exacted as a tax, as we have seen.[34] There were strictures against dealers charging rates higher than the government would pay but there is no doubt that this must frequently have happened.[35] As an illustration of this we may note that the city authorities of Oxyrhynchus bought gold for the presentation of a crown to Licinius junior (yet another form of exaction) at a price well above that which the government was using in payment for goods about seven years later.[36]

This selection of evidence (by no means exhaustive) for some of the major aspects of taxation in the early fourth century suggests that a major ingredient in the health of Egypt as a producer of revenue was the ability to maintain a balance between the natural and the monetary economy. By the 'natural' economy I mean commodities including not only foodstuffs, but also clothing and gold and silver bullion; the monetary economy is limited, at this period, almost entirely to the copper currency for silver and gold coinage did not play a great part in it.[37] The government did operate in kind to a large extent but I do not believe that it is legitimate to relegate the role of the ever-depreciating copper currency to the area of market transactions between private individuals. The government continued to collect it in significant quantities and to disburse it as stipendium to soldiers, as salaries to officials and as payment for requisitions. Such requisitions included bullion, clothing and foodstuffs and it was frequently the case that prices paid for these items were well below market rates.[38] This is equivalent to saying that when the government did operate with the depreciating copper currency it tried to make sure that such transactions worked in its favour.

Two important general issues remain to be considered briefly. First, the overall burden of tax in the early fourth century and second, the proportion of that burden levied in kind. It is difficult to be sure whether the populace was taxed more heavily in the early fourth century. Lactantius observes that the number of consumers was greater than the number of providers and there is no doubt that the late empire nurtured a much-enlarged and parasitical civilian and military bureaucracy.[39] There is little evidence, though, in this period for a precipitate decline in prosperity caused by over-taxation. Presumably the level of agricultural productivity was held constant, if not perhaps increased (see below, on Landholding). One must assume that the rate of taxation was not so high as to render the taxpayers incapable of meeting their own needs as well as those of the government. A most important document has recently been published which shows that in the early fourth centrry the Oxyrhynchite Nome produced almost half a million artabs of wheat in taxes on private land and rents on public.[40] The private land (4/5 of the total area) is taxed at a low rate, about 0.7 artab per aroura, whilst the rent on public land averages about 8 artabs per aroura (much higher than the average of about 4½ in the earlier empire).[41] The total for an area of somewhat over 200,000 arouras[42] can be compared with the figure of six million artabs cited by Aurelius Victor for the reign of Augustus,[43] but it is difficult to calculate what proportion of Egypt's revenues in wheat the Oxyrhynchite will have supplied. At any rate, the considerations advanced in the following section combine to suggest that the majority of landholders were not taxed at a very heavy rate on the major proportion of their holdings (i.e. private land). It is almost impossible to make a guess at the volume of revenue in cash in this period from scattered bits of evidence which I have mentioned and it is probably wise to suspend judgement. But it might be as well to add that one area in which we can be fairly certain that revenue will have increased is the unseen income of liturgical service demanded by the government of the curial classes in Egypt; from the early fourth century the heavy burden of liturgical service is aimed at those functions essential to the government rather than the local towns.[44]

It is generally assumed that the fourth century saw a greater emphasis on taxation in kind but this is not easy to justify. Taxes in kind predominated at all periods and the tax records from the earlier principate might lead us to conclude that a very high proportion of the total revenues of Egypt were extracted in kind.[45] It would then be hard to imagine a very dramatic increase in the fourth century. Diocletian's systematisation of the tax system, the integration of the annona militaris into the land tax and the more direct methods of collection and supply do not necessarily, in themselves, either prove or disprove an overall increase in the tax burden (I here specifically exclude requisitions as a means of obtaining commodities cheaply) or an increase in the proportion of revenue extracted in kind. They need imply no more than rationalisation. But the tax rates were in principle variable from year to year and it is therefore difficult to draw any generally valid conclusion. It may well be that the revenues in staple agricultural produce (wheat, barley, lentils) did not rise dramatically but that there was a higher level of supplementation in other produce and commodities from levies and requisitions.

3. Landholding

It hardly needs emphasising that the basis of wealth in the province of Egypt was the land and that consequently questions about tax-rates and taxability, about the role of currency and the nature of monetary transactions depend heavily upon our conception of the nature and role of the landholder. It was not simply that revenues in kind were based on landholding. As we have seen, compulsory purchase of bullion by the government was based on the quantity of taxes paid in kind.[46] The prosperity of Egypt's landholders was therefore always a crucial aspect of the government's ability to draw sufficient revenue from the province. There is plenty of evidence from the early empire—not all of it relating to Egypt—of landholders having difficulty in meeting their tax obligations. The problem is chronic; we can cite the edict of Tiberius Julius Alexander, the existence of the μερισμὸς ἀνακεχωρηκότων designed to meet the obligations of those who had fled, the enforced cultivation of abandoned land.[47] How had the situation changed by the early fourth century?

The most important single change is to be observed in the categories in which land was classified from the reign of Diocletian onwards. Instead of the numerous and complex categories of the earlier principate we now find that the majority of land is described as either ἰδιωτική or δημοσία. The Imperial House still owned land but even this may have been reduced in quantity; land is sometimes described as belonging to a town (πολιτική).[48] Some (perhaps a great deal) of the public land was assigned for compulsory cultivation, now called ἐπινέμησις or ἐπιβολή .[49] By encouraging private ownership to a much greater extent the government no doubt hoped to give the landholders a closer and more permanent attachment to their holdings. My impression is that this might well have worked. The owners themselves could continue to lease out parts of their property. A landholder who found difficulty in meeting the obligations on his holdings might lease from another in order to make up his deficit or might go into partnership with someone else. Hence, an individual's holdings might increase or decrease, as did those of Aurelius Isidorus.[50] There is little evidence to suggest the wholesale abandonment of land. The tax records attest payment on behalf of ἄπορα ὀνόματα but land thus abandoned might be reassigned.[51] It is worth noting that the villagers of Theadelphia claimed in A.D. 331-2 that various Theadelphians who had abandoned their land in the village were to be found farming elsewhere (P. Thead. 17 = P. Sakaon 44); they were therefore reacting not against farming as such, but against particular problems in one locality. On the whole the evidence, or lack of it, supports Jones' view that this phenomenon will only have affected a small amount of marginal land at this time.[52]

We are fortunate in being able to analyse the pattern of landholding in the early fourth century by considering the evidence of the extensive Hermopolite land-lists.[53] Jones' analysis of P. Flor. 71 is most revealing.[54] Of the total holdings of over 21,000 arouras, almost 19,000 consist of private land. The holdings are generally small; over 2/3 of the Hermopolite (as opposed to Antinoite) owners have under 30 arouras and the holdings of the larger owners are scattered rather than consolidated. Of the 233 Hermopolite owners living in the Sorth Fort district, 7 own between them over half the total area and a further 7 another quarter. These statistics are not significantly affected by the new data in P. Giss. 117. Several interesting conclusions may be drawn. The gap between small and large landholder is very great and the concentration of wealth in the hands of a few is marked. But there is no very clear tendency towards the build-up of very large consolidated estates; in other words, whilst the preconditions for the development of patrocinia may have existed there is no sign that this development had yet begun. If the plots were fragmented the basic agricultural pattern of labour and production will have changed little from the earlier principate. The great predominance of private ownership is marked, in a proportion of about 13:1. Jones argued that this imbalance was probably not typical of the nome as a whole but peculiar to the land closer to the metropolis (though he appears to have overlooked the fact that 17 pagi are attested and this must account for almost all the nome divisions) and that in rural areas the proportions will have been more nearly equal. A comparison with the Oxyrhynchite Nome, which yields a proportion of public to private land at 1:4.2,[55] reveals that the imbalance is not quite so severe but still marked. The rentals from the public land in the Oxyrhynchite average 8.2 artabs per aroura whilst the tax on private land averages 0.7 artabs per aroura. If the yield per aroura was about 13 artabs the high rental on public land does not offer subsistence to a peasant family.[56] But public land in the Hermopolite is held in small lots and almost exclusively by people who also own private land. In the Oxyrhynchite the public land (1/5 of the total) provides 3/4 of the total revenue in wheat. The high rentals therefore appear to be subsidising the low rate of tax on private land. We might therefore conclude that the public land was assigned in small lots to private owners who were enabled, by their private holdings, to offset the disadvantageous terms on which they held the public land. If it is true that the town-dwelling landlords held less public land than those resident in the outlying villages of the nome, it would follow that the town-population was proportionately better off than the rural.

Land continues to be leased and sold in the first half of the fourth century. Some scholars have concluded to a reduction in the scale of this activity since the evidence is less plentiful than for the earlier empire.[57] However, a comparison of the two Hermopolite lists suggests that a good deal of land was still changing hands. We have no precise date for either list,[58] but a rough count of the discrepancies between the lists of Hermopolite owners at the points where they are directly comparable reveals that almost a fifth of the owners appear in one list but not the other.[59] Sale of land may not account for all these differences but it would be remarkable if it did not account for a fair proportion. Similarly, a random check of individual owners who do appear in both lists shows, in a minority of cases, significant discrepancies in the quantity of land held. In almost all these cases the differences relate to the holdings of private, not public land.[60] The few documents which record prices paid for land in the early fourth century show considerable variation, but given the normal lack of information about differences in the quality of the land, it is not safe to draw any conclusions about the effects of inflation.[61] But it clearly did not inhibit entirely the movement of private land both in small and fairly large lots.[62] Examples of leases of private land from the early fourth century show a tendency to short-term leasing with variable rentals, from 9 artabs down to 1 artab per aroura, the amount depending partly on whether the owner or the lessee paid the taxes. Rentals paid in cash are now exceptional.[63] The taxpayer, whether owner or lessee, is thus protected against increases in the price of produce and, by his short-term lease, against drastic rises in the rate of tax from one year to another. Whatever the reasons for these changes, we are certainly entitled to conclude that in the first half of the fourth century the agricultural economy of Egypt still depended to a very large extent on a great number of small landowners and lessees. The so-called Byzantine feudal estate still lies in the future.

4. Money

In A.D. 308 Aurelius Isidorus of Karanis and the other members of his pittakion sold, in advance of delivery, 100 artabs of beans for a sum of 15 talents (P. Cair. Isid. 89). The sum of money was to be used for the purchase of gold and silver bullion to meet an assessment on their estates. This transaction, which is in effect a loan, reveals much about the relationship between money, commodities and taxation in the early fourth century. Isidorus needed the cash to buy the bullion which he was compelled to provide for purchase by the government and since he did not have it he borrowed on the strength of a forthcoming crop. Other documents of this kind often contain built-in interest and anti-inflation devices by specifying that the loan is to be repaid in kind at the price current at the time of repayment less one third (i.e. 50 per cent interest).[64] Isidorus presumably had to buy the bullion from a gold- or silversmith (or merchant) at current market rates which might well be higher than the rates paid by the government.[65] He might, therefore, have borrowed 15 talents, spent it on gold which he sold to the government for 12 talents and at the end of the transaction he would have a sum of depreciating copper currency instead of his crop. The moneylender is protected by the fact that he receives his payment in kind. Of the four principal figures in this transaction, government, moneylender, seller of gold and farmer it is only the latter who obviously stands to lose. The government gains most, especially if it bought the bullion with money levied as tax for the purpose (above, p. 27).

Whatever we might say about the later predominance of gold currency, it seems clear that gold coins were available to the average person only in very limited quantities in the earlier part of the century.[66] Isidorus had to buy gold and silver; if he had possessed aurei, he would presumably have been able to use them since their purity and value was guaranteed. We might note in this connection that in A.D. 296 we have an example of the use of three ὁλοκοττινοί to make a piece of jewellery (P. Mich. 218). It is obvious that bullion was available on the open market and the government is found distributing silver to soldiers in A.D. 300 (P. Beatty Panop. 2). In A.D. 304 a church at Oxyrhynchus declared that it possessed μήτε χρυσὸν μήτε ἄσημον μήτε ἀργύριον κτλ. But it seems that gold coins were never available in great abundance. Two fourth century letters, both unfortunately undated, contain instructions to the addressee to purchase gold coins, ἐαν εὕρῃς (P. Herm. Rees 11, PSI 825). References to the purchase or possession of gold coins are generally in single figures: a centurion bequeathed eight of them, Theophanes bought seven, loans of two or three solidi are recorded.[67] In fact, it is not until about A.D. 340 that we find gold coinage appearing at all in loan contracts.[68] It is also notable that the price of solidi on the open market appears to have fluctuated considerably in very short periods of time.[69] We are forced to conclude, therefore, that gold coinage did not figure heavily as a medium of exchange in Egypt in the earlier part of the century. The fluctuations in price make it clear that the market value of gold coins was not fixed by the government, no matter what official rate might theoretically have been in force. But for most people this will have had very little significance except in terms of their need to meet government assessments.

Silver coin was produced only at certain periods and in limited quantities in Egypt and it seems clear to me that the copper currency (whose volume of circulation appears very difficult to gauge from Egyptian numismatic evidence) was the principal medium of exchange in monetary transactions.[70] That its use was not limited to the private sector can be seen from a brief examination of some relevant papyrological evidence.

First, the use of copper currency in transactions in which the government was involved. It continued to pay its soldiers' stipendium in copper currency. P. Beatty Panop.2 clearly shows that the large amounts of coin were physically handled by soldiers and officials. Admittedly, the stipendium was now only a part of the soldier's income, but there is evidence for annona payments commuted into coin and for the payment of donatives in cash.[71] Diocletian's complaint about the reduced purchasing power of the soldier's stipendium should be taken seriously;[72] the soldier was a participant in the economic life of a province and if he bought and sold he did so, for the most part, with copper currency like the rest of the populace. The accumulated wealth of a retired centurion included 8 aurei and 199 1/2 talents (see below, p. 33). Similarly, in the second and third decades of the century Theophanes, a government official, was paid in copper currency and conducted his daily transactions in it whilst on official business.[73] Even at this time, the prices for individual items do not suggest the need for ridiculously large amounts of copper coin but as prices rose it is likely that the government simply renamed old coins and assigned higher nominal values to them.[74] As we have already seen, the government continued to collect significant amounts of copper currency in the form of tax. Apart from payment of salaries, it was used to pay for requisitions on terms generally favourable to the government (above, pp. 26-9). It seems to me unlikely that, by and large, the government minted new copper currency, put it into circulation and did not take it back again; this is not only out of tune with the evidence of the papyri, but it does not take account of the limited availability of the metal itself.[75]

Important questions regarding the use of money in the private sector are equally obscured by our inability to compile a plausible cost-of-living index.[76] We can be clear on the general point that the use of copper currency was pervasive, though supplemented to an increasing extent by payments in kind. An account of wages from A.D. 308 shows payment by a grammaticus for unspecified services in a mixture of cash and kind.[77] Aurelius Isidorus arranged a substitute for his brother in a liturgy in A.D. 297 at a rate of 200 drachmas per day and rations for the two-month period (P. Cair. Isid. 81). We can document a fivefold increase in the wages paid to a rhabdouchos in A.D. 301 and 325, which keeps pace with the increase in the price of gold but not with the depreciation of the currency in which he was paid.[78] When viewed in terms of purchasing power, rates for labour at Hermopolis in the early fourth century compare very badly with the earlier empire but the rates quoted may be misleading because of the tendency to supplement with payments in kind.[79] By A.D. 338 an account for a large estate at Hermonthis shows the predominance of payments in kind to agricultural workers, protecting their level of subsistence but not necessarily providing them with any purchasing power (P. Lips. 97).

It is difficult to gauge the effects of price increases expressed in terms of denarii or drachmas when we have so little information about the means by which individuals obtained money, especially if these increases are partly the result of nominal revaluation. There is not even complete agreement about the periods which saw very sharp price increases, though it seems clear that one such phase occurred about the middle of the century.[80] But throughout the period individuals continue to make loans in copper currency, generally for fairly short terms, sometimes with payment of interest in kind and often with illegally high rates of interest in cash hidden in the terms of the contract.[81] A loan contract of A.D. 337 specifies interest at the rate of 24 per cent per annum for a period of eight months, increasing to 40 per cent if the capital is not paid at the agreed time (P. Oxy. 3266). Evidence of this type seems to indicate quite clearly that people took steps to protect themselves against rising prices in the copper currency which they generally used, even though they might prefer the safer and less cumbersome gold coinage![82] The centurion's will of A.D. 320 which I have already mentioned (above, p. 32) shows what an individual of moderate status might accumulate: eight aurei, 199 1/2 talents and a long list of routine domestic and other objects. Reckoning at the current market price for gold ca. A.D. 316-8 (P. Oxy. 3307), just under 20 per cent of his monetary wealth is accounted for by the gold. It is difficult to estimate the purchasing power of his talents in A.D. 320 because of the lack of reliable evidence for prices. At the various prices attested for wheat in A.D. 314, they would have bought between 100 and 150 artabs (more than 8 years' normal food allowance in the earlier empire).[83] If we accept that the fluctuations in commodity prices represent the reality of market, we will abandon our attempts to plot a predictable inflation and recognise that the monetary transactions which are attested reflect the genuine uncertainty (at least in the short term) of the people who used the currency. It may not be a neat solution but it is, I submit, a plausible one.

NOTES

1. I do not attempt to provide comprehensive bibliographical references here. Recent important works which utilise the evidence of the papyri include: Jones, LRE and RE, chs. IV, IX, X and XIII especially, Callu, La Politique monétaire, ch. V, R. MacMullen, The Roman Government's Response to Crisis (1976). There is no recent book or monograph on the economy of early Byzantine Egypt; we still rely to a considerable extent on A. C. Johnson and L. C. West, Byzantine Egypt, Economic Studies and Currency in Roman and Byzantine Egypt. Much of the source material which I cite in this paper has been discussed by earlier scholars but I have not referred to such discussions except where they make points important for my argument; this omission may seem to minimise my debts to earlier research but anyone familiar with the material will realise the extent of my dependence on the papyrological scholarship of recent decades.

2. See for example, Callu, La Politique monétaire, ch. V, Jones, RE chs. IV, IX, MacMullen, Roman Government's Response to Crisis, chs. V, VI, Johnson and West, Byzantine Egypt, Economic Studies, ch. II (for a fairly optimistic picture of the condition of the peasantry in the earlier fourth century).

3. JRS, 66, 1976, 160ff.

4. See the citations in note 1. Less recent examples are, A. Déléage, La Capitation du bas-Empire, 1945, G. Mickwitz, Geld und Wirtschaft im römischen Reich des vierten Jhdts n. Chr., 1932. An unfortunate contrast is presented by W. Goffart, Caput and Colonate (Phoenix, Suppl. 12, 1974) which completely ignores the evidence of the papyri.

5. The evidence: Erim, Reynolds, Crawford, JRS, 61, 1971, 171ff., R. and F. Naumann, Der Rundbau in Aezani, Istanbuler Mitteilungen, Beiheft 10, 1973, 57, cf. Crawford and Reynolds, ZPE 34, 1979, 176-7. The bibliography is already fairly large. The views cited below are variously represented in the following principal contributions to the discussion: Jahn, JNG, 26, 1976, 91ff., Ruschenbusch, ZPE, 26, 1977, 193ff., Crawford, ANRW, II.2, 560ff., Lafaurie, RN ser. 6, 17, 1975, 73ff., Bruun, Annali Ist. Ital. di Numismatica, 23-4, 1976-7, 225ff., Callu in Les "Dévaluations" à Rome 107ff. and 187ff.

6. P. Beatty Panop. 2. 215-21, P. Oxy. 2106, see Rea, CE, 49, 1974, 163ff.

7. Naumann, loc. cit., note 5.

8. For the calculation see JRS, 61, 1971, 175 and Crawford, ANRW II.2, 580. The ratio of 12:1 for silver:gold is derived from the prices of 6,000 denarii per pound and 72,000 denarii per pound respectively given by the Aezani copy of the Maximum Price Edict (Naumann, loc. cit., note 5).

The face value of the argenteus was 100 denarii, as the Currency Reform inscription attests; the value of the aureus must have been 1,200 denarii in December 301 since the Price Edict clearly sets the price for a pound of gold at 72,000 denarii, whether in bullion or coin (the coins were struck at 60 per pound). An adjustment of Jones' calculations to allow for the new evidence (see RE, 200ff.) suggests that gold and silver continued to appreciate in approximately the same ratio in relation to the bronze coinage. It is worth noting the similar ratio in PSI 310 (8,263 den. per pound of silver) and P. Oxy. 2106 (100,000 den. per pound of gold) which must be approximately contemporary (see Rea, CE, 49, 1974, 164ff., in preference to Lafaurie, RN, ser. 6, 17, 1975, 122ff.).

9. The latter explanation seems preferable to me since it attributes significance to the occurrence of the phrase '[aurum] obryzae in regulis sive [in] solidis' in connection with the price of gold but not of silver (cf. Crawford and Reynolds, ZPE, 34, 1979, 164).

10. The contrast between "real" and "artificial" refers to the fact that gold and silver bullion might appreciate at the same rate (see above note 8) whereas the ratio between gold and silver coin is bound to become distorted if the value of gold coin is tied to the price of bullion, but silver not. Thus, if we assume (see note 8, above) that PSI 310 and P. Oxy. 2106 are roughly contemporary, the ratio of value in bullion is very close to 12:1; the argenteus is still tariffed at 100 denarii, as far as we know, but the aureus must be worth 1,666 denarii (100,000 ÷ 60).

11. Used by Lafaurie, RN, ser. 6, 17, 1975, 109. For the correct date see Manfredi, Atti XI Congresso Internazionale di Papirologia, Milano 1965, 1966, 243ff., cf. Crawford and Reynolds, ZPE, 34, 1979, 164.

12. P. Beatty. Panop. 2. 301-2 (see note ad loc. and Jones, RE, ch. XVI). As several commentators have seen, frag. b of the Currency Reform Edict must be restored to refer to a value of 25 denarii: '... vigin]ti quinque den[ari]orum potentia vige[...', but there does not seem to be agreement on which denomination this must represent (cf. the remarks of Callu, Les "Dévaluations" à Rome, 107ff. and compare, e.g. Ruschenbusch, ZPE, 26, 1977, 208).

13. The texts are P. Ryl. 607, P. Osl. 83 and PSI 965, discussed briefly by Jones, RE, 226-7, by Ruschenbusch, op. cit. (n. 12), 206-8 and by Crawford, ANRW II.2, 589 (amongst many). Ruschenbusch restores PSI 965 so as to refer to the Diocletianic reform against Crawford's view that the papyri reflect the change introduced by Licinius. It is not clear to me that PSI 965.6 can be referring to a reduction in face value from 25 to 12 1/2 den. (of course, the three texts need not all refer to the same event).

14. E.g. Callu, Les "Dévaluations" à Rome, 108-9. Crawford, ANRW II.2, 588 supposes an increase back to 25 den. in A.D. 307, followed by Licinius' reduction a decade or so later; Callu, loc. cit. argues for this in A.D. 318 followed by a reduction to 12 1/2 for the nummus between A.D. 320 and 324.

15. The status of the old Alexandrian coinage remains dubious. West and Johnson, Currency in Roman and Byzantine Egypt, 157 suggest that it lost its status as legal tender, pointing out that pre-296 coin does not appear in hoards with post-296 coin. It may nevertheless have continued to be used in private transactions quite extensively, even if the government refused to accept it in payment. A papyrus of A.D. 300 (SB 7338) refers to a legal dispute arising from a παραθήκη of old coinage, but it is not entirely clear that the dispute arose because the coinage was old.

16. Jones, RE, 187.

17. E.g. Callu, La Politique monétaire, 406, West and Johnson, Currency in Roman and Byzantine Egypt, 168 and cf. Whittaker in the present volume, p. 3.

18. On the physical limitation see Jones, RE 225. It seems to me crucial to ask not only whether the government was simply assigning higher face values to already existing coins, as it clearly was (see the works cited in n. 17 and Callu, Les "Dévaluations" à Rome, 107ff.) but also whether there was enough coinage available in a given area (this raises the question of forgeries on which see most recently Gara, Quaderni ticinesi di num. e ant. class., 1978, 229ff.).

19. See in general, Jones, RE, ch. XIII, Cerati, Caractère annonaire et assiette de l'impot foncier au bas-empire, 1975, 191ff., 243ff., and for Egypt Johnson and West, Byzantine Egypt, Economic Studies, 231. Note particularly the reference in P. Ryl. 658 to ἀρουρηδὸν καὶ ἀνδρισμός (cf. P. Thead. 17 = P. Sakaon 44) which suggests assimilation in principle, if not in detail to the practices introduced elsewhere in the empire.

20. P. Cair. Isid. 1-8. In general cf. Jones, LRE, 62ff.

21. For the relationship between the land-tax and the annona militaris Carrié, Armées et fiscalité, 379, Browne, HSCP, 75, 1971, 184 n. 7 and P. Mich. 643-6 introd. On the commissariat, Bowman, BASP, 15, 1978, 34-8, Van Berchem, Armées et fiscalité, 331ff.

22. On the increase in the soldiery see Bowman, op. cit. (n. 21), Duncan-Jones, Chiron, 8, 1978, 541ff.; on the economic effects of the presence of the army see Carrié, Armées et fiscalité, 377ff., Les "Dévaluations" à Rome, 227ff. For other calls upon the land-tax, Johnson and West, Byzantine Egypt, Economic Studies, 234.

23. P. Cair. Isid. p. 105; for assessments on poor land see, for example, P. Thead. 17 (= P. Sakaon 44), Youtie, ZPE, 32, 1978, 237ff.

24. For contrasting views on adaeratio see, for example, MacMullen, Aegyptus, 42, 1962, 98ff., Carrié, Armées et fiscalité, 378. For the variety of taxes to which the procedure might be applied, P. Cair. Isid. 59 (A.D. 316-8). In P. Abinn. 5 payment in hay is commuted into wheat (it is relevant that taxes could be imposed in wheat and barley on land which produced neither crop).

25. In P. Beatty Panop. 2 soldiers sometimes receive their annona in the form of cash (e.g. 11.36-42). For requisitions see, for example, P. Oxy. 3194 (A.D. 323), P. Cair, Isid. 54 (A.D, 314), 58 (A.D. 315) and cf. the remarks below, p. 33 .

26. This I take to be the fear which underlies the sentiments expressed in P. Reinach 56, οὐ θέλομεν γὰρ ἄχυρον μὴ πως μὴ λημφθῇ καὶ ἀναγκασθῶμεν τὴν τιμὴν διαγράψαι (badly misunderstood, I think, by S. Mazzarino, Aspetti sociali del quarto secolo, 1951, 137ff. as tendency against adaeratio). It is not clear under what circumstances adaeratio might be prohibited by the government to protect its own revenues against inflation. It is prohibited in P. Beatty Panop. 2.230ff. because the collectors are extorting more from the taxpayers than their due.

27. For pittakia (corporations of landholders) see P. Cair. Isid. 24-6 and cf. Bagnall, CE, 52, 1977, 322ff. Flight: Boak and Youtie, Studi Calderini-Paribeni II, 1957, 325ff., Jones, LRE 813ff., Whittaker, Studies in Roman Property (ed. M. I. Finley, 1976), 147ff., 152. P. Thead. 17 (= P. Sakaon 44) shows Theadelphians who had fled and were farming elsewhere in A.D. 331-2; twenty years earlier the plight of the village had been described as a state of 'total desertion' (P. Thead. 41 = P. Sakaon 38, A.D. 312).

28. But it is clear, even from a cursory glance at P. Cair. Isid. 41, 59-62, for example, that the government continued to collect a lot of money from adaeratio (see above, pp. 26ff.). For emphasis on currency in the private market sector see Jones, RE, 198 (cf. Liebeschuetz, Rh. Mus., 104, 1961, 242).

29. For personal taxation see P. Oxy. 3036-45, P.NYU 14, BGU 21, WChr. 253, P. Thead. 17, 48, SB 7622-3. On the epikephalaion and the introduction of capitatio see Jones, RE, 289ff., Rémondon, Proc. XIIth International Congress of Papyrology (American Studies in Papyrology, 7, 1970), 431ff. It is supposed that if the epikephalaion was an urban poll-tax, introduced in the 290s, it was abolished before ca. A.D. 320 (though the arguments for its removal do not seem strong). For other cash payments see e.g. P. Mert. 88, P. Cair. Isid. 71, P.NYU 12-14.

30. Reckoning the price of gold in this document at 110,000 den. per pound on the basis of col.ii.10, see Rea, CE, 49, 1974, 165.

31. For transportation taxes see e.g. P. Cair. Isid. 51, 55; for collection of taxes on trade in gold (the forerunner of the collatio lustralis?) see P. Panop. 15, 19 (ZPE 8, 1971, 207ff.). P. Oxy. 3307 appears to attest flat rate exactions in gold in the early fourth century.

32. See P. Mich. 645, Youtie, ZPE, 33, 1979, 206. For further comment on requisitions see below, p. 32 and cf. Vanags in Hassall and Ireland, De rebus bellicis (BAR Int. Ser., 63, 1979).

33. P. Cair. Isid. 89, see Rea, CE, 49, 1974, 163ff., Bagnall, CE, 52, 1977, 322ff.

34. See above this page and n. 32.

35. SB 9253.

36. P. Oxy. 3121 (ca. A.D. 316-8), a price of 432,000 den. per pound, compared to 300,000 den. in P. Oxy. 1430 (A.D. 324).

37. The term ἀργύριον in the papyri, often misleadingly translated as 'silver', refers simply to 'money', i.e. copper currency. For the small amount of silver coinage in Egypt see West and Johnson, Currency in Roman and Byzantine Egypt, 107 and for gold ibid. 109 (but see Callu, Les "Dévaluations" à Rome, 107ff., saying that gold coinage was not struck in Egypt). On the use of gold coin see below, pp. 31ff.

38. On governmental use of copper coin see below, p. 32ff. For requisitions of bullion, above, pp. 27ff.; barley, P. Cair. Isid. 58 (A.D. 315), at 1000 dr. per artab (for comparative prices see introd. at p. 237); clothing, P. Cair. Isid. 54, P. Oxy. 3194, P. Ant. 39, BGU 620 (it is evident that as late as the 320s the government was paying prices very close to those prescribed in the Maximum Price Edict and still deducting 6 1/2 per cent, cf. Rémondon, Rev. Phil., 32, 1958, 244-60 and P. Oxy. 3194 introd.).

39. See Lactantius, De mort. pers. 7.3, Jones, LRE, 1053ff. In the present volume Whittaker pp. 8ff. argues that the cost of the army and bureaucracy is not a sufficient explanation of the decline of the empire.

40. Youtie, ZPE, 32, 1978, 237ff.

41. Figures for the earlier empire in Johnson, Roman Egypt, 504. For rates of taxation on private land and royal land (now effectively in private ownership, P. Cair. Isid. p. 39) see P. Cair. Isid. 11 introd.: wheat 1/2 artab (private), 1 1/2 artabs (royal) plus 10 per cent per aroura; barley, 3/4 artab plus 10 per cent plus the epikouria; chaff, 25 lbs per aroura. Cf. Bagnall, CE, 52, 1977, 330. Of course, the Oxyrhynchite text records only wheat taxes and therefore does not give complete tax returns. See next note.

42. My rough calculation of the total area of the Oxyrhynchite yielded a figure of about 1/4 million arouras; if this is at all close to the mark it suggests that the proportion of land on which taxes were paid in wheat (not necessarily wheat-bearing land, see P. Cair. Isid. p. 109) was about five-sixths of the total. It also suggests, as was assumed by the editor, that the returns in this text are not likely to be partial ones.

43. Victor, Epit. 1.6 (20 million modii).

44. Bowman, The Town Councils of Roman Egypt (American Studies in Papyrology, 11, 1971), 123ff.

45. See S. L. Wallace, Taxation in Egypt from Augustus to Diocletian, 1938, 336ff. Johnson, Roman Egypt, ch. IV whose calculations (pp. 481ff.) underline the fragility of any attempt to divine the total revenues in cash and kind. The principal taxes in kind were paid in wheat, barley, chaff and lentils.

46. Bagnall, CE, 52, 1977, 322ff.

47. G. Chalon, L'édit de Ti. Julius Alexander, 1964, Lewis, JEA, 23, 1937, 63ff., G. Poethke, Epimerismos (Papyrologica Bruxellensia, 8, 1969).

48. On the land categories see Johnson and West, Byzantine Egypt, Economic Studies, 40ff., P. Cair. Isid. p. 39; on imperial ownership, Millar, The Emperor in the Roman World, 1977, Appendix 3; for sales of estates belonging to the fiscus SB 9883.

49. Jones, LRE, 814ff., cf. Lewis, JEA, 29, 1943, 71ff., P. Cair. Isid. 11, introd.

50. For the holdings of Isidorus see most recently Bagnall, CE, 52, 1977, 322ff. For another example of farming in partnership to meet tax obligations, P. Abinn. 50.

51. P. Princ. Roll xiv. 8, P. Thead. 17, 41 (= P. Sakaon 44, 16), cf. the items cited in n. 49 above. Note that twenty years earlier Theadelphia had been described as totally deserted (see above note 27).

52. Jones, LRE, 812ff.

53. Recently re-edited by Sijpesteijn and Worp, Zwei Landlisten aus dem Hermupolites. (P. Landlisten), 1978, for the date see n. 58, below.

54. Jones, RE, 244ff.

55. Youtie, ZPE, 32, 1978, 237ff.

56. The yield is calculated on the basis of Crawford, Kerkeosiris, 1971, 125ff., converting Ptolemaic to Roman artabs. The surplus of 5 art. per year compares badly with the workman's rate of 12 artabs in the principate (Crawford, op. cit., 130). For inability to meet the rents on public land see P. Cair. Isid. 64 (A.D. 298).

57. For the evidence see Johnson and West, Byzantine Egypt, Economic Studies, 78ff.

58. The editors' dating of the texts between 313 and 325 has been challenged by Bagnall, BASP, 16, 1979, 159ff. who proposes to date them in the 340s or perhaps the 350s (accepting the view that P.Giss 117 precedes P.Flor 71). Our inability to date the texts precisely does not significantly affect my analysis, if it is accepted that these texts reflect conditions prevailing in the first half of the fourth century.

59. The lists warrant a detailed statistical analysis which cannot be undertaken here.

60. Some small discrepancies are clearly due to differences in the survey, others to uncertainties or lacunae in the texts. The differences in holdings of public land affect a very small number of people. Our view of gains and losses depends, of course, on the chronological order of the texts (above, note 58).

61. For examples see Johnson and West, Byzantine Egypt, Economic Studies, 78ff., CPR VII.IV 14.

62. The largest holding which I noted as appearing in P. Giss. but not in P. Flor. was one of 383 1/4 arouras; the largest certain discrepancy between the holdings of an owner listed in both texts was 56 arouras. These observations are based on a random check.

63. For a list of leases see Johnson and West, Byzantine Egypt, Economic Studies, 80ff. Noteworthy additions in the archive of Leonides (P. Oxy. 3254-62, A.D. 315-334). SB 7675 exemplifies the fairly common practice of tenants (of village-owned land in this case) paying all taxes in lieu of rent.

64. Bagnall, GRBS, 18, 1977, 85ff.

65. See above note 36.

66. See above, note 37.

67. The centurion's will: Lewis, *Akten des XII int. Papyrologenkongresses*, 1973, 225. Theophanes: *P. Ryl.* 643. Loans: *P. Abinn.* 21, 37.

68. *SPP* 20.139, *P. Abinn.* 21, 37.

69. See *ZPE*, 22, 1976, 97ff., an undated text assigned to the mid-fourth century, which records prices of 36, 17 and 12 1/2 talents for a *solidus* (*cf.* *P. Ryl.* IV p. 107).

70. As Whittaker argues in this volume, pp. 2 the copper coinage now functioned essentially as token money.

71. See Jones, *RE*, 216, Duncan-Jones, *Chiron*, 8, 1978, 541ff.; for annona payments and donatives in cash, *P. Beatty Panop.* 2.36ff., 160ff., and *ZPE*, 22, 1976, 97-106 provide examples.

72. *Edictum de pretiis* (ed. **S.** Lauffer), *praef.* 10-12.

73. Centurion's will, Lewis, *loc. cit.* (in note 67). Archive of Theophanes, *P. Ryl.* 617-651.

74. West and Johnson, *Currency in Roman and Byzantine Egypt*, 166, Jones *RE* 215, Bagnall and Sijpesteijn, *ZPE*, 24, 1977, 120.

75. Jones, *RE* 217ff. talks of the government putting excessive quantities of denarii into circulation as pay for the troops or in the purchase of supplies, using money-changers (p. 219) but he then takes the view (p. 225) that the inflation from the reign of Constantine onwards was caused by the device of assigning higher nominal values to the coins.

76. See the remarks of Bagnall and Sijpesteijn, *ZPE*, 24, 1977, 114-6.

77. *ZPE*, 34, 1979, 81ff.

78. Bagnall and Sijpesteijn, *ZPE*, 24, 1977, 116ff.

79. Duncan-Jones, *Les "Dévaluations" à Rome*, 160ff.

80. Callu, *Les "Dévaluations" à Rome*, 114 sees a turning point *ca.* A.D. 338, Bagnall-Sijpesteijn, *ZPE*, 24, 1977, 120 note a new wave of sharply higher prices about A.D. 350.

81. Pestman, *JJP*, 16-17, 1971, 1ff., Bagnall, *GRBS*, 18, 1977, 85ff.

82. The writer of *P. Herm. Rees* 11 points out that gold coinage is much more convenient to carry, instructing the addressee to buy *solidi* ἵνα εὐχρεῶς κατέλθῃς μετ᾽αὐτῶν πρός με.

83. Crawford, *Kerkeosiris*, 130, Johnson, *Roman Egypt*, 220ff.

RÔLE ET DISTRIBUTION DES ESPÈCES DE BRONZE DE 348 A 392

INTRODUCTION

En 1973[1] avaient été traitées les années 313-348. Maintenant nous parcourons l'autre versant du siècle. On s'arrêtera pourtant à l'avénement d'Honorius, quand le choc des évènements commence à brouiller le paysage monétaire. Au demeurant la décennie 392-402 a déjà été largement étudiée,[2] ce qui n'est pas le cas de la période précédente où cependant se dessine l'évolution qui aboutira en 402 en Occident à l'interruption généralisée et durable du monnayage de bronze.[3]

Ayant à considérer deux générations, celle de Constance II et celle des Valentiniens, par un apparent paradoxe nous prendrons notre départ avec la seconde. C'est qu'il importe de resituer à leur exact terminus de thésaurisation plusieurs dépôts à enfouissement différé.

LES TRÉSORS VALENTINIENS (364-392)

I. Pour cette tranche, comme pour celle qui suivra, l'état de la recherche infléchit les dénombrements: il est, par exemple, hors de doute que beaucoup de trouvailles balkaniques échappent à nos statistiques;[4] en revanche la prépondérance de la Bretagne et de la Pannonie, tout en étant fondée sur une réalité historique, a certainement été accentuée grâce aux enquêtes systématiques des numismates anglais et hongrois.

Nous avons déterminé trois zones: les provinces bretonnes, le limes rhéno-danubien, enfin, le reste de l'Empire, divisé à son tour en secteur occidental, italo-africain et oriental. En principe 70 trouvailles sont à comptabiliser; cependant avant d'en présenter la répartition par origine et volume, il convient d'examiner, comme on vient de le noter, le problème posé par les trésors dits "à queue". De fait, il n'est pas toujours aisé de déterminer s'il faut ou non tenir compte de la dernière pièce pour dater un dépôt. Une position systématique est à proscrire. Aussi bien adopterons-nous tour à tour deux attitudes a priori contradictoires: d'une part, étant donnée la situation en Bretagne, en Germanie et dans la Gaule Septentrionale dans les années 353-367, on admettra qu'un <u>Aes</u> 3 des Valentiniens fournit une bonne date, même s'il est précédé d'un vide durant un laps de temps parfois prolongé. Nous allons y revenir.

Au contraire, la paix revenue à l'intérieur de l'Empire, l'observation permet de replacer plus haut l'arrêt du processus thésaurisateur pour certaines trouvailles où manifestement des monnaies ont été ajoutées après coup. Rentrent dans cette catégorie:

1) <u>avant 378</u>, les dépôts qui réunissent deux conditions minimales:

a) détenir un très faible contingent des années 364-378;
b) détenir un très faible contingent ou aucun exemplaire pour les années 358-361;

2) après 378, les dépôts qui ne détiennent aucun exemplaire des années 364-378;

3) après 388, les dépôts qui n'ont guère que 1% de monnaies pour trente ans, de p. 358 à p. 388 (l'incertitude demeurant pour les petites trouvailles).

Par conséquent, nous éliminons 9 trésors qui doivent être remontés c. 351,[5] c. 352,[6] c. 353,[7], c. 358,[8] c. 360[9] ou c. 363.[10] Ils seront étudiés plus avant avec leur homologues. Demeurent 61 ensembles.[11] (Tableau 1. et Notes 12-21).

Du total, les 3/5 contiennent plus de 100 ex. et de ce sous-groupe les 2/3 appartiennent aux territoires pourvus de garnisons.

1) On ne s'attardera pas sur un premier groupe datable des débuts de la dynastie valentinienne. La logique voudrait que fussent bien représentés les contingents immédiatement précédents. La réalité est moins simple. Tout d'abord, à l'exception d'un seul dépôt italien, le no. 87, les Aes 3 des deux Augustes Julien et Jovien sont quasiment absents de l'épargne: d'un poids relativement lourd, ils ont été avec rapidité démonétisés et refondus.[22]

Du moins sous leur forme officielle, les Aes 3, Fel Temp Reparatio et Aes 4, Spes Reipublice, ne sont pas, non plus, partout majoritaires. (Tableau 2.) S'il en est ainsi, semble-t-il, en Afrique et en Asie,[23] le faciès en Bretagne et sur le limes de Germanie[24] diffère beaucoup.

Dans ces régions, la crise post-magnentienne, puis les troubles postérieurs à la mort de Julien avaient fortement réduit les importations des types au cavalier: on vit donc, en les prolongeant jusqu'après 364 par des copies massives, sur les Aes 3 introduits de façon syncopée entre 354 et 359 (trésors d'Heslington, Oldcroft, Bourton-on-the-Water, Poundbury, Duston, Covesea, Lydney II). Ou bien, on continue à utiliser le numéraire constantinien dont la phase d'imitation paraît cependant en régression (trésors de Silchester VII, Wörschweiler et, secondairement, de Pevensey Castle). Ou bien même, parfois concurremment, recours est fait à nouveau aux radiés du IIIe s. (trésors d'Icklingham IV, Duston, Colchester, Carrawburgh, Mablethorpe, Taviers et, d'une manière partielle, de Laslea). En définitive, l'absence ou le petit nombre d'espèces valentiniennes ont même signification et il est ainsi permis d'ajouter à notre liste les neuf premiers dépôts du tableau ci-dessus qui autrement eussent été classés avant 358.[25]

II. Nous pouvons maintenant aborder l'époque centrale des temps valentiniens, celle dont les limites sont grosso modo fournies par le règne de Gratien de 367 à 383. Les lignes de force se dessinent avec assez de fermeté. Pour cette période, la distribution des trésors est comme suit: Bretagne, 3; limes rhéno-danubien, 19; Espagne, 2; Afrique, 3; Italie, 4; Grèce, 1; Turquie, 1; Egypte, 2.

A de rares exceptions près[26] et avec des variations d'intensité, le limes rhéno-danubien, la Bretagne, l'Egypte, voire la Turquie et l'Italie partagent une même tendance qui est donc dominante: presque partout dans ces zones l'apport des Valentiniens est déterminant, atteignant tôt, semble-t-il,[27] un pourcentage tel qu'il réduit en général à moins de 20% la part des Aes 3 et 4 antérieurs (Tableau 3).

Les travaux de M. R. Alföldi, G. Sonnevend, V. Lányi et S. Soproni[28] ont précisé la chronologie des émissions de Siscia, ce qui est capital, puisque cet atelier alimente la frontière de Pannonie. On constate qu'après un sommet en 367, la production des officines reste haute jusqu'en 370, ceci à proximité même du limes, car l'hinterland présente davantage de continuité. Si donc la fourchette établie à partir des trésors de Wilfleinsdorf et de Brigetio d'une part, de Jabing et de Kazsok, d'autre part, est la bonne, la différence entre les taux de de fabrication et de thésaurisation indique que quelque quatre à cinq ans ont suffi pour renouveler quasiment le circuit monétaire, une accélération s'effectuant de 372 à 374.

Ce numéraire frais injecté sans lenteur est d'une grande signification pour le problème que nous avons à résoudre. Sans entrer dès à présent dans le champ de l'interprétation, bornons-nous pour le moment à opposer 1) aux provinces militaires de Bretagne, du Rhin et du Danube; 2) aux centres d'importance stratégique ou économique que peuvent être l'Italie, la Turquie, l'Egypte,[29] la circulation moins rapide qui paraît caractériser l'Afrique et surtout l'Espagne où les monnayages de 354-361, sinon même de 340-348, n'ont pas encore cédé leur primauté:

Trésors Valentiniens (Afrique et Espagne c. 370-378): Répartition Chronologique des Types

Trésors	Date	avant 348	Fel Temp Reparatio	Spes Reipublice	Aes 3 Valent. 364-378
Afrique ?	c. 370	81.49	8.67	2.89	6.93
Sfax I	376	6.17	38.80	33.20	17.03
Bimeda	p. 378	32.80	57.29		6.77
Caldas II	p. 378	52.62	15.78	15.78	10.52

Reste, avant de passer à la troisième phase de notre période, à évoquer brièvement[30] les dépôts d'Aes 2 émis à partir de 378. D'habitude, ceux-ci s'agglomèrent avec les pièces de même module frappées après 392. Il en existe cependant quelques uns d'antérieurs: nous citerons ceux du Laurion (no. 117) et d'Aguntum I (no. 122) qui sont homogènes ou presque.

III) Après 378 et pendant les 14 ans qui suivent, la situation devient moins claire. Les raisons en sont que tout à la fois la documentation se clairsème et surtout que les troubles intérieurs et extérieurs, en s'aggravant, ont dû modifier les bases géographiques des implantations monétaires. De là une juxtaposition des situations antérieures et de nouvelles données, déjà caractéristiques de l'ère post-théodosienne.

A la première tendance ressortissent quatre types de circulation: a) La série des ensembles d'Aes 2 se poursuit, sans mixité sensible dans l'arrière pays rhénan: Zweibrücken (no. 127) et Hemptinne (no. 130);

b) En Bretagne et en Panonnie, de grosses concentrations se font encore autour des Aes III valentiniens: ainsi p. 383 à Shapwick III (no. 123: 84,29%) et Veszprem (no. 125: 71,67%), p. 388 à Wiveliscombe (no. 138: 75,76%);

c) Toujours aussi retardaire en Espagne, le mouvement des espèces l'est également dans les pays voisins, placés apparemment dans les mêmes conditions, telles la Lusitanie et, à moindre degré, la Gaule:[31]

Trésors Valentiniens (Gaule et Péninsule Ibérique p. 387-388): Reparition Chronologique des Types

Trésors	Date	avant 348	Fel Temp Reparatio	Spes Reipublice	Aes 3 Valent. 364-378
La Peneda	p. 388	55.00	25.00	-	-
Monte Mozinho II	p. 388	48.20	27.20	12.00	3.20
St-Martory	p. 387	24.98	37.50	4.68	1.56
Paris	p. 388	19.23	76.92	-	-

d) Enfin à mi-distance des groupes b et c, le deuxième dépôt de Sfax offre l'image d'une progression régulière des émissions de 364-378: en une douzaine d'années, cette fraction a doublé, passant de 17,03 à 35,66%.

Il y a, parallèlement des changements, qui sont de deux sortes:

a) Le ravitaillement sur le limes occidental[32] s'appauvrit: à Pesche (no. 134), Carlsruhe (no. 132), Fürstenfeldbrück (no. 126) les nummi constantiniens sont les plus nombreux. A vrai dire, la comparaison avec la phase précédente reste malaisée, car on n'y dispose à son terme que du seul dépôt d'Oudenburg, (no. 120 avec 87,5% d'Aes 3 de 364-378). Cependant on a l'impression que la masse en circulation privilégiait ou bien les Aes 2 p. 378 ou bien les modules antérieurs à 348.

b) Signe avant-coureur du Ve s., le trésor de Bundle, peut-être plus oriental que britannique (no. 140) fait cavalier seul: les nouveaux Aes 4, émis depuis 388, y apparaissent pour la première fois en proportion notable. On sait qu'ils étaient destinés à rapidement accaparer le marché.

Par contre, il suffit de considérer nos colonnes pour constater que les grands absents sont les Aes 3 frappés de 378 à 383/387:[33] ce fait, qui mérite d'être analysé de plus près, nous conduira à nous interroger sur le rôle du bronze. Mais auparavant il nous faut revenir en arrière, puisqu'aussi bien nous avons remonté neuf de nos trésors entre 351 et 363.

LES TRÉSORS CONSTANTIENS (348-363)

La fin des Constantinides est riche d'événements monétaires: en 348 une réforme conjointe aux deux Partes impose trois pieds, des Aes 2 de deux modules (1/60e et 1/72e) et un Aes 3 au 1/120e. A l'Ouest, l'épisode magnentien rompt l'unité avec une pièce lourde qui, évoluant selon plusieurs avatars du 1/60e au 1/36[3], se voit démultipliée par une série divisionnaire et des imitations en grande quantité.[34] A l'Est et au Centre, sans doute au plus tard vers 352, le 1/72e devient le seul Aes 2, cependant qu'est repris, sur une vaste échelle, l'Aes 3, cette fois au type du cavalier.[35] Puis, au printemps 354,

Constance II tire la leçon de la crise: il lui faut restaurer le marché monétaire sur des bases saines, expulser, par conséquent, le numéraire de l'usurpateur occidental mais aussi décrier ses propres Aes 2 sous-cotés et dès lors traités comme marchandise et non comme monnaie. Ce fut l'objet de la loi du Code Théodosien, IX, 23, 1.[36]

Les Aes 3 Felix Temporum Reparatio, au type du cavalier, même si leur diffusion dans une partie de l'Occident fut alors empêchée par les longues sequelles des invasions germaniques, eut ensuite le monopole des émissions jusqu'à ce qu'en 358, vraisemblablement au même moment où était créée la "silique" d'argent, l'Aes 4 Spes Reipublice fut l'instrument d'une nouvelle politique.

Enfin, dans le champ de la numismatique comme ailleurs, Julien, au pouvoir, devait réagir contre son cousin et rétablir en 362, outre un Aes 1 au 1/36e, un Aes 3, majoré en poids, à la légende des Vota: initiatives maintenues durant le court règne de Jovien:

Pour ces quinze années, notre documentation, si on y ajoute les 9 trésors à datation rectifiée, équilibre celle des temps valentiniens.[37] (Tableau 4.)

Fondamentalement, si on poursuit la comparaison, il n'y a pas, dans la répartition globale, de modification. Toutefois, la part faite au limes—qui en l'occurrence est celui de Rhin—est plus forte, avec davantage de petits ensembles ponctuels, reflets de circonstances troublées.[47]

I) La division la plus simple est livrée par la nomination de Julien comme César en Novembre 355. La première phase s'achève par conséquent quelque dix-huit mois après la loi de démonétisation. Il est donc intéressant de voir le comportement des monnaies de Magnence et celui des Aes 2 des Constantinides pour préciser le rythme de leur disparition.

Jusqu'en 353, on constate quatre formes principales d'accumulation: (Tableau 5)

1) dans les premières années, la masse principale provient souvent comme on doit s'y attendre, des émissions constantiniennes de 330-348 (trésors d'Halifax, Appleford, Great Weldon, Mitrovic, Rouvroy-les-Merles, Lugenfeld, Metternich, Hanham, Mackviller);[48]

2) dès l'avènement de Magnence ou quasiment, il existe une catégorie de trouvailles à numéraire frais;[49] les monnaies de l'usurpateur atteignent ainsi des pourcentages écrasants dans les dépôts de Brétigney, Kaiseraugst I, Chamoson, de la région lyonnaise, de Kopstukken, de Skellow, de Mayence I, du Palatinat, d'Herkenbosch, de Tarragone et sans doute de Theux;[50]

3) l'Orient et, semble-t-il, le Centre manifestent une semblable tendance à l'homogénéité, mais cette fois au profit des Aes 2 gravés depuis 348: notre information malheureusement se limite à cinq ensembles, 3 d'Egypte, 1 de Syrie, 1 d'Autriche; les profils y sont identiques;

4) la quatrième catégorie concerne des découvertes faites en Grande-Bretagne, en France de l'Est et en Suisse: dans le Berkshire, à Byard's Leap, Villing, Pizokel, Bassecourt, ainsi qu'à Cobham, voire à

Croydon, un relatif équilibre s'institue entre les Aes 2 des Constantinides et ceux de Magnence: les épargnants sont passés des uns aux autres, sans apparemment de difficultés.

Cette situation, somme toute, très régulière, se brouille après 353 et du changement est certainement responsable la démonétisation de 354. A la lisière des deux périodes, le dépot des Fontaines Salées est encore le seul à posséder un gros contingent de pièces magnentiennes. A Perbal, de même, on est à la veille du décri des espèces lourdes. Les autres trésors, eux, n'ont plus désormais de hauts pourcentages en Aes 2. A l'exception de celui d'Aes, en zone danubienne, où les opérations militaires ont dût introduire, par acheminement direct, les Aes 3 au cavalier, le centre de gravité s'y situe en amont de 348: prépondérance des années 330-340 à Regensburg, Hemel, Michelfeld, moins certainement à la Théodule Pass,[51] apports plus anciens encore à Silchester V et Mayence II.[52]

Avant de disparaître, sauf réflexes thésaurisateurs, les "moyens bronzes" avaient ainsi largement irrigué les circuits monétaires durant au moins quatre ans.

II) La répartition des trésors engage à un commentaire géographique. (Tableau 6.) Il est clair, de fait, qu'entre 355 et 363, Bretagne, Gaule septentrionale et Germanie ressentent cruellement l'absence de numéraire neuf. Pour l'analyste, il en résulte une grande difficulté à fixer le terminus ante quem des ensembles. L'exemple le plus notable, à cet égard, est fourni par la trouvaille de Freckenham: les pourcentages encore hauts en Aes 2 de Magnence mais aussi des Constantinides inciteraient à remonter la chronologie de même que l'absence de toute monnaie au nom de Julien César; par contre, le contingent en Aes 3 au cavalier est important avec sur le nombre plus de la moitié d'imitations: Freckenham, par là, s'apparente à Heslington, les deux découvertes ayant aussi en commun de rares frappes de Carausius II.[53]

Dès lors nous avons été obligés à des choix qui pourraient paraître subjectifs. Cependant, quand nous classons dans ce laps de temps des trésors composés pour l'essentiel de copies constantiniennes (Mayence V, Reims, sans doute aussi White Woman's Hole), nous nous y sentons autorisés par les parallèles rhénans (Rheinzabern 1 et II, Niederingelheim) qui, postérieurs à 355, se regroupent autour des années 330-348, en augmentant quelque peu la masse par des monnaies de nécessité.[54]

Les trois derniers dépôts de la zone occidentale ne contredisent pas ces conclusions: Mayence IV est encore davantage tourné vers le passé, Mayence III se nourrit d'importations d'Orient, Epiais Rhus traduit une fidélité politique à Magnence.[55] Les difficultés d'approvisionnement n'ont pas joué, en revanche, sur le front danubien; les Felix Temporum Reparatio au cavalier caractérisent par leur volume les trois dépôts du Banat publiés par E. Chirila et ses collaborateurs.[55bis] Dans chacun d'entre eux cependant, les Aes 2 de 348-354 subsistent de façon appréciable. On ne s'étonnera donc pas qu'en Serbie, à Boljetin et à Kosmaj on ait pu encore thésauriser, en grande proportion, les "moyens bronzes".[56] Phénomène retardateur qui s'estompe définitivement dans les années suivantes.[57]

Il reste à dire quelques mots sur l'Occident méridional et les pays de la Méditerranée centrale et orientale. A Conimbriga et à Caldas, les Aes 3 FTR tentent d'atténuer une lourdeur de circulation plus sensible ailleurs (Monte Mozinho I, l'Estrade). Mais en règle générale, sur le pourtour de la mer intérieure, le numéraire neuf arrive bien: on en a la preuve pour les secteurs d'Afrique (Malte, Affreville), d'Asie Mineure (Smyrne, Chaniâ), d'Egypte (trésor Milne) où à Minieh on a cependant été aussi épargnant qu'en pays serbe. Quand les Spes Reipublice relèvent les Felix Temporum Reparatio le processus n'est pas mis en défaut.

Ferme la marche le trésor de Vairano, aussi anormal que le no. 87 italien précédemment évoqué. Décidément sur le marché, on a tout fait pour abolir la restauration julienne.

LES USAGES DE LA MONNAIE DE BRONZE

Sans méconnaître l'interpénétration des populations, notamment sur les frontières,[58] il est commode et, en fin de compte, légitime de distinguer emplois civils et militaires.

I) Pour notre part, nous avons toujours attribué beaucoup d'importance aux monnayages de nécessité qui sont bien autre chose que des fraudes. Leur présence, à toute époque et dans tout secteur, plaide pour un besoin de monnaies: on ne fabrique pas par lucre des imitations qui ne sauraient tromper personne.[59] Or de 352 à 367, l'Occident breton, gaulois, germain a multiplié les copies d'abord des prototypes constantiniens,[60] ensuite de Fel Temp Reparatio au cavalier.[61] La zone couverte se superpose partiellement à celle touchée au III^{e}s. par le même phénomène. Les intéressés, par conséquent, ne doivent pas différer.

Sur les décennies valentiniennes, on est moins renseigné. Les travaux admirables de G. Boon ont démontré qu'en Bretagne la vague était quasiment retombée.[62] Il faudrait maintenant interroger les trouvailles africaines,[63] balkaniques,[64] orientales.[65] L'enquête n'a pas encore dépassé le niveau des observations ponctuelles.[66] Aussi, dans l'impossibilité de conclure pour le moment, nous tournons-nous vers un second argument: les mouvements interprovinciaux des espèces.

Ici tout naturellement—nous y conduit en particulier l'étude précédente des trésors—un texte majeur s'impose: la loi IX, 23, 1 du 8 Mars 354. Nous y avons déjà fait allusion. Il convient maintenant d'être un peu plus précis. (Annexe A)

Soumis à une décomposition logique, cette prescription reçue en Arles, ce "port de Trèves" selon l'Expositio totius mundi, en relations suivies avec l'Espagne, l'Afrique, sinon l'Orient, pourrait se résumer ainsi:

1) On rappelle que certaines monnaies sont interdites.[67] Il s'agit, vraisemblablement, des espèces de Magnence envoyées à la fonte dès le lendemain de sa défaite. Le public, même s'il doit être averti à nouveau, semble avoir vite obtempéré. Nous en voulons pour preuve notre figure 2, où les exceptions sont surtout des trésors britanniques de datation incertaine;

2) La loi constate un trafic sur la "grosse pièce" de "100" deniers.[68] Ce multiple contenait de l'argent[69] et sa valeur intrinsèque lui avait permis, au

début, d'être accueilli et donc imité.[70] Mais la crise de la Reconquête de l'Occident, en suscitant, on peut le supposer, une hausse des prix, avait eu pour résultat que l'estimation faciale, parce qu'elle n'avait pas été réajustée pour freiner l'inflation, était devenue inférieure à la couverture métallique. L'Aes 2 achetait moins sur le marché officiel mais se négociait plus cher que sa tarification par l'Etat. Bref d'instrument, il se transformait en "marchandise",[71] exportée par les négociants qui gagnaient la différence entre les cours public et privé;

3) La réaction de l'Empereur fut la démonétisation.[72] Nous avons, comme pour Magnence, traduit par une figure (no. 1) les effets de cette mesure. L'application fut un peu moins réussie que dans le premier cas. Outre les trésors de Bretagne, déjà mentionnés, d'autres dépôts, dans les Balkans mais aussi sur le pourtour de la zone méditerranéenne (Portugal, Grèce, Turquie, Egypte) capitalisent environ dix ans cette monnaie lourde qui sera reprise par Gratien, puis par Théodose;[73]

4) Une seule espèce dorénavant a le droit de circuler: l'Aes 3 au type du cavalier. Une distinction, capitale pour notre propos, est cependant introduite. Au marchand par voie de terre qui n'est qu'un simple colporteur, on oppose le mercator sur mer. Le premier n'a droit qu'à un viatique transporté animalibus propriis.[74] La somme est mince, puisqu'elle se monte à 1000 folles[75] et c'est ainsi au reste que nous apprenons le nom, peut-être nouveau, attribué à l'Aes 3. Le patron de bateau, lui, au contraire, ne subit aucune limitation:[76] il a le droit d'emporter l'argent dont il a besoin pour ses achats.[77a]

Nous voudrions prouver par quelques exemples qu'il en est bien ainsi et que dans plusieurs zones, il existe un relatif brassage de monnaies qui, selon toute apparence, n'étant pas justifié par le budget militaire,[77b] relève plutôt des opérations commerciales. Les faits concerneront des trouvailles ibériques, africaines et égyptiennes, c'est-a-dire qu'ils proviennent de diocèses peu militarisés et, pour deux d'entre eux, dépourvus d'atelier monétaire.

a) Egypte: Nous commençons par ce secteur, parce qu'on s'est souvent interrogé sur les importations monétaires qui s'y remarquent. De fait, Alexandrie fabrique de la monnaie; pourtant, si on se réfère à 7 trésors de notre période, plus de 40% de leurs espèces sont extérieurs au pays.

Alexandrie :	58.2%;	Antioche :	11.4%;	Détroits :	24.1%
Balkans :	1.4%;	Italie :	4.3%;	Gaule :	0.45%[78]

Mais est-ce nécessaire de supposer avec G. Mickwitz[79] que la monnaie était surévaluée en Egypte? Nous ne le croyons pas, car, dans un contexte sans doute différent, on voit de pareils partages dans l'approvisionnement.

b) Afrique: Telle est la situation en Algérie et en Tunisie.[80] Nous n'avons pas eu encore l'occasion d'examiner de ce point de vue les deux ensembles de Cherchel. A première impression néanmoins, ils confirment les statistiques tirées d'Affreville et de Sfax I et II.[81]

	Gaule	Italie	Orient
Affreville	17.50	32.50	50.0
Sfax I et II	6.46	41.38	52.1

La géographie amène nécessairement des variations: Affreville reçoit davantage d'Arles que Sfax, mais il est évident que les importations suivent trois canaux et que celui des ateliers des Détroits et d'Orient joue un rôle considérable.

c) Péninsule ibérique: L'échantillon mêle ici aux Aes 3 et 4 de trois petits dépôts espagnols des Aes 2 à la légende Reparatio Reipub. trouvés en Espagne et au Portugal.[82]

	Gaule	Italie	Orient
Aes 2 et 3	44.70	26.30	28.90
Aes 2	51.19	28.57	20.23

Les Reparatio Reipub. ont été moins frappés à l'Est et ceci minore le pourcentage. Celui-ci eût été très favorablement inversé, si on avait joint les Aes 2 théodosiens postérieurs à 392. Quoiqu'il en soit, à l'extrémité Ouest de la Méditerranée les officines orientales, de Siscia à Antioche, virent leurs émissions alimenter le marché, pour une part, qui, tout en étant plus faible qu'en Afrique, dépasse l'accidentel. Cessons donc d'estimer bizarre que sur un bord de la mer—à savoir l'Egypte—soit arrivé un numéraire de marchand qui parvient régulièrement en deux autres régions touchées par le commerce maritime.

Indépendamment de toute spéculation conjoncturelle sur la qualité de la monnaie, celle-ci voyage donc, servant aux échanges dans les ports. De ce rôle visible durant toute la période qui nous occupe nous voudrions, avant d'envisager des emplois moins pacifiques, offrir une dernière preuve. Des travaux de Codrington sur les monnaies découvertes en Inde et à Ceylan[83] il résulte que parallèlement à une pénétration de l'or, le bronze, en large quantité, était reçu jusque dans les débuts du Ve s. Ainsi la fonction de ce métal n'était pas limitée aux transactions quotidiennes, usuelles surtout dans les villes,[84] il gardait assez de valeur—et c'est une surprise, avouons-le—pour financer les achats de Rome à l'Extrême Est.[85]

II) Nos cartes et tableaux, nous y avons déjà fait allusion, orientent dans une seconde direction, le bronze au service de la défense de l'Empire. Sur ce point, nous n'avons pas à être originaux mais seulement à souscrire aux thèses des numismates de l'Ecole Hongroise.[86] Il faudrait, de fait, s'aveugler pour ne pas voir que les Aes 3 émis par Valentinien Ier ont fondamentalement une mission militaire.

Dans le prolongement de nos devanciers, nous soulignons ce qui, à nos yeux, constitue trois évidences:

1) L'Aes 3 a financé la reconstruction du limes: Alors que les campagnes d'Afrique[87] et de Germanie[88] ne sont pas ou à peine traduites par le témoignage des trésors, en Bretagne, la restauration du pouvoir central[89] et surtout sur le Danube, presque tout au long du fleuve, en fait jusqu'à l'Olt, la remise en état des fortifications ont amené près des côtes ou à proximité du Barbaricum la masse de nombreux dépôts. En Pannonie, ce grand travail, entrepris dès 366 s'arrête avec la mort de l'Empereur d'Occident; or c'est bien à cette décennie qu'appartient la plupart de nos dépôts;[90]

2) L'Empire d'Orient qui n'avait que peu de frontières à protéger en Thrace et qui, ailleurs, n'est guère inquiété,[91] ne s'est pas associé à la politique de Valentinien Ier. Là est, pensons-nous, l'explication d'un phénomène monétaire qui mérite l'attention. Pearce a remarqué qu'à partir de 367 la totalité des ateliers orientaux stoppait leur production jusqu'en 378.[92] Alors se manifestait un fait connexe: tandis qu'à l'Ouest, les Aes 3 frappés de 378 à 383/387[93] sont à peu près absents des trésors et des fouilles,[94] on les rencontre en Orient.[95] Une simple loi de bascule rend compte de ces anomalies symétriques. La Pars Occidentis, bien pourvue en numéraire durant le règne de Valentinien 1, était nourrie grâce à ce stock; au contraire, après une fermeture de près de dix ans, l'Empire oriental avait besoin d'émissions et les nouveaux revers rétablissaient un niveau normal dans la circulation;

3) Grâce aux inventaires de monnaies de site, une comparaison peut être développée entre plusieurs centres, villes de garnison et cités de l'intérieur. On a choisi de mesurer les variations entre les temps constantiens et ceux de la dynastie suivante. Les conclusions ne manquent pas de clarté, à condition bien sûr de faire jouer le correctif suivant: une région mal alimentée auparavant attire plus de numéraire qu'une autre, largement irriguée les années précédentes:

forte augmentation: Richborough, Vindonissa;[96]
très légère augmentation: Carnuntum, Brigetio;[97]
légère baisse: Antioche;[98]
baisse sensible: Athènes, Corinthe;[99]
baisse très sensible: Conimbriga.[100]

Qu'est ce à dire, sinon que le secteur frontalier a été favorisé au détriment des zones plus "civiles". Jointes en un faisceau, ces trois séries de constatations permettent d'affirmer qu'aux temps valentiniens, le follis, volontairement désargenté, avait en priorité pour destination l'armée.[101]

L'Etat, en ces ultimes décennies du IVe s., poursuit ainsi ses frappés de bronze, parce qu'il les sait encore utiles à son commerce et à sa logistique. N'imaginons pas toutefois que cette situation pourra longtemps durer. En cette année 392 qui nous offre notre terminus, paraît le De mensuris et ponderibus d'Epiphane de Salamine. Or du miliarensis, cette monnaie d'argent, bientôt l'étalon du commerce oriental,[102] on nous dit qu'elle est le στρατιωτικὸν δόμα.[103] L'Empereur pouvait payer ses murailles avec des Gloria Romanorum ou des Securitas Reipublicae.[104] Les soldats, eux, préféraient de plus en plus des pièces blanches,[105] quand ce n'était pas déjà cet or sous lequel Rome allait mourir ensevelie.[106]

NOTES

1. J. P. Callu, "La circulation monétaire de 313 à 348", Actes du 8ème Congr. Int. Num., New York-Washington, 1973 = Bale, 1976, 227-242.

2. R. Reece, 'Numerical Aspects of Roman Coin Hoards in Britain,' Coins and the Archaeologist, BAR 4, 1974, 78-94. Add. pour la Belgique les travaux de J. Lallemand et pour la France ceux, en cours, de R. Delmaire.

3. Ceci à l'exception de Rome—Réapparition mineure des Aes 3 vers 408/413 à Lyon, Arles, Aquilée et Siscia. Les Aes 4 ne sont plus frappés jusqu'à la mort d'Honorius.

4. Le déficit est particulièrement grave pour la Bulgarie: v.g., BIAB, 12, 1938, 450; 17, 1950, 320; 20, 1955, 611, B. Soc. Arch. Varna, 9, 1953, 114. Il est de même bien évident que nous ne citons que les dépôts où une statistique est possible. D'où des omissions regrettables mais volontaires.

5. no. 99 (Kaiseraugst II).

6. no. 128 (Damas).

7. no. 96 (Palatinat).

8. no. 131 (Orşova II); 137 (Jupa); 101 (Orşova I); 113 (Kosmaj).

9. no. 89 (Smyrne).

10. no. 114 (Vairano).

11. A ces 61 trésors, add. 9 de Bretagne, sans ex. des Valentiniens mais postérieurs sans doute à 364, cf. infra.

12. no, 71 (Milan).

13. no. 119 (Caldas II); 136 (La Peneda); 75 (Taviers); 127 (Zweibrücken); 117 (Laurion).

14. no. 73 (Mablethorpe); 80 (Silchester VII); 83 (Pevensey Castle); 100 (Ickham); 107 (Aylesbury); 140 (Bundle); 82 (Laslea); 91 (Stielings); 112 (Bregenz-Lochau); 122 (Aguntum I); 124 (Medgidia); 135 (Paris).

15. no. 72 (Carrawburgh); 103 (Kits Coty House); 90 (Carnuntum VI); 120 (Oudenburg); 132 (Carlsruhe); 129 (St Martory).

16. no. 74 (Wroxeter); 105 (Vienne Krottenbach); 134 (Pesche); 116 (Bimeda); 133 (Monte Mozinho II); 84 (Monte Guspini); 93 (Afrique ?); 77 (Cherchel II); 78 (Priène).

17. no. 81 (Wörschweiler); 58 (Gelse); 94 (Wilfleinsdorf), 98 (Lupoglav); 104 (Gölle); 118 (Carnuntum V); 121 (Enns I); 126 (Fürstenfeldbrück); 76 (Cherchel I); 79 (El Beida); 87 (Italie); 115 (Delta).

18. no. 95 (Brigetio); 102 (Kazsok); 85 (Grand Saint Bernard).

19. no. 123 (Shapwick III); 138 (Wiveliscombe); 97 (Jabing); 106 (Oregcsem); 109 (Vinkovci); 130 (Hemptinne); 86 (Turquie).

20. no. 110 (Arpas); 111 (Öcsöd); 108 (Sfax I); 139 (Sfax II); 92 (El Kab).

21. no. 125 (Veszprem).

22. no. 87 (Italie): 156 ex, 47. 8%; no. 92 (El Kab): 192 ex, 6.8%; no. 97 (Jabing): 46 ex, 3.2%; no. 108 (Sfax I): 44 ex, 1%. Voir aussi no. 114 (Vairano) où on aurait deterré 14 aes 1 de Julien, 21. 53%. Par ailleurs, les fouilles de Carnuntum ont livré 66 ex. de Julien Auguste (26 aes 1, 40 aes 3) et 30 de Jovien (aes 3).

23. Afrique: no. 76 (Cherchel I) 70. 1% FTR, 20. 28% Spes; no. 77 (Cherchel II), 75. 3% FTR, 9.87% Spes; no. 79 (El Beida) 47.8% FTR, 25.8% Spes; Asie: no. 78, Priène, données moins évidentes à cause de l'imprécision du dénombrement, mais FTR et Spes paraissent bien représentés.

24. Add. le no. 82, Laslea, hors du limes, en Transylvanie, où l'environnement explique une circulation ralentie et l'emploi de bronzes du Haut-Empire—Pour la crise du milieu du IVe s. consulter notre article cité infra n. 60.

25. 5 sont inférieurs au palier de 100 ex, 4 le dépassent, dont 2 de plusieurs milliers. Add. la trouvaille d'Ehl, Bull. Soc. Conserv. Mon. d'Alsace, 7, 1865, 87-94.

26. Au début de la période se situe l'ensemble du Grand St Bernard, no. 85, où très normalement les espèces valentiniennes sont encore loin avec 10.5% d'avoir expulsé les FTR (38.7%) et les Spes (28.5%); à l'autre bout de la chaîne, le dépôt d'Enns I (no. 121) pourrait bien être en fait la juxtaposition de deux épargnes séparées dans le temps. A noter le défaut quasi absolu de documentation sur la Gaule: R. Delmaire veut bien nous signaler la découverte dans une tombe à Vron (Somme) d'une bourse de 77 ex. dont 72 des Valentiniens, terminus: 374.

27. Le no. 71 (Milan) est trop peu probant, vue son exiguité.

28. M. R. Alföldi, "Fragen des Münzumlaufs im 4. Jahrhundert n. Chr.", JNG, 13, 1963, 75-104; G. Sonnevend, "Adatok az I Valentinianus Korbeli Sisciai Kisbronzak Kronologiajahoz", NK, 54-55, 1955-1956, 7; V. Lanyi, 'The Coinage of Valentinian I in Siscia', Acta Arch. Hung., 21, 1969, 33-38; S. Soproni, "Über den Münzumlauf in Pannonien zu Ende des 4. Jahrhunderts", Fol. Arch., 20, 1969, 69-78: organisation rationnelle des officines de Siscia à partir de 371.

29. La prudence s'impose: pour l'Italie, on ne dispose que du trésor atypique étudié par M. Amandry; le dépôt turc a été vu à Istanbul, mais d'où provient-il?; les faits égyptiens, au contraire, sont très clairs: dès 370, à El Kab, en Thébaïde, c'est-à-dire en un territoire où l'armée est présente, les espèces valentiniennes tournent autour des 80%, mais, un peu plus tard, dans le Delta, on retrouve le même pourcentage.

30. A ce monnayage en définitive assez répandu nous avons consacré un article "Reparatio Reipub: un problème de circulation monétaire", Nummus, 2, 1, 1978, 99-119 (Add., Budapest, NK, 21-22, 1922-1923, 30; plusieurs trouvailles isolées dans le Sud de la France).

31. Dans la péninsule ibérique, les constantiniennes l'emportent, en Gaule les Fel Temp Reparatio—Pour Paris et la Peneda il est impossible d'exclure totalement l'hypothèse de 'trésors à queue'. [Add. (?) l'ensemble de Crozon, Finistère, doc. inédite G. Aubin].

32. Peut-être aussi sur le Danube inférieur: la trouvaille de Medgidia dans la Dobroudja présente un exemple de récupération de monnaies très anciennes (no. 124).

33. Les aes 3 p 378 sont présents dans 9 trésors, de 1 à 8 ex.

34. La métrologie des années 350-353 a été étudiée par P. Bastien, Le monnayage de Magnence, Wetteren, 1964; pour les fractions voir G. Fabre et M. Mainjonet, "La trouvaille monétaire des Fontaines-Salées (Yonne)", Gallia, 23, 1965, 151-233.

35. J. P. C. Kent, "Fel Temp. Reparatio", NC, 7, 7, 1967, 83-90. L'adoption du 1/72e est chose faite à Aquilée en 352. Le trésor de Damas (no. 128) qui comporte 1 aes 3 paraît se limiter à des 1/60e: il y aurait donc une certaine synchronisation entre les 1/72e et les 1/120 e au type du cavalier. Il est, en effet, indubitable que les aes 3 FTR n'ont pas succédé aux aes 2 FTR. Si certains dépôts, v.g. Boljetin (no. 52) et Kosmaj (no. 113) donnent cette impression, ils le font à cause de leur tendance thésaurisatrice. En réalité, les statistiques de Perbal (no. 34) le prouvent, en 354, dans une trouvaille, les aes 3 atteignent en volume les 3/5e des aes 2. On peut donc risquer l'hypothèse que vers 352 le 'cavalier' de petit module a remplacé les 'phénix' , 'galère' et assimilés si bien qu'en 354 à côté de la maiorina circulait pourrait-on dire une 'minorina pecunia'.

36. J. P. Callu,'Denier et nummus (300-354)"in Les 'Dévaluations' à Rome," Rome, 1978, 107-121.

37. Constantiens: 63 + 9; Valentiniens: 61 + 9 bretons.

38. no. 24 (Skellow); 35 (Silchester V); 53 (Mayence V).

39. no. 6 (Berkshire); 7 (Byard's Leap); 5 (Lugenfeld) ; 15 (Pizokel); 20 (Kopstukken); 27 (Mayence I); 28 (Herkenbosch); 37 (Michelfeld); 40 (Nirès); 41 (Mayence III); 54 (Reims). Add. no. 94 (Palatinat); 4 (Rouvroy-les-Merles); 29 (Tarragone); 32 (Collonge-en-Charolais); 43 (Conimbriga C); 44 (Monte Mozinho I); 61 (Chaniâ).

40. no. 11 (Brétigney); 13 (Theux); 14 (Villing); 23 (Fussach); 30 (Regensburg); 38 (Théodule Pass); 39 (Acs). Add. no. 99 (Kaiseraugst II); 58 (Caldas I); 47 (Affreville); 57 (Malte). Add. no. 114 (Vairano).

41. no. 9 (Hanham); 31 (Hemel); 16 (Bassecourt); 17 (Chamoson); 18 (Strasbourg); 36 (Mayence II), 48 (Mayence IV); 59 (Kaiseraugst I); 21 (Fayoum). Add. no. 128 (Damas).

42. no. 3 (Great Weldon); 55 (White Woman's Hole); 10 (Mackviller); 33 (Fontaines Salées); 46 (L'Estrade); 22 (Egypte I).

43. no. 25 (Cobham); 56 (Freckenham); 3a (Mitrovic); 34 (Perbal); 50 (Rheinzabern II); 51 (Niederingelheim). Add. no. 101 (Orşova I) et 137 (Jupa); 60 (Egypte II).

44. no. 1 (Halifax); 52 (Boljetin). Add. no. 131 (Orşova I); 12 (Kom Denchal); 45 (Minieh).

45. no. 26 (Croydon); 49 (Rheinzabern I); 19 (Région lyonnaise); Add. no. 89 (Smyrne).

46. no. 2 (Appleford); 4a (Vranic); 8 (Metternich); Add. no. 113 (Kosmaj).

47. Les trésors orientaux, en majorité égyptiens, sont de masse importante, pour la simple raison que les petits dépôts n'ont pas été recueillis dans les transactions numismatiques.

48. En complément, on joindra un cinquième groupe où les aes 3 de la réforme de 348 (types du phénix ou de la galère, séries de Vétranion) constituent un pourcentage signifiant: 91.68% à Vranic, 31.8% à Lugenfeld, 15.8% à Mackviller, 13.3% à Kaiseraugst II, 49.5% à Strasbourg. Add. le trésor énigmatique de Damery (en dernier lieu cf. nos "Cachettes monétaires multiples", Studien zu Fundmünzen der Antike, 1, 1979, 5-16, no. 36) où, selon un décompte hélas approximatif, un des vases aurait contenu, outre un denier d'Antonin, 5 Urbs Roma ou Constantinopolis, 100 Victoriae D D Augg Q N N et Fel Temp Reparatio (types de la hutte et de la galère), le chiffre aussi impressionnant qu'à Vranic de c. 3900 aes 3 Fel Temp Reparatio au phénix. Ces monnaies furent refondues avant 354 et souvent même en Bretagne surfrappées par le revers au cavalier. Par la suite, elles ne laissent, pour ainsi dire, aucune trace dans la circulation.

49. Il y a pour ce tableau comme pour les autres une part d'arbitraire dans la fixation de l'hinterland du limes.

50. A Strasbourg, les ex. de Magnence sont un peu minorés à cause des aes 3 de 348 cf. supra n. 48; à Kaiseraugst II, un reliquat constantinien important atténue la concentration autour des monnaies de l'usurpateur, au surplus, il s'agit d'un trésor 'à queue'. —Nous n'avons pu exploiter les dépôts de Gaboš et de Ljubljana signalés par A. Jeločnik in RN, 6, 9, 1967, 228, n. 8 et 229, n. 8.

51. Les renseignements sont très incertains; à voir seulement les pièces recueillies, les FTR au cavalier dominent et d'ailleurs rien ne les empêchait de parvenir dans le Valais.

52. Add. la circulation normalement atypique de Nirès en Transylvanie.

53. Cf. infra Annexe B, Notes 69 et 76. A Heslington, Oldcroft, voire à Pevensey Castle, les Magnence comptent encore.

54. Cf. infra Annexe B, Notes 49 à 65. Les espèces constantiniennes de 330-348 n'avaient pas été décriées en 354, pas plus au reste qu'elles ne l'avaient été en 348. A propos de cette réforme antérieure, il faut bien préciser que le Bas Empire a connu deux types de mutations monétaires.

Ou bien, comme en 301 (Edit d'Aphrodisias) et en 318 (démonétisation), on attribue une nouvelle valeur à un poids inchangé, ou bien, comme en 295 ou en 348, on introduit des espèces lourdes mais sans éliminer les espèces légères précédentes, radiées du III s., Aes 3 et 4 des Constantinides.

55a. Cf. infra Annexe B, Notes 42 et 43.

55b. Add. le trésor de Dalboşeţ cf. Tibiscus, 1972, 53-60.

56. A Boljetin et Kosmaj, les aes 4 de 340-348 ont été dédaignés.

57. 9.4% à Smyrne (c. 360); 7.1% à Chaniâ (363); 8.69% à Heslington (355/364); 7.5% à Pevensey Castle, et 6.06% en Turquie (p. 367).

58. Garnisons proprement dites et environnement des cabanae, troupes d'élite et 'territoriale', soldats de l'intérieur et barbares. Distinguer de même les dépenses de personnel et celles d'infrastructure.

59. J. P. Callu, "La fonction monétaire dans la société romaine sous l'Empire", 5e Congrès Hist. Eco., Léningrad, 1970 = Moscou, 1977, V, 197-235.

60. J. P. Callu et J. P. Garnier, "Minimi constantiniens trouvés à Reims", Quaderni Ticinesi, 6, 1977, 281-315—Pour la survie de ces séries cf. notre Fig. 3.

61. G. C. Boon, "Counterfeit Coins in Roman Britain", Coins and the Archaeologist, BAR 4, 1974, 95-170, en particulier 130-135, dont nous adoptons les conclusions chronologiques.

62. Ibid. 135. Selon G. Boon la raison en est 'the abandonment of the silver proportion in the small-change alloy'. Il est certes nécessaire de se préoccuper du titre—et à cet égard, nous espérons bientôt confirmer sur plus grande échelle l'élimination de l'argent à partir des Valentiniens, telle que la suggèrent les travaux d'A Ravetz, Archaeometry, 6, 1963, 45-55 et plus récemment de L. H. Cope et G. R. Gilmore, "Gold, Antimony, Arsenic and Indium in the Copper-Based Roman Imperial Coinage Alloys", Universities Research Reactor, 5, Risley, 1976. Cependant, l'absence d'imitations me paraît due à une reprise normale des approvisionnements cf. infra.

63. Le dossier pour l'Afrique est à peine entrouvert. Il n'est pas exclu toutefois que des imitations aient pu prolonger la circulation des Fel Temp Reparatio cf. infra n. 87.

64. M. R. Vasić, 'A IVth and Vth Centuries Hoard of Roman Coins and Imitations in the Collection of the National Museum in Belgrade', Sirmium, VIII, 113-132: à l'heure actuelle, on ne note pas de monnayage irrégulier entre les aes 2 de Constance (une trentaine à Belgrade) et les aes 4 du début du Ve s. A priori, la masse du numéraire, dans la période intermédiaire, rend cette absence non fortuite.

65. En Egypte, rognage et imitations entre 367 et 378, cf. infra.

66. Le seul cas occidental qui ait une certaine surface est celui des aes 2 de 378-388. Ce grand module a été imité dans la partie Nord des Gaules et ceci sur des sites qui n'obligent pas toujours à postuler une occupation

militaire. Sur cette monnaie, de bonne diffusion et sans doute plus à l'usage des marchands que de l'armée, voir notre article supra n. 30 et infra.

67. C. Th., IX, 23, 1: Pecunias vero nulli... fas erit... vetitas contrectare; ...praeter... ceteras quas vetitas esse cognoscunt. cf. infra annexe A pour le texte complet. [Pour une bonne datation cf. PLRE, p. 783, no. 25: l'erreur est explicable par une confusion entre le VIIe (=354) et le VIIIe (=356) consulat de Constance II, entraînant à son tour la substitution du César Julien au César Gallus; on sait, en effet, par Ammien, XIV, 10, 4 que Rufin auquel est adressée la loi, était préfet du prétoire en Gaule au printemps 354].

68. Ibid.: ...pecunias... ad diversa vendendi causa transferre..., pecunias vero nulli emere omnino fas erit...

69. C. Th., IX, 21, 6, du 12 Février 349: Comperimus nonnullos flatuarios maiorinam pecuniam non minus criminose quam crebre separato argento ab aere purgare. A rapprocher de ces flatuarios, le début de la loi de 354: ...conflare pecunias. Nous espérons promouvoir une recherche sur l'aloi des aes 2 de 348 à 354 pour préciser cette donnée du problème en comparaison des aes 3 de 348 à 358.

70. Dans notre article supra cit. n. 36, 117, nous nous sommes referé à Thémistius, Orat. XXXIII, 367 b-c. Les monnaies, y est-il dit, ne conservent pas toujours leur pouvoir d'achat initial, ὥσπερ δὴ κἀκεῖνα τὰ πρώην, ἅ ἔναγχος ἐξελήλαται τῆς ἀγορᾶς. ἦ οὐ μέμνησθε ὡς αὐτίκα μὲν, ἡνίκα τὸ πρῶτον ἐξεφοίτησε τῶν χαλκοτύπων, σεμνόν τι χρῆμα καὶ μεγάλη ἡ δύναμις καὶ πολλὰ ἂν ὀλίγου ἐπρίω; προϊὸν δὲ καὶ ταῦτα ἐ οὐ πολλῷ χρόνῳ οὐδ' ἰσαρίθμως...οὕτωσ ἀχρείως εἰς τὰ πωλητήρια ἀφικνεῖται.

On le voit, il n'y a pas contradiction entre l'analyse de Themistius et celle du législateur. Même si s'est affirmée une diminution du poids (vers 352) et du titre—hypothèse qui demande vérification, l'aes 2, en lui-même, n'a pas subi de dégradation. Le maintien de sa 'dynamis', aboutit par contre dans la réalité à une diminution de la contrepartie en produits achetables. Plusieurs dépôts (Kom Denchal, Egypte I, Fayoum, Damas) traduisent un accaparement de la nouvelle monnaie. Nous avons déjà parlé (cf. supra n. 64) des imitations balkaniques: à Boljetin comme à Kosmaj elles sont l'oeuvre de faux-monnayeurs spéculant sur la demande du public. D'ailleurs, leur masse plutôt restreinte montre qu'on n'a pas affaire à un numéraire de nécessité.

71. C. Th., IX, 23.1: pecunias... in usu publico constitutas pretium oportet esse, non mercem.

72. Ibid.: ...praeter pecunias quas more solito maiorinas vel cententionales communes appellant. Selon nous, le vel réunit les deux noms d'une même monnaie.

73. A Affreville, enfoui en 358, les aes 2 par usure sont tombés pour 16 ex. à une moyenne de 3.52 g.

74. C. Th., IX, 23, 1: et itineris tramites statuimus custodiri... Nec vero aliquis negotiatorum plus mille follibus pecuniae in usu publico constitutae animalibus propriis sumptuum gratia portare debebit.

75. Comment comprendre les mille follibus? Si l'on entend par follibus un sac, l'usage du IVe s. est d'envisager une somme de 125 monnaies (cf. notre étude, 'Une constante arithmétique dans la métrologie du Bas-Empire', à paraître in PACT, 1980). Comme l'aes 3 est frappé c. au 1/120e de la livre, on parviendrait à un poids énorme. Il paraît donc plus convenable de voir dans le follis le contenu et non plus le contenant, d'autant que sous Julien Auguste deux textes règlementaires l'emploient dans cette acception (C. Th., XIV, 4, 3 et CIL, VIII, 24 609 cf. notre article, Pensa et follis sur une inscription d'Afrique', à paraître in Antiquités Africaines, 1980, où nous nous sommes efforcé d'établir un rapport entre la monnaie d'or et celle de cuivre, à vrai dire, dans la métrologie du IVe s., le maillon le plus fragile.

76. C. Th., IX, 23, 1: Portus enim litoraque, quo facilior esse navibus consuevit accessus...Nam pecuniae navibus vectas non omnes iudicamus mercatores debere promere, quippe in usu tantum publico pecunias constitutas permittimus convehi...Et si forte cum mercibus ad quascumque provincias venerint naves, cuncta solita licentia mercabuntur.

77a. Il est donc vain de conclure, comme on le fait parfois, que la loi de 354 limitait au troc les échanges maritimes. Le Sommaire du Code Vatican pour ce même texte se rapporte à une époque beaucoup plus tardive où on n'autorisait les transferts de fonds que pour l'équipement des domaines d'outre-mer: Altero capite naves iubet pro commercio tantum entecae portare pecunias. cf. Dig., 33, 7, 2, 1: dotes praediorum quae Graeco vocabulo ἐνθῆκαι appellantur.

77b. A la différence des envois de monnaies fabriquées à Siscia et dirigées en 374 sur la region de Trèves et la Bretagne cf. V. Lányi, art. cit., 45.

78. Documentation concernant Kom Denchal (351), Fayoum et Egypte I (c. 352), Minieh (p. 355), Egypte II (361), El Kab (370), Delta (p. 378). Premier dénombrement par J. Schwartz, "La circulation monétaire dans l'Egypte du IVe siècle", SMB, 33, 1959, 11-17. Les pourcentages pour Alexandrie sont respectivement de 55; 51.9; 55.6; 44.6; 80.2 et de 48.3%. El Kab, qui fait exception, est plus profondément à l'intérieur des terres.

79. G. Mickwitz, Geld und Wirtschaft im römischen Reich des vierten Jahrhunderts p. Ch., Helsingfors, 1932, 110-111.

80. Nous le démontrerons encore davantage dans notre étude, en cours, des trésors constantiniens d'Afrique du Nord (enfouissements c. 340).

81. Affreville (358), Sfax I (376), Sfax II (p. 388).

82. Aes 3 et 4: Caldas I (c. 360), Caldas II (p. 378), la Peneda (p. 388), aes 2: trésors de Conimbriga A, Fiães I, Tarifa, fouilles de Conimbriga cf. art. cit. supra n. 30.

83. H. W. Codrington, "Ceylon Coins and Currency", Memoirs of the Colombo Museum, A, 3, Colombo, 1924, 31-32 et 252-253: solidi de Constance II, Valentinien, Valens. Pour le bronze, en Inde: 'quantities of copper coin at Madura'; à Ceylan: 'Imperial bronze in large quantities of most of the Emperors from Constantine the Great to Marcian, the order of

frequency being 1) Arcadius; 2) Théodosius I or II; 3) Honorius; 4) Constantius II; 5) Valentinian II and 6) Constans; the coins are with few exceptions "third brass" ' [add. Coin Hoards, III, RNS, London, 1977, no. 219] A noter à cet égard qu'en Orient la frappe de l'aes 3 reprend en 393.

84. Prix de la viande et du bois en folles cf. supra n. 75; pour le vin et le nummus voir Annales, 5, 1960, 166-183; aumônes en nummi, Ambroise, De off. min., I, 11,38, c. 386,...

85. En dernier lieu, M. G. Raschke, 'New Studies in Commerce with the East', ANRW, II, 9, 2, Berlin, 1978, 604-1361.

86. Cf. supra n. 28.

87. A l'heure actuelle l'insurrection de Firmus ne peut être mise en relation avec une découverte monétaire. Les fouilles montrent la présence de bronzes valentiniens, mais l'arrivée de ceux-ci n'est pas datée. Voir supra n. 63.

88. Ici règne la même disparité. Nous parlerons plus avant (cf. infra n. 96) du fort volume des émissions de Valentinien 1er à Vindonissa. Cependant les pays rhénans, pris dans une acception large, n'ont livré que deux trouvailles au reste de faible ampleur: Oudenburg, en Flandre Occidentale, Stielings en Souabe. Le témoignage des monnaies de fouilles est par conséquent utile: v.g. Bonn (camp légionnaire), BJ, 151, 1951, 229, ou Roisdorf (fontaine), ibid., 159, 1959, 471.

89. Aux 5 trésors post 367 d'Ickham et Kits Coty House dans le Kent, d'Aylesbury dans le Buckinghamshire, de Shapwick III et de Wiveliscombe dans le Somerset, add. la trouvaille probable de Lydney (Glos.), NC, 5, 1939, 139: 1296 ex. et tout récemment celle d'Holybourne (Hants), SCMB, 1976, 204: 117 ex. Pour sa part, au vu des monnaies recueillies sur un échantillon de sites bretons, R. Reece, "Bronze Coinage in Roman Britain and the Western Provincies, AD 330-402', Scripta Nummaria Romana, Essays Presented to Humphrey Sutherland, (ed. R.A.G. Carson, C. M. Kraay), Spink, 1978, 124-142 en particulier, 140, fig. 3, observe que les émissions de 364-376, y sont très communes. Voir aussi infra n. 96.

90. Par les travaux de M. R. Alföldi (cf. supra n. 28) nous savons que dans les provinces danubiennes les invasions quades et sarmates ont entrainé une vague d'enfouissements autour des années 375. On compte 6 trésors en Autriche: sauf Bregenz, ils sont concentrés à l'Est: Vienne-Krottenbach, Carnuntum V et VI, Wilfleinsdorf et Jabing—Hongrie: 8 trouvailles, Gelse, Arpas, Brigetio, Oregcsem, Ocsöd, Veszprem, Gölle et Kazsok—Yougoslavie: Lupoglav et Vinkovci.

91. On a deux dépôts égyptiens dont l'un à El Kab, en Thébaïde, est peut-être dans un contexte militaire.

92. RIC, IX, 189, 200-201, 237, 248-249, 264, 296. Pearce y voyait 'the revolt against the claim of the West to impose a uniform bronze coinage upon the whole empire'.

93. A Trèves, Lyon, Arles, ainsi que dans les 6 ateliers orientaux la frappe des aes 3 ne dépasse pas 383. Au contraire, Valentinien II les poursuit de 383 à 387 dans ses officines d'Aquilée, Rome Siscia et Thessalonique.

94. Trésors cf. supra n. 33; Monnaies de fouilles: Conimbriga: (I. Pereira, J. P. Bost et J. Hiernard, Fouilles de Conimbriga, III, les Monnaies, Paris, 1974): 3 aes 3; La Grande Baume: (Acta Numismatica, 6, 1976, 73-106): 4 ex; Fontaines Salées: (Gallia, 23, 1965, 151-233): 1 ex; Vindonissa: (T. Pekáry, Die Fundmünzen von Vindonissa, Brugg, 1971): 4 ex; Carnuntum: (FMRÖ, III, 1, 1976): 12 ex; Brigetio: (K. Bíró-Sey, Coins from Identified Sites of Brigetio and the Question of Local Currency, Budapest, 1977): 4 ex; R. Reece veut bien nous informer qu'à Richborough, on ne dénombre que 12 aes 3.

95. Athènes: (M. Thompson, The Athenian Agora, II, Coins from the Roman through the Venetian Period, Princeton, 1954): 365 ex; Antioche (D. B. Waagé, Antioche on the Orontes: Greek, Roman, Byzantine and Crusaders' Coins, Princeton, 1952: 98 ex—Egalement plusieurs exemplaires à Curium et Apamée. Ces centres ont, on le remarquera, une vocation civile.

96. Richborough: cf. R. Reece, art. cit. supra n. 89, 134 et 142, fig. 5, 348-364: 333 ex, 364-375: 1221 ex-Vindonissa, 348-364: 167 ex, 364-375: 628 ex. Dans les deux occurrences la crise post-magnentienne avait creusé un vide qu'il importait de combler.

97. Carnuntum, 348-364: 791 ex, 364-378: 844 ex.—Brigetio, 348-364: 258 ex.,364-378: 279 ex. Le rythme monétaire est donc maintenu sur le limes danubien, déjà bien approvisionné.

98. Antioche, 348-361: 1177 ex, 364-375: 1080 ex.

99. Athènes, 348-363: 2807 ex, 364-375: 801 ex. —Corinthe, cf. K. M. Edwards, Corinth. The Coins, 1896-1929, Cambridge, 1933. 348-360: 696 ex, 364-378: 273 ex.

100. Conimbriga, 348-363: 1724 ex., 364-378: 228 ex. Cette fois le mouvement jouait en sens inverse. La mécanique ainsi décrite n'explique pas tout cependant. Déjà entre 330 et 348 Conimbriga avait reçu 2099 monnaies. Le dégonflage à l'époque valentinienne n'était donc pas fatal et se comprend parce qu'alors le numéraire était dirigé ailleurs.

101. Sur l'actuel territoire français, les monnaies valentiniennes, sans être rares (v.g. La Grande Baume, supra n. 94, la trouvaille de Vienne, R A Est, 24, 1973, 375-395, fouilles inédites des Bolards, etc) ne sont pas arrivées en priorité, car la zone n'était pas stratégique.

102. La drachme sassanide est égale au miliarensis cf. Cosmas Indicopleust., XI, 14-15.

103. Texte assuré par la version syriaque, lignes 25-29, col. 69 a, 109 de l'édition J. E. Dean, Chicago, 1935 (confirmation par le R. P. P. Devos).

104. La légende Securitas Reipublicae est éclairante.

105. Les trésors d'argent de Bretagne et de Roumanie le prouvent. Il est probable toutefois, comme l'indiquent les trouvailles dans les camps de ces régions (v.g. Wiveliscombe, Sucidava), que la monnaie de bronze continuait à circuler dans le milieu des garnisons, soit comme complément de soldes, soit à cause des relations avec la population civile qui,

par ailleurs, associée au moins indirectement aux entreprises de fortification, devait par conséquent être rétribuée.

106. Pour l'or, l'étape décisive est vers 384 cf. notre étude in Ktema, 3, 1978, 301-316.

Nous adressons nos remerciements à tous ceux qui nous ont procuré des documents inédits ou malaisés d'accès: K. Bíró-Sey, C. King, C. Metzger, C. Brenot, A. Jeločnik, H. Cahn, P. Salama, F. Dolbeau, M. Amandry, J. P. Garnier ainsi que l'ANS de New York, E. Demougeot, G. Dembski, G. Aubin, E. Chirila, R. Reece, R. Delmaire.

[Add. Döbrönte, c. 375, A Veszprém Megyei Múzeumok Közleményei 13, 1978, p. 51-88; Novae, c. 370 et Bodrovo, c. 372, Chiron, 9, 1979, p. 607-620; Gherla, c. 372-375, Acta Musei Porolissensis, 3, 1979, p. 525-533.]

Tableau 1 Trésors Valentiniens: Répartition générale par volume et origine
Size and geographical distribution of bronze-hoards A.D. 364-392

Nombre d'exemplaires	Bretagne	Limes rhéno-danubien	Autres Provinces: Occident	Autres Provinces: Italie-Afrique	Autres Provinces: Orient	Total	Note
de 1 à 10				1		1	(12)
de 11 à 20		2	2		1	5	(13)
de 21 à 50	6	5	1			12	(14)
de 51 à 100	2	3	1			6	(15)
de 101 à 200	1	2	2	3	1	9	(16)
de 201 à 500		8		3	1	12	(17)
de 501 à 1000		2		1		3	(18)
de 1001 à 2000	2	4			1	7	(19)
de 2001 à 5000		2		2	1	5	(20)
de 5001 à 9000		1				1	(21)
Total	11	29	6	10	5	61	
				21			

Table 2 Chronological composition of hoards buried c. 364-367

Tableau 2 Trésors Valentiniens (Bretagne et Limes Rhéno-Danubien c. 364-367); Répartition chronologique des types

Noms	Date	avant 330	330-340	340-348	FTR	Spes	Valent.
Heslington	355/p. 364	0.46	6.40	4.99	63.50		
Oldcroft	355/p. 364	0.33	4.60	1.50	70.90		
Icklingham IV	359/p. 364	57.00	9.50	-	33.30		
Duston	359/p. 364	58.30	-	-	41.60		
Colchester	359/p. 364	77.50	2.50	-	20.00		
Covesea	359/p. 364	-	3.90	2.10	24.01		
Lydney II	359/p. 364	-	0.42		17.10		
Bourton on W.	359/p. 364	-	-	-	100.00		
Poundbury	359/p. 364	-	1.10	-	83.30		
Carrawburgh	p. 364	95.34	-	-	-	-	3.44
Mablethorpe	p. 364	75.73	-	-		5.15	6.06
Wroxeter	p. 364	6.06	87.10	-	-	-	0.75
Taviers	p. 364	73.30	6.6		-	-	6.60
Silchester VII	p. 367	5.55	38.80	52.70	-	-	2.77
Wörschweiler	p. 367	2.74	42.20	50.80	-	-	1.37
Laslea	p. 367	89.24	3.57	-	3.57	-	3.57
Pevensey C.	p. 367	-	25.00	12.50	5.00	-	17.50

Table 3 Chronological and geographical distribution of Valentinianic bronze hoards 367–378

Tableau 3 Trésors Valentiniens (Bretagne, Limes Rhéno-Danubien, Italie et Orient c. 367-378: Répartition chronologique des types

		Bretagne				Limes rhéno-danubien				Autres secteurs			
Trésors	Date	Av. 348	FTR	Spes	Val.	Av. 348	FTR	Spes	Val.	Av. 348	FTR	Spes	Val.
Monte Guspini	p. 367 ?									-	21.05	7.00	34.20
Turquie	367									22.55	19.70	10.03	41.40
Italie	p. 367									-	-	-	52.10
Gelse	p. 367					-	2.80	2.10	67.30				
Carnuntum VI	p. 367					-	6.17	9.87	83.90				
Stielings	p. 368					-	4.34	-	78.20				
El Kab	370									1.58	2.19	3.75	82.30
Wilfleinsdorf	370					4.66	34.70	21.50	30.80				
Brigetio	372					29.60	17.87	13.15	23.27				
Jabing	374					0.84	5.18	5.04	81.06				
Lupoglav	374						3.20	1.92	73.39				
Iekham (28)	374-375	-	-	-	100.00								
Kazsok	374-375					1.86	4.95	8.96	80.30				
Kits Coty H.	a. 375	22.44	-	-	77.55								
Gölle	375					11.61	-	-	86.70				
Vienne K.	375					0.59	6.58	4.79	76.64				
Oregcsem	375					1.38	8.57		87.55				
Aylesbury	c. 376	-	5.55	-	91.66								
Vinkovci	376					1.12	5.10	7.00	85.28				
Arpas	376					0.81	3.73	2.89	92.36				
Ocsöd	376					1.57	4.99	10.59	81.10				
Bregenz L.	p. 378					6.75	-	2.21	70.40				
Delta	p. 378									2.73	3.87	10.02	78.58
Carnuntum V	p. 378					1.83	11.00		77.29				
Oudenburg II	p. 378					1.13	5.68	-	87.50				

Table 4 Size and geographical distribution of Constantinian bronze hoards
Tableau 4 Trésors Constantiens: repartition genérale par volume et origine

Nombre d'exemplaires	Bretagne	Limes Rhéno-danubien	Autres provinces Occident	Italie-Afrique	Orient	Total	Note
de 1 à 10						0	
de 11 à 20	2	1				3	(38)
de 21 à 50	2	10	6		1	19	(39)
de 51 à 100		8	1	3		12	(40)
de 101 à 200	2	6			2	10	(41)
de 201 à 500	2	1	2		1	6	(42)
de 501 à 1000	2	6			1	9	(43)
de 1001 à 2000	1	2			2	5	(44)
de 2001 à 5000	1	1	1		1	4	(45)
de 5001 à 9000	1	3				4	(46)
Total	13	38	10	3	8	72	
				21			

Table 5 Chronological and geographical distribution of bronze hoards buried A.D. 348 to 354

Tableau 5 Trésors Constantiens (Bretagne, limes Rhéno-Danubien, Gaule, Espagne, et Orient, c. 348-354); Répartition chronologique des types

Trésors	Date	Bretagne						Limes rhéno-danubien						Autres Secteurs					
		pre 330	330-340	340-348	Ae 2	Magn.	F TR	pre 330	330-340	340-348	Ae 2	Magn.	F TR	pre 330	330-340	340-348	Ae 2	Magn.	F TR
Halifax	p. 348	0.09	47.6	51.5	0.55														
Appleford	p. 348	29.40	28.7	41.7	0.01														
Great Weldon	p. 348	0.43	40.8	52.6	-														
Mitrovic	p. 348							-	7.61	88.99	-								
Rouvroy-les-M.	p. 348													-	69.6	24.2	-		
Vranic	350							-	0.38	0.36	0.32	-							
Lugenfeld	350							-	31.80	22.7	11.3	2.2							
Berkshire ?	350	8.3	16.60	-	41.6	33.3													
Byard's Leap	350	-	-	-	45.0	22.5													
Metternich	350							0.18	42.6	55.9	0.35	0.49							
Hanham	350	3.0	12.06	77.8	0.5	1.5													
Mackviller	350							12.78	33.9	26.4	5.9	2.9							
Brétigney	350							-	-	-	-	100.0							
Kom Denchal	351													-	-	-	100.0		
[Kaiseraugst I]	[351]							-	-	-	-	[98.75]							
[Kaiseraugst II]	[351]							[1.33]	[13.33]	[18.66]	[8]	[36]							
Theux	352							-	-	-	-	19.6							
Villing	352							-	-	-	52.05	47.9							
Pizokel	352							-	-	-	46.6	46.6							
Bassecourt	352							6.84	-	-	38.2	54.9							
Chamoson	352							1.98	3.4	1.3	4.08	85.0							
Strasbourg	352							-	-	0.9	11.9	34.8							
Reg. lyonnaise	352													-	-	-	-	100.0	
Kopstukken	352							-	-	-	8.6	91.3							
[Damas]	[352]													[4]	-	-	[93.6]	-	[0.8]
Fayoum	c. 352													-	-	-	98.03	-	1.9
Egypte I	c. 352													-	-	-	99.09	-	0.9
Fussach	c. 353							-	-	-	94.5	4.05							
Skellow	353	-	-	-	15.7	84.2													
Cobham	353	0.11	-	-	48.2	51.4													
Croydon	353	-	-	-	74.1	25.8													
Mayence I	353							-	-	-	13.7	86.2							
[Palatinat]	[353]							-	-	-	[7.69]	[79.48]							
Herkenbosch	353							-	4.5	-	-	95.4							
Tarragone	353													-	-	-	19.04	80.9	
Regensburg	p. 353							1.02	45.9	18.3	26.5	7.1	1.02						

Tableau 5 (cont.)
Table 5 (contd.)

		Bretagne						Limes rhéno-danubien						Autres secteurs					
Trésors	Date	pre 330	330-340	340-348	Ae 2	Magn.	F TR	pre 330	330-340	340-348	Ae 2	Magn.	F TR	pre 330	330-340	340-348	Ae 2	Magn.	F TR
Hemel	p. 353	10,8	59,6	8,6	-	1,1	-												
Collonge	p. 353													16,3	30,6	4,08	14,2	14,2	6,1
Fontaines Salées	353-354													2,4	6,5	3,6	3,6	48,7	5,6
Perbal	354							-	-	-	67,8	3,2	28,3						
Silchester V	p. 354	83,2	11,1	-	-	-	5,5												
Mayence II	p. 354							52,3	10,6	34,9	0,9	-	0,9						
Michelfeld	p. 354							3,5	60,7	28,5	-	-	3,5						
Théodule Pass	p. 354							+11,9	-55,4?	-	-	2,1?	30,4?						
Acs	p. 354												94,73						
Nires	p. 354?							96,6	-	-	3,3?	-	-						

Table 6 Chronological and geographical distribution of bronze hoards buried c. A. D. 355-363

Tableau 6 Trésors Constantiens (Bretagne, limes Rhéno-Danubien, Gaule, Espagne, Afrique, et Orient, c. 355-363); Répartition chronologique des types

Trésors	Date	Bretagne						Limes rhéno-danubien						Autres secteurs					
		pre 330	330-348	Aes 2	Mag.	FTR	Spes	pre 330	330-348	Aes 2	Mag.	FTR	Spes	pre 330	330-348	Aes 2	Mag.	FTR	Spes
Mayence III	p. 355							36,3	13,6	-	-	50							
Epiais Rhus	p. 355													6,88	48,27	-	20,68	17,24	
Conimbriga C	p. 355													3,8	49,9	15,3	-	26,9	
Monte Mozinho I	p. 355													93,0	3,4	-	-	3,4	
Minieh	p. 355													-	-	66,1	-	33,8	
L'Estrade	356													2,51	91,2	-	0,22	0,68	
Affreville	c. 358													-	-	27,28	-	72,41	
[Jupa]	[c. 358]							[0,61]	[0.41]	[7,41]	-	[90,3]							
[Orşova II]	[c. 358]							[1,63]	[0,97]	[22,44]	-	[73,7]							
Mayence IV	p. 358							86,8	10,38	-	0,86	-	0,86						
Rheinzabern	p. 358							4,85	94,7	0,08	0,14	-	0.02						
Rheinzabern II	p. 358							1,05	87,37	2	0,46	-	0,15						
Niederingelheim	p. 358							-	94	-	-	--	0,18						
Boljetin	p. 358							3,73	5,52	65,2+	1,7	2,8	0,05						
[Kosmaj]	p. 358							[6,73]	[5,18]	[79,83]	[1,49]	[3,42]	[0,09]						
[Orşova I]	p. 358							[0,95]	[0,67]	[19,17]	-	[77,67]	[0,54]						
Mayence V	a. 359							-	100	-	-	-	-						
Reims	a. 359							-	94,7	-	-	-	-						
White Woman's Hole	a. 359	38,3	10,08	-	-	0,22	-												
Freckenham	353-p. 359	0,55	1,65	28,3	34,4	34,8	-												
Malte	360													-	-	-	-	58,4	41,5
Caldas I	c. 360													3,1	44,3	-	-	22,2	9,5
[Smyrne]	[c. 360]													[0,04]	[1,37]	[9,4]	-	[81,9]	[4,8]
Egypte II	361													-	2,27	-	-	37,5	28,9
Chaniâ	363													-	3,5	7,1+	-		-75,0
[Vairano]	[p. 363]													-	-	-	-		[63,07]

ANNEXE A

APPENDIX A

<u>CTH</u> VIIII, 23, 1

354 Mart. 8).

IMP. CONSTANTIVS A. ET IVLIANVS CAES. AD RVFINVM
P(RAEFECTVM) P(RAETORI)O. Quicumque vel conflare pecunias
vel ad diversa vendendi causa transferre detegitur, sacrilegii sen-
tentiam subeat et capite plectatur. Portus enim litoraque diversa,
quo facilior esse navibus consuevit accessus, et itineris tramites
statuimus custodiri per idoneos officiales ac praepositos a praesidi-
bus et nonnullis praeditis dignitate, ut cognita veritate provinciarum
rectores obnoxios legibus puniant. Officia quoque inmenso periculo
1 subiacebunt. Nec vero aliquis negotiatorum plus mille follibus pecuniae
in usu publico constitutae animalibus propriis sumptuum gratia
portare debebit. Aut si ampliorem modum quisquam vehere detegatur,
facultates eius fisci dominio vindicentur et ipse adficiatur exilio.
2 Nam pecunias navibus vectas non omnes iudicamus mercatores
debere promere, quippe in usu tantum publico pecunias constitutas
permittimus convehi itidemque eas solas species emi, quae merca-
toribus more sollemni ad diversa portantur. Pecunias vero nulli
emere omnino fas erit nec vetitas contrectare, quia in usu publico
3 constitutas pretium oportet esse, non mercem. Placet denique, ut,
si quis forsitan nummus praeter eum, qui in usu publico perseverat,
aput aliquem mercatorem fuerit inventus, fisci dominio cum omnibus
delinquentis facultatibus vindicetur. Et si forte cum mercibus ad
quascumque provincias venerint naves, cuncta solita licentia merca-
buntur praeter pecunias, quas more solito maiorinas vel centenionales
communes appellant, vel ceteras, quas vetitas esse cognoscunt.
ACC. VIII ID. MAR. CONSTANTINA CONSTANTIO A. VIII ET IVLIANO
CAES. CONSS.

Appendix B Table 7 Chronological distribution of the coins from 142 bronze hoards A. D. 348-392
Annexe B Tableau 7 Répartition des monnaies des 142 trésors 348-392

Abbreviations: p. post, a. pre, c. circa

Nom Name	Date	3rd cent.	295-318	318-330	330-340	340-348	A3 348	A2 348-354	Magn.	A3 FTR	A4 Spes	JuA JoA	A3 364-378	A2 378-388	A3 p. 378	A4 p. 378	A4 388-392	? Ind.	Total
1 Halifax	p. 348	1			512	554	1	6										1	1075
2 Appleford	p. 348	16	19	1659	1654(1)	2399(2)	4	1(3)											5752
3 Great Weldon	p. 348			1	94(4)	121	9											5	230
3a Mitrovic	p. 348				65	760(4a)	29												854
4 Rouvroy. L. M.	p. 348				23(5)	8(6)	1											1	33
4a Vranic	350				19	18	4479	16										353	4885
5 Lugenfeld	350				14	10	14	5	1										44
6 Berkshire?	350	2			4			10(7)	8(8)										24
7 Byard's Leap	350							18	9									13	40
8 Metternich	350	1(9)		9	2174(10)	2849(11)	8	18	25(12)									7	5092
9 Hanham	350	1		5	24	155	3	1(13)	3									7	199
10 Mackviller	350	4	2	46	137	107	64	24	12									1(15)	404
11 Brétigney	350								90										90
12 Kom Denchal	351							1062											1062
13 Theux	352								12(16)									48	61
14 Villing	352							38	35										73
15 Pizokel	352							21	21									3(17)	45
16 Bassecourt	352	4	1	2				39(18)	56(19)										102
17 Chamoson	352		1	2	5	2	1	6	125(20)									5(21)	147
18 Strasbourg	352					1	54	13	38(22)									3(23)	109
19 Rég. lyonnaise	352								2358(24)										2358
20 Kopstukken	352							4	42										46
21 Fayoum	c. 352							100		2									102
22 Egypte I	c. 352							220		2									222
23 Fussach	c. 352						1	70	3										74(25)
24 Skellow	353							3	16										19
25 Cobham	353		1				2	403	430(26)										836
26 Croydon	353							2072	724										2796(27)
27 Mayence I	353							4(28)	25										29
28 Herkenbosch	353				1				21(29)										22
29 Tarragone	353							8	34										42
30 Regensburg	p. 353			1	45	18		26	7	1									98(30)
31 Hemel	p. 353	10(31)	4	5	103(32)	15	6		2(33)									28	173
32 Collonge	p. 353		3	5	15	2	7	7	7	3(34)									49
33 Fontaines Salées	353-354	2	3	1	16	9(35)		9	120(36)	14								72	246
34 Perbal	354						3	357(37)	17(38)	149									526
35 Silchester V	p. 354	1		14	2					1(39)									18
36 Mayence II	p. 354		16	38	11	36		1		1									103
37 Michelfeld	p. 354			1	17	8				1								1	28
38 Theodule P.	p. 354	11		1 + c. 50?(40)					2	28									42+c. 50
39 Acs	p. 354									90								5	95
40 Nirès	p. 354?	29						1											30(41)

	Nom	Date	3rd cent.	295–318	318–330	330–340	340–348	A3 348	A2 348–354	Magn.	A3 FTR	A4 Spes	JuA JoA	A3 364–378	A2 378–388	A3 p. 378	A4 p. 378	A4 388–392	Ind. ?	Total
41	Mayence III	p. 355		1	7	3					11(42)									22
42	Epiais R.	p. 355	1		1	10	4	2		6	5									29(43)
43	Conimbriga C	p. 355	1			4	9		4(44)		7								1	26
44	Monte Mozinho I	p. 355		4	23	1					1									29
45	Minieh	p. 355						1	981		502									1484
46	L'Estrade	c. 356	1		10	221(45)	176(46)	2		1(47)	3								21	435
47	Affreville	358							16		42									58
48	Mayence IV	p. 358	90	5	5	7	5	1(48)		1		1								115
49	Rheinzabern I	p. 358	85	31	56	1535(49)	1814(50)	4	3	5		1								3534
50	Rheinzabern II	p. 358	1	2	4	236(51)	332(52)	2	13	3		1							56(53)	650
51	Niederingelheim	p. 358				228(54)	283(55)	29				1							2	543
52	Boljetin	p. 358	5+	12	51	97	4	8	177(56)	31	51	1							-366(57)	1803
53	Mayence V	a. 359				15(58)														15
54	Reims	a. 359	1(59)			36(60)													1(61)	38
55	White W. H.	a. 359(62)	171(63)			45(64)					1								228(65)	446 ?
56	Freckenham	353–p. 359		3		6		3(66)	153(67)	186(68)	188(69)								1	540
57	Malte	360									38	27								65
58	Caldas I	c. 360	2			8	20				14	6							13	63
59	Kaiseraugst I	351–361						1		159			1 ?(70)							161
60	Egypte II	361				8	7	1			244	188							202	650
61	Chaniâ	363					1		2+		21-		1						3	28
62	Heslington	355–p. 364	2	2	9(71)	177(72)	138(73)	17	240(74)	385(75)	1755(76)								36(77)	2761
63	Oldcroft	355–p. 364	3(78)	3	5	150(79)	49(80)	21	222(81)	373(82)	2312(83)								122(84)	3260(85)
64	Icklingham IV	359–p. 364	11		1	2					7									21(86)
65	Duston	359–p. 364	7								5									12(87)
66	Colchester	359–p. 364	31			1					8									40(88)
67	Covesea	359–p. 364				9(89)	5(90)			2	55(91)								158(92)	229
68	Lydney II	359–p. 364					7				282								1357	1646(93)
69	Bourton on W.	359–p. 364									23									23(94)
70	Poundbury	359–p. 364				1					75(95)								14	90
71	Milan	p. 364									1	1	1	3						6
72	Carrawburgh	p. 364	82(96)	1										3					1(97)	87
73	Mablethorpe	p. 364	24(98)	1							5(99)			2					1(100)	33
74	Wroxeter	p. 364	8(101)			115			1				1(102)	1					6	132
75	Taviers	p. 364	11(103)			1								1					2 ?	15 ?
76	Cherchel I	p. 364				6	11			1	197	57		2					7	281
77	Cherchel II	p. 364	1			1	16	1	1		122(104)	16		4						162
78	Priène	p. 364	3(105)			3	4				21	37		1					112(106)	181
79	El Beida	365				11	8				124	67	1	1					47	259
80	Silchester VII	p. 367	2(107)			14	19							1						36
81	Worschweiler	p. 367		4	4	123	148	4	3	1				4						291(108)
82	Laslea	p. 367	23(109)	1	1	1					1			1						28

Nom	Date	3rd cent.	295–318	318–330	330–340	340–348	A3 348	A2 348–354	Magn.	A3 FTR	A4 Spes	JuA JoA	A3 364–378	A2 378–388	A3 p. 378	A4 p. 378	A4 388–392	Ind. ?	Total
83 Pevensey C.	p. 367				10	5	1	3	7(110)	2			7					5(III)	40
84 Monte Guspini	p. 367 ?									24	8		39(112)					43	114
85 Grdt St Bernard	p. 367			3	19	6		2	20(113)	235	173	4(114)	64					80	606(115)
86 Turquie	p. 367	1	10	18	234	61(116)		87		283	144	2	595(117)						1435
87 Italie	p. 367											156(118)	170						326
88 Gelse	p. 367									8	6		192(119)					79	285
89 Smyrne	p. 367 ? (120)		1		19	12	1	212		1849(121)	110		1					50	2255
90 Carnuntum VI	p. 367									5	8		68						81
91 Stielings	p. 368									1			18					4	23
92 El Kab	370			1	14	30				62	106	192(122)	2324(123)					92	2821
93 Afrique ? (124)	c. 370				32	109				15	5		12						173
94 Wilfleinsdorf	370				9	9	1	14	2	134	83	15(125)	119						386
95 Brigetio	372	19(126)	5	15	84	53	3	11		106	78	5	138					76	593(127)
96 Palatinat	374 ? (128)							3	31				4 ?					1(129)	39 ?
97 Jabing	374		1		7	4				74	72	46(130)	1156(131)					66	1426
98 · Lupoglav	374									10	6	2(132)	229					65	312
99 Kaiseraugst II	374 ?			1	10	14	10	6(133)	27(134)				5					2	75
100 Ickham	374–375												29(135)						29
101 Orşova I	374–375 ?	6(136)		1	4	1	3	140		567	4		3					1	730
102 Kazsok	374–375		1		7	6	1	4		37	67	3(137)	600					21	747
103 Kits Coty H.	a. 375	2 ?			20 ?								76						98 ?
104 Gölle	375	12(138)	6	1		16(139)	1		1				261					3	301
105 Vienne K.	375				1					11	8		128(140)					19(141)	167
106 Oregcsem	375					16+				104–(142)		3(143)	1062					27	1213
107 Aylesbury	c. 376								1	2			33						36(144)
108 Sfax I	376	11(145)	1		55	203			4(146)	1688	1444	44(147)	741					157(148)	4349
109 Vinkovci	376		1		5	15	1			100	137	6(149)	1669					23	1957

Nom	Date	3rd cent.	295–318	318–330	330–340	340–348	A3 348	A2 348–354	Magn.	A3 FTR	A4 Spes	JuA JoA	A3 364–378	A2 378–388	A3 p. 378	A4 p. 378	A4 388–392	Ind. ?	Total
110 Arpas	376	2		1	24	13				182	141	9(150)	4500(151)						4872
111 Ocsöd	376	2			16	14	4			100	212	9(152)	1623					21	2001
112 Bregenz. L.	p. 378				2	1					1		31			6 ?		6	44
113 Kosmaj	p. 378 ?		226(153)	321(154)	398	23	243	6472(155)	121(156)	278	8	4(157)		1				12	8107(158)
114 Vairano	p. 378 ?										41(159)	14(160)		1				9(161)	65
115 Delta	p. 378				12					17	44	19	345		2				439
116 Bimeda	p. 378		1		43	19					110		13			6			192
117 Laurion	p. 378													16					16
118 Carnuntum V	p. 378	1			4	3					48	3	337	2				38(162)	436
119 Caldas II	p. 378				4	6				3	3		2		1				19
120 Oudenburg	p. 378			1				1		5			77		1			3(163)	88
121 Enns I	p. 378	280(164)		1	3						11	2(165)	21	1				6	325
122 Aguntum I	p. 378							1						29					30
123 Shapwick III	p. 383	4		2	42	59			4(166)		32(167)	1	945		4	16		12(168)	1121
124 Medgidia	p. 383	12(169)	6	1	7					2		1	1	1					31
125 Veszprem	p. 383	3	2	1	51	45		2	1	316	484	24(170)	5863		8			1380(171)	8180
126 Furstenfeldbruck	p. 383	12	45	8	71	26				31			25	1				1(172)	220(173)
127 Zweibrücken	p. 383	1	1											10					12
128 Damas	p. 383 ?	1	1	3				117		1				2					126
129 St-Martory	p. 387	3	2		6	5	1			24(174)	3		8	1(175)	1	3		6	64(176)
130 Hemptinne	p. 387													1041(177)				1?	1042
131 Orşova II	p. 388 ?	19(178)		1	5	7	7	274(179)		900			4			3	1		1221
132 Carlsruhe ?	p. 388	16(180)			43(181)	15(182)							2		1		2	5	85
133 Monte Mozinho II	p. 368	4			23(183)	37				34(184)	15(185)		4				2	6	125
134 Pesche	p. 388		2	3	59(186)	30(187)			1	18(188)			5	1			2	5	126(189)
135 Paris	p. 388				5(190)					20(191)							1		26
136 La Peneda	p. 388	1		10						5							1	3	20
137 Jupa	p. 388 ?	4(192)	1	1	4		5	72		877			5			1	1		971
138 Wiveliscombe	p. 388	10(193)		3(194)	36(195)	39	2		6(196)	46(197)	4(198)	2(199)	863(200)		7	20(201)	71(202)	29(203)	1139
139 Sfax II	p. 388	14(204)			6	101(205)				377	599	21(206)	871(207)	2	2	178(208)	61(209)	212	2442
140 Bundle	p. 388									3	2		1		4(210)	3	8(211)		21

Notes du tableau 7 en annexe

1. Dont 13 imitations de 330-335 et 74 de 337-340=87 (1.5%).
2. Dont 31 imitations (0.53%).
3. Galère avec phénix, imitation (0.01%).
4. Dont 4 imitations de 335-340 (1.7%).

4a. Dont 1 imitation (0.11%).

5. Dont 1 imitation (3.03%).
6. Dont 1 imitation (3.03%).
7. Dont 1 imitation, galère (4.1%).
8. Dont 1 imitation (4.1%).
9. Imitation de Tétricus (0.01%).
10. Dont 601 imitations (11.8%).
11. Dont 196 imitations (3.8%).
12. *Add.* 1 *argenteus*.
13. Galère, imitation (0.5%).
14. Dont 6 imitations (1.4%).
15. 317-340.
16. *Add.* 1 *aureus*.
17. *Aes* 2.
18. Dont 12 imitations (11.7%).
19. Dont 5 imitations (4.9%); dans le lot de 473 ex. du Mt. Terrible, il y avait 103 Magnence-Décence (21.7%).
20. Dont 2 imitations (1.3%).
21. 330-348.
22. Plus de la moitié des *aes* 2 et 3 sont des imitations.
23. 2 *aes* 2 dont 1 Constant, 1 *aes* 3.
24. Dont 237 imitations (10.05%); le trésor dans son intégralité aurait été de c. 10.000 *aes* 2.
25. Lot de 74 sur 130 ex, avec les restes d'une bourse.
26. Quelques pièces ont le module de l'*aes* 1.
27. 2796 monnaies ont été examinées sur un total de 3600 ex.
28. Révolte de Trèves en 353.
29. 12 *aes* 1 et 9 *aes* 2.

30. Lot de 98 sur 140 monnaies initiales.

31. Dont 7 imitations (4.04%).

32. Dont 32 imitations (17.3%).

33. Dont 1 imitation (0.5%).

34. Dont 1 imitation (2.04%); il y avait aussi une copie d'Urbs Roma.

35. Dont 4 imitations post magnentiennes.

36. Dont 11 imitations (4.4%) et 54 de module réduit.

37. Dont 1 imitation (0.19%).

38. Dont 1 imitation (0.19%) et un ex. de module réduit.

39. Imitation au nom de Constant (5.5%).

40. *Cf. supra* note du texte no. 51.

41. Lot de 30 sur 150; il y avait 29 deniers de Néron à Sévère Alexandre.

42. Dont 1 Antioche, 7 Alexandre, 1 Nicomédie.

43. J. P. Garnier doit étudier cette trouvaille importante qui comportait: a) 2 *aes* 1 au chrisme de Magnence dans les deux orbites du mort; b) 1 *aes* 2 de Magnence sous le poignet gauche; c) une bourse contenant 26 monnaies et 22 anneaux, la plupart en potin; 3 des FTR sont des imitations (10.34%), dont 2 de module réduit.

44. Dont 1 imitation, galère (3.8%).

45. Dont 7 imitations (1.6%).

46. Dont 2 imitations (0.45%).

47. Imitations (0.22%).

48. Galère, peut-être *aes* 2.

49. Dont 121 imitations (3.42%).

50. Dont 26 imitations (0.7%).

51. Dont 28 imitations (4.3%).

52. Dont 3 imitations (0.46%).

53. Dont 2 de 337-348.

54. Dont 6 imitations (1.1%).

55. Dont 1 imitations (0.18%).

56. Dont 13 imitations (0.7%).

57. Il y avait au moins 4 radiées du IIIe s. et une pièce illyrienne d'où un maximum, semble-t-il, de 366 monnaies indéterminées qui toutes paraissent avoir été au type Fel Temp Reparatio.

58. *Minimi*.

59. Imitation de Tétricus.

60. Imitations.

61. Imitation.

62. Ou 394/395 si la pièce d'Arcadius n'a pas été ajoutée.

63. Dont 80 imitations de Tétricus (17.9%) ; 85 ex. officiels ont été coupés en 1/2, 1/4, etc.

64. Imitations (10.08%).

65. Flans, rondelles coulées, résidus.

66. Dont 1 imitation, galère (0.18%).

67. Dont 38 imitations (7.03%), il y avait 13 Constance II de l'insurrection de Trèves en 353.

68. Dont 25 imitations (4.6%, 11 de module réduit); il y avait 10 ex. à 7.53 g.

69. Dont 100 imitations (18.5%); il y avait 3 Galle et 3 Carausius II.

70. Silique de Julien, il n'est pas assuré pourtant que cette pièce d'argent fasse partie du trésor. Un autre dépôt—le 3ème de bronze—a été découvert à Kaiseraugst, Westd. Zeits, 25, 1906, 175-176: sur 454 ex, un lot de 157 dont 26 de 330-340, 78 de 340-348, 52 constantiniennes illisibles, 1 Magnence.

71. Dont 1 imitation (0.03%).

72. Dont 22 imitations (0. 79%).

73. Dont 3 imitations (0.1%).

74. Dont 46 (?) imitations, galère (1.6%, 1 ex. surfrappé).

75. Dont 284 imitations (10.2%, 2 ex. surfrappés).

76. Dont 834 imitations (30. 2%, 294 surfrappés dont 1 Tetricus, 1 Requies Opt. Merit., 135 de 330-340, 69 de 240-348, 22 FTR, soit 10.6%); il y avait 1 Censeris et 2 Carausius II.

77. FTR, aes 2 ou 3.

78. Dont 1 imitation (0.03%).

79. Dont 6 imitations (0.18%).

80. Dont 2 argentei, Pax Augustorum, TR et Victoria Augustorum, SISω.

81. Dont 43 imitations (1.3%); un FTR au cavalier est surfrappé sur un aes 2 de Magnence.

82. Dont 255 imitations (7.8%); il y avait 30 ex. à module réduit.

83. Dont 1217 imitations (37.3%); il y avait 95 surfrappés, 1 radié, 78 de 330-340, 14 de 340-348, 1 aes 3 de 348-350, 1 Magnence.

84. dont 11 surfrappes sur Gloria Exercitus à 2 enseignes.

85. Add. 4 barres d'AR: 9.68; 7.86; 3.04 et 2.25 g.

86. Les 21 ex. sont des imitations.

87. Les 12 ex. sont des imitations; trois FTR en surfrappe.

88. Les 40 ex. sont des imitations; un FTR en surfrappe.

89. Dont 5 imitations (2.1%).

90. Dont 3 imitations (1.3%).

91. Dont 54 imitations (23.5%).

92. Imitations (68.9%).

93. Tous les ex. identifiés sont des imitations.

94. Les 23 ex. sont des imitations.

95. Dont 24 imitations (26.6%).

96. Dont 78 imitations (89.6%);

97. Flan.

98. 4 aes d'Auguste à Commode, 20 radiés.

99. 4 imitations FTR (12.1%) et un PB de Julien.

100. Pb de Constance II.

101. Dont 6 imitations (4.5%).

102. Silique fourrée de Julien.

103. Dont 10 imitations des Tetrici (66.6%).

104. Plusieurs imitations FTR de module réduit.

105. Trois ex. grecs: 2 Priène; 1 Antiochus IV.

106. Aux types de FTR, Spes et Securitas Reipublicae.

107. Dont 1 imitation (2.77%).

108. 291 ex. conservés sur 600.

109. 13 aes de Tibère à Marc Aurèle, 4 deniers d'Antonin à Septime Sévère, 6 radiés.

110. 3 ex. à module réduit.

111. Minimi.

112. Un des ex. de Valentinien I est reféré à Coh. 42, Victoria Auggg, AR ? qui en fait appartient à Valentinien II après 378 (RIC, IX, 36 b). Date par conséquent incertaine.

113. Dont 1 aes 1.

114. 1 aes 1, 2 aes 3 de Julien.

115. Les aes 3 sont de provenance italienne et orientale.

116. Dont 1 imitation (0.06%).

117. Dont 3 Procope.

118. 118 aes 3 de Julien (36.1%), 38 Vota de Jovien (11,6%).

119. Dont 1 Procope.

120. Selon R. A. G. Carson, JNG, 21, 1971, 137-154, la thésaurisation s'arrête avec les Spes et on a ajouté 1 Gloria Romanorum de 367-375 et 2 Virtus Exerciti de 395-402. Il est provisoirement possible de ne faire cette hypothèse que pour les deux dernières pièces.

121. Dont 13 imitations (0.57%).

122. Julien: 49 aes 3, Vota, 3 aes 4, Vir. Exerc. Romanor.; Jovien: 140 aes 3, Vota.

123. Restitutor Reip: 34 ex., 5, à 1.9 g, 29 à 2.79 g; 169 Gloria Romanorum, 1976 Securitas Reipublicae, 143 imitations (5.06%), dont 5 surfrappes (2 sur FTR, 1 sur Spes, 2 sur Vot V de Jovien); il y avait 2 Procope.

124. Les monnaies viennent d'Arles, Rome, des Détroits, de l'Orient: cette répartition des ateliers fait penser a une origine africaine.

125. Julien: 7 aes 1, 3 aes 3; Jovien: 1 aes 1, 4 aes 3.

126. 1 monnaie greque, 3 dupondii de Trajan, Commode, Galle, 15 radiés.

127. Add. 1 monnaie byzantine.

128. Il n'est pas certain du tout que les 4 aes 3 valentiniens appartiennent au trésor.

129. Aes 2.

130. Julien: 1 aes 1 (coulé), 34 aes 3; Jovien: 11 aes 3.

131. Vota 3, Restitutor Reip. 7, Gloria Romanorum 543, Securitas Reipublicae 603; il y avait 2 surfrappés sur FTR.

132. Vota 1 Julien, 1 Jovien.

133. Dont 1 imitation (1.35%).

134. Dont 1 imitation (1.35%).

135. Dont 1 imitation (3.44%).

136. 1 quadrans de Trajan, 1 denier fourré, 1 aes de Nicée pour Sévère Alexandre, 3 radiés dont 2 fourrés.

137. Julien: 2 aes 3, Jovien: 1 aes 3.

138. Trois sesterces (Domitien, Nerva, Faustine), 2 bronzes coloniaux (Trajan, Antonin), 7 radies.

139. Dont 3 Gloria Exercitus à 1 enseigne.

140. Dont 1 Procope.

141. Dont 1 de la moitié du IVe s., 17 de la 2 ème moitié du IVe s.

142. Les 80 Constance II peuvent ne pas tous appartenir à cette période.

143. Aes 3 Jovien.

144. "une poignée" prise dans un récipient.

145. Dont 7 imitations (0.16%); outre les radiés, il y avait un ex. de Judée (Maccabées).

146. Dont, semble-t-il, 2 imitations (0.04%).

147. Julien: 3 aes 3, Vota, 37 aes 4 Virt. Exerc. Romanor,; Jovien: 4 aes 3 Vota.

148. Dont 12 imitations (0.027%) et 2 faux.

149. Julien, 4 Virt. Exerc. Romanor., Jovien, 2 Vota.

150. Julien: 4 Vota, Jovien: 5 Vota.

151. Dont 1 Procope.

152. Julien: 8 Vota; Jovien: 1 Vota.

153. Dont 23 impériales grecques et coloniales.

154. Dont 4 imitations (0.04%).

155. Dont 37 imitations (0.45%) et 44 tréflées.

156. Dont 2 imitations (0.02%).

157. Aes 3: 3 Vota Julien, 1 Jovien.

158. Premier décompte.

159. 34 Constance II, 4 Galle, 3 Julien César; ce trésor doit être étudié par J. P. C. Kent.

160. 14 maiorinae dont 1 imitation (1.53%).

161. Dont 1 imitation (1.53%).

162. Dont 21 aes 4 qui peuvent être des années 330-348, 358-361 ou 378-383.

163. Dont 1 Constantin Ier incus.

164. De Valérien à Dioclétien dont 45 postérieurs à la réforme d'Aurélien.

165. Aes 3 Vota, 1 Julien, 1 Jovien.

166. Dont 2 imitations (0.17%).

167. Dont 10 imitations (0.89%); il y avait 6 modules réduits et 4 surfrappés.

168. De Constance II.

169. De Vespasien à Philippe, plus 7 coloniales du IIIe s.

170. Vota, 12 Julien, 11 Jovien; une monnaie d'Isis.

171. Dont 20 ex. indéterminés de Constance II-Julien et 2 imitations (0.002%).

172. Constance II, Gloria Romanorum, Coh. 138-139.

173. Lot de 220 sur 800/1200.

174. Dont 4 imitations (6.25%).

175. *Add*. une silique de Maxime.

176. Lot de 64 sur 77 ex.

177. Dont 164 imitations (15.7%).

178. IIe s.: 1 as, 1 quadrans, 2 deniers dont 1 fourré; IIIe s.: 3 coloniales de Bithynie, 1 denier fourré, 11 antoniniani dont 1 fourré.

179. Dont 1 imitation (0.08%).

180. Dont 10 imitations (11.76%).

181. Dont 10 imitations (11.76%).

182. Dont 2 imitations (2.35%).

183. Dont 1 imitation (0.8%).

184. Dont 3 imitations (2.4%).

185. Un ex. peut-être du type FTR.

186. Dont 13 imitations (10.3%).

187. Dont 4 imitations (3.17%).

188. Dont 6 imitations (4.76%).

189. Lot de 126 ex. sur 350.

190. Imitations (19.23%).

191. Imitations (76.92%).

192. De Trajan à Claude II; il y avait une coloniale de Viminacium et un antoninianus fourré.

193. Dont 2 imitations (0.17%).

194. Dont 1 imitation (0.08%).

195. Dont 3 imitations (0.26%);

196. Imitations (0.52%).

197. Dont 17 imitations (1.49%); il y avait aussi 5 surfrappes.

198. Dont 1 imitation (0.08%).

199. *Vota*, 1 Julien, 1 Jovien; *add*. une silique de Julien.

200. Dont 2 ?imitations (0.17%).

201. Aux 13 *Vota* sont ajoutés 7 *Spes* de Maxime c. 387.

202. 18 *Salus*, 53 *Victoria*; il y avait 7 imitations (0.61%).

203. Dont 5 constantiniennes, 1 Gratien et 2 imitations (0.17%).

204. 1 Judée, 13 antoniniani dont 11 imitations (0.45%).

205. dont 48 *Victoriae*, 46 *Vota*.

206. Julien: 13 Virt. Exerc. Romanor.; Jovien: 8 Vota.

207. 226 Gloria, 645 Securitas.

208. Dont 163 Vota, 2 Gloria Reipublice (camp), 2 Victoria Aug (2 Victoires), 9 Spes.

209. 13 Salus, 48 Victoria.

210. Dont 2 imitations (9.52%).

211. Dont 2 imitations (9.52%); il y avait aussi 2 Cyzique, 1 Thessalonique; les 3 Vota de c. 383 étaient 2 Antioche et 1 Alexandrie; 1 des 3 FTR provient de Nicomédie. Donc coloration orientale du trésor.

RÉFÉRENCES DES TRÉSORS
HOARD BIBLIOGRAPHY *

1. Halifax (Yorks), YAJ, 33, 92, 1915, 444-451.
2. Appleford (Berks), RBN, 123, 1977, 41-100.
3. Great Weldon (Northants), Rep. Res. Com. Soc. Ant. London, 31, 1974, 104-106.

3a. Mitrovic (Croatie), VHAD, 2, 1896-1897, 82-93.

4. Rouvroy-les-Merles (Oise), BSFN, 24, 6, 1969, 418.

4a. Vranic (Croatie), VHAD, 6, 1902, 170-178.

5. Lugenfeld (Pfalz), FMRD, IV, 2, no. 2070.
6. Berkshire, NC, 6, 14, 1954, 211-213.
7. Byard's Leap (Lincs), NC, 6, 1942, 107-108.
8. Metternich (Rheinland), BJ, 145, 1940, 180-226.
9. Hanham (Glos), NC, 6, 14, 1954, 213-215.
10. Mackviller (Bas-Rhin), Cah. Alsaciens d'Arch, d'Art et d'Hist., 1957, 33-50, 69-73, 95-96.
11. Brétigney (Doubs), R. A. Est, 19, 1968, 177.
12. Kom Denchal (Delta), Annales Service Antiquités Egypte, Supplt. 7, 1948, 1-28.
13. Theux (Liège), M. Thirion, Les trésors monétaires gaulois et romains trouvés en Belgique, Bruxelles, 1967, 156-157, no. 291.
14. Villing (Moselle), Cah. Alsaciens d'Arch. d'Art et d'Hist., 1957, 35-36 et 46-47.
15. Pizokel (Grisons), RNS, 30, 1943, 104-105.
16. Bassecourt (Jura suisse), Actes Soc. jurassienne d'Émulation, 1945, 1-12.
17. Chamoson (Valais), SMB, 64, 1966, 150-151.
18. Strasbourg (Bas-Rhin), Cah. Alsaciens d'Arch, d'Art et d'Hist., 1957, 33-35.
19. Région lyonnaise, ibid. p. 48-49 et P. Bastien, Le monnayage de Magnence (350-353), Wetteren, 1964, 121-122.

---

* This section has not been translated into English as it seemed unnecessary.

20. Kopstukken (Groningue), W. A. van Es, De romeinse mundtvondsten uit de drie noordelijke provincies, Groningue, 1960, 102.

21. Fayoum, SMB, 34, 1959, 43-44.

22. Egypte I, Cercle d'Et. Num., 2, 1, 1965, 2-4.

23. Fussach (Vorarlberg), NZ, 91, 1977, 40, G 3.

24. Skellow (Yorks), NC, 6, 7, 1947, 83-84.

25. Cobham (Kent), NC, 3, 5, 1885, 108-117.

26. Croydon (Surrey), NC, 4, 5, 1905, 36-62.

27. Mayence I (Rheinland), FMRD, IV, 1, no. 1196.

28. Herkenbosch (Limbourg), Jaarb. voor Munt- en Penningkunde, 52-53, 1965-1966 , 52-58.

29. Tarragone (Catalogne), Principe de Viana, 32, 1971, 27-34.

30. Regensburg (Oberpfalz), Germania, 56, 1958, 96-103.

31. Hemel (Herts), Rep. Res. Com. Soc. Ant. London, 31, 1974, 104 et 115-117.

32. Collonge-en-Charolais (Saône et Loire), La Physiophile, 35-36, 1953, 2-22.

33. Fontaines Salées (Yonne), Gallia, 23, 1965, 152-233.

34. Perbal (Pest), Folia Arch., 16, 1964, 63-77.

35. Silchester V (Hants), NC, 6, 20, 1960, 248-249.

36. Mayence II (Rheinland), FMRD, IV, 1, no. 1169.

37. Michelfeld (Nord Wurtt.), FMRD, II, 4, no. 4446.

38. Theodule Pass (Valais), NC, 3, 17, 1897, 127-130.

39. Acs (Vaspuszta), Arch. Ert., 99, 1972, 232-239.

40. Nirès (Transylvanie), D. Protase, "Les trésors monétaires de la Dacie romaine, leur signification sociale, économique et ethnopolitique," Congr. Int. Num., Atti, Rome 1961, (1965), 423-434.

41. Mayence III (Rheinland), FMRD, IV, 1, no. 1156.

42. Epiais Rhus (Val d'Oise), doc. inédite J. P. Garnier.

43. Conimbriga C (Coimbra), Fouilles de Conimbriga, III, Les monnaies, Paris, 1974, 325-326.

44. Monte Mozinho I (Porto), Conimbriga, 13, 1974, 75-91.

45. Minieh (Moyenne Egypte), NC, 6, 16, 1956, 179-188.

46. L'Estrade (Aude), Trésors monétaires, 1, 1979, 93-107.

47. Affreville (Chélif), BSFN, 15, 8, 1960, 465-467 et doc. inédite P. Salama.

48. Mayence IV (Rheinland), FMRD, IV, 1, no. 1201.

49. Rheinzabern 1 (Pfalz), FMRD, IV, 2, no. 2076.

50. Rheinzabern II (Pfalz), FMRD, IV, 2, no. 2077.

51. Neideringelheim (Rheinhessen , FMRD, IV, 1, no. 1093.

52. Boljetin (Serbie), Sirmium VIII, Rome, 1978, 135-177.

53. Mayence V (Rheinland), FMRD, IV, 1, no. 1188.

54. Reims (Marne), Quaderni Ticinesi, 6, 1977, 281-315.

55. White Woman's Hole (Somerset), Proc. Univ. Bristol Spelaeol. Soc., 13, 1, 1972, 61-69.

56. Freckenham (Suffolk), NC, 6, 13, 1953, 69-73.

57. Malte, Annual Rep. of the Museum Department, Malte, 1961, 8-10.

58. Caldas I (Pontevedra), Studia Arch., Valladolid, 12, 1973, 5-14.

59. Kaiseraugst I (Bâle), SMB, 18, 66, 1967, 50-57.

60. Egypte II, JRS, 10, 1920, 169-184.

61. Chaniâ((Crête), Archaeologicon Deltion, 26, 1961, 11.

62. Heslington (Yorks), NC, 7, 11, 1971, 207-225.

63. Oldcroft (Glos), NC, 7, 14, 1974, 65-75.

64. Icklingham IV (Suffolk), NC, 5, 14, 1934, 262-266.

65. Duston (Northants), NC, 5, 14, 1934, 266-268.

66. Colchester (Essex), NC, 5, 11, 1934, 255-262.

67. Covesea (Moraysh.), PSAS, 65, 1930, 209-212.

68. Lydney II (Glos), NC, 6, 10, 1950, 256.

69. Bourton-on-the-Water (Glos), ibid., and BGAST, 1934, 133-139.

70. Poundbury (Dorset), NC, 6, 12, 1952, 96-98.

71. Milan (It.), Boll. Num, 9, 1911, 66-67.

72. Carrawburgh (Chester), NC, 5, 13, 1933, 82-84.

73. Mablethorpe (Lincs), NC, 6, 5, 1945, 165-166.

74. Wroxeter (Shrops), NC, 1, 20, 1857, 79-83.

75. Taviers (Namur), M. Thirion, op. cit., 155, no. 287.

76. Cherchel I (Alger), doc. inédite P. Salama.

77. Cherchel II (Alger), doc. inédite P. Salama.

78. Priène (Aydin), K. Regling, Die münzen von Priene, Berlin, 1927, 176-178.

79. El Beida (Cyrénaïque), Libya Antiqua, 3-4, 1966-1967, 202-211.

80. Silchester VII (Hants), NC, 6, 20, 1960, 251-252.

81. Würschweiler (Saarland), FMRD, III, no. 1180.

82. Laslea (Transylvanie), E. Chirila, N. Gudea, G. Moldovan, Münzen aus der Sammlung des Museums der Stadt Sighisoara, Sighişoara, 1972, 31-34.

83. Pevensey Castle (Sussex), NC, 1, 3, 1841, 65.

84. Monte Guspini (Cagliari), Annali, 1, 1954, 90-91.

85. Grand St Bernard (Aoste), M. Orlandini, Catalogo della raccolta numismatica dell'Accademia di S. Anselmo, Aoste, 1971, 286-302, no. 882-1407.

86. Turquie, Jaarb. voor Munt- en Penningkunde, 56-57, 1969-1970, 25-48.

87. Italie, doc. inédite M. Amandry.

88. Gelse (Zala), NK, 48, 1949, 58.

89. Smyrne (Ismir), Jb Num, 21, 1971, 137-154.

90. Carnuntum VI (Basse Autriche), FMRÖ, III, 1, 1976, 206.

91. Stielings (Swaben), FMRD, 1, 7, no. 7197.

92. El Kab (Thébaïde), CE, 45-46, 1948, 162-180.

93. Afrique ?, NC, 6, 17, 1957, 240-241.

94. Wilfleinsdorf (Basse Autriche), Jahresschrift der öster. Gesel. für Arch., 5-6, 1977-1978, 15-40.

95. Brigetio (Komaron), Folia Arch., 25, 1975, 147-150.

96. Palatinat, FMRD, IV, 2, no. 2331.

97. Jabing (Burgenland), NZ, 29, 69, 1936, 60-68.

98. Lupoglav (Croatie), VHAD, 12, 1912, 284-286.

99. Kaiseraugst II (Bâle), RSN, 42, 1962-1963, 21-31.

100. Ickham (Kent), Coin Hoards, 2, 1976, 53-55.

101. Orşova I (Banat), E. Chirila, N. Gudea, I. Stratan, Drei Münzhorte des 4. Jahrhunderts aus dem Banat, Lugoj, 1974, 17-29.

102. Kazsok (Somogy), NK, 66-67, 1967-1968, 3-22.

103. Kits Coty House (Kent), NC, 15, 1853, 59.

104. Gölle (Somogy), Folia Arch., 20, 1969, 63-68.

105. Vienne-Krottenbach (Vienne), FMRÖ, IX, 1978, 145-149.

106. Oregcsem (Komaron), NK, 41, 1942, 11-23.

107. Aylesbury (Bucks), NC, 6, 1, 1941, 95-96.

108. Sfax I (Tunisie), Jaarb. voor Munt- en Penningkunde, 55, 1968, 19-27.

109. Vinkovci (Croatie), VHAD, 12, 1912, 272-284.

110. Arpas (Sopron), NK, 32-33, 1933-1934, 3-27.

111. Ocsöd (Szolnok), NK, 28-29, 1929-1930, 30-44,

112. Bregenz-Lochau (Vorarlberg), NZ, 91, 1977, 47, H11.

113. Kosmaj (Serbie), doc. inédite F. Dolbeau, C. Metzger, C. Brenot.

114. Vairano (Tessin), SMB, 46, 1962, 39.

115. Delta (Egypte), NC, 6, 5, 1945, 163-164.

116. Bimeda (Asturies), Numisma, 25, 1975, 9-17.

117. Laurion (Attique), Archaeologicon Deltion, 19, 1964, 73-74.

118. Carnuntum V (Basse Autriche), FMRÖ, III, 1, 1976, 204-206.

119. Caldas II (Pontevedra), Studia Arch., Valladolid, 19, 1973, 14-18.

120. Oudenburg (Flandre Occ.), M. Thirion, op. cit., p. 134, no. 233.

121. Enns I (Linz), Der römische Limes in Österreich, 9, 1908, col. 162-176.

122. Aguntum I (Tyrol), Beitr. z. römerzeitl. Bod. Forsch. in Öst., 2, 1974, 54-55.

123. Shapwick III (Somerset), NC, 5, 19, 1939, 128-142.

124. Medgidia (Dobroudja), Pontica, 5, 1972, 537-547.

125. Veszprem (Veszprem), NZ, 42, 1909, 117-136 et NK, 40-41, 1961-1962, 29-48.

126. Fürstenfeldbrück (Ober-Bayern), FMRD, I, 1, no. 1078.

127. Zweibrücken (Pfalz), FMRD, IV, 2, no. 2329.

128. Damas (Syrie), doc. inédite A. R. Ebeian, ANS, New York.

129. St-Martory (Hte Garonne), Révue de Comminges, 90, 1977, 159-171.

130. Hemptinne (Namur), Ann. Soc. Arch. Namur, 54, 1967, 6-59.

131. Orşova II (Banat), E. Chirila, N. Gudea, I. Stratan, op. cit., 29-47.

132. Carlsruhe? (Süd Baden), FMRD, II, 2, no. 2334.

133. Monte Mozinho II (Porto), Conimbriga, 13, 1974, 93-110.

134. Pesche (Namur), RBN, 104, 1958, 45-61.

135. Paris (F.), RN, 5, 8, 1944, 34, n. 22bis.

136. La Peneda (Pontevedra), Studia Arch., Valladolid, 19, 1973, 18-22.

137. Jupa (Banat), E. Chirila, N. Gudea, I. Stratan, op. cit., 5-15.

138. Wiveliscombe (Somerset), NC, 6, 6, 1946, 163-165.

139. Sfax II (Tunisie), Jaarb. voor Munt- en Penningkunde, 55, 1968, 19-27.

140. Bundle (Lancs), NC, 6, 7, 1947, 216.

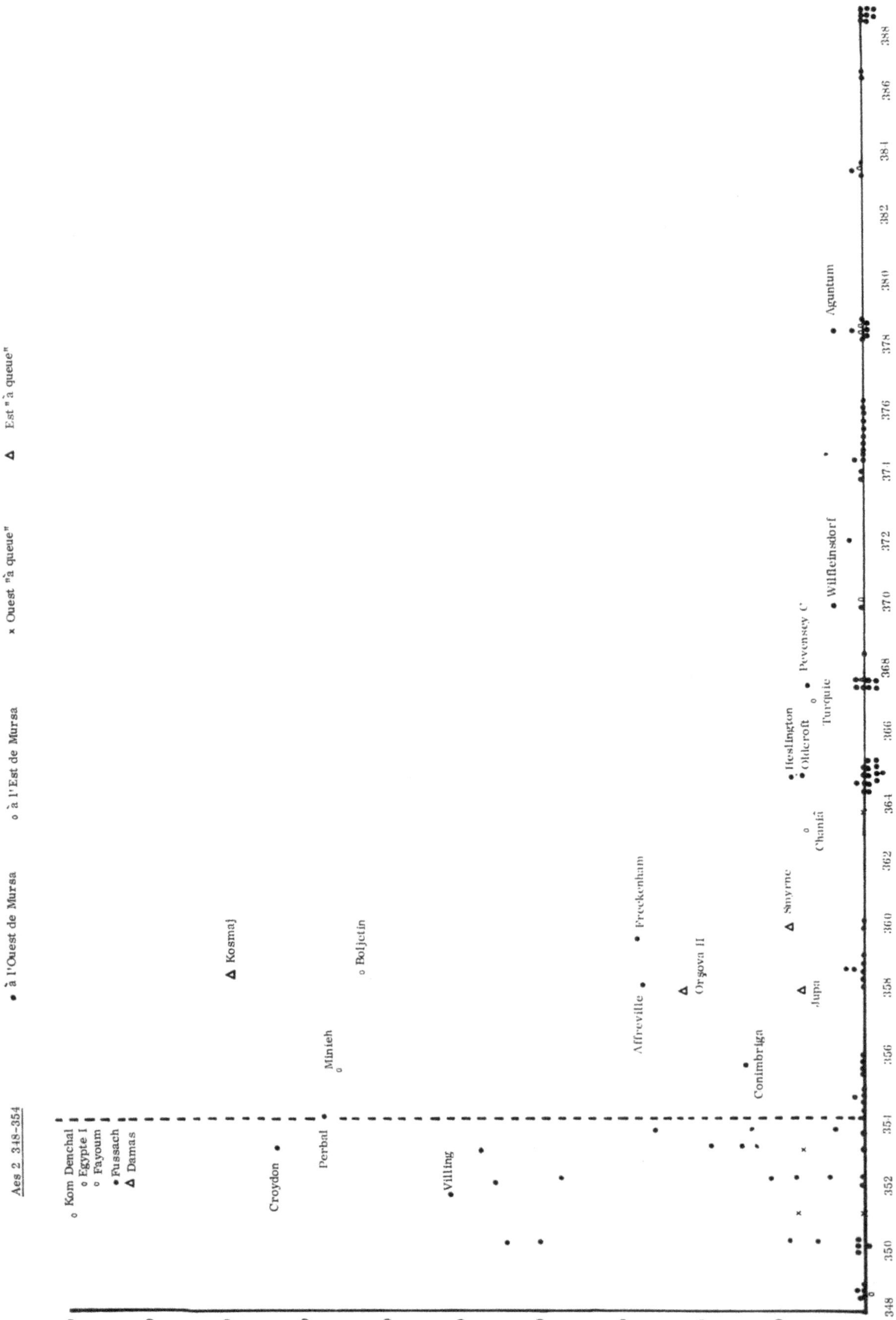

Aes 2 348-354
• à l'Ouest de Mursa
o à l'Est de Mursa
x Ouest "à queue"
Δ Est "à queue"
Kom Denchal
Egypte I
Fayoum
Fussach
Damas
Croydon
Perbal
Minieh
Villing
Kosmaj
Boljetin
Affreville
Freckenham
Orsova II
Conimbriga
Jupa
Smyrne
Chania
Heslington
Oldcroft
Turquie
Pevensey C
Wilfleinsdorf
Aguntum
100
90
80
70
60
50
40
30
20
10
0
348
350
352
354
356
358
360
362
364
366
368
370
372
374
376
378
380
382
384
386
388

• Aes de Magnence à l'Ouest de Mursa x " à queue")

Fig. 2

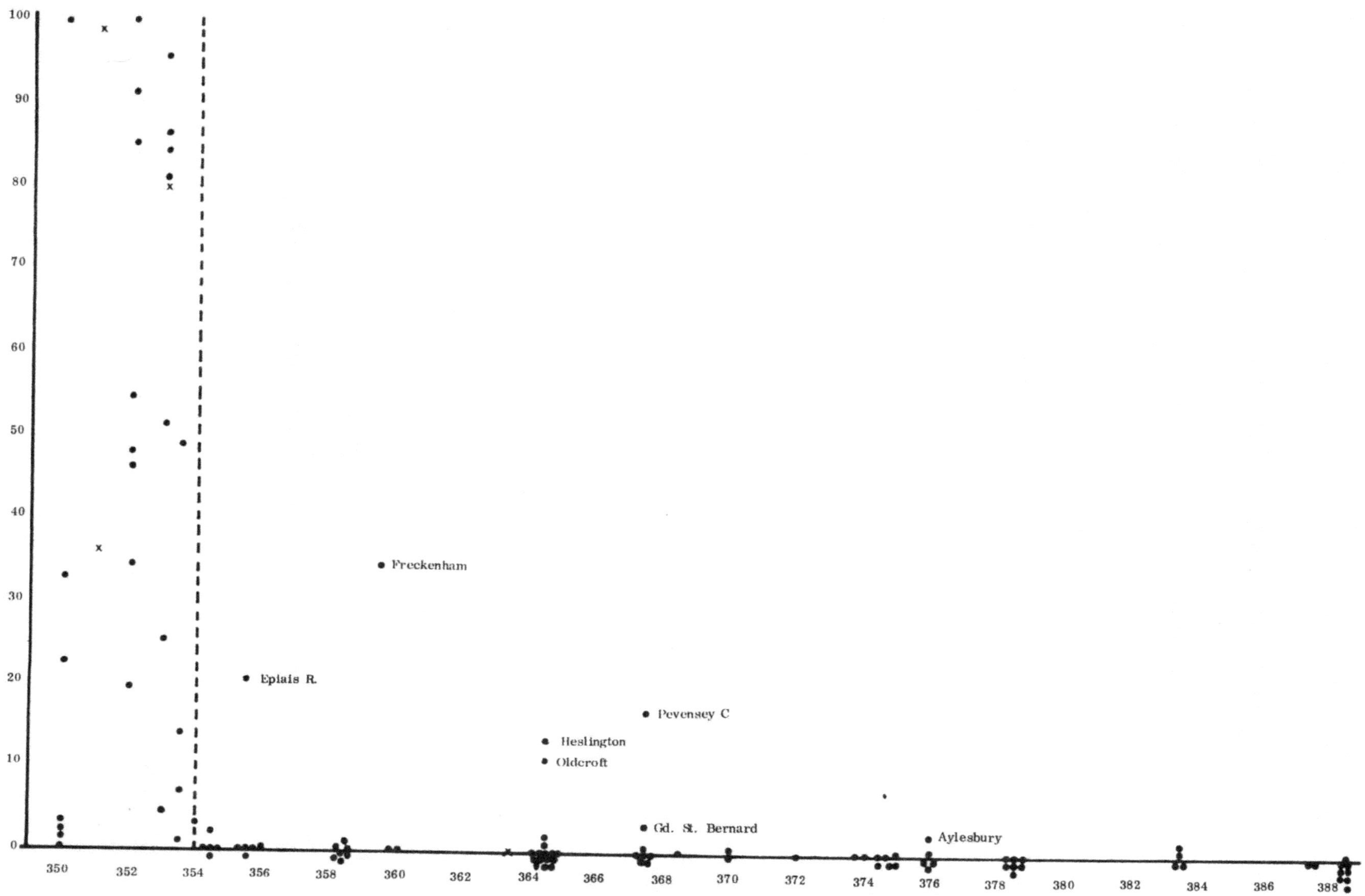

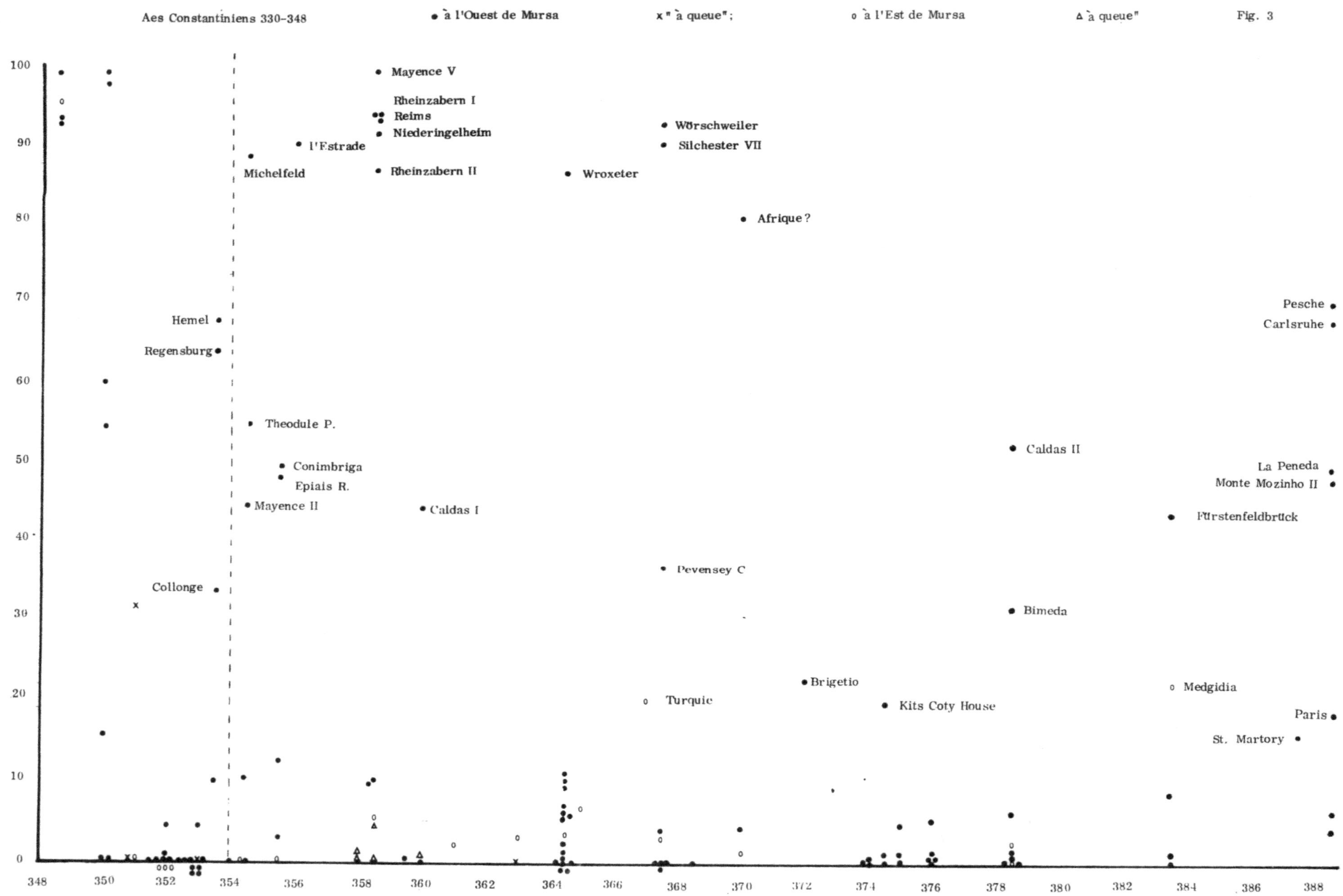
Aes Constantiniens 330-348
• à l'Ouest de Mursa
x " à queue";
o à l'Est de Mursa
Δ à queue"
Mayence V
Rheinzabern I
Reims
Niederingelheim
l'Estrade
Michelfeld
Rheinzabern II
Wroxeter
Wörschweiler
Silchester VII
Afrique ?
Hemel
Regensburg
Theodule P.
Conimbriga
Epiais R.
Mayence II
Caldas I
Collonge
Pevensey C
Turquie
Brigetio
Kits Coty House
Caldas II
Bimeda
Pesche
Carlsruhe
La Peneda
Monte Mozinho II
Fürstenfeldbrück
Medgidia
Paris
St. Martory
100
90
80
70
60
50
40
30
20
10
0
348
350
352
354
356
358
360
362
364
366
368
370
372
374
376
378
380
382
384
386
388
Fig. 3

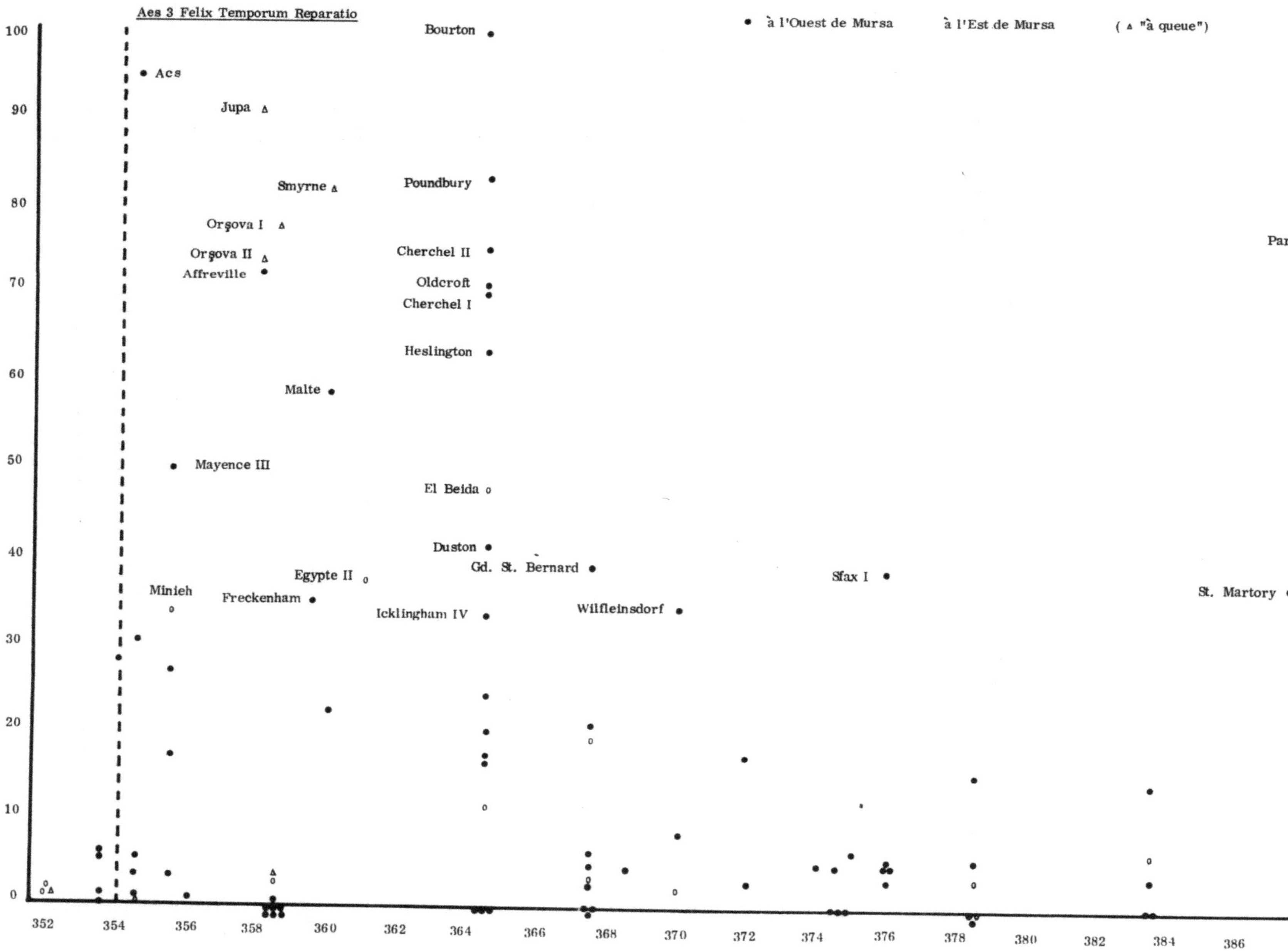
Aes 3 Felix Temporum Reparatio
● à l'Ouest de Mursa
à l'Est de Mursa
(▵ "à queue")
Acs
Jupa
Smyrne
Orşova I
Orşova II
Affreville
Malte
Mayence III
Minieh
Freckenham
Egypte II
Bourton
Poundbury
Cherchel II
Oldcroft
Cherchel I
Heslington
El Beida
Duston
Gd. St. Bernard
Icklingham IV
Wilfleinsdorf
Sfax I
St. Martory
Paris
100
90
80
70
60
50
40
30
20
10
0
352
354
356
358
360
362
364
366
368
370
372
374
376
378
380
382
384
386
388

Fig. 4

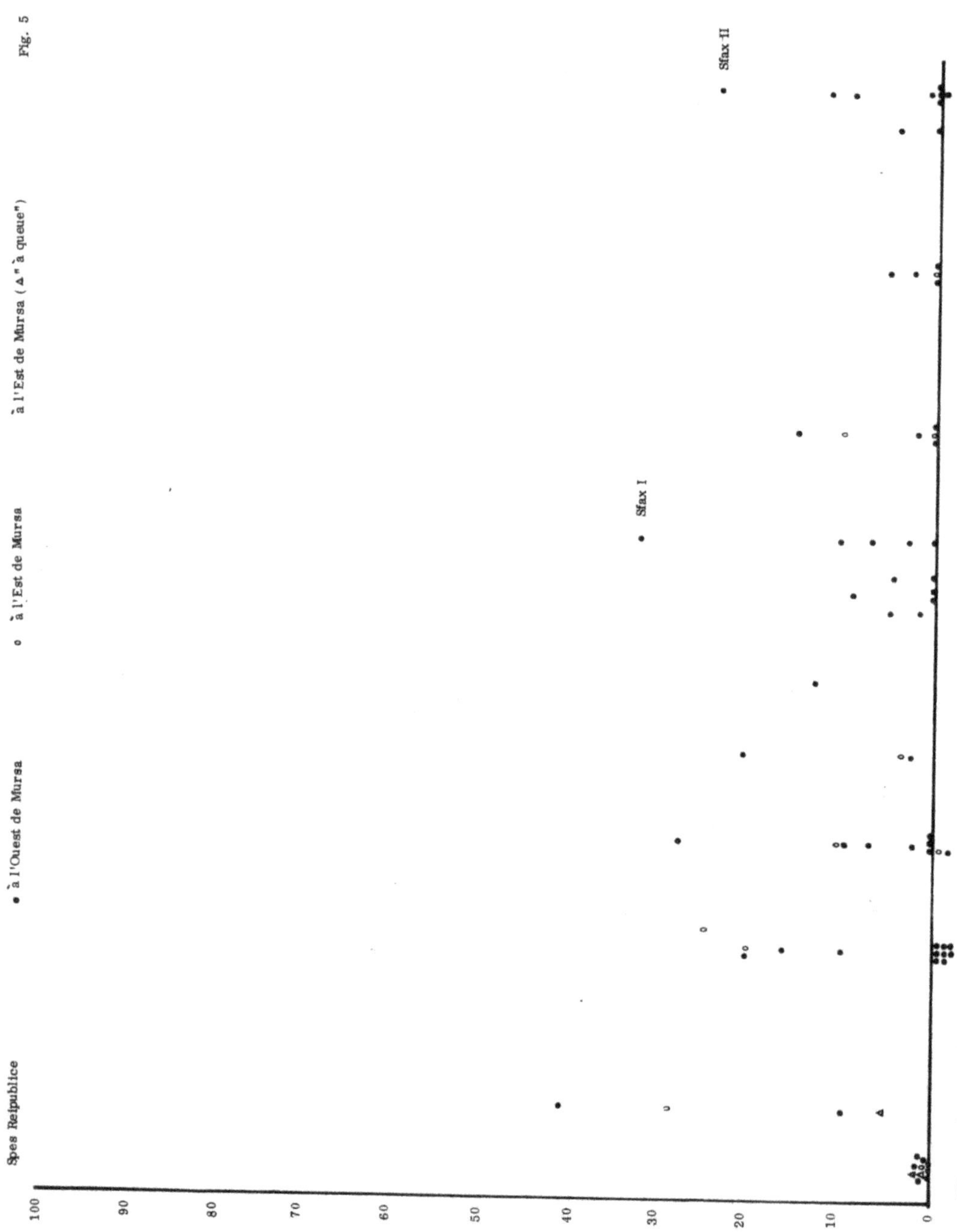
Spes Reipublice
• à l'Ouest de Mursa
○ à l'Est de Mursa
à l'Est de Mursa (Δ " à queue")
Sfax I
Sfax II
100
90
80
70
60
50
40
30
20
10
0
358
360
362
364
366
368
370
372
374
376
378
380
382
384
386
388
Fig. 5

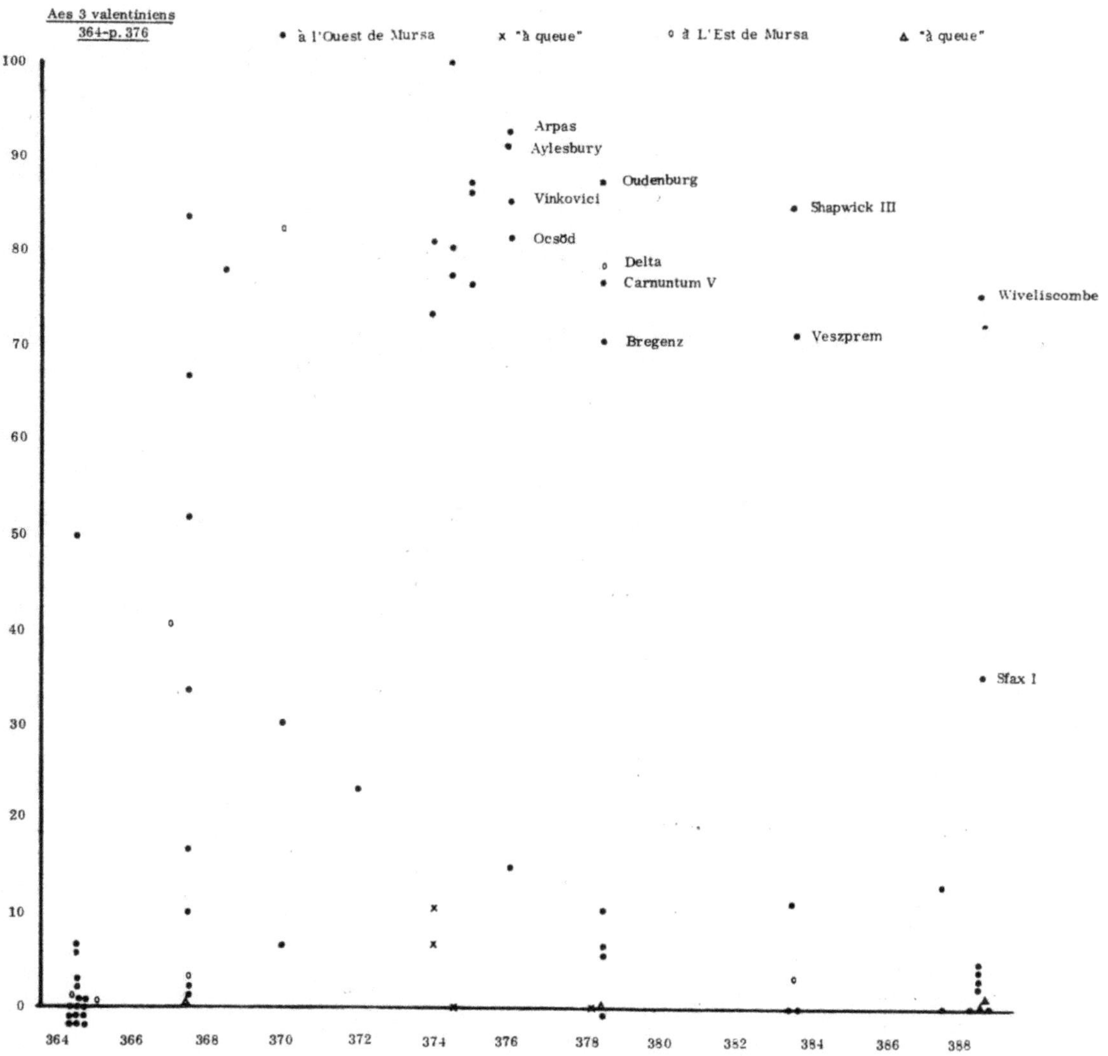
Aes 3 valentiniens
364-p. 376
• à l'Ouest de Mursa
x "à queue"
o à L'Est de Mursa
▲ "à queue"
Arpas
Aylesbury
Oudenburg
Vinkovici
Shapwick III
Ocsöd
Delta
Carnuntum V
Wiveliscombe
Bregenz
Veszprem
Sfax I
100
90
80
70
60
50
40
30
20
10
0
364
366
368
370
372
374
376
378
380
382
384
386
388

Fig. 6

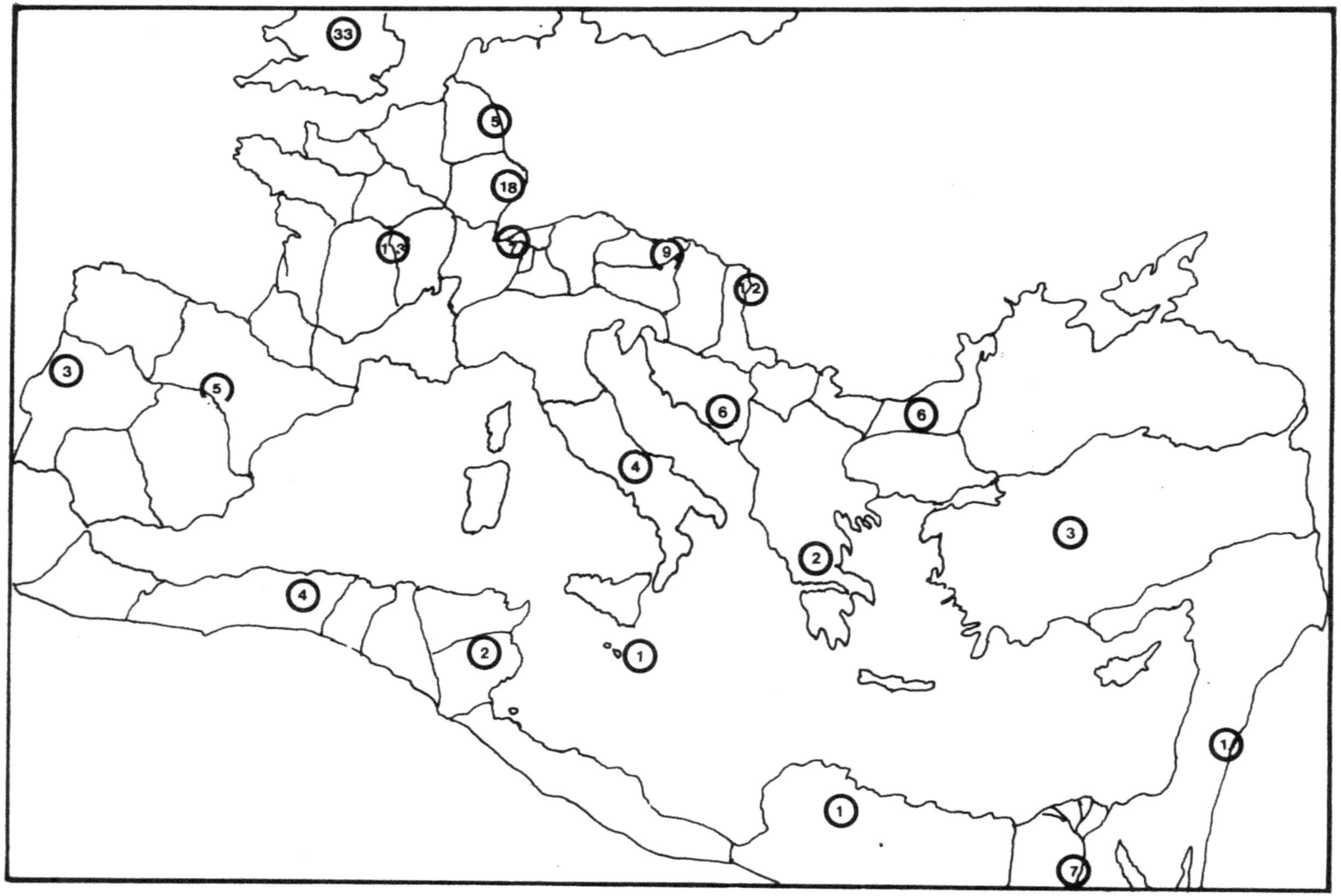

Carte 1 Répartition schématique des 142 trésors exploités 348–392

Map 1 Geographical Distribution by Region of the 142 Hoards Examined in this Study

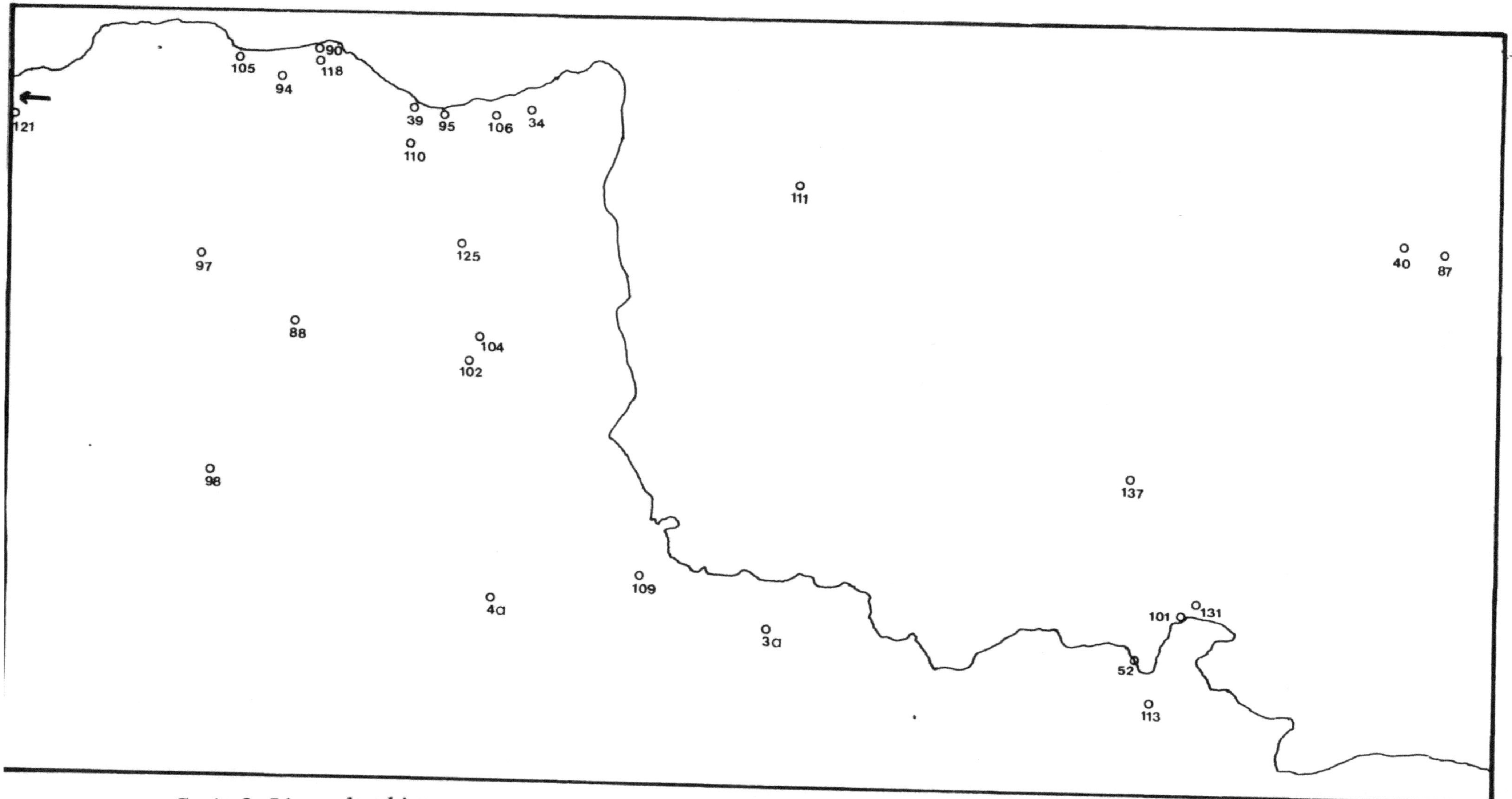

Carte 2 Limes danubien

Map 2 Hoard Distribution on the Danube Frontier

THE DISTRIBUTION AND THE ROLE OF
THE BRONZE COINAGE FROM A.D. 348 TO 392 *

J. P. Callu

INTRODUCTION

The bronze coinage of the years 313-348 was examined in 1973.[1] Now the bronze issued minted during the second half of the century will be investigated but only from 348 to the accession of Honorius in 392 when the pressure of events begins to obscure the monetary picture. Although the decade 392-402 has already been studied in some detail the preceding period has not.[2] Nonetheless it was during those years that the coinage was evolving in a manner which was to result after 402 in an almost complete break in the production of bronze coins in the West.[3]

There are two generations of bronze coinage to consider: 1) that of Constantius II and 2) that of the house of Valentinian and, although it may seem paradoxical, the discussion will begin with the latter. First, indeed, it is important to establish the precise terminal date of several hoards buried at a date significantly later than the period during which they were accumulated.

VALENTINIAN HOARDS (364-392)

I. For this period, as for the one which follows, certain difficulties resulting from the current state of research must be enumerated. For example, it has not been possible to include many of the Balkan hoards in the statistical analyses.[4] Equally, the predominance of Britain and Pannonia, although based on historical reality, has almost certainly been enhanced as a result of the systematic studies made by English and Hungarian numismatists.

Three areas of circulation can be isolated: 1) the British provinces; 2) the Rhine-Danube frontier and 3) the remainder of the empire which can be subdivided into a Western zone, an Italo-African zone, and an Eastern zone. In theory, seventy hoards have been recorded in sufficient detail to be utilized in statistical analyses, but before analysing their distribution in terms of their size and their provenance, it is necessary to examine the difficulty presented by those hoards which have a "tail". Indeed, it is not always easy to know whether one ought to rely on the date of the latest coin in a hoard in order to fix the date of a find, or not. A consistent position in regard to this problem is impossible by definition. Instead it is necessary to adopt two points of view, one after the other, which are 'a priori' contradictory. On the one hand, given the situation in Britain, Germany and Northern Gaul during the years 353-367, it must be agreed that an aes 3 coin of the house of Valentinian provides an accurate terminal date even if it was preceded by a period, sometimes of rather long duration, from which there are no coins.

* Tables 1-6, Appendices A and B, the hoard bibliography, figs. 1-6 and maps 1-2 are printed at the end of the French version of this paper, pp. 61ff.

This point will be discussed more fully below. On the other hand, once peace had returned to the interior of the empire the situation was somewhat different. Investigation of the contents of certain hoards suggests that the bulk of the hoard was accumulated in an earlier period, the end of which provides the hoard's terminal date and that the latest coins were obviously added after a break. The following hoards belong in this category:

1. Pre 378. Those hoards which meet two minimal conditions:-
   a) they contain a very small proportion of pieces datable to 364-378.
   b) they contain an extremely small number or no coins at all of 358-361.

2. Post 378. Hoards which have no coins datable to 364-378.

3. Post 388. Hoards in which scarcely 1% of the coins are datable to c. post 358-c. post 388 (the uncertainty arises in the case of small hoards).

By applying these criteria nine hoards can be eliminated from this period and redated to c. 351,[5] c. 352,[6] c. 353,[7] c. 358,[8] c. 360,[9] and c. 363.[10] These will be studied below in the section on Constantinian hoards. The remaining sixty-one finds will now be analysed in more detail.[11] (Table 1 and notes 12-21).

Sixty percent of the hoards contain more than one hundred coins and two-thirds of the finds in this sub-group were found in areas which had garrisons.

1. There is no need to linger over the first group of hoards which can be dated to the beginning of the Valentinianic period. Logic suggests that the issues immediately prior to 364 ought to be well represented. The facts, however, are less simple. Firstly, with the exception of a single Italian find (no. 87) aes 3 coins of the two Augusti, Julian and Jovian, are almost never found in hoards; their relatively heavy weight must have led to their rapid demonetization and recoinage.[22]

In any case, the official issues of the aes 3 'Fel Temp Reparatio' and aes 4 'Spes Reipublice' were not particularly dominant in all parts of the Empire. Although they seem to predominate in Africa and Asia,[23] the picture in Britain and on the German frontier is very different.[24] (Table 2)

In these provinces the post-Magnentian crisis, followed by the troubles after Julian's death, had significantly lowered the number of the falling horseman reverses entering these areas. The lack of new coin is evident from the prolonged circulation of these coins which continued until after 364 and which was made possible only the by widespread imitation of the aes 3 issues imported sporadically between 354 and 359 (as seen in the Heslington, Oldcroft, Bourton-on-the-Water, Poundbury, Duston, Covesea and Lydney II hoards). Alternatively, the situation can be seen as one in which Constantinian issues continued in circulation for a long time, although the period when they were imitated marked a regression (as, for example, in the Silchester VII and Wörschweiler hoards in the first instance and the Pevensey Castle hoard in the second). An even more dramatic instance of the shortage of new coinage can be seen in the fact that 3rd century radiates were again circulated contemporaneously with Fel Temp copies and genuine pieces, (they are found in the Icklingham IV, Duston, Colchester, Carrawburgh, Mablethorpe and Taviers hoards and, on a smaller scale, in the Laslea find). Certainly the complete lack of coins of the Valentinianic period in hoards, or their presence only in very small numbers must have the same significance and one can therefore add nine finds to the hoards examined in Table 2 which would otherwise have been grouped in the period before 358.[25]

II. Having dealt with the early finds it is now possible to discuss the middle years of the Valentinianic period whose limits roughly approximate to those of the years of Gratian's reign, i.e. 367-383. The areas in which the hoards are concentrated emerge very clearly. In this period the distribution of hoards by region can be summarized as follows: Britain 3, the Rhine-Danube frontier 19, Spain 2, Africa 3, Italy 4, Greece 1, Turkey 1, Egypt 2.

With rare exceptions,[26] and with varying intensity, the Rhine-Danube frontier, Britain, Egypt, and even Turkey and Italy had the same find pattern which thus was dominant everywhere. Bronze coins of the house of Valentinian predominate in almost every region and soon reached a high percentage level in hoards. This phenomenon was accompanied by a reduction of the number of aes 3 and 4 pieces from the preceding period to less than 20% on average.[27] (Table 3).

The studies by M. R. Alföldi, G. Sonnevend, V. Lányi and S. Soproni[28] have established an accurate chronology for the issues from Siscia, which is of great significance since this mint supplied the Pannonian frontier. It has been ascertained that production reached a peak in 367 and remained high until 370 in the frontier area, while the interior of the province demonstrated more continuity in output. If the differences between the Wilfleinsdorf and Brigetio hoards on the one hand, and the Jabling and Kazsok hoards on the other represent a valid distinction, then the contrast between the rate of production and the speed at which hoards were concealed suggests that c. 4-5 years were sufficient to resupply almost the entire monetary circuit, and that there was an acceleration of the process between 372 and 374.

The fresh supply of money which was so rapidly put into circulation is of great significance in the discussion of a problem which must now be resolved. Without attempting at this point to interpret the data, the argument will be limited to demonstrating the contrast between: 1) Africa and Spain on the whole and the military provinces of the Rhine and the Danube; 2) centres of strategic or economic importance which could include Italy, Turkey and Egypt.[29] The first two areas are characterized by what seems to be a much slower rate of circulation: the coinage of 354-361 and even that of 340-348 continued to predominate during the years 367-383. (See Table on next page).

Before proceeding to the third and final phase of the bronze coinage of the Valentinianic period the hoards of aes 2 coins which were issued after 378 should be briefly mentioned.[30] In general these coins tend to cluster in hoards with pieces of the same module struck after 392. There exist, however, some earlier hoards such as Laurion (no. 117) and Aguntum I (no. 122) which are homogeneous in composition or nearly so.

Chronological distribution of types in Spanish and African hoards c. 370-8.

Hoards	Date	pre 348	Fel Temp Reparatio	Spes Reipublice	Aes 3 Valent. 364-378
Africa?	c.370	81.49	8.67	2.89	6.93
Sfax I	376	6.17	38.80	33.20	17.03
Bimeda	p.378	32.8	57.29		6.77
Caldas II	p.378	52.62	15.78	15.78	10.52

III. After 378 and during the next fourteen years, the circulation pattern of the bronze coinage becomes less clear. Not only does the find evidence become sparse but increasing internal and external difficulties led to an inevitable alteration of the geographical distribution of hoard burial, which had been characteristic of the earlier part of the century. Given this fact, a view of the changed circulation pattern emerges by juxtaposing the picture which had prevailed earlier with the current one, by now very like that of the post-Theodosian period.

The prevailing trends in the earlier period are illustrated by four types of circulation: a) in the area behind the Rhine frontier the series of aes 2 finds continued without significant addition of other coins (Zweibrücken (no. 127) and Hemptinne (no. 130)); b) in Britain and Pannonia the largest concentration of coins were still composed of Valentinianic aes 3 coins, for example, post 383 there is the Shapwick hoard with 84.29% (no.123) and the Veszprem hoard with 71.67% (no.125); and post 388 there is the Wiveliscombe hoard with 75.76% (no.138); c) the circulation of new coins in Spain always lagged behind that of other provinces but in this period nearby areas such as Lusitania and, to a lesser extent, Gaul, also show a decline in the circulation of new coin which probably resulted from their finding themselves in much the same situation as that prevailing in Spain.[31]

Chronological distribution of types in French and Iberian hoards post 387/8.

Hoards	Date	pre 348	Fel Temp Reparatio	Spes Reipublice	Aes 3 Valent. 364-378
La Peneda	p.388	55.00	25.00	-	-
Monte Mozinho II	p.388	48.20	27.20	12.00	3.20
St.Martory	p.387	24.98	37.50	4.68	1.56
Paris	p.388	19.23	76.92	-	-

Finally, midway between Groups b and c, the Sfax II find contains a regular progression of the emissions produced from 364-378 and in a twelve year period the proportion doubled, from 17.03% to 35.66%.

At the same time there were changes of two different kinds: a) the supply of coin on the western frontier declined,[32] in the Pesche (no. 134), Carlsruhe (no.132) and Fürstenfeldbrück (no.126) finds Constantinian nummi predominate. In fact, it is difficult to establish a comparison with the preceding period with any certainty because there is only one hoard, Oudenburg (no.120) which contains 87.5% aes 3 coins datable to 364-378. Nonetheless, one has the impression that the majority of the coins in circulation consisted of either aes 2 pieces minted after 378 or Constantinian types produced before 348. b) the Bundle hoard (no. 140) which anticipates the pattern which was characteristic of fifth century hoards, is perhaps more Eastern than British in composition and is unique in its make-up; the new aes 4 pieces, minted from 388 onwards, appear in it in appreciable numbers for the first time. As is well known, these small pieces were destined to monopolise the money market very quickly.

By contrast, it is sufficient simply to look at the figures presented in Table 6 to assert that there is a large void which ought to be filled by aes 3 pieces struck between 378 and 383 to 387.[33] This fact, which is worth investigating more closely, leads inevitably to the question of what the role of the bronze coinage may have been. But before discussing this, it is necessary to deal with the earlier period, especially since nine hoards have been redated to the years 351-363.

HOARDS OF CONSTANTIUS A.D. 348-363

The end of the Constantinian period was very eventful in monetary terms. In 348 there was a joint reform of the coinage in both halves of the empire which consisted of the introduction of three denominations on different weight standards; two aes 2 denominations struck at 1/60th and 1/72nd of the Roman pound respectively, and a aes 3 piece at 1/120th. In the West the Magnentius episode destroyed the unity of the system by introducing a heavy piece which evolved in several stages from 1/60th to 1/36th of the Roman pound, but was rapidly outnumbered by an issue of fractional coins and large numbers of imitations.[34] In the Eastern and Central empire, no later than c. 352, the bronze denomination minted at 1/72nd of the pound became the only aes 2 coin while the aes 3 piece was again produced on a very large scale, this time with the falling horseman reverse.[35] Then, in the spring of 354, Constantius II came to terms with the lesson imposed by his monetary crisis; he had to restore the monetary system on a sound footing, and he therefore had to drive out the coin produced by the Western usurper. But he also had to deny a place in the system to his own aes 2 pieces which were undervalued and from that point onwards treated as merchandise and not coin. This explains the point of the statute in the Theodosian Code (IX, 23, 1).[36]

The aes 3 Felix Temporum Reparatio pieces with the falling horseman reverse were dominant from 354 until 358 although their diffusion in parts of the West was still impeded by the severe consequences of the Germanic invasions. Thereafter it is possible that the aes 4 Spes Reipublice type became the instrument of a new policy in regard to the bronze coinage at the same time as the introduction of the silver siliqua.

Finally, in the numismatic field as elsewhere, once Julian was in power, he had to react against the policy of his cousin. He therefore re-established in 362, both an aes 1 piece at 1/36th of the pound and an aes 3 denomination of heavier weight, with a vota reverse. These innovations were continued during the short reign of Jovian.

During these fifteen years the number of extant hoards, if the nine redated finds are included, is nearly equal to the number for the Valentinianic period.[37] (Table 4).

Basically, if one carries the comparison further there is no modification in the geographic distribution of hoards buried in this and the later period. However, the coin destined for the limes, which effectively meant the Rhine frontier, forms a larger proportion and there are more scattered small finds which reflect the disturbances of the times.[47]

I. The simplest sub-division of this period is marked by the nomination of Julian as Caesar in November 355 and it ended eighteen months later after the law on demonetisation had been issued. It is therefore useful to examine the behaviour of the bronze coins of Magnentius and that of the aes 2 pieces of the house of Constantine in order to establish the rate at which they disappeared.

Until 353 four major types of hoards can be distinguished (Table 5):

1. Those datable to the early years contain coins of the years 330-348 which often compose the bulk of the find, as one might expect (i.e. the Halifax, Appleford, Great Weldon, Mitrovic, Rouvroy-les-Merles, Lugenfeld, Metternich, Hanham and Mackviller finds).[48]

2. From the accession of Magnentius, or virtually so, a new category of hoards came into being with new specie,[49] and the coins of the usurper reached almost overwhelming percentages in the hoards from Bretigny, Kaiseraugst I, and Chamoson, the Lyons region find, Kopstukken, Skellow, Mainz I, the Palatinate, Herkenbosch, Tarragona and no doubt from the Theux hoard as well.

3. The East and, it would seem, the Central Empire show a similar tendency to homogeneity, but this time in favour of the aes 2 pieces produced after 348. Unfortunately the information on which these statements are based is limited to only five finds (3 from Egypt, 1 from Syria and 1 from Austria) but the picture each presents is identical.

4. The fourth category consists of discoveries made in Great Britain, Eastern France and in Switzerland. In the Berkshire, Byard's Leap, Villing, Pizokel and Bassecourt hoards as well as in the Cobham and even the Croydon finds their composition is marked by a relative balance between the aes 2 pieces of the house of Constantine and those of Magnentius.[50] Exchanges from one into the other were apparently effected without difficulty.

In sum, this situation, which had been in fact very regular, was distorted after 353 and the change certainly resulted from the demonetization of 354. Lying in the borderland between the two periods, the Fontaines Salées hoard is still the only one to contain a large number of Magnentian pieces. In the Perbal hoard, moreover, the heavy denominations are on the verge of disappearing altogether. The remaining hoards no longer have high percentages of aes 2 pieces. With the exception of the Acs hoard in the Danubian zone, where military operations made the direct supply of the aes 3 falling horseman type necessary, the mass of coins predated 348; the years 330-340 predominate in the Regensburg, Hemel and Michelfeld hoards, and less clearly in the Théodule Pass find.[51] Even earlier coins form the bulk of the Silchester V and Mainz II hoards.[52]

By the time of their permanent disappearance, the "middle bronzes" had thus furnished the bulk of bronze coinage in circulation for about four years.

II. The geographical distribution of the hoards requires comment. It is clear in fact that between 355 and 363 (Table 6) Britain, Northern Gaul and Germany suffered acutely from a lack of new specie. Great difficulty arises for the individual attempting to analyse the chronology of hoards from these years in fixing their 'terminus ante quem'. The most outstanding example in this context is provided by the Freckenham hoard: not only are there high percentages of aes 2 pieces of Magnentius and also of the house of Constantine but the total absence of any coins of Julian might suggest an early date, while the large number of aes 3 Fel Temp falling horseman coins of which nearly half are imitations must also be taken into consideration. Freckenham on this evidence is closely related to the Heslington hoard and both also contain some rare pieces of Carausius II.[53]

At this point certain choices must be made which may seem subjective. However, the dating of hoards composed largely of Constantinian imitations (Mainz V, Rheims, and certainly White Woman's Hole as well) to this period is justified by the similar picture on the Rhine where hoards clearly buried post 355 (i.e. Rheinzabern I and II, Niederingelheim) are largely composed of pieces minted c. 330-348 which were slightly supplemented by contemporary imitations.[54]

The evidence of the last three hoards in the Western zone does not contradict these conclusions; Mainz IV is based still further on past issues, Mainz III was fed by imports of coin from the East and Epiais Rhus betrays a political fidelity to Magnentius.[55a]

Difficulties in the supply of coin do not seem to have been experienced on the Danube frontier, there the Fel Temp Reparatio pieces with the falling horseman reverse are characteristically found in large numbers in the three Banat hoards published by E. Chirila and his colleagues.[55b] In each of them, however, aes 2 of 348-354 also exist in appreciable quantity. It is therefore not surprising that in Serbia, at Boljetin and at Kosmaj "middle bronzes" could be hoarded in significant quantities.[56] This somewhat anachronistic burial pattern definitely disappeared in the next period.[57]

The Southern parts of the Western part of the Empire, and its Central and Eastern areas, have yet to be discussed. At Conimbriga and at Caldas, the aes 3 Fel Temp pieces seem to speed up slightly the slow circulation of coin within the province which is even more apparent elsewhere (Monte Mozinho I, l'Estrade). In general however, new coin was well supplied around the circumference of the Mediterranean. This can be seen in the material from Africa (Malta, Affreville), Asia Minor (Smyrna, Chania), Egypt (Milne hoard, Minieh), where, there was the same saving processus as in the Serbian region. When the Spes Reipublice pieces replaced the Fel Temp Reparatio reverses, the circulation of coin suffered no disturbance.

This section will close with a brief discussion of the Vairano hoard which was as atypical as the Italian hoard (no. 87) previously mentioned. There is no doubt that in the market place everything possible was done to abolish Julian's reformed pieces.

THE FUNCTION OF THE BRONZE COINAGE (TABLE 7, APPENDIX B)

It is both convenient and legitimate to distinguish between the civil and military use of bronze coin, bearing in mind the difficulties posed by their intermixing, most notably on the frontiers.[58]

I. Contemporary imitations have always, in my view, played an important role in the circulating currency and they signify something quite different from simple fraud. Their existence in every era and in every part of the empire argues for a lack of coin; imitations which would not have deceived anyone were not produced solely for gain.[59] Thus from 352 to 367 copies proliferated in the West in Britain, Gaul and Germany, first of Constantinian prototypes[60] and later of Fel Temp Reparatio falling horseman reverses.[61] The area affected can be partly superimposed over that which experienced the same phenomenon in the third century. The same interests therefore must have been involved.

There is less information for the Valentinianic period. The admirable studies by G. Boon have demonstrated that in Britain the practice of counterfeiting had nearly ceased.[62] It is necessary next to examine the finds from Africa,[63] the Balkans,[64] and the East.[65] Since it is not yet possible to reach a valid conclusion on the basis of the existing evidence[66] the interprovincial movements of bronze coinage should also be investigated.

There is a law in the Theodosian Code which is significant to this discussion: C. Th. IX, 23, 1 of 8 March 354, to which reference was made above in the section on the Constantian period. It is now necessary to examine this law in more detail.

A systematic analysis of this text shows that the law was applicable to Arles (the port of Trier according to the Expositio totius mundi) and was concerned with the trading relations between Arles and Spain, Africa, and possibly the Eastern half of the empire. It can be summarized as follows:

1. As mentioned above, certain coins were banned.[67] These no doubt were the bronze coins of Magnentius which were ordered to be melted down immediately after his defeat. The public seem to have complied quickly even though they had to be informed twice. The data in Fig. 2 support this suggestion, since the only exceptions are British hoards of uncertain date.

2. The law describes speculation in the large coin equal to 100 denarii.[68] This multiple had some silver in its composition[69] and its intrinsic value

would have led to its initial acceptance and subsequent imitation.[70] It seems reasonable to assume that the crisis resulting from the reconquest of the West, by causing a rise in prices, would have led to the face value of the pieces being less than their intrinsic value because it had not been re-adjusted in order to restrain the inflation. The aes 2 denomination purchased less on the official market but it did sell at a higher rate than that imposed by the government. In brief, it had been transformed into "merchandise" and was exported by traders who pocketed the difference between the official and unofficial tariffs.[71]

3. The emperor's reaction was to demonetize the coins.[72] Fig. 1 demonstrates the effect of this measure on the hoarding pattern. The application of the law was not as successful as it had been in regard to Magnentius' coinage, In addition to the British hoards previously mentioned, other finds in the Balkans and around the circumference of the Mediterranean (Portugal, Greece, Turkey and Egypt) demonstrate that this heavy denomination was saved for approximately ten years, after which it was issued again by Gratian and later by Theodosius.[73]

4. Only one denomination was allowed to circulate freely: the aes 3 Fel Temp Reparatio falling horseman piece. However, a significant distinction was made between the trader who transported goods overland by road, i.e. a simple pedlar and the merchant who shipped goods by sea. The former was entitled to a travelling allowance only for animalibus propriis.[74] The sum was small since it amounts to only 1000 folles[75] and so we learn moreover the name given, perhaps for the first time, to the aes 3 piece. The ship owner, on the other hand, was subjected to no currency limits;[76] he was entitled to import the amount of money necessary to make his purchases.[77a]

It can now be demonstrated by a number of examples that there was a relative mixture of bronze coins in several areas of the empire which was not apparently linked to military expenditure[77b] but rather was related to commercial transactions. The coin evidence to support this assumption is based on Spanish, African and Egyptian hoards, i.e. finds from provinces which had had small numbers of troops and, in the case of two of them (Spain, Africa), no mint.

a) Egypt. It is perhaps best to begin with this area because the significant number of pieces found in Egypt which were minted in other parts of the empire has long been a subject of discussion. Despite the fact that Alexandria had a mint, more than 40% of the pieces in the seven hoards belonging to this period came from mints outside the province.[78]

Alexandria	58.2%
The Bosporus	24.1%
Antioch	11.4%
The Balkans	1.4%
Italy	4.3%
Gaul	0.45%

But is it necessary to assume on the basis of this fact as G. Mickwitz[79] has done that bronze coin was overvalued in Egypt? The theory seems unlikely since in an altogether different context it is possible to see similar distribution patterns in the monetary supply.

b) Africa. The find pattern has been established for Algeria and Tunisia.[80] It has not yet been possible, however, to study the two hoards from Cherchel in this context. At first glance, though, they support the mint distribution figures in the Affreville and Sfax I and Sfax II hoards.[81]

	Gaul %	Italy %	The East %
Affreville	17.50	32.50	50.00
Sfax I and II	6.46	41.38	52.10

Variations in the distribution pattern result from the differences in the geography of the find spots. Affreville for example had many more coins minted in Arles than Sfax but it is clear that coin travelled by three main routes and that the Eastern mints and those on the Bosporus played a significant role in supplying Africa with coin.

c) Spain. The pattern combines aes 3 and 4 pieces from three small hoards of Spanish provenance with aes 2 coins bearing the Reparatio Reipub reverse found in Spain and Portugal. [82]

	Gaul %	Italy %	Eastern mints %
Aes 3 and 4	44.70	26.30	28.90
Aes 2	51.19	28.57	20.23

The Reparatio Reipub type was struck less heavily in the East, which accounts for its lower percentage in the Spanish hoards. This pattern is reversed if one adds to the Reparatio Reipub type the Theodosian aes 2 pieces struck after 392. On the western edge of the Mediterranean, therefore, the Eastern mints from Siscia to Antioch sent their issues to supply the marked need for coin. Although the amount of coin involved is considerably less than that found in Africa, the percentages are too high for the importation of Eastern coins to have occurred accidentally. It can consequently no longer be considered strange that a 'merchant' coin which is known to have travelled by sea to these 2 areas was regularly supplied to Egypt which was also involved in the maritime trade.

The coin which did travel by sea, regardless of its hypothetical value, was used in commercial exchanges in the port cities. A final argument can be adduced in support of the obvious role this coinage played in its commercial aspects during the period under discussion. From the studies of Codrington of the Roman coins discovered in India and Ceylon the influx of gold into these countries was accompanied by a parallel influx of bronze in vast quantity up to the beginning of the fifth century.[83] Thus it can be seen that the function of the bronze coinage was not limited simply to daily transactions of the sort that normally took place in cities,[84] it also preserved enough of its value, surprisingly enough, to finance Roman purchases in the extreme orient.[85]

II. The maps and tables to which reference has already been made suggest another function of the bronze coinage; the defence of the empire. There is nothing new that this paper can contribute on this point, the theories of the Hungarian numismatists are clearly valid.[86] In fact, only a blind man could deny that the aes 3 coins minted by Valentinian I were not intended for military purposes. The following evidence supports this view:

1. The aes 3 issues financed the reconstruction of the limes. (However, the African campaigns[87] and those in Germany[88] did not affect the hoard pattern in those areas—or only very slightly). The restoration of central power in Britain[89] and, above all, the repair of the fortifications along the entire length of the Danube as far as the Olt, explains the large number of hoards found on the shores of the sea or in the vicinity of the Barbaricum. In Pannonia this extensive rebuilding programme, begun in 366, ceased with the death of the Western emperor and it is precisely in this decade that the majority of the hoards occur.[90]

2. The Eastern Empire, which had only a small frontier area to protect in Thrace, did not really figure in Valentinian's frontier policy.[91] This fact explains a monetary phenomenon which is worth noting briefly. Pearce noticed that after 367 all of the Eastern mints ceased production until 378.[92] Related to this development is the fact that in the West the aes 3 issues struck from 378 to 383/7[93] are almost entirely missing from hoards and site finds[94] while they are to be found in the East.[95] A simple law of balance will serve to explain these anomalies. The Western part of the empire had been well supplied with coin during the reign of Valentinian I but in the East, a ten year mint closure led to a need for new coin which was supplied by the introduction of the new reverse types which re-established the normal level of circulation.

3. Thanks to the published lists of site finds, a comparison can be made between the garrison cities on the frontier and those of the interior part of the empire. The variations between the Constantian period and that of the house of Valentinian have been analysed and certain conclusions emerge quite clearly as long as the following corrective is applied to the data: an area poorly supplied with coin during an earlier period attracts more coin later than an area which had been well supplied initially;

large increase:	Richborough, Vindonissa[96]
very slight increase:	Carnuntum, Brigetio[97]
slight decrease:	Antioch[98]
significant decrease:	Athens, Corinth[99]
very large decrease:	Conimbriga[100]

This evidence strongly supports the theory that the frontier areas were supplied with coin to the detriment of the more "civilian" areas. Thus, the hoard and find material demonstrate that in the Valentinianic period the follis, by this time deprived of any silver in its alloy, was minted in the first instance to pay the army.[101]

The state, therefore, continued to produce bronze coins during the last decades of the fourth century because they were useful administratively and commercially. However, it cannot be assumed that this situation lasted for long. In 392, which marks the terminus of this study, the Treatise on Weights and Measures (De mensuris et ponderibus) of Epiphanius appeared. In it the miliarensis, the silver coin which served as the standard in Eastern trade,[102] is described as the στρατιωτικὸν δόμα.[103] The emperor could pay for his fortifications with the Gloria Romanorum or Securitas Reipublicae pieces[104] but the troops increasingly preferred to be paid in silver,[105] if not by this time in the gold under which Rome was to buried alive.[106]

NOTES

1. J. P. Callu, "La circulation monetaire de 313 a 348," Proceedings of the 8th International Congress of Numismatics, N.Y., Washington, 1973 (Basle 1976), 227ff.

2. R. Reece, "Numerical Aspects of Roman Coin Hoards in Britiain", Coins and the Archaeologist, (Ed. J. Casey, R. Reece), BAR 1974, 78ff. In addition the works of J. Lallemand on Belgian sites should be noted, and in France, the studies of R. Delmaire which are now in progress.

3. With the exception of Rome. There was a brief reappearance of aes 3 pieces about 408/413 at Lyons, Arelate, Aquileia and Siscia. Thereafter aes 4 coins were no longer struck until the death of Honorius.

4. The lack of material is particularly severe in Bulgaria; see for example BIAB 12, 1938, 450; 17, 1950, 320; 20, 1955, 611; and B. Soc. Arch. Varna, 9, 1953, 114. (Add. K. Dimitrov, Zwei, Schaftzfunde des 4 Jahrhunderts u. Z. aus Bulgarien, Chiron, 9, 1979, 607ff). Obviously only hoards with sufficient information to allow statistical analyses have been cited which means that there are a number of regrettable but deliberate omissions.

5. Hoard no. 99 (Kaiseraugst II).

6. Hoard no.128 (Dames).

7. Hoard no.96 (Palatinate).

8. Hoards nos. 131 (Orşova II), 137 (Jupa); 101 (Orşova I), 103 (Kosmaj).

9. Hoard no. 89 (Smyrna).

10. Hoard no.114 (Vairano).

11. To these 61 hoards, 9 from Britain should be added that have no pieces of Valentinian or Valens but are undoubtedly post 364 in date.

12. Hoard no. 71 (Milan).

13. Hoards nos. 119 (Caldas II); 136 (La Peneda); 75 (Taviers), 127 (Zweibrücken); 117 (Laurion).

14. Hoards nos. 73 (Mablethorpe), 80 (Silchester VII), 83 (Pevensey Castle), 100 (Ickham), 107 (Aylesbury), 140 (Bundle); 82 (Laslea), 91 (Stielings), 112 (Bregenz-Lochau), 122 (Aguntum I), 124 (Medgidia); 135 (Paris).

15. Hoards nos. 72 (Carrawburgh), 103 (Kits Coty House); 90 (Carnuntum VI), 120 (Oudenburg), 132 (Carlsruhe); 129 (St. Martory).

16. Hoards nos. 74 (Wroxeter); 105 (Vienne Krottenbach), 134 (Pesche); 116 (Bimeda), 133 (Monte Mozinho II); 84 (Monte Guspini), 93 (Africa ?); 77 (Cherchel II); 78 (Priene).

17. Hoards nos. 81 (Wörschweiler), 58 (Gelse), 94 (Wilfleinsdorf), 98(Lupoglav), 104 (Gölle), 118 (Carnuntum V), 121 (Enns I), 126 (Fürstenfeldbrück); 76 (Cherchel I), 79 (El Beida), 87 (Italy); 115 (Delta).

18. Hoards nos. 95 (Brigetio), 102 (Kazsok); 85 (Grand Saint Bernard).

19. Hoards nos. 123 (Shapwick III), 138 (Wiveliscombe); 97 (Jabing), 106 (Oregcsem), 109 (Vinkovici), 130 (Hemptinne); 86 (Turkey).

20. Hoards nos. 110 (Arpas), 111 (Öcsöd), 108 (Sfax I), 139 Sfax II); 92 (El Kab).

21. Hoard no. 125 (Veszprem).

22. Hoards nos. 87 (Italy): 156 ex. 47.8%; no. 92 (El Kab): 192 ex. 6.8%; no. 97 (Jabing): 46 ex. 3.2%; no. 108 (Sfax I): 44 ex. 1%. See also no. 114 (Vairano): from which 14 aes 1 pieces of Julian (21.53%) were recovered as well. In addition, 66 examples of Julian Augustus (26 aes 1, 40 aes 3) and 30 of Jovian (aes 3) have been recorded in the site finds from Carnuntum.

23. Africa: hoard no. 76 (Cherchel I) 70, 1% Fel Temp reverses, 28% Spes; no. 77 (Cherchel II) 75.3% Fel Temp reverses, 9.87% Spes; no. 79 (El Beida) 47.8% Fel Temp reverses, 25.8% Spes; Asia: no. 78 (Priene) presents a less clear pattern owing to inaccuracies in the numbering of the coins but the Fel Temp and Spes types seem to be well represented.

24. Hoard no. 82 (Laslea), beyond the limes in Transylvania where the non-Roman environment explains the much slower circulation of coin and the continued use of bronze coins of the earlier empire. On the mid-4th century crisis see the article cited in note 60.

25. Five hoards fall below the level of 100 examples; four exceed it and two of them contain several thousand coins. See also the Ehl hoard, Bull. Soc. Conserv. Mon. d'Alsace 7, 1865, 87ff.

26. No. 85 (Grand Saint Bernard) can be placed at the beginning of the period since bronzes of the house of Valentinian (10.5%) had a long way to go before replacing the Fel Temp (38.7%) or Spes reverses (28.5%). At the other extreme the Enns I find (no. 121) could in fact represent the juxtaposition of two separate savings hoards amassed at different times. The almost complete lack of documentation on Gallic finds should be noted. However, R. Delmaire has recently informed me that in a tomb at Vron (Somme) a purse was found with 77 coins of which 72 are of the house of Valentinian with a terminal date of 374.

27. Hoard no. 71 (Milan) is inconclusive, because of its small size.

28. M. R. Alföldi, "Fragen des Münzumlaufs im 4 Jahrhundert n. Chr." JNG 13, 1963, 75 ff; G. Sonnevend, "Adatok az 1 Valentinianus Korbeli Sisciai Kisbronzak Kronnológiájahoz, " NK, 54-55, 1955-56, 7; V. Lanyi, "The Coinage of Valentinian I in Siscia," Acta Arch. Hung. 21, 1969, 33ff; S. Soproni, "Uber den Münzumlauf in Pannonien zu Ende des 4 Jahrhunderts," Fol. Arch., 20, 1969, 69 ff.discusses the organisation of *officinae* at Siscia after 371.

29. Caution is necessary in interpreting these data: for Italy, there is only one atypical hoard studied by M. Amandry, while the Turkish hoard was seen in Instanbul but is of unknown provenance. The Egyptian evidence on the other hand is very clear; from 370 onwards at El Kab in the Thebaid, i.e. an area in which the army was present, coins of the Valentinianic period number approximately 80%. However, a little later the same percentage is found in the Delta.

30. On these coins, which certainly had a generalized circulation, see J. P. Callu, "Reparatio Reipub: un problème de circulation monétaire", Nummus, 2, 1, 1978, 99ff. See also, for the Budapest hoard, NK 21-22, 1922-23, 30. There are also several isolated finds in the South of France.

31. In Spain coins of the house of Constantine are dominant, in Gaul the *Fel Temp Reparatio* pieces. It is impossible to exclude entirely the theory that the Paris and La Pineda finds may be hoards with a 'tail'. The Crozon, Finistère hoard (an unpublished study by G. Aubin) may also belong in this category.

32. Possibly on the lower Danube as well; the find from Medgidia in Dobroudja (no. 124) is an example of the survival of very old coins.

33. *Aes* 3 coins datable to post 378 are present in nine hoards ranging from 1 to 8 pieces.

34. The metrology of the coinage of 350-353 has been studied by P. Bastien *Le monnayage de Magnence*, Wetteren, 1964. On the fractions see G. Fabre and M. Mainjonet, "La trouvaille monétaire des Fontaines-Salées (Yonne)", Gallia, 23, 1965, 151 ff.

35. J. P. C. Kent, "Fel Temp Reparatio", NC, 7, 7, 1967, 83ff. Aquileia adopted the 1/72nd standard in 352. The Damas hoard (no. 128) seems to contain specimens struck at 1/60th of the pound with the exception of a single *aes* 3. There would have been, consequently, a certain synchronization between pieces minted at 1/72nd of the pound and those at 1/120th with the falling horseman reverse. There is in fact no doubt whatever that *aes* 3 *Fel Temp* pieces did not succeed the *aes* 2 *Fel Temp* coins. If certain hoards (Boljetin (no. 52) and Kosmaj (no. 113)) tend to give that impression, it is the result of their aberrant character. In fact the figures for the Perbal hoard (no. 34) demonstrate that by 354 the volume of *aes* 3 pieces had reached a level equal to nearly 60% of the *aes* 2 coins. It can therefore be tentatively suggested that *c.* 352 the falling horseman type of small module had replaced the phoenix and galley reverses and by 354 they could be labelled *minorina pecunia*, side by side with the *maiorina*.

36. J. P. Callu, "Denier et nummus (300–354)", Les Dévaluations à Rome époque républicaine et impériale, Rome, 1978, 107ff.

37. Constantian: 63+9; Valentinian: 61+9 from Britain.

38. Hoards nos. 24 (Skellow), 35 (Silchester V); 53 (Mainz V).

39. Hoards nos. 6 (Berkshire), 7 (Byard's leap); 5 (Lugenfeld), 15 (Pizokel); 20 (Kopstukken), 27 (Mainz I), 28 (Herkenbosch), 37 (Michelfeld), 40 (Nirès), 41 (Mainz III); 54 (Rheims). [See also no. 94 (Palatinate)]; no. 4 (Rouvroy-les-Merles); 29 (Tarragona), 32 (Collonge-en-Charolais), 43 (Conimbriga C), 44 (Monte Mozinho I), 61 (Chania).

40. Hoards nos. 11 (Brétigney), 13 (Theux), 14 (Villing), 23 (Fussach), 30 (Regensburg), 38 (Theodule Pass), 39 Acs). [See also no. 99 (Kaiseraugst II)]; 58 (Caldas I); 47 (Affreville), 57 (Malta); [See also no. 114 (Vairano)].

41. Hoards nos. 9 (Hanham), 31 (Hemel), 16 (Bassecourt), 17 (Chamoson), 18 (Strasbourg), 36 (Mainz II), 48 (Mainz IV), 59 (Kaiseraugst I); 21 (Fayoum). [See also no. 128 (Damas)].

42. Hoards nos. 3 (Great Weldon), 55 (White Woman's Hole); 10 (Mackviller); 33 (Fontaines Salées), 46 (L'Estrade); 22 (Egypt I).

43. Hoards nos. 25 (Cobham), 56 (Freckenham); 3a (Mitrovic), 34 (Perbal), 50 (Rheinzabern II), 51 (Niederingelheim). [See also nos. 101 (Orşova I) and 137 (Jupa)]; 60 (Egypte II).

44. Hoards nos. 1 (Halifax); 52 (Boljetin). [See also nos. 131 (Orşova II); 12 (Kom Denchal), 45 (Minieh).

45. Hoards nos. 26 (Croydon); 49 (Rheinzabern I); 19 (Région Lyonnaise); [see also no. 89 (Smyrna)].

46. Hoards nos. 2 (Appleford); 4a (Vranic), 8 (Metternich). [See also 113 (Kosmaj)].

47. Recorded Eastern hoards, most of which are Egyptian, are large, for the simple reason that small finds have not been published.

48. There is a fifth group of hoards which complements this picture in which the aes 3 pieces minted after the reform of 348 (with the phoenix or the galley reverse and the series issued by Vetranio) form a significant part of the total: Vranic: 91.68%, Lugenfeld: 31.8%, Mackviller: 15.8% Kaiseraugst II: 13.3%, Strasbourg: 49.5%. See also the enigmatic Damery hoard (cf. J. P. Callu, "Cachettes monétaires multiples," Studien zu Fundmünzen der Antike, 1, 1979, 5ff. no. 36) in which, according to a reckoning which is unfortunately only approximate, one of the hoarding vessels contained not only 1 denarius of Antoninus Pius, 5 Urbs Roma or Constantinoplis reverses, 100 Victoriae D D Augg Q N N and Fel Temp Reparatio (hut and galley types) but also the impressive figure of c. 3,900 aes 3 Fel Temp Reparatio pieces with the phoenix reverse. These pieces were recoined before 354 and are often overstruck with the

49. The delineation of the area beyond the frontier has been designated somewhat arbitrarily in this and the other tables.

50. In the Strasbourg find examples of Magnentius are somewhat fewer owing to the incidence of aes 3 pieces of 348 (cf. note 48). The Kaiseraugst II hoard contains a significant number of Constantinian pieces which diminishes the percentage of pieces of the usurper. Moreover, it is again a hoard with a 'tail'. The Gaboš and Ljubljana hoards published by A. Jeločnik in RN, 6, 9, 1967, 228 no. 8 and 229 no. 8 have not been used in this discussion.

51. The data are very uncertain. To judge only by the pieces which have been recovered, the Fel Temp Reparatio pieces predominate, added to which there is no factor which would have prevented their arrival in the Valais region.

52. The atypical circulation pattern of Nirès in Transylvania should also be mentioned.

53. See below Appendix B notes 69 and 76. In the Heslington, Oldcroft and even the Pevensey Castle finds, coins of Magnentius still exist in measurable quantities.

54. See below, Appendix B notes 49-65. The Constantinian coins minted between 330 and 348 had not been any more discriminated against in 354 than they had in 348. With regard to the earlier reform, the late empire had experienced two kinds of monetary manipulation. Either as in 301 (in the Aphrodisias Edict) and, later, 318 (demonetization) a new value was assigned to a coin of unchanged weight, or, as in 295 and 348 new heavy weight pieces were introduced without withdrawing from circulation the lightweight pieces which immediately preceded them, i.e. in 295 the 3rd century radiates and in 348 the aes 3 and 4 of the house of Constantine.

55a. See below, Appendix B notes 42 and 43.

55b. See also the Dalboşeţ hoard in Tibiscus, 1972, 53ff.

56. The aes 4 of 340-348 was not considered worthy of inclusion in the Boljetin and Kosmaj hoards.

57. 9.4% in the Smyrna hoard (c. 360); 7.1% in the Chaniâ find (363); 8.69% in the Heslington hoard (355-post 364); 7.5% in the Pevensey Castle find and 6.06% in the hoard from Turkey (post 367).

58. Including those found in full-scale garrisons, or in the area of the cabanae, i.e. in the vicinity of elite troops, or 'territorial' soldiers; of troops stationed in the interior and 'barbarians'. It is necessary to distinguish the expenditure made on personnel from that involving the materials required for the infrastructure.

59. J. P. Callu, "La fonction monétaire dans la société romaine sous l'Empire", 5th International Congress of Economic History, Leningrad, 1970 (Moscow 1977) V, 197ff.

60. J. P. Callu and J. P. Garnier, "Minimi constantiniens trouvés à Reims," Quaderni Ticinesi, 6, 1977, 281ff. For the survival rate of these series see Figure 3.

61. G. C. Boon, "Counterfeit Coins in Roman Britain", Coins and the Archaeologist, (ed. J. Casey, R. Reece) BAR 4, 1974, 95ff., and especially 130-135 for the chronology which has been followed in this study.

62. ibid. 135. According to Boon the reason for this was "the abandonment of the silver proportion in the small-change alloy." It is certainly necessary to take the silver fineness of the alloy into consideration. It is hoped that the absence of any silver content in the bronze coinage of the house of Valentinian will shortly be confirmed on a larger scale than that suggested by A. Ravetz, Archaeometry, 6, 1963, 45ff; and L. H. Cope and G. R. Gilmore "Gold, Antimony, Arsenic and Indium in the Copper Based Roman Imperial Coinage Alloys," Universities Research Reactor, 5, Risley, 1976. However, in my view the lack of imitations was probably the result of the resumption of normal supplies of coin. See below.

63. The material from Africa has only just begun to be examined. The possibility cannot yet be excluded, therefore, that imitations could have prolonged the circulation of the Fel Temp Reparatio pieces. See below note 87.

64. M. R. Vasić, "A IVth and Vth centuries hoard of Roman Coins and Imitations in the Collection of the National Museum in Belgrade," Sirmium VIII, 113ff. There are no contemporary imitations from the period between the aes 2 of Constans (c. 30 pieces in Belgrade) and the aes 4 at the beginning of the 5th century. A priori the lack of bronze coins datable to the intermediate period suggests this absence was not fortuitous.

65. In Egypt coins were clipped and imitated between 367 and 378. See below.

66. The single case of which one can be certain in the West is that of the aes 2 of 378-388. This coin had been imitated in the Northern part of Gaul and on sites which need not always be linked to military occupation. On this coin, which is found widely distributed and no doubt was used more by merchants than the army, see the article referred to in note 30 above, and below.

67. C. Th., IX, 23, 1: Pecunias vero nulli. . . fas erit. . . vetitas contrectare. . . praeter. . . ceteras quas vetitas esse cognoscunt. For the complete text of the law see Appendix A. [For the correct date see PLRE, 783 no. 25: the error can be explained by a confusion between the 7th consulate of Constantius II (354) and his eighth consulship (356) which involved the necessary substitution of the Caesars Julian and Gallus. In fact it is known (Amm. XIV, 10, 4) that Rufinus, to whom the law was addressed was Praetorian Prefect in Gaul in the spring of 354].

68. C. Th., IX, 23, 1: . . .pecunias ... ad diversa vendendi causa transferre ... pecunias vero nulli emere omnino fas erit ...

69. C. Th., IX, 21, 6 of 12 February 349: Comperimus nonnullos flatuarios maiorinam pecuniam non minus criminose quam crebre separato argento ab aere purgare. The problem of these 'flatuarii' is touched on in the beginning of the law of 354 (C. Th. IX, 23, 1): ... conflare pecunias. I hope to be able to undertake a study of the alloy content of the aes 2 pieces

from 348 to 354 in order to utilize this information in comparing it with aes 3 coinage minted between 348 and 358.

70. In my article which is cited above (note 36) I have referred to Themistios, Orat, XXXIII, 367 b-c. This states that coins did not always preserve their original purchasing power, ὥσπερ δὴ κἀκεῖνα τὰ πρώην, ἅ ἔναγχος ἐξελήλαται τῆς ἀγορᾶς. ἢ οὐ μέμνησθε ὡς αὐτίκα μὲν, ἡνίκα τὸ πρῶτον ἐξεφοίτησε τῶν χαλκοτύπων, σεμνόν τι χρῆμα καὶ μεγάλη ἡ δύναμις καὶ πολλὰ ἂν ὀλίγου ἐπρίω; προϊὸν δὲ καὶ ταῦτα ἐν οὐ πολλῷ χρόνῳ οὐδ' ἰσαρίθμως... οὕτως ἀχρείως εἰς τὰ πωλητήρια ἀφικνεῖται.
it can be readily seen that there is no contradiction between the analyses of Themistius and that of the legal codes. Even if there were a reduction in weight (c.352) and of the silver fineness (a theory which is in need of verification), the aes 2 coins did not intrinsically suffer a debasement. The fact that its dynamis was preserved, however, resulted in a diminution of the goods if could purchase. Several hoards (Kom Denchal, Egypt I, Fayoum, Damas) are characterized by a large proportion of the new coin. The imitations from the Balkans have already been discussed (see above, not 64); at Boljetin as at Kosmaj they represent the work of counterfeiters speculating on public demand. Their rather restricted issue demonstrates that there was no question of these imitations being produced to compensate for an insufficient quantity of official coin.

71. C. Th., IX, 23, 1: pecunias ... in usu publico constitutas pretium oportet esse, non mercem.

72. Ibid. : ... praeter pecunias quas more solito maiorinas vel centenionales communes appellant. In my view, the conjunction vel unites two names for a single coin.

73. In the Affreville find, buried in 358, the aes 2 pieces were so worn that the average weight of sixteen examples is only 3.52g.

74. C. Th., IX, 23, 1: et itineris tramites statuimus custodiri ... Nec vero aliquis negotiatorum plus mille follibus pecuniae in usu publico constitutae animalibus propriis sumptuum gratia portare debebit.

75. How is mille follibus to be understood? If one takes the term follibus to refer to a bag, then the customary 4th century use of the term entails the sum of 125 coins (see my study 'Une constante arithmétique dans la métrologie du Bas-Empire', to appear in Pact in 1980). Since the aes 3 pieces were struck at 1/120th lb. an enormous amount of coin would have been involved. It therefore seems more sensible to see the follis as the contents rather than the container, especially as the legal texts under Julian already use the term in this sense (C. Th., XIV, 4, 3; and CIL VIII, 24, 609). See also my forthcoming article "Pensa and follis in an African inscription", Antiquités Africaines, in which I have tried to establish the relationship between gold and copper coin in the context of the metrology of the 4th century, a fragile framework at the best of times.

76. C. Th., IX, 23, 1: Portus enim litoraque, quo facilior esse navibus consuevit accessus ... Nam pecunias navibus vectas non omnes iudicamus

mercatores debere promere, quippe in usu tantum publico pecunias constitutas permittimus convehi ... Et si forte cum mercebus as quascumque provincias venerint naves, cuncta solita licentia mercabunter.

77a. It is therefore useless to conclude as some have done that the law of 354 limited maritime commerce to barter. The Summary of this text in the Vatican Code belongs to a much later period when the transfer of funds overseas was authorized only for the supply of estates. Altero capite naves iubet pro commercio tantum entecae portare pecunias. cf. Dig., 33, 7, 2, 1: dotes praediorum quae Graeco vocabulo ἐνθῆκαι appellantur.

77b. For the difference between this practice and the despatch of coin minted in Siscia and sent to the region of Trier and Britain in 374 see V. Lányi, art. cit., 45 (cf. note 28).

78. The geographical distribution of coins from Kom Denchal (351), Fayoum and Egypt I (c.352), Minieh (post 355), Egypt II (361), El Kab (370) and Delta (post 378) has been discussed by J. Schwartz, "La circulation monétaire dans l'Egypt du IVe siecle", SMB 33, 1959, 11ff. The respective percentages of Alexandrian coins are: 55, 51.9, 55.6, 44.6, 80.2, and 48.3. The exception to this pattern, El Kab, is a site deep in the interior of the province.

79. G. Mickwitz, Geld und Wirtschaft im römischen Reich des vierten Jahrhunderts n. Ch., Helsingfors, 1932, 110ff.

80. This will be demonstrayed in greater detail in my study now in progress, on Constantinian hoards of North Africa (buried c. 340).

81. Affreville (358), Sfax I (376), Sfax II (post 388).

82. Aes 3 and 4: Caldas I (c. 360), Caldas II (post 378), La Peneda (post 388). Aes 2: Conimbriga A, Fiães I, Tarifa, for the site finds from Conimbriga, see the article referred to above, note 30.

83. H. W. Codrington, 'Ceylon Coins and Currency' Memoirs of the Colombo Museum, A, 3, Colombo, 1924, 31-2 and 252-3; for solidi of Constantius II, Valentinian and Valens. On the bronze coinage in India: "Quantities of copper coin at Madura", in Ceylon: "Imperial bronze in large quantities of most of the emperors from Constantine the Great to Marcian, the order of frequency being 1) Arcadius, 2) Theodosius I or II, 3) Honorius, 4) Constantius II, 5) Valentinian II and 6) Constans; the coins are, with few exceptions, "third brass"." [See also Coin Hoards III, RNS, London, 1977, no. 219] It should be mentioned in this context that aes 3 coins began to be struck again in the Eastern half of the empire in 393.

84. For prices of meat and wood in folles see above note 75; for wine prices and the nummus see Annales, 5, 1960, 166ff.; for charitable distributions in nummi see Ambrose, de off. min. I, 11, 38, c. 386.

85. The most recent contribution to this subject is that made by M. G. Raschke, 'New Studies in Commerce with the East,' ANRW, II, 9, 2, Berlin, 1978, 604ff.

86. See above note 28.

87. The exact moment when the rebellion of Firmus took place cannot be correlated with any hoard. Casual finds demonstrate the presence of Valentinianic bronzes but the date of their arrival has not been established. See above note 63.

88. The same disparity is dominant here as well. The high volume of the bronze issues of Valentinian I at Vindonissa will be discussed later (see note 96). However, in the area of the Rhine, even when its extent is most liberally interpreted, only two hoards have been discovered containing relatively small quantities of coin; Oudenburg in Western Flanders and Stielings in Swabia. The evidence from casual finds is therefore useful e.g. Bonn (a legionary camp), BJ, 151, 1951, 229; and Rolsdorf (a fountain) ibid, 159, 1959, 471.

89. There are five hoards datable to after 367; Ickham and Kits Coty House in Kent, Aylesbury in Buckinghamshire, Shapwick III and Wiveliscombe in Somerset. To these can be added the hoard which was probably found at Lydney (Glos.) NC 5, 1939, 139 (1296 pieces) and, most recently, the Holybourne (Hants) hoard, SCMB, 1976, 204 (117 pieces). R. Reece, in a study of Roman coins recovered from a number of Roman sites has noted that emissions of 364-376 are very common, 'Bronze Coinage in Britain and the Western Provinces, A.D. 330-402', Scripta Nummaria Romana: Essays Presented to Humphrey Sutherland, (ed. R. A. G. Carson, C. M. Kraay), Spink, 1978, 124ff. and especially 140, fig. 3.

90. From the studies of M. R. Alföldi (see above note 28) it is known that in the Danubian provinces the invasions by the Quadi and Sarmatae resulted in a wave of hoard burials c. 375. There are six hoards from Austria and with the exception of Bregenz they are concentrated in the East; Vienna-Krottenbach, Carnuntum V and VI, Wilfleinsdorf, and Jabing. From Hungary there are eight hoards: Gelse, Arpas, Brigetio, Oregcsem, Öcsöd, Veszprem, Gölle and Kazsok. From Yugoslavia there are two hoards: Lupoglav and Vinkovci.

91. There are two Egyptian finds of which one, El Kab from the Thebaid, may possibly belong in a military context. See, however, Themistius, Or. X, 136a.

92. RIC, IX, 189, 200-1, 237, 248-9, 264, 296. Pearce interpreted this phenomenon as "the revolt against the claim of the West to impose a uniform bronze coinage upon the whole empire."

93. At Trier, Lyons and Arles as well as in the six eastern mints the striking of aes 3 coins did not continue beyond 383. By contrast, Valentinian II maintained the minting of these pieces from 383 to 387 in Aquileia, Rome, Siscia and Thessalonica.

94. For the hoards see note 33 above; Site finds: Conimbriga (I. Pereira, J. P. Bost and J. Hiernard, Fouilles de Conimbriga III, Les Monnaies, Paris 1974); 3 aes 3; La Grande Baume (Acta Numismatica 6, 1976, 73ff); 4 pieces; Fontaines Salées (Gallia 23, 1965, 151ff); 1 example; Vindonissa (T. Pekary, Die Fundmünzen von Vindonissa, Brugg,1971);

4 examples; Carnuntum (FMRÖ, III, 1, 1976); 12 examples; Brigeto (K. Bíró-Sey, Coins from Identified Sites of Brigetio and the Question of Local Currency, Budapest, 1977); 4 examples; R. Reece informs me that only 12 aes 3 pieces were found at Richborough.

95. Athens: (M. Thompson, The Athenian Agora, II, Coins from the Roman through the Venetian Period, Princeton 1954); 365 pieces; Antioch: (D. B Waage, Antioch on the Orontes: Greek, Roman, Byzantine, and Crusader Coins, Princeton, 1952); 98 pieces. There are also several examples from Curium and Apamea. These cities, it should be noted, functioned in a civil context.

96. Richborough: cf. the article cited above in note 89, 134 and 142, fig. 5, 348-364: 333 pieces; 364-375: 1221 pieces. Vindonissa: 348-364: 167 pieces: 364-375: 628 pieces. In both instances the post-Magnentian crisis had created a void which had to be filled.

97. Carnuntum: 348-364: 791 pieces; 364-378: 844 pieces. Brigetio: 348-364: 258 pieces; 364-378: 279 pieces. The monetary flow was therefore maintained on the Danubian frontier, which was already well supplied.

98. Antioch: 348-361: 1177 pieces; 364-375: 1080 pieces.

99. Athens: 348-363: 2807 pieces; 364-375: 801 pieces. Corinth: (K. M. Edwards, Corinth, the Coins 1896-1929, Cambridge 1933) 348-360: 696 pieces; 364-378; 273 pieces.

100. Conimbriga: 348-363: 1724 pieces; 364-378: 228 pieces. On this occasion the movement operated in an inverse sense. The mechanism which I have described does not provide a complete explanation however. Earlier, between 330 and 348 Conimbriga had received 2099 coins. The reduction in the Valentinianic period was not therefore fatal and is comprehensible since the coinage was directed elsewhere.

101. On present French territory coins of the house of Valentinian, without being rare (e.g. La Grande Baume, note 94 above; the Vienna hoard, R. A. Est, 24, 1973, 375ff; unedited finds from the Bolards etc.) never achieved dominance because the area was not important strategically.

102. The Sassanian drachma was equal to the miliarensis, cf. Cosmas Indicopleustes, XI, 14-15.

103. The text is certain in the Syriac version (lines 25-29, col.69a) on p.109 of the edition by J. E. Dean, Chicago, 1935 (confirmed by R. P. P. Devos).

104. The legend Securitas Reipublicae is enlightening in this respect.

105. The silver hoards from Britain and Romania prove it. It is therefore probable as the hoards from the camps in these regions demonstrate (e.g. Wiveliscombe, Sucidava), that bronze coinage continued to circulate in the area surrounding military garrisons, either to complement military pay, or because of the soldiers' relationships with the civil population. The latter would, moreover, have been associated indirectly with the task of strengthening the fortifications and thus would have had to be remunerated.

106. In the case of gold, the turning point occurred about 384. See my study in Ktema, 3, 1978, 301ff. I should like to thank all those who obtained unpublished documents for me or published studies which are difficult of access: Mme. K. Bíró-Sey, Mlles. C. King, C. Metzger, C. Brenot, MM H. Cahn, A. Jeločnik, P. Salama, F. Dolbeau, M. Amandry, J. P. Garnier; as well as the ANS in New York, E. Demougeot, G. Dembski, G. Aubin, E. Chirila, R. Reece and R. Delmaire.

NOTES ON TABLE 7

1. Of which 13 are imitations from 330-335 and 74 from 337-340 = 87 (1.5%).
2. Of which 31 are imitations (0.53%).
3. Galley with phoenix imitation (0.01%).
4. Of which 4 are imitations from 335-340 (1.7%).

4a. Of which one is an imitation (0.11%).

5. Of which one is an imitation (3.03%).
6. Of which one is an imitation (3.03%).
7. Of which one is an imitation (galley) (4.1%).
8. Of which one is an imitation (4.1%).
9. Imitation of Tetricus (0.01%).
10. Of which 601 are imitations (11.8%).
11. Of which 196 are imitations (3.8%).
12. Also one argenteus.
13. Galley, imitation (0.5%).
14. Of which six are imitations (1.4%).
15. 317-340.
16. Also one aureus.
17. Aes 2.
18. Of which 12 are imitations (11.7%).
19. Of which 5 are imitations (4.9%); in the portion of 473 examples from Mt. Terrible there are 103 pieces from the period Magnentius - Decentius (21.7%).
20. Of which two are imitations (1.3%).
21. 330-348.
22. More than half of the aes 2 and 3 pieces are imitations.
23. Two aes 2 of which is of Constans, one aes 3.
24. Of which 237 are imitations (10.05%); the entire hoard consisted of about 10,000 aes 2 coins.
25. 74 from a total of 130 pieces, in a purse.

26. Some pieces have the form of _aes_ 1.

27. 2796 coins have been examined from a total of 3600.

28. The rebellion at Trier in 353.

29. 12 _aes_ 1 and 9 _aes_ 2.

30. 98 coins from an initial 140.

31. Of which seven are imitations (4.04%).

32. Of which 30 are imitations (17.3%).

33. Of which one is an imitation (0.5%).

34. Of which one is an imitation (2.04%); there is also a copy of an _Urbs Roma_ coin.

35. Of which 4 are post-Magnentius imitations.

36. Of which 11 are imitations (4.4%) and 54 are of reduced module.

37. Of which one is an imitation (0.19%).

38. Of which one is an imitation (0.19%) and one coin is of reduced module.

39. Imitations with the name of Constans (5.5%).

40. _Cf_. above note 51 of the text.

41. 30 coins from a total of 150; there are 29 _denarii_ dating from the period Nero - Severus Alexander.

42. Of which one is from Antioch, 7 from Alexandria and one from Nicomedia.

43. J. P. Garnier has studied this important find which consisted of the following: a) Two _aes_ 1 with the chi-rho reverse in the eye sockets of the skeleton, b) one _aes_ 2 of Magnentius under the left wrist, c) a purse containing 26 coins and 22 rings, the majority of pewter; 3 of the _Fel Temp_ coins were imitations (10.34%), and 2 of these were of reduced module.

44. Of which one is an imitation (galley) (3.8%).

45. Of which 7 are imitations (1.6%).

46. Of which two are imitations (0.45%).

47. Imitations (0.22%).

48. Galley, perhaps _aes_ 2.

49. Of which 121 are imitations (3.42%).

50. Of which 26 are imitations (0.7%).

51. Of which 28 are imitations (4.3%).

52. Of which 3 are imitations (0.46%).

53. Of which two are from the period 337-348.

54. Of which 6 are imitations (1.1%).

55. Of which one is an imitation (0.18%).

56. Of which 13 are imitations (0.7%).

57. There were at least four third century radiates, one Illyrian coin, and a maximum number of 366 unidentified coins which seem to have had Fel Temp Reparatio reverses.

58. Minimi.

59. Imitation of Tetricus.

60. Imitations.

61. Or 392/395 if the coin of Arcadius is not included.

62. Imitation.

63. Of which 80 are imitations of Tetricus (17.9%). 85 coins have been officially clipped into 1/2s, 1/4s etc.

64. Imitations (10.08%).

65. Flans, cast blanks, residue.

66. Of which one is an imitation (galley) (0.18%).

67. Of which 38 are imitations (7.03%). There are 13 Constans II coins from the rebellion at Trier in 353.

68. Of which 25 are imitations (4.6%, 11 of reduced module); there are 10 pieces of 7.53 g.

69. Of which 100 are imitations (18.5%); there are 3 of Gallus and 3 of Carausius II.

70. Siliqua of Julian, but it is not clear whether this coin formed part of the hoard. Another find, the third, was a bronze hoard discovered at Kaiseraugst, Westd- Zeits. 25, 1906, 175ff. Out of a total of 454 pieces, there was a group of 157 coins which were listed: A.D. 330-40, 26; A.D. 340-348, 78. There were 52 illegible Constantinian pieces, and one of Magnentius.

71. Of which one is an imitation (0.03%).

72. Of which 22 are imitations (0.79%).

73. Of which three are imitations (0.1%).

74. Of which 46 (?) are imitations, (galley, 1.6%, one coin is overstruck).

75. Of which 284 are imitations (10.2%, two coins overstruck).

76. Of which 834 are imitations (30.2%, 294 overstruck of which 1 is of Tetricus, 1 Requies Opt. Merit; 135 are from 330-340, 69 from 340-348, 22 are Fel Temp Reparatio (10.6%)), there is one coin of Censeris and two of Carausius II.

77. FRT, aes 2 or 3.

78. Of which one is an imitation (0.03%).

79. Of which six are imitations (0.18%).

80. Of which 2 are argentei, Pax Augustorum, TR and Victoria Augustorum, SISU.

81. Of which 43 are imitations (1.3%); one FTR horseman is overstruck on an aes 2 coin of Magnentius.

82. Of which 255 are imitations (7.8%); there are 30 reduced module pieces.

83. Of which 1217 are imitations (37.3); there are 95 overstrikes, one radiate, 78 from the period 330-340, 14 from 340-348, one aes 3 of 348-350 and one coin of Magnentius.

84. Of which 11 are overstruck on Gloria Exercitus with two standards.

85. Also, four silver ingots: 9.68, 7.86, 3.04 and 2.25 g.

86. The 21 examples are imitations.

87. The 12 examples are imitations; 3 are FTR overstruck pieces.

88. The 40 examples are imitations; one is an FTR overstruck piece.

89. Of which 5 are imitations (1.3%).

90. Of which three are imitations (1.3%).

91. Of which 54 are imitations (23.5%).

92. Imitations (68.9%).

93. All the identified coins are imitations.

94. The 23 examples are imitations.

95. Of which 24 are imitations (26.6%).

96. Of which 78 are imitations (89.6%).

97. Flan.

98. 4 aes ranging in date from Augustus to Commodus, 20 radiates.

99. Four are imitations (FTR, 12.1%) and one is a small bronze coins of Julian.

100. Small bronze of Constantius II.

101. Of which 6 are imitations (4.5%).

102. Plated siliqua of Julian.

103. Of which ten are imitations of Tetricus (66.6%).

104. Several FTR imitations of reduced module.

105. Three Greek examples, 2 of Priene, 1 of Antiochus IV.

106. With FTR, Spes and Securitas Reipublicae types.

107. Of which one is an imitation (2.77%).

108. 281 coins are preserved from a total of 600.

109. 13 aes from the period Tiberius-Marcus Aurelius, 4 denarii from Antoninus-Septimus Severus, 6 radiates.

110. 3 reduced module pieces.

111. Minimi.

112. One of the pieces of Valentinian I was given a Cohen reference (42) VICTORIA AVGGG, AR ? This type in fact belongs to Valentinian II and was minted after 378 (RIC IX, 36b). As a result the date of the hoard is uncertain.

113. Of which there is one aes 1.

114. Two aes 1, two aes 3 of Julian.

115. The aes 3 pieces are from Italian and Eastern provenance.

116. Of which one is an imitation (0.06%).

117. Of which 3 are of Procopius.

118. 118 aes 3 of Julian (36.1%), 38 Vota of Jovian (11.6%).

119. Of which one is of Procopius.

120. According to R. A. G. Carson, JbNum, 21, 1971 137 ff. The hoard stops with Spes and later Gloria Romanorum of 367-375 and two Virtus Exerciti of 395-402 were added. Its possible that this theory applies only to the last two pieces.

121. Of which 13 are imitations (0.57%).

122. Julian: 49 aes 3, Vota; three aes 4 Virt. Exerc. Romanor; Jovian: 140 aes 3, Vota.

123. Restitutor Reip: 34 pieces, 5 weigh 1.9 g, 29 weigh 2.79 g; 169 Gloria Romanorum 1976 Securitas Reipublicae, 143 imitations (5.06%), of which five are overstrikes (2 on FTR, 1 on Spes, 2 on Vot V of Jovian); there are two coins of Procopius.

124. These coins come from Arles, Rome, the Bosporus, and the East; this distribution of mints could suggest an African origin.

125. Julian: seven aes 1, three aes 3; Jovian: one aes 1, four aes 3.

126. One Greek coins, three dupondii of Trajan, Commodus and Gallus, 15 radiates.

127. Also one Byzantine coin.

128. It is not certain that all the 4 aes 3 coins of Valentinian belong to the hoard.

129. Aes 2.

130. Julian: One aes 2 (cast), 34 aes 3; Jovian: 11 aes 3.

131. Vota 3, Restitutor Reip. 7, Gloria Romanorum 543, Securitas Reipublicae 603; there are two overstrikes on FTR.

132. Vota 1 Julian, 1 Jovian.

133. Of which one is an imitation (1.35%).

134. Of which one is an imitation (1.35%).

135. Of which one is an imitation (3.44%).

136. One quadrans of Trajan, one plated denarius, one aes of Nicea for Severus Alexander, three radiates of which two are plated.

137. Julian: two aes 3, Jovian: one aes 3.

138. Three sestertii (Domitian, Nerva, Faustina) two colonial bronzes (Trajan, Antoninus), seven radiates.

139. Of which three are Gloria Exercitus with one standard.

140. One of Procopius.

141. Of which one is from the first half of fourth century, 17 from the second half of the fourth century.

142. The 80 coins of Constantius II may possibly not all belong to this period.

143. Aes 3 of Jovian.

144. 'A handful' taken in a container.

145. Of which seven are imitations (0.16%); besides the radiates there is one piece of Judas Maccabeus.

146. Of which, it seems, two are imitations (0.04%).

147. Julian: three aes 3, Vota, 37 aes 4 Virt. Exerc. Romanor; Jovian: four aes 3 Vota.

148. Of which twelve are imitations (0.27%) and two forgeries.

149. Julian, 4 Virt. Exerc. Romanor, Jovian, two Vota.

150. Julian, 4 Vota, Jovian, 5 Vota.

151. One of which is of Procopius.

152. Julian, 8 Vota, Jovian, 1 Vota.

153. Of which 23 are Greek imperial and colonial.

154. Of which four are imitations (0.04%).

155. Of which 37 are imitations (0.45%) and 44 trefoils.

156. Of which two are imitations (0.02%).

157. Aes 3; 3 Vota of Julian, 1 of Jovian.

158. First reckoning.

159. 34 Constantius II, 4 of Gallus, 3 of Julian as Caesar, this hoard will be studied by J. P. C. Kent.

160. 14 maiorinae of which one is an imitation (1.53%).

161. Of which one is an imitation (1.53%).

162. Of which 21 are aes 4 pieces which may be dated to 330-348, 358-361 or 378-383.

163. There is one incuse of Constantine I.

164. From Valerian to Diocletian. 45 pieces are after the reform of Aurelian.

165. Aes 3 Vota, one of Julian, one of Jovian.

166. Of which two are imitations (0.17%).

167. Of which ten are imitations (0.89%); there are six reduced module coins and four overstrikes.

168. Of Constantius II.

169. From Vespasian to Philip, plus seven third century Greek imperials.

170. Vota, 12 of Julian, 11 of Jovian; one Isis piece.

171. Of which 20 are uncertain pieces dating from Constantius II to Julian and two are imitations (0.002%).

172. Constantius II, Gloria Romanorum Coh. 138-39.

173. A group of 220 from a total of 800/1200.

174. Of which four are imitations (6.25%).

175. Also one siliqua of Maximus.

176. A group of 64 from a total of 77.

177. Of which 164 are imitations (15.7%).

178. Second century pieces: 1 as, 1 quadrans, 2 denarii of which one is plated. Third century pieces: 3 colonial coins from Bithynia, 1 plated denarius, 11 antoniniani of which one is plated.

179. Of which one is an imitation (0.08%).

180. Of which 10 are imitations (11.76%).

181. Of which 10 are imitations (11.76%).

182. Of which two are imitations (2.35%).

183. Of which one is an imitation (0.8%).

184. Of which three are imitations (2.4%).

185. One piece, perhaps FTR type.

186. Of which 13 are imitations (10.3%).

187. Of which four are imitations (3.17%).

188. Of which six are imitations (4.76%).

189. A group of 126 from a total of 350.

190. Imitations (19.23%).

191. Imitations (76.92%).

192. From Trajan to Claudius II; There is one colonial coin from Viminacium and one plated antoninianus.

193. Of which two are imitations (0.17%).

194. Of which one is an imitation (0.08%).

195. Of which three are imitations (0.26%).

196. Imitations (0.52%).

197. Of which 17 are imitations (1.49%); there are also five overstrikes.

198. Of which one is an imitation (0.08%).

199. Vota, one of Julian, one of Jovian; also one siliqua of Julian.

200. Of which two (?) are imitations (0.17%).

201. to 13 Vota coins we can add 7 Spes of Maximus c. 387.

202. 18 Salus, 53 Victoria; there are 7 imitations (0.61%).

203. Of which five are Constantinian coins, one is of Gratian and there are two imitations (0.17%).

204. One Judaea, 13 antonininai of which 11 are imitations (0.45%).

205. Of which 48 are Victoriae coins and 46 are Vota.

206. Julian; 13 Virt. Exerc. Romanor; Jovian: 8 Vota.

207. 226 Gloria, 645 Securitas.

208. Of which 163 are Vota coins 2 Gloria Reipublice (camp), 2 Victoria Aug (2 victories), and 9 Spes.

209. 13 Salus, 48 Victoria.

210. Of which two are imitations (9.52%).

211. Of which two are imitations (9.52%); there are also two coins from Cyzicus and one from Thessalonica. The 3 Vota coins of 383 comprise 2 from Antioch and 1 from Alexandria; one of the three FTR types comes from Nicomedia. These show the eastern bias of this hoard.

THE *PRIVATA* FROM DIOCLETIAN TO THEODOSIUS: DOCUMENTARY EVIDENCE

Fergus Millar

Few areas of the history of the empire present more complex problems of definition than do the finances and properties of the emperors. Indeed even that sentence has its obscurities: at what point should we think of 'imperial' properties as ceasing to be in any private-law sense the 'property' of the emperor and as becoming 'state' or 'crown' property? Alternatively, should we—at any rate from the late second century onwards—see some 'imperial' properties as 'crown property' (*Krongut*) and others as in some sense still 'private'. If so, which is which? How are the uses and meanings of words like *fiscus*, *fiscalis*, *ratio privata*, *res privata* *patrimonium*, *patrimonialis* and the Greek terms 'tam(i)eion', 'tamiakos', 'idios logos', 'despotikai ktēseis' related?

Some aspects of these problems of definition cannot be avoided, since they affect the origins and meaning of the term *privata*. They will be discussed briefly later. Some wider questions, not attempted here, equally affect the evolution and nature of the Late Roman state. What will be discussed here is one of the frameworks within which the state, in the person of the emperor and his agents, acquired landed or movable property, disposed of it by way of *beneficia*, administered what it kept, and exploited it for revenues in cash or kind. One non-economic function of this process will be clear throughout, that is the important role of confiscation in the apparatus of punishment at the disposal of the state. This is parallelled, though less prominently in our sources for the fourth century, by the process of the acquisition of vacant property (*bona vacantia* or *caduca*). We can also see clearly the opposed process—again of an only partially economic character—whereby these properties functioned as a store of value for the emperor, from which he could make *ad hoc* grants of cash, recurring grants of revenues or outright gifts of property. Valentinian I began the intermediate process of granting imperial land as private property, but subject to a perpetual rent. His successors used this land as a source of capital in cash, by selling it subject to such a rent.[2]

What remains much less clear is whether there was any overall purpose or policy in the exploitation of these estates. The revised and supplemented list of the documentary evidence for the *privata*, which is given in the Appendix and is the main contribution of this paper, shows very clearly the piecemeal and haphazard process by which the *privata* acquired wealth, and also the complexity of the administrative procedures involved. It also gives some indication of the cash revenues (and their acute liability to peculation) and of the rather obscure functions of the privata in collecting goods in kind. It is far less clear whether either the cash revenues or the goods were designed for specific uses either by the privata itself, by other branches of the civil administration or (perhaps) by the army.

Before these questions are approached in more detail a few essential definitions need to be attempted. Firstly, therefore, in the period concerned fiscus and its cognates, once (in the author's view) associated with the financial claims and the properties of the emperor as such, as opposed to the Roman res publica, had become general terms which could be applied to any aspect of the finances, revenues, or possessions of the state.[3] 'Fiscus' did not denote (and never had) any branch of the administration. It was thus, like what appears to be its Greek equivalent 'tam(i)eion', an abstract general term with no specific reference.

By contrast patrimonium was used in the early empire for the wealth which was in some (now undefinable) sense private to the emperor, and also came to refer to specific properties in particular parts of the empire. Up to the early third century, but not after that, we also find officials of the patrimonium, sometimes for specific areas. By the fourth century some 'imperial' properties were still designated as 'patrimonial', but there is no trace of any organisation or administrative hierarchy devoted to them. It is impossible to define 'patrimonial' properties in terms of the means by which they passed into imperial possession (or in any other way). All that can be said is that this label came into existence for some imperial properties in the earlier empire and continued to be used in the fourth century.[4]

As regards the privata the essential background can be summarised as follows. The term used in documents of the later second and the earlier third century is invariably ratio privata. A central procurator rationis privatae is attested under Marcus Aurelius, and local officials of it from Severus to towards the middle of the third century. By the middle of the third century we also find a central magister summae privatae.[5]

There are only two clues to the nature of this development. Firstly the Historia Augusta (Sept.Sev. 12) gives an account of confiscations by Severus, and then continues by saying that the privatarum rerum procuratio was first established then. The terminology is that of the second half of the fourth century. But the dating is at least partially justified by the appearance under Severus of local officials of the ratio privata, and there is a clear implication that the properties concerned derived from confiscation.

The second clue is that the meaning of ratio privata is identical with that of 'idios logos', the 'private account' inherited by the Roman emperors from the Ptolemies, headed in Egypt by the Idiologos, operative only in Egypt, and concerned above all with the reception of confiscated or vacant property. On present evidence it is not attested after A.D. 239.[6] The identity of meaning of 'idios logos' and ratio privata cannot be accidental, and is extremely relevant to the operations of the privata as we find them in documents of the tetrarchic period and after (see Appendix). But there is no evidence for the actual functioning of the ratio or summa privata outside Egypt in the second half of the third century. When the institution re-appears in the Egyptian evidence it is, with one possible exception (App., doc. 1), not until 298, and designated by the Latin term privata, apparently functioning as a noun, and transliterated into Greek as '(hē) privatē'—(the) privata.

There is thus both an acute discontinuity in our evidence, and a perfectly clear (if roundabout) derivation of nomenclature, combined with a definite continuity of function: the concern of the 'privatē' with confiscated property is the most striking feature of the relevant papyrus evidence for the tetrarchic period (App., docs. 2.4.6-7, 12-14, 17 and cf. 27).

One other partial form of continuity is also visible in these documents. The forms of landed property in Egypt in the first three centuries included a number of 'treasury estates' ('ousiai tamiakai'). Without venturing here on the complex evidence relating to these properties,[7] it will be enough to say that they were conceived of as belonging to the 'tameion' (fiscus?), seem to have been acquired on occasion by confiscation, were worked by tenants, and were managed by a hierarchy of local officals apparently nominated by the local town councils.[8] In the tetrarchic period it is clear that the overall control of these 'ousiai' has come into the hands of the officials of the privata (App., docs. 6, 9-12, 27). The 'estates account' ('ousiakos logos') now disappears, as does the office of 'epitropos ousiakos' (procurator of estates), which seems to have lasted until the 280s.[9]

From 298 until the end of the fourth century, where the present survey stops, a variety of evidence, papyri, inscriptions, the law-codes and the Notitia Dignitatum, shows that the privata, under a constantly evolving variety of titles (see below), denoted both a range of 'imperial' properties, ultimately at least spread all over the empire, and a hierarchy of tenants, local managers, procuratores, provincial officials (magistri and then rationales) and, at least from towards the middle of the century, a single (?) comes (rei privatae or rerum privatarum). In the Notitia Dignitatum we find one comes rerum privatarum in the East (Or. XIV) and another in the West, the latter supported by two further comites, of the largitiones privatae and of the patrimonium of Gildo, confiscated in 398 (Oc. XII).

The overall structure of posts concerned with the privata is sufficiently well known[10] and it may be enough to emphasise a few points of terminology which emerge from the strictly documentary evidence. From the beginning of this evidence in 298 we find in Egypt a procurator ('epitropos') of the privata, concerned with regions of very varying size: of the Thebaid in 298 (App., docs. 9 and 11) and 301/2 (12); of Egypt in 305/6 (14) and 309 (17); of the Oxyrhynchite and Cynopolite nomes in 360 (32). Above him stands a 'magistros (tēs) privatēs' (magister privatae) attested in 298 (2-8) and 304-7 (13; 15-16) and at an uncertain date (27), with however no regional designation. Doc. 21, of about 314, shows a magister privatae 'of Egypt and Libya'. If these magistri are all (as it seems) regional (diocesan?) officials, it remains very unclear whether there existed in the tetrachic period one or more 'central' officials, and if so what their titles were (see App., docs. 18, 19, 22, 25). It is more important to stress that the documents can already show an extended hierarchy: so for instance doc. no. 14 of 305/6 involves successively an Imperial edict, a letter of the magister privatae, an order of the procurator privatae of Egypt, and action by two boards of officials in Oxyrhynchus.

The term *magister* for regional officials of the *privata* was replaced quite soon by the more general term *rationalis* ('katholikos'), and appears only three times in legal sources.[11] Both a regional *rationalis* of imperial properties and a *comes* who is certainly a *comes rei privatae* are securely attested for the first time in doc. 32 of 360. With his mention of the 'kanōn' (rent in cash) the writer of the document reveals by implication a hierarchy extending up from the tenants to himself as *procurator* of the imperial properties of the Oxyrhynchite and Cynopolite nomes, to the 'katholikos' and ultimately the *comes*. It is likely in fact that the full hierarchy extending up to the *comes* had been in existence since the 340s. Both Ammianus and the Theodosian Code apply the title to Eusebius, to whom Constantius wrote in 342 to say that gifts made out of the *res privata* by 'our divine progenitor' (Constantine) should be valid and unquestioned.[12] The terminology used for both the various offices and the properties concerned is highly variable, sometimes as a result of conscious *variatio* (most evident in Symmachus' *Relatio*, doc. 36). The details are perhaps not worth pursuing, but it may be noted that *ratio privata* never reappears in this period, and the expression most often used by modern scholars to denote this category of imperial possessions, *res privata*, makes its earliest appearance in a document in no. 34 of A.D. 371. It seems clear that the singular, *res privata*, and the plural, *res privatae*, were used interchangeably in the later fourth century.

What the documentary evidence reveals very clearly is the importance of condemnation and confiscation as processes leading to the inclusion of property in the *privata*. Confiscation could of course be used deliberately as a penalty, as in the Great Persecution (App., doc. 13) or in Julian's letter (App., doc. 33) about the property of the Arian church in Edessa. Theodosius I was also to use the threat of confiscation of properties on which meetings of pagans or heretics were held; but in August 395 Arcadius and Honorius are found expostulating over the audacity of heretics who met on 'our properties' (*possessiones nostrae*) secure in the knowledge that these could not be 'conjoined to the *fiscus*' because they were in its ownership (*dominium*) already.[13] More often, the documents, especially the papyri of the early period, illustrate the random effects of the acquisition of minor items of property following condemnations: thus a quantity of wine (App., doc. 6), a single slave (7), or a nil return of the property of one soldier (17). This pattern is also reflected in the fears of some peasants, about which Libanius wrote to the *comes* Euagrius (under doc. 32). Alternatively, property might be reported as being vacant and thus be liable to seizure by the *privata*, and often (as in doc. 36) to being claimed for himself by the delator.

Since the documents show one case (27) where confiscated properties are being re-sold, and a number (see below) where goods are being delivered on the orders of the *privata*, we must be open to the possibility that there were some principles of selection in the use made of the random kinds of landed or movable property which came in by way of confiscation or vacancy. Nonetheless, what the documents reveal more clearly is the possibility of peculation by the hierarchy of officials involved (App., docs. 32, 34) and the burden which the process of tracing, acquiring, administering and exploiting the properties of the *privata* placed both on the town councils and on the general civil (and in one case military) administration of the provinces.

At the city level we find the officials of Panopolis having to despatch a slave to the magister (App., doc. 7) or look for persons sought by the privata (8); those of Oxyrhynchus receiving declarations of confiscated church property (13), corresponding with each other about confiscated property (14, 17) or delivering persons and documents to the magister (24). On an individual level the secretaries, accountants and officials of treasury estates in office in September 298 (6) will still, as a decade before (p. 126ff. above) have been nominated by the council. This is confirmed by the abortive exchange which takes place later in the same month, in which the procurator privatae, via the unhappy 'stratēgos', gives orders for the council of Panopolis to appoint extra superintendants for 'treasury estates', and the council replies defiantly claiming exemption for men of curial status. By an inversion typical of the empire, with its complex and contradictory pattern of obligations and exemptions, Constantius was to write in 340 to Nemesianus, comes, to say that curiales should indeed not be subject to obligations (munera) on behalf of 'our res privata'.[14] By a further inversion Julian (so Valentinian and Valens write) laid down that actores 'of our res privata' should not be subject to obligations laid on them by the principales or councils of the cities.[15] Actores, as is clear from doc. 34 and legal sources,[16] were agents for the collection of rents. But actual tenancies of the privata's properties could also be put to good use, and it emerged under Constantius that curiales in the diocese of Oriens were deliberately seeking such tenancies in order to be protected from city obligations.[17]

The burden placed on the provincial administration and (in Egypt at least) its sub-divisions can be simply illustrated from P. Beatty Panopolis 1, which shows that the 'stratēgos' sent an average of roughly one letter about the affairs of the privata every day. Since the privata embraced a large range of properties, with tenants and (like other imperial properties) with persons of servile status attached (see CTh IV, 12, 3), it was inevitable that imperial pronouncements affecting it would need on occasion to be directed to other officials, the Praetorian Prefects, the vicarii and so forth. So for instance the pronouncement of Valentinian and Valens, mentioned above on the immunity of actores of the privata was addressed to the vicarius urbis, and another of theirs, on the production in court of coloni or conductores of the privata, to the vicarius Africae. It is not necessary to multiply examples. The existence of large quantities of imperial property, whether in large or small units, was an acute complicating factor not only in the network of obligations and exemptions (see above) but in both the juridical and administrative structure and the ownership- and taxation-patterns of the Late Empire. This is very clear for instance in the letter of Constantius sent in 349 to Eustathius, perhaps a deputy of the Praetorian Prefect:

> Let the actores and other personnel of our res privata be compelled with the authority of due serverity to the delivery of the established taxes in kind (species sollemnes) lest the immunity of our res privata should be a burden to the provincials.

So did the privata emjoy immunity or not? If Jones is right, it was liable to the ordinary taxes but not to superindictiones or extraordinaria munera. If the immunity tended to be extended to the regular taxes this would place an greater burden on the other tax-payers in each locality.[18] We may reasonably doubt whether these fine distinctions were always perceived in identical terms by the ordinary provincials, those of them who had roles as tenants or actores of the privata, the procuratores or rationales of the privata, the Praetorian Prefects and their staff, or the emperors themselves (for whom such questions involved conflicting interests).

One of the documents (30) also involves the intervention of military forces in order to assist the collection of Imperial rents. The demand is made by the procurator of imperial properities with reference to an order from the dux of Egypt, Flavius Felicissimus; the offical sent to collect the troops is described as having been sent both by the dux and by the 'katholikos' (rationalis), who may have been either the general financial official of Egypt or a rationalis of the privata. In either case the document again illustrates the complexities and ambiguities created by the existence of imperial properties. Similarly the important and difficult imperial letter of 371 (doc. 34),[19] the most extensive and detailed evidence for the privata outside Egypt, shows an attempt by the emperors to re-allocate to the cities some of the revenues of that category of the privata's land (that which was iuris rei publicae) which had originally been confiscated from the cities. Their action is prompted both by a report from the proconsul and by an embassy from Ephesus. The instructions— to control the actores, and divide the appropriate revenues between the cities and the res privata, and also to prepare a detailed report on the productivity of the estates of the res privata in Asia—are given to the proconsul, and bypass any higher officials of the privata who may have been operating in the province.

The documentary evidence does little to illuminate the process of the disposal of the properties of the privata by gift or sale—though the latter is alluded to in the fragmentary doc. 27. But the function of the imperial properties, in providing a reserve fund for imperial liability is clear in no. 20, where the funds for the Catholic church of Africa will come first from the rationalis, who controlled the general revenues. If supplementation was needed, the bishop of Carthage was to turn to the 'procurator of our properties'. Such properties could of course be granted outright. In 330, when the Catholics of Cirta required a new church to replace the one occupied by the Donatists, Constantine could assume without question that there would be available a house 'belonging to our properties' (nostrorum bonorum), elsewhere called a 'fiscal site' (locus fiscalis), which could be granted for the construction of a church at fiscal expense (sumptu fiscali). It is noticeable that the emperor affirms that he has sent a letter of authorisation to the rationalis to transfer full ownership to the church (cum omni iure suo ad dominium ecclesiae catholicae).[20] Legal sources make abundantly clear that the ownership of such grants was liable to subsequent challenge both by officials of the privata and by others.[21] Naturally enough, even greater insecurity attended such grants when made under the regime of a usurper. For instance, Arcadius and Honorius wrote in 395 to Eulogius, comes r(erum) p(rivatarum), to say that property which had been granted by the order of the usurper Maximus (therefore in Gaul, Spain, Britain or Italy in 383-8), if transferred not by governors (praesides) but by rationales should be recovered and restored to the res privata.[22]

What the documents, or rather the papyri of the early period, do show is the puzzling phenomenon of the delivery on the orders of the magister privatae of quantities of goods in kind, or in one case silver bullion (no. 15). In this latter instance what is concerned is a purchase of uncoined silver, following a procedure attested by other papyri of the early fourth century, namely as an obligation laid on the cities. But the official normally concerned is the rationalis, not the magister privatae. A similar puzzle arises in no. 16, where it is clear that the city of Oxyrhynchus has a collective obligation to provide two mules for the magister. In these two instances it is certain that the process concerned has no connection with the raising of revenues from the estates of the privata. This is less certain where the magister is accepting delivery of ship-loads of matting (3), or has ordered the delivery to Alexandria of ship-loads of charcoal (26?; 29). But if the text were more secure, it would appear in no. 28 that a village could by obliged by the magister to make a collective contribution of wool; and a similar obligation is evident in no. 23 where a cash payment is collected by village officials in lieu of woad to go to the office of the privata. If there were clear indications that these products in kind actually derived from estates of the privata, then it might be suggested that the magister is seeing to the collection of the taxes in kind (see p. 129 above) from the privata's properties. One papyrus of the earlier fourth century (P. Oxy. 2154) refers to the collection of wool and tow for the anabolicum, for which a 'soldier of the procurator' has come, and also to security given to a praepositus of the treasury estates ('tōn tamiakōn'). Alternatively, some of the supplies mentioned (wool, woad, charcoal, matting?) might have been required for imperial dye-works. We have evidence for the existence of an imperial dye-works at Tyre already in the last quarter of the third century;[23] and on the other hand a pronouncement of Constantine from A.D. 333 shows that dye-works and woollen mills under procuratores could then form part of the privata.[24] Unfortunately the Notitia Dignitatum for Oriens provides no equivalent to the list of woollen-mills, linen-mills and dye-works in the West, and at that time under the comes sacrarum largitionum (Occ. XI); the comes privatarum in the West still, however, had two woollen-mills at Trier and at one other unidentifiable place (Occ. XII, 26-7). It is therefore not impossible that the magister privatae in Egypt might have collected materials and fuel either for use in a putative dyeworks in Alexandria, or perhaps for shipment to Tyre. Donkeys too might have been requisitioned either for the use of officials of the privata or for the transport of goods. Finally, while the reasons for official purchases of gold and silver bullion are clear, there seems no way of explaining why (on the one attested occasion) this was done at the orders of the magister privata.

It may be noted that a very similar puzzle, relating to Egypt in the 320s, and 330s, is presented by the revenues of imperial properties (possessiones) in Alexandria and Egypt (and elsewhere), granted by Constantine for the support of churches in Rome and listed in the Liber Pontificalis XXXIV. The list gives no indication of the formal status of these properties (as belonging for instance to the privata or the patrimonium), but it does at one point seem to indicate that a property in Alexandria had been caduca (XXXIV, XX), and at another, of a property near Rome, that it had been confiscated (XXXIV, XXV). There is therefore some resemblance to the properties of the privata. Furthermore some of the properties are listed as providing a revenue calculated both in solidi and in a variety of relatively valuable products, which include papyrus, pepper, saffron, stroax, incense, oil, balsam, linen and myrrh. If it is correct that these goods could not all have literally been products of estates in Egypt,[25] and if, as seems clear from the mechanical listing of the revenues, the estates had already been providing revenues in this form before they were granted to the churches, we may have a parallel case of the regular acquisition of valuables by requisition or purchase. But, while the evidence of the Liber Pontificalis demands investigation in its Egyptian context (and other local contexts), for the moment it merely adds further puzzles in our conception of the forms in which revenues in cash and kind were extracted.

It cannot therefore be pretended that even the relatively plentiful papyrus evidence gives us any clear conception of the frameworks within which these revenues were raised in the name of the privata, or of whether the privata used the products for its own operations (as perhaps in dye-works) or passed them on to some other agency. Furthermore, if there was any policy of using the extensive imperial properties as a means of guaranteeing the supply of either useful or valuable commodities, our evidence is not such as to demonstrate it. Such a policy was in any case hardly needed, since the required commodities could be, and were, raised by means of direct taxation in kind.

It is better therefore to see the landed properties of the privata primarily as a source of revenue, paying both rent and the established taxes. Whether the acquisition and exploitation (as opposed to re-sale) of innumerable items of property in all regions of the empire was on balance worth the disturbance to local patterns of ownership and tenancy, the confusion of local obligations (munera) and exemptions, the ample opportunities for peculation, and the complex administrative hierarchy required, may well be doubted. What is clear is that the land held by the privata represented a store of capital value on an enormous scale, which by the fifth century seems to have amounted in some regions to about a sixth of the total area.[26] Whether such a proportion was typical or not, the Notitia Dignitatum shows that the apparatus of the privata was established in all parts of the empire. These complex administrative arrangements which we find in the fourth century were the product of a long development beginning in the first, whereby confiscated and vacant properties came to be claimed for the fiscus, and (for reasons which are not wholly clear) were retained rather than being sold. The privata thus belongs as much in the sphere of punishments as it does in that of state finance. Confiscation of property was an important weapon in the hands of the state, and the presence of imperial properties everywhere will have served as a constant reminder to the individual subject of the possibility that his own property might join them.

If it did not, the emperor could always issue further reminders, as Valentinian II, Theodosius and Arcadius did in the matter of the aqueducts of Rome, which in itself illustrates a remarkable aspect of the continuity from the first century to the fourth. In the first century, as we know from Frontinus, the inhabitants of Rome were liable to tap the aqueducts illegally, for which the penalty was a fine. It could be done legally, however, by making a petition to the Emperor, and obtaining permission to draw water from one of the reservoirs (castella) and not directly from a pipe.[27] In 389, more than a century after the emperors had ceased to reside there regularly, a pronouncement of Valentinian, Theodosius and Arcadius makes clear that it was still an imperial prerogative to grant permission to tap the aqeuducts of Rome.[28] Illegal tapping persisted also, even though the penalty risked had become significantly more severe. A few years earlier the emperors had described both the wrongdoing and the penalty in expostulatory terms typical of the period:[29]

> If moreover anyone, with the audacity of forbidden madness, presumes to damage the amenities of the most flourishing city by drawing water into his own property from a public aqueduct, let him be aware that the said property is to be sealed with a fiscal notice and conjoined to our res privatae.

If the res privatae thus acquired further properties in Rome it will have been as a result of the random effects of private wrongdoing, delation and the activity of officials—very similar effects to those which led in doc. 36 to a conflict of jurisdiction between Symmachus as Praefectus Urbis and the privatae rei comes. The real economic advantage to the state is much less evident than the scale and ubiquity of property-ownership by the privata, and its importance as one vehicle for the constant exchange of wealth between state and subject.

NOTES

1. Throughout the text Latin terms are underlined, and transliterated Greek words or phrases placed in inverted commas.

2. See A. H. M. Jones, The Later Roman Empire, 1964, 412ff. (needless to say, the clearest exposition of the subject). This paper aims to touch on a number of themes, without attempting to go over all the ground covered by Jones.

3. For this view see F. Millar, 'The Fiscus in the First Two Centuries', JRS LIII, 1963, 29; The Emperor in the Roman World, 1977, 189ff. and App. 2 (henceforward ERW). For a different view, P. A. Brunt, 'The 'Fiscus' and its Development', JRS LVI, 1966, 75.

4. ERW, 625ff.

5. Ibid., 627ff.

6. See P. R. Swarney, The Ptolemaic and Roman Idios Logos, 1970; ERW, 158ff; 166; 170-4.

7. For recent discussions see H. C. Kuhnke, Ousiakē Gē (Diss. Köln, 1971; S. M. Parassogiou, Imperial Estates in Egypt, American Studies in Papyrology 18, 1978. See D. J. Crawford, 'Imperial Estates', M. I. Finley (ed.), Studies in Roman Property, 1976, 35.

8. See e.g. Wilcken, Chrestomathie, no. 174 (A.D. 199); 177 (under Aurelian); 378 (A.D. 288).

9. The 'ousiakē epitrōpe' appears in P.Oxy, 2228, 1.38, which dates to 283 or 285. See A. K. Bowman, The Town Councils of Roman Egypt, 1971, esp. 80.

10. See Jones, loc. cit. (n. 2) and PLRE I, 1062-4.

11. CTh, X, 1, 2 (319) on grants of imperial property; X, 1, 4 (320), addressed to Domitius, mag(ist)er privatae rei Africae, on cases between the fiscus and private persons; CTh XII, 1, 14 (326), on the curial status of sons of comites, praesides, rationales and magistri privatae. For the date see O. Seeck, Regesten der Kaiser und Päpste, 1919, 177.

12. Ammianus XV, 5, 4; CTh, X, 10, 6.

13. CTh, XVI, 10, 13.

14. CTh, XII, 1, 30 = CJ X, 32, 21.

15. CTh, X, 4, 2.

16. Actores: CTh X, 4, 1 = CJ III, 26, 9, + XI, 72, 1 (313?); CTh XI, 7, 6 = CJ X, 19, 4 (346).

17. CTh XII, 1, 33.

18. CTh XI, 7, 6 = CJ X, 7, 6. See Jones, LRE, 419-20.

19. See also F. F. Abbott and A. C. Johnson, Municipal Administration, 1926, no. 157; A.C. Johnson, F. C. Bourne, P. R. Coleman-Norton, Ancient Roman Statutes, 1961, no. 317 (translation and notes); Jones, LRE, 415, 732-3. Many obscurities remain in this text.

20. Optatus, App. X.

21. E.g. CTh X, 1, 2 (319).

22. CTh XV, 14, 10.

23. Eusebius, HE VII, 32, 3; cf. Ammianus XIV, 9, 7.

24. CTh I, 32, 1.

25. ERW, 186-7, following L. Duchesne, Le Liber Pontificalis I, p. CL.

26. Jones, LRE, 415-16.

27. Illegal tapping: Frontinus, de aquae ductu 9; 65; 75-6; 88; 115. beneficium from emperor: praef. 3; 88; 94; 99; 105; 111; 118; cf. Statius, Silv. III, 1, 61-4; Martial, Epig, IX, 18.

28. CTh XV, 2, 5 = CJ XI, 43, 3.

29. CTh XV, 2, 4 = CJ XI, 43, 2 (date uncertain, but perhaps 381/2).

APPENDIX

DOCUMENTARY REFERENCES TO THE PRIVATA, LATE THIRD TO LATE FOURTH CENTURY

This list offers a revision, supplementation and extension in time of that in The Emperor in the Roman World (1977), App. 3.2. Documents which should be accepted as referring to the privata, though not using this specific term, are inset in their appropriate place. Imperial and other letters from MS sources are included, but not literary references or the extensive material from the Codex Theodosianus or Codex Justinianus.

1. Third Century (?) — F. Bilabel, Griechische Papyri (Veröff. bad. Pap.-Samml. 4) (1924), no. 90. List of properties and taxes. L.2 has 'epitropou privatēs' (procurâtor privatae), but provides no context.

2. 298 Aug. 16 — P. Oxy. 3247. Fragments of a petition, probably addressed to the 'stratēgos', Aurelius Zenagenes (see P. Oxy 3246), and mentioning property (?) apparently allotted to the account ('taxis') of the '[magistros t]ēs privatēs' (possibly Pomponius Domnus, see below). The expression 'formerly of Akontios' in l.5 suggests that confiscated property is in question.

    298 September — P. Beatty Panop. 1. (correspondence of 'stratēgos' of Panopolite nome).

3. Sept. 14 — LL.120-7. Letter addressed 'to Pomponius Domnus' (see below); second copy, ll.160-6, addressed 'to the magistros'. On despatch of ships carrying matting.

4. Sept. (15?) — LL.149-52. Letter of 'stratēgos' to Pomponius Domnus on arrest of a man and his slave and their despatch to his office.

5. Sept. 16 — LL.192-200. Letter of 'stratēgos' on arrests ordered by the 'magistros privatēs' and referring (l.200) to the interests of 'the most sacred treasury' ('to hierōtaton tameion') (cf. also. l.204).

6. Sept. 17 — LL.205-12. Order of 'stratēgos' following letters from the 'magistros privatēs', Pomponius Domnus, for reports from secretaries ('grammateis') accountants ('cheiristai') and officials ('pragmateutai') of treasury estates ('tamiakai ousiai') on the amount of wine included among confiscated goods accruing to the treasury ('tameion').

7. Sept. 17 — LL.225-9. Letter of 'stratēgos' to the President of the Council of Panopolis ordering the arrest and despatch to the office of the 'magistros privatēs', Pomponius Domnus, of a slave formerly owned by Theognostos, now condemned, and now owned by 'the most sacred Treasury'.

8. Sept. 19 — LL.338-41. Letter of 'stratēgos' to nominators of the metropolis (Panopolis) on persons being sought in the interests of 'the most sacred treasury' on the orders of Pomponius Domnus 'magistros preivatēs' (sic).

9. Sept. 23 — LL.365-8. Letter of 'stratēgos' to council (of Panopolis) referring to a letter from Valerias Melas, 'epitropos privatēs' (procurator privatae) of the Thebaid on the appointment of four extra superintendents ('pronoētai') of the treasury estates ('ousiai tamiakai').

10. Sept. 23 — LL.369-73. Letter of 'stratēgos' to Melas, 'epitropos privatēs', reporting his order to the city council, and their reply that no-one of curial status should be subjected to a 'treasury duty' ('tamiakē phrontis') and referring to the orders of the 'hēgoumenos' (praeses) of the Thebaid.

11. Sept. 24 — LL.400-4. Letter of 'stratēgos' to council acknowledging theirs, and referring to a further letter of Valerius Melas, 'epitropos privatēs', repeating his previous order.

12. 301/2 — P. Lond. 1271 (ed. T. C. Skeat, Two Papyri from Panopolis, 156-7). Letter from the 'epitropos privatēs' of the Thebaid referring to confiscated property ('now of the most sacred treasury', l.8, and cf. l.10), and probably concerning its lease ('misthōsis', l.5).

13. 304 Feb. 5 — P. Oxy. 2673 see J. R. Rea, ZPE XXXV, 1979, 128. Declaration to officials of the city of Oxyrhynchus by the lector of a village church concerning the surrender of church property following instructions from Aurelius Athanasius, 'epitropos privatēs', on the orders of Neratius Apollonides, 'magistros tēs privatēs'.

14. 305/6 — P. Oxy. 2665. Letter from one board of city officials in Oxyrhynchus to another concerning an order from Aurelius Athanasius, 'epitropos tēs kat' Aigupton privatēs', in conformity with an imperial edict and a letter of Neratius Apollonides (see no. 13), that the property of a man condemned by the praeses of the Thebaid should be 'adjudged to the accounts of the treasury ('tameion').

15. 306 Aug. 11 — PSI 310. see J. R. Rea, 'P.S.I. 310 and Imperial Bullion Purchases', CE XLIX, 1974, 163 (for the date).

Acknowledgement to a banker 'of the office of the privata ('taxeōs privatēs') from an official of Heracleopolis of payment for uncoined silver delivered on the orders of the 'magistros'.

16. 307 May 9 — P. Oxy. 3192. Declaration to a city official of Oxyrhynchus by a man who states that he has been molested by the donkey-traders of the town in connection with the supply of two donkeys sent to the 'magistros tēs privatēs', and swears that he has never been a donkey-trader.

17. 309 June-July — Mitteis, Chrestomathie, no. 196. Letter from one group of officials in Oxyrhynchus to another on confiscations carried out on the orders of Valerius Asterius, 'epitropos privatēs Aiguptou' of the property of a soldier condemned by the dux, reporting that the archives showed no property of his.

18. ?310/320 — CIL VI, 1704-5 = ILS 1214-15 (Rome). L. Caelius Saturninus (PLRE I, Saturninus 9), rationalis privatae between being vicarius summae rei rationum and praefectus annonae urbis. The date is uncertain, but perhaps early in the second decade of the fourth century.

19. ?312/24 — CIL VI, 36952 (Rome). Appius Primianus, v.p., rationalis summae privatae.

20. 313 first half — Eusebius, Hist. Eccl. X, 6. Letter of Constantine to Caecilianus, bishop of Carthage, recording his order to Ursus, 'katholikos' (rationalis) of Africa, to make payments to the clergy, and authorising further requests to Heracleides, 'tou epitroupou tōn hēmeterōn ktēmatōn' (procurator nostrarum possessionum = procurator privatae ?).

21. c. 314 — CIL III 18 = 6586 (Alexandria). Valerius Epifanius, magister privatae Aegypti et Libyae.

22. 314 — FIRA I², no. 94. Edict of Constantine repressing accusations by informers, and mentioning letters on the subject sent to the Praetorian Prefects, governors (praesides), the rationalis and the magister privatae. cf. CIL III, 13569 = Ins. Cret. I. XVIII, 189 (Lyttos), probably also Constantinian, and also mentioning instructions sent to officials, including the magister privatae.

23. 319 — SB 10264. revised by D. Hagedorn, 'Waid für die Res Privata', ZPE XVII, 1975, 91. Two village officials give a receipt for money paid as a substitute for woad "to go to the office of the privata' (tē taxi tēs privatēs').

24. 325 — P. Oxy. 3125. Letter from two officials of Oxyrhynchus to Flavius Graphicianus, 'magistros privatēs', sending persons and documents (receipts?).

25. 325/30 — CIL VI, 1135 (Rome). Dedication to Helena, mother of Constantine, by L. Pi[st]ius, v.p., p(rae)p(ositus) rerum privatarum.

26. 326 Jan. 9 — Mitteis, Chrestomathie, no. 342. Declaration by shipper addressed to the 'stratēgos' that he has received on his boat 20,000 lb of charcoal to transport to Alexandria on the instructions (?) of the office of the 'magistership' ('magistriōtes—of the privata? cf. no. 29).

27. Early fourth century — SB 9883, from N. Lewis, 'A New Document on the Magister Rei Privatae', JJP XV, 1965, 157. Document of uncertain character mentioning (l.3) the 'magistros privatēs' and (l.4) 'ousiai tamiakai' ('treasury estates') and 'chōria venti ...? ' which have come into the possesion of the most sacred treasury' and (ll. 9-11) will be sold by it.

28. Diocletian-Constantine? — Wilcken, Chrestomathie, no. 178 (BGU 927, conjecturally restored in Archiv V, 185-6). Note by two village officals recording delivery of wool as a 'synteleia' in accordance with the orders of the 'magistros tēs privatēs' (conjectural reading).

29. 338 Dec. 24 — P. Vindob. Sijpesteijn 1, re-discussed by H. C. Youtie, Scriptiunculae I, 1973, 400-4. Two receipts by shippers for loading of charcoal, and undertaking on oath to deliver it at Alexandria in accordance with the orders of Eudaimon, a centurion from the office of the 'privatē'.

30. 345/7 — Wilcken, Chrestomathie, no. 179 = P. Abinn. 3. Flavius Macarius, 'epitr(opos) despotik(ōn) ktēseōn' (procurator of imperial properties), writes to Flavius Abinnaeus, praepositus (or praefectus) of the fort at Dionysias, to say that on the orders of the dux and comes, 'taking thought for the 'despotikos oikos' ('imperial estate'?), he should send troops to assist in the collection of the 'despotikoi kanōnes' (imperial rents). Further on there is a reference to the 'katholikos' (rationalis). For the identification of 'despotic' properties with those of the privata see no. 32.

31. 359-64 — Basil, Ep 15. Letter addressed to Arcadius, 'komēti privatōn (comes rerum privatarum), and making an obliquely-worded request on behalf of the city of Caesarea in Cappadocia. For the date see PLRE I, Arcadius 3.

32. 360 P. Oxy. 2267. Complaint by Flavius Heraclides, a former 'epitropos tōn despot(ikōn) ktēseōn' (procurator of the imperial properties) of the districts ('nomoi') of Oxyrhynchus and Cynopolis, who protests as to the integrity with which he has served the interests of the 'despotikos logos' ('imperial account') and the intrigues against him of Flavius Diodotus, 'katholikos tōn despotikōn pragmatōn' (rationalis of the imperial affairs'), including the claims that he had demanded more than the due 'kanōn' (rent). L.29 refers to Euagrius, the 'komēs tōn despotikōn'. This is the earliest documentary reference to the comes rerum privatarum/rei privatae, and the identification is made certain by the reference to Euagrius as comes rei privatae in 361 by Ammianus XX.3.7. Note also Libanius, Ep. 126, addressed to Euagrius, on the fears of peasants that they might be exposed to accusations as having wronged 'the emperors' estate' ('ton basileōs oikon').

33. 362 Julian, Ep. 43 Hertlein/112 Bidez-Cumont/40 Loeb. Letter ordering confiscation of the property of the Arian church in Edessa, and attachment of its landed possessions to 'our res privatae' ('tois hēmeterois privatois').

34. 371 FIRA[2] I, no. 108 (Ephesos). Letter of Valentinian, Valens and Gratian to Eutropius, as proconsul of Asia on the provision of funds for the restoration of city walls. Funds had been granted from the revenues of estates iuris re[i privatae or (possibly) publicae]; but it was reported that these revenues were being held back by the actores (agents) privatae rei nostrae, even though they were simultaneously raising rents above the established canon (see nos. 30 and 32) and producing no profit for 'our treasury' (aerarium nostrum). Management of the relevant estates was therefore to be transfered to the city councils, and after the due portion of the revenues had been paid to each city Eutropius was to see that the balance was paid to 'our res privata'. A catalogue was also to be made of all the relevant properties in Asia and of their annual payments to 'our res privata', and indicating which were infertile 'with loss to res nostra'.

35. 370-8 Basil, Ep. 303. Letter addressed to an unnamed 'komēs privatōn' (comes rerum privatarum), protesting about false accusations over the requisitioning of broodmares ('phoradōn telesma') and asking for abuses to be stopped.

36. 384 — Symmachus, *Relatio* 41, see R. H. Barrow, *Prefect and Emperor: the Relationes of Symmachus*, 1973, 210ff. Symmachus, as *Praefectus Urbis* of Rome, writes to the Emperors (Theodosius I, Valentinian II and Arcadius) about the case of an estate delated as being *vacantia* and therefore falling to the *fiscus* (*in ius fisci*), and requested as a reward by the *delator*. Symmachus mentions the advocates (*defensores*) and *rationales* of the *augustissima domus* ('imperial estate'?), and in one place a *rationalis patrimonii*, and protests about a hearing before a *rationalis*, allegedly (but in his view improperly) delegated by the *privatae rei comes*.

37. Fourth Century — *AE* 1900, 158 (Thessalonica). Tomb inscription of Flavius Kallistus, 'epitropos choriōn despotikōn' (*procurator* of imperial properties). See nos. 30 and 32.

THE *SACRAE LARGITIONES*: REVENUES, EXPENDITURE AND THE PRODUCTION OF COIN

C. E. King

Relatively little has been published about the emergence and function of the *largitiones* or its chief officer the *Comes Sacrarum Largitionum* (who will be referred to hereafter as the CSL).[1] Given the importance of this treasury particularly in the later fourth century it is somewhat surprising that the subject has not occasioned more attention. This neglect may in part be explained by the obscurity in which the origins of the CSL are shrouded, the apparent areas of overlap with the *res privata* and the difficulties in elucidating how the diocesan and provincial structures operated.

Of central importance to the understanding of the workings of Roman treasuries is the fact that from the second century onwards there was a recurrent tendency for the emperor's private income and public funds to be assimilated to one another. Septimius Severus separated the *privata* from the *patrimonium* but during the third century the *privata* reabsorbed it and the *rationalis summarum rationum* emerged as the chief financial official.[2]

The original function of the *res summa* had been the unification of procuratorial accounts. The first individual to appear with the title *rationalis summarum rationum* (i.e. *rationalis summae rei*) was Aurelius Eubolus.[3] About A.D. 250 two important subordinates of the *rationalis* had begun to emerge at the central level, the *magister summarum rationum*, directly responsible to the *rationalis* and the *magister privatae*, the latter being responsible as might be expected for domain accounts.[4] *Magister privatae* continue to be mentioned until the mid-4th century and the office existed at both the central and diocesan level.

Unfortunately very little evidence exists regarding the *officium summarum rationum* at Rome. The one surviving inscription suggests that as late as the reign of Carinus the servile grades which had traditionally served procurators continued to do so.[5]

The existence on the diocesan level in the 4th century of both the *res summa* and the *privata* is attested by a number of sources, and here, as on the central level, the *rationalis* seems to have had authority over the *magister*.[6] However, either there was a considerable overlap in function at this time since the two departments were not yet separate, or the use of the title *rationalis* as opposed to *magister privatae* (which came to be the normal designation) when referring to the official in charge of matters relating to domain lands was not fixed.[7] Analysis of the existing evidence suggests that the institutions themselves were in a state of evolution, and rigid distinctions in function cannot be drawn in the early fourth century although the general developmental pattern is clear.

The officia of the magistri privatae at the provincial level included beneficiarii, stratores, tabularii, praecones, principes, and Caesariani but unfortunately with the exception of the Caesariani, who were responsible for the incorporation of confiscated property, there is little information regarding the functions of specific officials.[8]

The rationalis summarum rationum had two subordinates: the magister summarum whom Kent has described as relatively unimportant since the title is rarely attested and the magister rei privatae whose existence can be documented from c. 250-350.[9] It is signigicant that diocesan magistri occurred as well as central ones and that the latter survived into the sixth century.[10]

THE COMES SACRARUM LARGITIONUM AND HIS OFFICIUM

The CSL, as noted above, was the direct successor of the rationalis rei semmae. He controlled the mints, mines (gold and probably silver), and a number of state factories: linyfia, gynaecea, baphia, and barbaricarii basically concerned with the production of fabrics and clothing. He also collected money taxes and other levies in gold and silver including the compulsory purchase of bullion. The structure of the ministry is given in skeletal form in the Notitia Dignitatum, and is far more complete for the West than for the East.[11]

About A.D. 340 the two rationales, i.e. that of the res summa and the emerging res privata, were absorbed into the comitatus and appear with new titles: comes largitionum and comes rei privatae. The development in the East differed somewhat from that of the West. In the East by the time of the Notitia, comites largitionum existed in every diocese, but in the West they are attested only for Illyricum, Italy, Africa, and Gaul.[12] Their restricted geographical distribution in the West has led Kent to argue that this is the reason for the survival there of rationales on the diocesan level.[13] Both Eastern and Western officials played a role in the exaction of taxes, which will be discussed below.

Various other functions originally under the control of the rationalis rei summae were subdivided and allocated to special officials, i.e. the comes metallorum who was in charge of mines, and the comites commerciorum who in the East dealt with external trade.[14]

The structure of the officium of the comes sacrae largitionum has been preserved not only in the Notitia Dignitatum but also in one of the laws of the Theodosian Code which is a corrupt form of one in the Code of Justinian dated to A.D. 384.[15] Before this time, or in any case by 352, the officium had been subdivided into two sections, the largitionales comitatenses and the largitionales civitatum or singularum urbium.[16] The latter seem to have been permanently stationed in the provinces and after 354 to have enjoyed a lower status than the largitionales comitatenses.[17]

The various bureaus of the largitionales comitatenses and their functions have been discussed in detail by Kent and more briefly by Jones; they can be summarized as follows.[18]

The Non-Financial Bureaus

1) The scrinium totius officii was the general branch of the and dealt with the organization of the bastaga, fiscal cases (libelli and instrumenta), and handled the inspections resulting from the discovery of financial abuses.[19]

2) The scrinium numerorum probably dealt with the issue of stipendia and donativa to the troops.

3) The scrinium tabulariorum was the accounting branch and would have played an important part in any financial inspections undertaken by the CSL. It may also have audited the accounts of the other scrinia.[20]

4) The scrinium canonum appears to have been responsible for the receipt of all taxation related to the largitiones and the dues from the state factories, one of its sub-departments, the scrinium mittendariorum, was responsible for sending officials into the provinces annually to supervise the collection of the largitionales tituli.[21]

5) The scrinium vestiarii sacri whose function, although doubtful, may have been to organize the distribution of uniforms to military and civil personnel.

The Financial Bureaus

6) The scrinium auri massae seems to have been the treasury into which the gold bullion was deposited; some if not all of which was later minted as solidi.[22] The structure of this bureau was complex since it had two and probably three sub-departments which are summarized below. The officials have been arranged in order of decreasing importance; the information in parentheses refers either to rank or the number of personnel recorded as existing in a given bureau.

THE STRUCTURE OF THE SCRINIVM AVRI MASSAE

primicerius
scrinii aureae massae

secundarius (vp)

tertiocerius (duc)

quartiocerius (duc)
centenarii (4)
epistulares (4)

aurifices specierum	aurifices solidorum	sculptores et ceteri aurifices
vp (1) primicerius	ducenarius (1)	centenarius (1)
ducenarii (2)	centenarii (7)	epistulares (5)
centenarii (6)	epistulares (6)	formae primae (6)
formae primae (18)	formae primae (9)	formae secundae (18)
formae secundae (4)	formae secundae (30)	

The problem is whether the aurifices solidorum and sculptores et ceteri aurifices were subordinate to the aurifices specierum as Kent has suggested in his arrangement of this material, or whether the three sub-bureaus were more or less independent of one another, and the presence of a vir perfectissimus as head of the aurifices specierum simply a result of that particular subdepartment being more important than the others. Their respective functions, while variously interpreted may have been as follows: the aurifices specierum may have been the gold workers who made the brooches, rings etc. given by the emperors as gifts on aniversaries; they may also have produced other ornamental gold objects. The aurifices solidorum were obviously responsible for the production of gold coin, but the function of the sculptores et ceteri aurifices is less clear. Judging by their title and lower standing, since the highest ranking official in this department was only a centenarius, they may have been responsible for the production of the dies from which gold coins were made and other engraved objects. This would support the notion of their having been subsidiary to the aurifices solidorum and perhaps to the aurifices specierum as well.

7) The scrinium auri ad responsum seems to have been divided into three subdepartments each headed by a vir perfectissimus although the text is not clear in this regard. Kent has reconstructed their organization as follows:[23]

primicerius
scrinii auri ad responsum
(vp ord (?) prim)

	vp ord (?) sec	vp ord (?) sec
ducenarius	ducenarius	ducenarius
centenarius	centenarius	- - - - - - - -
epistularis	epistularis	epistularis
formae primae (1)	formae primae (1)	formae primae (1)
formae secundae (1)	formae secundae (1)	formae secundae (1)

The function of this bureau remains obscure. Kent has suggested that it may have represented the original department of benefactions; Jones postulated that it dealt with the return of gold stocks to regional treasuries, and Hendy thinks it could have been the equivalent of the two monetary scrinia (a miliarensibus and ad pecunias) and as such dealt with some aspect of the gold coinage.[24] Kent's suggestion seems the most reasonable, but admittedly there is no evidence on which to be certain.

8) The scrinium a miliarensibus by its title should have had something to do with coined silver money, but precisely what is not certain, possibly it dealt with larger silver denominations. Kent has suggested that it may have had some share in deciding the amount of silver to be coined and in its distribution.[25] Its infrastructure was smaller and simpler than most of the bureaus discussed up to this point and can be summarized as follows:

primicerius scrinii
a miliarensibus
(vp ord (?) prim)

ducenarius

- - - - - - - -

formae primae (1)

formae secundae (2)

formae tertiae (3)

9) The scrinium ab argento is similar in structure to the scrinium auri massae if Kent's suggestion is accepted that the argentarii comitatenses and barbaricarii have been incorrectly classed under the scrinium ad pecunias and rightly belong to the scrinium ab argento.[26] This would certainly seem a reasonable assumption after the bronze coinage had lost its silver content entirely, since on the surface it seems anomalous to have silver workers in a scrinium whose basic function was the production of bronze coin. It is not inconceivable, however, that this arrangement had come into being in the earlier part of the fourth century and by 384 was an anachronism, but in accepted bureaucratic tradition was allowed to continue. The structure of the scrinium was as follows:

primicerius scrinii
ab argento
(vp ord (?) sec)

formae primae (2)

formae secundae (2)

formae tertiae (5)

Its very truncated nature, i.e. the absence of a ducenarius or centenarius seem to provide strong grounds for Kent's suggestion, unless the text of the law is somehow corrupt, since no other bureau completely lacks these intermediate grades.

10) The scrinium a pecuniis must have dealt with the production of bronze coin at the regional mints. Its structure can be summarized as follows:

primicerius scrinii a pecuniis

centenarius

epistularis

formae primae (4)

formae secundae (3)

formae tertiae (1)

The information presented above regarding the structure of the scrinia which formed the officium of the CSL while skeletal and at times frustratingly ambiguous when one is attempting to elucidate the function and operation of the fiscal scrinia is nonetheless illuminating. It presents a picture of a highly developed and specialized organization which was set up to deal with the collection of revenue, the transformation of bullion into coin or objects, and all the accounting procedures resulting from these activities. It also illustrates how schematic the information in the Notitia is, listing only the main departments and not the lower levels of the administration.

The general pattern of organization is one in which departments dealing with gold, silver, bronze, military uniforms, taxation, and accounting were all kept separate. In the case of gold and silver there was a further subdivision the precise nature of which remains unclear. It is in the context of this evolving and complex bureaucratic structure on the fiscal level that the collection of taxes, production of coin, and government expenditure must be considered.

REVENUES OF THE CSL

Collatio lustralis[27]

According to Zosimus this tax was instituted by Constantine and it was levied on all those engaged in commerce and those in cities who bought and sold goods or services. It was collected in cash and levied every five years.[28] The unit of assessment was probably the workman and his tools, and its base appears to have been related to the capitatio.[29] The meagre evidence that exists suggests that each workman and his tools were expressed as a specific monetary value.[30]

The 5-yearly incidence of this tax has led Kent to suggest that it was raised in order to pay the troops their quinquennial donative, and evidence does exist that a quinquennial cycle was operating after 297 although the actual indiction cycle began later, probably in 312.[31] The tax was collected by curials in each city or town who were themselves exempt from it unless they were negotiatores.

Exemptions from the tax were few. Veterans in 326 received a remission up to 100,000 folles and although the amount of exemption was changed from time to time during the course of the century, in principle veterans retained partial immunity.[32] Other groups known to have been exempted after 360 included coloni on senatorial estates indulging in internal trade in agricultural produce, rustic craftsmen, traders in their own agricultural produce, the clergy, doctors, and teachers.[33]

The tax was bitterly complained of as being intolerably heavy but unfortunately very little evidence exists regarding the rate of levy per city or per person.[34]

gleba senatoria [35]

The gleba senatoria was also instituted by Constantine and was paid annually.[36] It was a tax levied on the estates of Senators who were clarissimi and probably represents the only attempt made by the Romans to impose a graduated tax according to income. By 372, and perhaps before, senators were classified into three groups by wealth and paid 8, 4, or 2 folles of gold respectively.[37]

Unfortunately the meaning of the term follis in this context is not at all certain. The legal texts make it clear that in the 380s and after the tax was paid in gold and that the 7 solidi mentioned in CTh 6, 2, 15 (383) was less than 2 folles. The difficulty is to establish the value of the follis, and it is not certain whether the use of the term here refers to a gold follis or an abstract accounting unit expressed in terms of the current worth of the argentiferous bronze coinage. If the latter, then the actual amount of the tax paid in gold would have fluctuated as the value of the bronze coinage altered as a result of its frequent debasement and occasional imperial attempts at reform.[38]

All senators were required to make a complete tax declaration of their land holdings and the lists (glebae senatoriae breves) were kept by the scrinia palatina although the assessment and collection were the responsibility of the magister censuum and his censuales both of whom were subordinate to the praefectus urbi.[39] By the time of Symmachus the lists were brought up to date every three months.[40]

Exemptions from the tax were rarely granted, and in A.D. 428 those who were not liable included barristers of the high courts of the praetorian and urban prefects, court physicians, certain high-ranking palatine officials who held senatorial rank during their service or after retirement, notaries, decurions of the sacrii palatii, domestici and protectores, principes and agentium in rebus.[41]

oblatio senatoria[42]

Oblationes were certainly given in the third century to judge from the evidence of Dio; they were voluntary subscriptions by senators given on such public occasions as imperial accessions, or quinquennial anniversaries.[43]

In the West the offering was made in gold bullion and the only reference to the contribution from Constantinople in A.D. 357 alludes to its having been presented εἰς στεφανιας μετασκευήσαντο which demonstrates the close relationship this tax bore to the aurum coronarium.[44] The compulsory character of this so-called free-will offering emerges clearly from evidence dating to the late fourth century. Symmachus complains not only that the amount was arbitrarily fixed but that it was excessively heavy.[45] Further, it was not a standardized sum and seems to have grown larger over time.[46] It is known that at the end of the century senators living in Rome were expected to pay their contribution on the spot while those in the provinces paid there.[47]

A law in the Theodosian Code dated to 395 suggests that an annual oblatio may have existed as well and was presented at the New Year.[48] Unfortunately very little is known about it, the method by which it was assessed, or the amounts raised. Theoretically it too was voluntary but its relationship to the oblatio senatoria remains obscure.

aurum coronarium[49]

Again this was a voluntary levy in theory and originated in the gifts of gold crowns made by cities to Hellenistic monarchs, a practice which continued under the Roman empire.[50]

The custom of furnishing actual gold crowns had previously been attested as late as the reign of Aurelian and an Oxyrhyncus papyrus as yet unpublished proves that the custom still held in 316-318.[51] By and large however, payments tended to be made in coin or bullion rather than crowns and the incidence of the tax was probably quinquennial in the early fourth century, although the evidence is not entirely clear on this point.[52] It was regularly paid on occasions of public rejoicing such as imperial accessions, military victories, remissions of tax arrears etc.[53]

Curials were liable to the offering and this category probably included landowners with fairly modest holdings.[54] Since it was a voluntary offering the gold presented was exempted from the usual certification of weight and purity and deficit amounts could not be exacted.[55]

<u>aurum tironicum</u> [56]

The first known instance of this tax occurs about 370. It consisted of a levy in gold as a commutation for the provision of army recruits since the government preferred to enlist barbarian troops at this time.[57] The amount of gold demanded in place of a recruit is not certain and figures of 30, 25, and 80 solidi per man have been recorded.[58]

<u>militaris vestis</u> [59]

This tax was levied for the purpose of supplying the army with uniforms or an equivalent sum of money with which to purchase them.[60] The tax had its origin in compulsory purchases and indictions but must be distinguished from the <u>anabolicae species</u> which seems to have been levied in raw materials.[61]

Although the tax was levied annually, Kent has suggested that it may have been paid in monthly instalments and that collection was normally through city councils.[62] Assessment schedules have survived for Oriens based on a unit of <u>iuga seu capita</u> and Egypt where it was based on <u>arourae</u>. In practice the amounts actually levied on specific communities were often uneven, i.e. involving $\frac{1}{2}$ of a shirt or cloak which made this tax difficult to administer.[63]

<u>Compulsory purchase of gold and silver</u>

The compulsory purchase of gold and silver was not a tax in the narrow sense, but the practice of demanding gold and/or silver from individuals at a price fixed by the government which was lower than the market price was in effect a forced levy.[64]

Most of our information regarding the compulsory purchase of gold in the late third and early fourth centuries is derived from Egyptian papyri. Unfortunately there is considerable difficulty in distinguishing whether a number of these texts refer to compulsory bullion purchases or to a cash tax paid on land. There is no doubt that the Panopolis Papyrus refers to compulsory purchase and the use of the term 'purchase' (συνηνωνή) or a direct reference to the sale of bullion in a number of other papyri seems to support their having been receipts for compulsory purchase as well.[65]

The uncertain texts are receipts for payments in silver or gold but which do not specifically mention its sale or purchase.[66] They fall into two groups; those which employ the phrase τὸν χρύσιον καὶ ἀσήμον as the title of the assessment and those which refer to an <u>epibole</u> paid in gold and silver. What is not certain is whether all of these texts refer to the same or different taxes or to compulsory purchase.

Specific reference is made in some papyri to the assessment being levied on land and Rea has suggested in a re-interpretation of P Oxy 1653 a very plausible mechanism by which this was effected. The extra levy was shared out in proportion to the amount of grain tax paid by the individuals concerned.[67]

It is not clear from these documents however that they represent compulsory bullion purchase rather than a cash tax on land. The use of the term epibole found in P Merton 31, P Thead 33 and P Oxy 1653 might imply an extraordinary rather than normal levy but once again the precise meaning is not clear from the context.[68]

Reference should be made to the χρυσὸς τελωνικός attested in P Panop 19 (338-345) and possibly 15 (309) as well.[69] The problem is to establish what was being taxed. The earlier document is specific; the tax was levied on oil harvested the previous year and presumably was some sort of sales tax. This has led Rea to suggest that may have been identical with the collatio lustralis and he tentatively places the later receipts in this category also.[70]

His theory is certainly possible for No. 15 not only was a trade tax paid early in 309 on sales in 308 but correlates in time with the quinquennalia of Galerius. The later receipts, however, are annual and as was noted above the collatio lustralis was probably a five-yearly tax. Further, the later receipts give no precise indication of what was being taxed and while the editors that they may represent an oil tax, they could equally refer to something else.[71]

The relationship between the aurum comparaticium attested in the Theodosian Code for the diocese of Oriens and the compulsory purchases of bullion in Egypt is not clear.[72] By its name the aurum comparaticium should have been a compulsory purchase and the mention in the same law of the militaris vestis is puzzling. The code states that a fixed levy based on a land assessment (iuga seu capita) was to be established for Oriens accompanied by a reduction in the aurum comparaticium which was also assessed on land (iuga only). However, what is significant is that the aurum comparaticium is an attested instance of compulsory bullion purchase outside Egypt.

The papyri which definitely record the compulsory purchase of gold are almost all early 4th century in date and after c.310 the practice ceased almost entirely. This suggests that it was a short-lived financial measure employed by Diocletian and Galerius. How successful it was is difficult to assess but unless the compulsion imposed by the government was fairly severe it seems unlikely that very many individuals could be persuaded to sell bullion to the treasury at a personal loss to themselves.

The independent existence of a tax assessed on land but paid in bullion also seems attested by the papyri for this period while the χρυσὸς τελωνικός seems to have been based on capitatio as was the collatio lustralis. The difficulties in understanding the nature of these taxes are compounded by the uncertainties which surround the use of the terms iuga and capita.

Nonetheless, a policy existed and was put into practice whereby the government could supplement its precious metal stocks by buying bullion from the public at a fixed price below that of the open market price.

Revenue from state land

In the early fourth century the revenues from state land were collected and administered by the res summa and although later the collection was handled by agents of the res privata the income remained under the control of the sacrae largitiones.[73] Payment was made annually and took the form of gold, silver, and corn.[74]

Civic revenues [75]

At an uncertain date in the first half of the fourth century the revenues from land and taxes of the cities were confiscated by the state. Constantine also confiscated the fundi iuris templorum which provided a further source of revenue for the res summa.[76] The basic revenues in the early fourth century consisted of vectigalia and civic lands were added on a permanent basis after the reforms of A.D. 364-365.[77]

Fines [78]

The income from fines seems to have gone to the CSL in the later fourth century and thus to the res summa in the earlier period. By the end of the century this source of revenue had been almost entirely transferred to the CRP. Examples of the sorts of abuses which were punished by monetary fines included: tomb robbery, unauthorized exactions by the Praetorian Prefect, neglected appeals, and the diversion of public income.[79]

Indirect Taxes [80]

Revenue from indirect taxes falls into two major categories; customs taxes (portoria) and revenue from state-owned mines and quarries.

Mines and Quarries

State-owned mines were normally leased to contractors with the revenues being paid to the res summa in the early fourth century and later to the CSL.[81] By the fourth century the amount of income derived from state-owned mining had declined significantly from that of the principate. Some mines were still directly managed by the state, however, and in Macedonia, Dacia Mediterranea, Moesia, and Dardania they were controlled by procuratores of curial rank.[82] Their principal function was the collection of the amount owing to the treasury which possibly can be identified as the metallicus canon mentioned in the Theodosian Code.[83]

Quarries were both privately owned and state owned. By 376 all were subjected to a tax of ten percent except those belonging to senators.[84] Washing for gold was also regulated by the CSL in the later fourth century although its practice was in private hands. Control took the form of the issue of a license permitting the activity.[85]

The goldwashers fall into two groups: 1) the aurileguli who seem to have been itinerant gold washers and who were restricted geographically in the practice of their profession, normally to the diocese within which they were licensed; and 2) owners or inhabitants of metallica loca which seem in origin to have been estates of the res privata.[86]

Custom Dues

The tightening of the defensive system of the Roman frontier led to the restriction of trade with peoples outside the empire to a few carefully controlled entry points.[87] This made the collection of import and export dues relatively simple and the policing of the entry points was essentially military by the fourth century with the officials being drawn from the staffs of the provincial governors.[88]

The burden of tax collection rested on the curials who were officially designated conductores and contracts were auctioned locally for a period of three years.[89]

The standard charge on all goods exported or entering the empire was 12½% (octavae) and was collected at recognized entry points on the frontier and at specified ports.[90] There were exemptions to the tax but these were rare. Goods restricted to private or agricultural use were exempt as were those imported to pay taxes.[91] Navicularii and veterans were also excused from paying portoria.[92]

Symmachus mentions in protest that he had to pay a quadrigesima or quinquigesima on wild beasts imported for the games at Rome which led Jones to argue that these taxes were survivals of similar sorts of imposts dating to the principate.[93a]

Conclusions

A number of points worth consideration emerge as a result of this analysis of the sources of cash revenue of the res summa in the fourth century, much of which has been based on evidence dated to post 340. First, the government exacted a number of taxes in gold and/or silver, some of which were openly compulsory while others were theoretically voluntary. Second, the collatio lustralis seems to have had a five-year incidence and thus been intended to meet the costs of quinquennial donatives; this may well have been the function of the aurum coronarium and oblatio senatoria as well. The degree to which this correlates with an increased number or volume of gold and silver emissions on these occasions, ought to provide support or its opposite for this theory.

Third, the existence of an additional land tax possibly related to the militaris vestis and compulsory purchases of gold and silver suggest that the government had a real and ongoing need for precious metals which it attempted to supply by these additional levies.

THE MINT SYSTEM AND THE PRODUCTION OF COIN IN THE FOURTH CENTURY

Silver and Bronze Production in the 4th Century

One of the more important areas of responsibility of the CSL was his control of the mint system. While the principle that all mints were under the jurisdiction of the CSL and his officers is undeniable, the manner and extent to which control were exercised are less certain. What prompted the decision to coin and who took it? Current numismatic research suggests that in the ancient world coinage was produced by the state for political and administrative reasons.[93b] However, this view has been challenged and it has been asserted that in the 4th century A.D., at least, bronze coins were minted primarily for economic reasons.[94] Indeed it is argued that mint sites were also chosen with economic considerations in mind using much the same sort of evidence as that adduced to support the opposing view.[95]

These arguments are not as contradictory as they may appear since no matter what consideration prompted the issue of coin in the first instance, once coins were in circulation they would immediately be affected by economic factors. The problem is to determine the extent to which the decision to coin, the amount to be coined, the choice of metals, and when and where coins were to be issued were imperial decisions, and what prompted them.

In seeking an answer to these questions, two kinds of numismatic evidence must be considered, hoards and site finds. Both have been studied in isolation but are rarely examined together to see whether they demonstrate the same sort of pattern. Superficially there are good reasons for this. Hoards are composed of coins which their owner felt were worth saving and later concealing. Stray finds most commonly consist of coins of low value which were lost and not recovered. Thus hoards could and often did represent accumulations of great value while casual finds almost never do. Furthermore it is generally recognized that both kinds of evidence have their limitations.[96]

However the studies by Callu in this volume of the chronology, geographical distribution, and volume of issues of bronze and silver coinage in the fourth century strongly suggest that decisions about what to coin, when, and how much were often made at the highest level.[97]

The pattern of silver emissions which Callu has described can be summarized as follows: after the relatively abundant minting of Diocletian's argenteus, silver issues were extremely sparse until 324 and probably not very large between 324-337 since their survival rate in hoards is very low.[98] Between 337 and 350 policy differences can be seen among Constantine's sons both in regard to the amounts of silver they issued and the denominations they favoured while the size of issues increased. Between 350-358 the West, affected by the usurpation of Magnentius, began to produce substantial issues of silver coins at the Gallic mints. Hoards concealed during this period often contain plate and ingots as well.

Introduction of the siliqua in 358 led to the argenteus being immediately superceded. In 360 the elevation of Julian as Augustus was accompanied by an upsurge in silver production initially in the West and later in the East after he controlled the entire empire. At the beginning of the Valentinianic period (364-367) there seems to have been a large output of silver in the West followed by what seems to have been a sharp decline for approximately 5 years (see Tables 1-2). Again, in the West in the 370s silver production was high, in the East it was low. In the 380s silver output in the West was affected by the usurpation of Magnus Maximus who minted siliquae in abundance at Trier. At the time he moved into Italy Maximus lowered the weight standard of the siliqua from c. 1.9 to c.1.5 g. After the defeat of Maximus the weight standard again rose but was lowered by Eugenius between 392-395 and never again recovered its original weight.

Thus in the West, large silver issues seem to have been produced in periods of war—against barbarians and usurpers, while in the East silver issues seem to have been much smaller on the whole.[99] Differences in policy between the two halves of the empire could therefore result from political considerations and it is clear that decisions were often if not always taken at the highest level. The emission pattern also suggests that output was often linked (as in the case of the Vota issues) to imperial donativa.

Bronze coinage in Callu's view, again based largely on hoard studies, had both a military and a civil purpose.[100] As an instance of its military use, he cites the aes 3 coins minted by Valentinian I which financed the reconstruction of the limes especially on the Danube and in Britain. The civil use of bronze as a trading medium can be seen in the composition of hoards in such areas as Egypt, Africa and Spain.[101]

At times changes in the system of bronze coinage were paralleled by changes in the silver, as for example the introduction of the siliqua in 358 and the new aes 3 coin Spes Reipubice while the cessation of bronze issues c. 367–383 in the East was accompanied by a sharp diminution of silver output in the West and possibly the East as well.[102]

Fulford has charted the evolution of mint representation of the bronze coinage during the fourth century for a number of Western and Eastern sites.[103] His evidence demonstrates the predominance of Trier for the first half of the century and of Arles and Lyons jointly from the 360s onwards on British and Germanic sites. The volume of coinage for given periods is no less interesting and has some significant correlations with the hoard evidence.

Bronze coins of the years 348–364 exist in relatively small numbers on British and Germanic sites and are equally rare in hoards, especially if imitations are excluded.[104] For example the Western sites analysed by Fulford yield the following figures

Britain	%	Germany & Luxembourg	%
Canterbury	14.7	Dalheim-Ricciacus	7.2
Cirencester	4.7	Mainz	2.5
Nettleton	8.1	Rheinzabern	0.0
Portchester	4.3	Speyer	3.5
Verulamium	8.1	Trier	3.7
Wanborough	4.6		

Alps	%	Portugal	%
Bregenz	20.6	Conimbriga	32.8
Chur	23.5		
Vindonissa	6.6		

The variant pattern suggested for the Alpine areas and for Spain (Conimbriga) suggest that bronzes of 348–364 reached Chur and Bregenz in larger proportions than Vindonissa but the number of coins available for analysis (102, 136 and 1037 respectively) varies sufficiently in quantity to render inferences tentative.[106] Callu has noted substantial numbers of bronzes of these years in Africa, Asia and on the Danube and their relative rarity in German and British hoards which he ascribes to the effects of the Germanic invasions and the usurpation of Magnentius.[107] It seems reasonable to suggest, then, that any attempt to assess the effects of trade on mint output should be set within the context of contemporary political events. These could obviously obstruct the free circulation of coin, prevent its production, or lead directly or indirectly to increased production of issues.

Representation of bronze coins of 348-364 from Eastern sites again seem to correlate with Callu's statement that these coins are relatively abundant in hoards.[108]

Site	%
Antioch	19.2
Athens	21.9
Corinth	27.8
Curium	13.7
Troy	11.5

It must be stressed that these figures provide evidence of a general correlation but that as yet the number of sites is too few for these conclusions to be accepted without reservations. What it does suggest is that comparison of many more sites from all parts of the empire (a task rendered extremely difficult owing to the lack of published finds from the East) may compare well with the composition of hoards of similar dates.

The behaviour of the bronze coinage c. 367-383 does not unfortunately demonstrate any very clear correlation between the hoarding pattern and site finds since the latter are abundant in most areas while hoards are common only on the Rhine. During these years Spain and Africa apparently continued to use the coinage minted c.348-60 and the evidence suggests new specie was slow to arrive and circulate throughout the province.[109]

Finally Callu's evidence demonstrates very clearly that if one is ever to understand either the reasons underlying the issue of coins or their behaviour once they were in circulation, that it will be necessary to see how the production of gold, silver and bronze was interrelated, and whether for example silver tended to be produced in conjunction with bronze and/or gold or in their absence. The relationship between output in the 3 metals coupled with the sort of political considerations mentioned above and the economic implications which necessitated the frequent "reforms" of the coinage in the 4th century would have had a significant effect on the decision of what to coin, when and where.

Mint Location

It has long been realised that the location of mints bears a reasonably close but by no means absolute relationship to the diocesan structure.[110] The evolution of the regional mint system was clearly linked to the fiscal, and administrative reforms of Diocletian and since the res summa and later the sacrae largitiones would have needed a regional structure in order to perform many of their functions, it is scarcely surprising that it often paralleled the diocesan pattern. The areas of non-correlation between the diocesan and regional organization of the CSL are equally comprehensible in a broad sense since the functions and needs of the prefectural/diocesan system would have been different in many instances from those of the two main treasuries (res privata and sacrae largitiones).

How then did the regional structure of the res summa and sacrae largitiones function, how does the location of mints relate to this function and what changes and developments took place during the course of the 4th century? Much of our information is based on the entries in the Notitia Dignitatum under the CSL Orientis and Occidentis and from it we know the CSL included under his responsibilities not only the control of a number of mints, but treasuries and factories as well.[111]

Fourth century mints fall into two categories: 1) those which can be designated as 'stable', i.e. in operation for most if not the entire period, and 2) those which operated for a brief span of years and then ceased. Table 3 gives the pattern of mint opening and closures for the years 294-337, and from it several points emerge quite clearly: 1) mints could be opened, transferred, and closed for brief or longer periods of time (or even permanently) without seriously affecting the operation of the system; 2) the changing pattern in the West, for example, after 324 when London and Ticinum were closed more-or-less permanently (c. 325-6) suggests that alterations to the system were not haphazard and probably conformed to what would have been defined as general monetary policy; 3) the system was flexible enough to adapt readily to short-term needs as, for example, the establishment of the mint at Ostia (which subsequently moved to Arles) or at Serdica while Thessalonica was closed. Who made the decisions as to which mints worked and when is not known, unfortunately, but for the first half of the 4th century it almost certainly would have been a decision made by the res summa at the central level.

M. Hendy has demonstrated that the 'stable' mints correlate in an approximate way with the diocesan system. For example, in the first quarter of the 4th century, the main mints (by diocese) were:[112]

	DIOCESE	MINT	SUBSIDIARY MINTS	DATES
	BRITANNIAE	LONDON Closed c. 326		
	GALLIAE	TRIER		
		LYONS		
	VIENNENSIS	ARLES opens 313		
OCCIDENTIS	ITALIA	TICINUM Closed c.326		
		AQUILEIA		
	SUBURBICARIA	ROME	OSTIA	308-313
	AFRICA	CARTHAGE c. 297-307		
	PANNONIAE	SISCIA	SIRMIUM	320-326

cont....

	DIOCESE	MINT	SUBSIDIARY MINTS	DATES
	MOESIAE	THESSALONICA 298-303	SERDICA	303-307
	THRACIA	HERACLEA 294-5, 308-12		
ORIENTIS		CONSTANTINOPLE Opened 326		
	ASIANA	CYZICUS 294-9, 305-12		
	PONTICA	NICOMEDIA 294-7, 305-12		
	ORIENS	ANTIOCH 294-312		
	AEGYPTUS	ALEXANDRIA 294-312		

In the West the Notitia also lists 12 treasuries, most of which were located in the same cities as the mints: London, Trier, Arles, Rome, Aquileia and Siscia have both, only Ticinum was omitted, but Milan is included which may well reflect the fact that by the time the Notitia was drawn up Milan was an active mint and Ticinum had long been closed.[113]

Treasuries also existed where mints didn't; i.e. Salona (Dalmatia), Savaria (Pannonia), Augusta Vindelicarum (Raetia) and Remi (Gaul). Unfortunately the list of mints, treasuries and factories in the Eastern half of the empire is not given in the Notitia, only the fact that they existed, but it is reasonable to suppose that in many instances the location of a mint and treasury would coincide. Finally it should be pointed out that some dioceses either had no mint, i.e. Spain, or had one only briefly (Carthage in Africa) for reasons that are not altogether clear. Neither Spain nor Africa had a treasury either and were singularly lacking in factories (two in Africa, a gynaecium at Carthage and a baphium at Girba). The implication that mints, treasuries and factories are linked to army presence is unmistakable and they cluster fairly thickly in Gaul and N. Italy for example.[114]

The existence of a complex regional structure for Spain and Africa under the Pretorian prefects and its much less developed form under the CSL can probably be explained by the fact that tax collection in both dioceses certainly necessitated a structure by which this could be effected, but mints, treasuries, factories etc. would be located in areas where the government would be distributing coin as goods, normally to the army or high ranking officials.[115]

Thus both mints and treasuries seem to have been located in centres of administrative importance, not on the frontiers but not far from them, almost always on rivers or the sea which presumably made it easier to transport bullion and/or coin.

In the earlier 4th century most mints could and often did produce gold, silver, or bronze although there was a gradually increasing tendency for the striking of precious metal coinage to be restricted to the emperor's presence. Hendy has rightly pointed out that the so-called 'stable' mints are to be equated with monetae publicae whose main function in the later 4th century was the production of bronze coinage.[116] Indeed some like London and Lugdunum (294-c. 337) and Alexandria (post 312) never struck in gold while others did so only rarely. The transient mints in Hendy's view often served a specific short term military objective, as, for example, Sirmium which struck mainly gold but also small issues of copper and silver from 320-326 and was in operation sporadically during the second half of the 4th century.[117] The mints of Rome and later Constantinople stood somewhat outside the 4th century regional system since Rome had been, and Constantinople became, the principal residence of the emperor. Both were 'stable' mints and produced coins in gold, silver and bronze but Constantinople became increasingly important while Rome grew less so.

Between 363-368 a number of financial reforms were undertaken by Valentinian I and Valens which included the following measures: 1) taxes would hencefourth be exacted by the staffs of provincial governors and diocesan vicars; 2) all taxes were to be paid in bullion only and the metal was to be tested for purity; 3) any deficiency in weight or fineness would be made up by the taxpayer. Thus after 364 all gold was brought to the comitatus and the minting of gold coin was confined to the imperial residence.[118] These measures had far-reaching implications not only in terms of the mints which produced coins but on the power of the CSL.

The pattern of mint operation in the later 4th century illustrates that the *monetae publicae* continued in operation but that their main function was the production of copper coin. Certain mints like Milan which opened *c.* 364-402 have been distinguished from *monetae publicae* on grounds that they did not mint copper coins and can thus be considered comitatensian mints as can the brief reactivation of London under Magnus Maximus. Hendy has documented instances of the effect that rapid movement of the *comitatus* had on the production of gold at various mints which included movement of personnel, the minting of Eastern types at Western mints etc.[119] Equally prolonged imperial residence at Trier, Milan or Ravenna in the West and Constantinople and Antioch in the East resulted in a concentration of gold issues from these cities. Thus the mint system in operation from 364-395 can be briefly summarized as follows:

DIOCESE	MINT	METALS COINED	TRANSIENT MINT	METALS COINED	DATES
BRITANNIAE			LONDON	AV, AR	383-8
GALLIAE	TRIER	AV, AR, AE			
VIENNENSIS	LYONS	AV, AR, AE			
	ARLES	AV, AR, AE			
ITALIA			MILAN	AV, AR	364-83, 388-402
	AQUILEIA	AV, AR, AE			
SUBURBICARIA	ROME	AV, AR, AE			
PANNONIAE	SISCIA	AV, AR, AE	SIRMIUM	AV, AR, AE	364,
				AV, AR	378-83, 393-5.
DACIAE	THESSALONICA	AV, AR, AE			
THRACIA	HERACLEA	AV (364 only) AE			
	CONSTANTINOPOLIS	AV, AR, AE			
ASIANA	CYZICUS	AV, AR (364 only) AE			
ORIENS	ANTIOCH	AV, AR, AE			
AEGYPTUS	ALEXANDRIA	AE			

It can be readily seen that the production of gold was much more restricted in the East than the West after 364 and the difference is in part explicable by the more unsettled situation in the West.

Not only were the taxes of the CSL being collected in the form of gold bullion in the latter half of the 4th century but certain taxes paid to the praetorian prefect in kind were in process of being aedaerated, i.e. transmuted to money payments in gold. This, coupled with the responsibility for collection of the CSL's revenues which was now under the diocesan and provincial governor's jurisdiction, and thus within the control of the praetorian prefect, meant that the power of the latter slowly began to increase at the expense of the CSL and CRP. The Praetorian Prefects had the only variable income, depending on the amount of the yearly indiction, while the revenues of the CSL were fixed.

Certain changes in the coinage system itself were also taking place which must in some sense reflect the changes in the way taxes were being collected and more important, how the government was making its payments.

A direct result of Diocletian's reforms had been the gradual shift from paying taxes in debased argentiferous bronze coinage to paying in kind or in gold (and more rarely silver). Equally, the government expected to pay salaries in kind or in precious metals. By the 360s government interest in gold and in controlling it had increased sharply partly because it needed to collect taxes in gold in order to have a sufficient supply to pay out.

The earlier half of the century had seen the production of large issues of argentiferous bronze coinage from which the government had clearly derived a profit since the coins were overvalued in terms of their intrinsic worth. This fact, which had not failed to reach the public's attention, coupled with the the government's reluctance to reaccept these bronze coins in the form of taxes etc., had a number of disastrous results. The first was that since they did not have unstinting public acceptance they were revalued in terms of a 'market rate' which was substantially lower than the official rate. The official response to this seems to have taken two forms. Firstly, the government tried from time to time to 'reform' the coinage by increasing its weight and/or silver content but without success. The more highly silvered coins which one suspects were again unrealistically over valued were melted down and forged. The final attempt at the sort of reform which involved an increase in silver content took place c. 348 with the issue of the FEL TEMP series. Once the government had recognized the failure of this reform, it abandoned permanently any notion of adding minute quantities of silver to the bronze coinage.

As noted above from the 360s to the 380s bronze issues were abundant in Gaul and probably the West in general (output at Siscia seems to have been unusually high) except at Trier where production dropped after 348.[120] Much the same sort of process had overtaken the silver.

The 370s and 380s saw the undisputed dominance of Trier as the main silver producing mint in the West while in the late 380s and 390s the balance shifted to Milan. After c. 410 silver issues were very small and sporadic.[121] The silver issues produced in Italy c. 387–402 show a drop in the weight standard from c. 1.9 g to c. 1.5 g and fractions weighing 1 g were also minted.[122] The output of bronze at the western mints also seems to have declined sharply after A.D. 400 while the gold coinage saw the introduction of the tremis in the 380s. All of this attests a significant change in the monetary system in the West in which increasing emphasis was placed on minting gold while silver and bronze issues virtually lapsed.

The causes of the change are in part linked to the aedaeration of taxes in kind to gold but not entirely. The West was apparently unique in its minting of silver in abundant quantities from c. 350–400 since the same pattern does seem to be reflected in the East. As suggested above this difference probably resulted from somewhat different fiscal policies followed by the Eastern and Western halves of the Empire.[123] After 400 however, the West seems to have concentrated on producing gold coin.

The reasons for this shift in policy are obscure but must have been related to the decisions regarding the payments made to soldiers and state functionaries and the form in which they were made.

Unfortunately we are ill informed on this point. Such evidence as does exist quotes military and civil salaries in precious metals as in kind.[124] Accepting the testimony of the sources leaves one with the necessity of explaining the function and volume of the bronze coinage in the 4th century. Hendy has suggested that the survival of monetae publicae in the East minting copper arose from the government's need to ensure a stable gold coinage which could be recovered from the public through taxes.[125] The abundant 4th century bronze issues must have served some sort of similar exchange purpose although the precise workings of the system are not always clear. One obvious explanation, although unfortunately undemonstrable, is that if soldiers were paid in precious metals, the moment they wanted to buy things they would need to exchange it. The bronze coinage could be used as "change" and to the extent the government could control the exchange rate, they profited.

No discussion of the 4th century coinage system should exclude the role played by plate and bullion. Not only did it form a significant part of the "cash" and bullion reserve as, for example, the frequent occurrence of silver bowls,ewers, jewellery, candle-sticks, and ingots in hoards attests but its presence suggests an attitude toward precious metals including coinage which is mirrored in the structure of the officium of the CSL and its expenditure.[126] The insignia of the CSL (and the CRP for that matter) include bowls of coins, belt buckles, gold leaves etc.[127] Bowls, fibulae, and rings inscribed with imperial vota have been found and clearly formed part of high ranking individuals' salaries.[128] Thus any attempt to calculate salaries in the 4th century must also take into account payments made in this form since they seem to have been reckoned by weight and the implication is that they were carefully scaled to a person's rank.[129] It has been suggested earlier in this paper that the aurifices specierum who served in the scrinium auri massae may have been responsible for the production of these objects.

The decision to produce precious metal objects rather than coin would inevitably have affected the stocks of bullion available to be minted. Whether or not this was the reason for the decline in silver coinage in the 5th century (and its apparently more restricted emission in the East in the 4th) is problematical. The other obvious explanation for its dwindling importance could have been a shortage of silver. Current evidence does not indicate which of these alternatives may have resulted in a decision to coin less silver, or even if there was another cause altogether.

It would be extremely interesting to learn how large issues of gold, silver, and bronze were in the 4th century. Sadly, this is a topic on which numismatists have not spent much time. There are two possible approaches: the first is to attempt to estimate the amount produced by looking at the number of issues found in hoards and seeing how large they are. This can give the size of issues relative to one another but not an absolute figure.[130] A more profitable approach would be a die study since once all dies are collected one can make a mathematical estimate of the size of issues. Such an analysis could almost certainly be pursued with profit for 4th century gold coinage but a preliminary examination of the silver issues suggests that in many cases issues were really rather large since they do not die link readily.[131]

CONCLUSIONS

This paper has tried briefly to trace the emergence and development of the sacrae largitiones during the 4th century and to discuss the evolution of the mint system and the coinage. It seems clear that the mint system, particularly in regard to the production of issues of gold and silver underwent an evolution during the course of the 4th century which was linked to changes in the collection of taxes and an increasing government need to control the flow of gold in and out of the treasury.

The choice of when to coin and the amounts to be minted were apparently made at the central level as were major changes to the system. Political events seem to have had a significant effect on the output of coinage in the 4th century, particularly in the West. Differences in minting policy between the Western and Eastern halves can often be demonstrated, but rarely if ever seem to reflect purely economic consideration although once it had been put into circulation the coinage could be affected by economic factors.

The decision to open and close mints for shorter or longer periods of time seem to have been linked to administrative or political convenience. What emerges from an examination of their behaviour in the 4th century is the flexibility of the system. Mints could often be transferred, closed, or new ones pressed into service without any apparent dislocation of the distribution and circulation of coin. The dislocations that occurred seem to have been linked to the amount of coin supplied to an area rather than which mints produced it. Thus, for example, between 348 and 364 in Britain and on the Rhine there seems to have been a shortage of new coins which is reflected by their relatively small numbers in hoards and on sites and the relatively large amounts of contemporary imitations.

Further studies of 4th century hoards, site finds, and the chronology of gold, silver and bronze emissions and their interrelationship should help us understand more clearly how coin functioned in both a political/administrative context and an economic one. Whatever else seems true at this stage it is an oversimplification to define decline in terms of an inflation resulting from an overproduction of bronze coin.

Table 1 Regular Siliquae Issues in the West 364-395

Lustrum	Main Reverse Types	Trier	Lyons	Arles	Aquileia	Milan	Rome
363-368	RESTITVTOR REIP	V_I*	V_I, Val	V_I, Val	V_I, Val		
368-373							
373-378	VRBS ROMA (throne)	V_I, Val, Gr					
	VRBS ROMA (cuirass)	Val, Gr, V_{II}, Th	Gr		Val, Gr, V_{II}		
378-383	CONCORDIA AVGGG	Gr, Th	Gr, Th		Th		
	VICTORIA AVGGG	V_{II}	V_{II}		V_{II}		
	VICTORIA AVGG				Gr, V_{II}, Th		
	VIRTVS ROMANORVM (throne)	Gr, Th, V_{II}			Gr, V_{II}, Th		
	VRBS ROMA (throne)						Gr, Th, Ar
383-388	VIRTVS ROMANORVM (throne)	Th, MM, FV			FV		
	CONCORDIA AVGGG	Th, MM			V_{II}, Th, Arc, MM	V_{II}, Th	
	VICTORIA AVGVSTORVM				FV, MM		
388-393	VIRTVS ROMANORVM(cuir)	V_{II}, Th, Arc, Eug					
	VRBS ROMA (cuir)	V_{II}, Th, Arc	V_{II}, Th, Arc, Eug				
393-(398)	VIRTVS ROMANORVM(cuir)					Th, Arc, Eug	
	SPES ROMANORVM						Th
	VICTORIA AVGGG				Arc, Hon	Th, Arc, Hon	

*Abbreviations:
Arc - Arcadius
Eug - Eugenius
FV - Flavius Victor
Gr - Gratian
Hon - Honorius
Th - Theodosius
V_I - Valentinian I
Val - Valens
V_{II} - Valentinian II

Table 2 Siliqua Vota Coinages

Possible date		Trier	Lyons	Aquileia	Milan	Rome
368–9	VOTIS V MVLTIS **X**	V_I*				
	VOT V MVLT **X**	Val	Val	V_I		V_I Val
	VOT **X** MVLT XV	Val, Grat				
373–4	VOT **X** MVLT **XX**		Val			
or	VOTIS **X** MVLTIS **XX**			Val, Grat		
377–8						
380	VOTIS V MVLTIS **X**			V_{II}		
380	VOT V MVLT X	V_{II}, Th				
380	VOT V MVLTIS **X**	V_{II}				
382–4	VOT **X** MVLTIS XV	Gr, Th				
382	VOT XV MVLTIS **XX**	Gr				
382	VOT XV MVLT **XX**	Gr				
387–8	VOT V MVLT **X**				Arc	
392–3	VOT **X** MVLT XV				Hon, Arc	
388–9	VOT **X** MVLT **XX**				V_{II}, Th	

* For Abbreviations see Table 1

Mint Openings and Closures A. D. 294-337

Diocese and Mint		294-297	298-302	303-307	308-312	313-317	318-322	323-327	328-332	333-337
PARTES OCCIDENTIBVS										
Britanniae -	London	Not under imp. cont.	X	X	Closed 308 Open 310	X	X	Closed 325	-	-
Galliae	Lyons	X	X	X	Closed 310	Open 314	X	Closed 325	Open 330	X
	Trier	X	X	X	Closed 310 Open 312	Closed 314 Open 316	X	X	X	X
Viennensis	Arles	-	-	-	-	X	X	X	X	X
Hispaniae		-	-	-	-	-	-	-	-	-
Africa	Carthage	Open 296	X	X	Closed 311	-	-	-	-	-
Italia	Ticinum	X	X	X	Closed 310 Open 312	X	Closed 318 Open 320	Closed 327	-	-
	Aquileia	X	X	X	Closed 309 Open 312	Closed 315 Open 316	Closed 318 Open 320	Closed 322 Open 324-6	-	Open 337
Suburbicaria	Rome	X	X	X	X	X	X	Closed 322 Open 325 Closed 326	Closed 328 Open 330	Open 334
	Ostia	-	-	-	X	-	-	-	-	-
Pannoniae	Siscia	X	X	X	Closed 308 ?	X	X	X	X	X
	Sirmium	-	-	-	-	-	Open 320	Closed 326	-	-

Table 3 (contd.)

Diocese and Mint		294-297	298-302	303-307	308-312	313-317	318-322	323-327	323-327	333-337
PARTES ORIENTIS										
Moesiae	Serdica	-	-	X	-	Open 313-4	-	-	-	-
	Thessalonica	-	Open 298	-	X	X	X	Closed 322	X	X
Thracia	Heraclea	Closed 295	-	X	X	X	Closed 322	Open 324	X	X
	Constantinople	-	-	-	-	-	-	Open 326	X	X
Asiana -	Cyzicus	X	Closed 299	Open 305	X	X	X	X	X	X
Pontica -	Nicomedia	X	-	Open 305	X	X	X	X	Closed 331	Open 335
Oriens	Antioch	X	X	X	X	X	X	X	X	Closed 333/5
	Alexandria	X	X	X	X	X	X	X	Closed 330	Open 334

NOTES

1. Jones, Later Roman Empire (LRE) (2nd ed.) 427ff. gives a summary account of the CSL and his function. The most complete and best account is J. P. C. Kent's PhD thesis 'The Office of Comes Sacrarum Largitionum, London, 1951, hereafter referred to as CSL, unfortunately unpublished on on which I have drawn heavily in this paper. For specific aspects of the CSL's responsibilities in regard to the mint system see Kent in Essays in Roman Coinage Presented to Harold Mattingly, 1956, 190ff; Michael Hendy Univ. of Birmingham Hist. Journal, XII, 1971, 129ff. JRS 62, 1972, 75ff.; NC 1972, 117ff. Kent also has a brief discussion of the CSL in Dumbarton Oak Studies 1961, 35ff. as does Lafaurie in his discussion of the Chécy hoard, Gallia Supplement XII, 1958, 299ff. The most recent discussion is that of R. Delmaire in Les dévaluations a Rome, Collection de l'école française de Rome, 37, 1978.

2. Kent, the Office of CSL, 2ff. See also in this volume F. Millar, "The Privata from Dicletian to Theodosius: Documentary Evidence," 125ff. for a definition and assessment of the role of the privata in the 4th century which is an expansion of his discussion in The Emperor in the Roman World, 1977, Appendix 2.

3. Dio, 79 (80), 21 who refers to him as τοὺς.... καθόλου λόγους ἐπιτετραμμένος Masi, Res Privata, 1971, pp. 5ff. thinks that the ratio privata was in existence by the time of Pius and its autonomous existence can be documented in the reign of Commodus. See also Nesselhaus, HA Coll., 1963, pp. 73ff. and Millar, this volume, 126ff.

4. magistri rei summae: Dessau 1347 (CIL 8, 822); CIL 8, 23948 (Pflaum, Carrières, no. 327; CIL 6, 1618; 32045; Eus. HE, 8, 11, 2. According to Kent, CSL, p. 2, note 12 his subordination to the rationalis is established by Dessau 1214 (CIL 6, 1704). magistri rei privatae: Dessau 1347 (CIL 8, 822); CJ 3,22, 5; Lact. de mort pers, VII, 4; CIL 3, 18; CTh 10, 1, 4 (320); 11, 19, 1; 12, 1, 14 (date disputed); Firm Mat. IV, 21, 9; Athan. ap ad const 10, 12. Millar (see note 2) has observed that the use of the term ratio privata is much more common in the 3rd and early 4th centuries. The expression res privata in the singular is rarely found in the legal codes until after c. 340.

5. CIL 6, 1115.

6. See Jones, LRE, Chap XIII, note 43 (p. 1174). The list in note 11 which includes some references mentioned by Jones does not distinguish between the diocesan and central officials.

7. Jones, LRE, Appendix I. The overlap in function apparently continued since Jones lists and discusses certain laws in the Theodosian Code addressed to the CSL and CRP in the later 4th and 5th centuries which suggest that a certain ambiguity of function existed. Kent, CSL, 5-6

lists instances of the rationalis dealing with matters technically in the jurisdiction of the res privata between A.D. 260-330 but Jones has argued that CJ 3, 22, 5 and CTh 10, 1, 2 indicate sufficient flexibility in the use of titles at this time to make it difficult to draw rigid distinctions. See also Masi, Res Privata, pp. 80ff. and Millar, this volume, 126ff.

8. Kent, CSL, pp. 7-8 and notes, cites the following texts: Pliny, Ep, 10, 27-8; CIL 3, 1099; 1477=7979 (establishing beneficiarii in provincial officia rationum at an early date); CTh 8, 7,7, (361); beneficiarii; C Th 9, 3, 1, (320) stratores; CTh 12, 6, 2; tabularii; Amm. 28, 2, 13; CTh 5, 15, 18 (368) praecones; CTh 6, 30, 2 (379) princeps officii of the comes domorum; CJ, 10, 1, 5 (285-93); CTh 10, 8, 2 (319); CTh 10, 1, 5 (326) Caesariani.

9. Kent, CSL, 5 and note 20; Millar, this volume, 126ff. notes the discontinuity of the evidence in the 3rd century within Egypt and its absence outside Egypt.

10. ibid. 9ff.

11. Not. Dig., Or. XIII; Occ. XI.

12. ibid.; for Gaul see CTh 6, 19, 1 (400). Kent notes that the usual term for these officials in the east is comes thesaurorum (CTh 8, 7, 14 (377); 23 (426).

13. Kent, CSL, 15ff. He regards Seeck's insertion of rationales summarum in the East as unjustified.

14. Kent, CSL, 9-15 and note 94 from which this account has been summarized. Also CTh 10, 19, 3 (370); 19, 1 (320).

15. CJ, 12, 23, 7 (384); CTh 6, 30, 7 (384).

16. CTh 6, 35, 3 (352); the date is contested. See Kent, CSL, 8.

17. Kent, CSL, 33ff. and CTh 8, 7, 6 (354). The date of this constitution is disputed (Kent, CSL, 250ff.).

18. Kent, ibid., 35ff.; Jones LRE, 427ff. This account is based on theirs and I have cited the relevant sources.

19. CTh 2, 30, 5 (386); 10, 20, 18 (436).

20. CTh 10, 20, 18 (436).

21. CTh 6, 30, 8-9 (385); 22 (419); 23 (422); cf. Gloss Basil, ap du Cange gloss med et inf graec.

22. Amm 22, 9, 11; CTh 6, 26, 18 (426).

23. Kent, CSL, 40.

24. Kent, ibid., 39; Jones LRE, 428; Hendy NC, 1972, 124. Hendy states that the technicians aurifices specierum solidorum etc. did not form scrinia but doesn't group them where they seem logically to belong, i.e. under the control of the scrinium auri massae. Accepting the latter arrangement would seem to weaken his suggestion that the scrinium auri ad responsum also dealt with coin, although it doesn't exclude it.

25. Kent, CSL, 40. CJ 12, 23, 7 (384) reads scrinium ad militum.

26. Kent, ibid., 42.

27. For the basic discussion of this tax see Seeck, collatio lustralis, PW, IV, 370ff.; Kent, CSL, 69ff.; Jones, LRE, 4ff. and notes; Karayannopulos, Finanzwesen, 129ff.; Chastagnol, HA Coll., 1964/5, 43ff.

28. Zos II, 38, 2; supported by CTh 7, 20, 3 (320/5). Contra see Evag. HE, 3, 39. The Syro-Roman law book, FIR, 2nd ed. II, p. 794 states that Constantine gave the clergy immunity from the tax; Chron. Pasch., p. 525 a. a. 325 states that he remitted it on his vicennalia.

29. Kent, CSL, p. 71 citing Zon XIV, 3, 11 ff. On capitatio see Déleage, la capitation, Jones LRE, 62ff. and notes; Jones, JRS, 1957, 90ff; Karayannopulos, Finanzwesen, 28ff.; Lact de mort pers, XXIII, 2. The unit of taxation for capitatio appears to have been men and animals but was in the late fourth century, if not sooner, assessed in the form of cash. Kent, ibid., 69 and note 5; Jones, LRE, 63; Varady, Acta Archaeologica, 1962, 408ff. offers a stimulating discussion of the meaning of capitatio.

30. CTh 7, 20, 3 (326 ?); CTh 13, 1. 2 (360); 11 (379); 14 (385).

31. Kent, CSL, 71ff.; Amundsen, Ostraca Osloënsia, 64-8; on the indiction cycle see Kase, A Papyrus Roll, 25ff.

32. CTh 7, 20, 3 (326 ?); 13, 1, 2 (360); 7, 20, 9 (366); 13, 1, 7 (369); 14, (385); 7, 21, 3 (396).

33. Kent, CSL, 75ff. and notes; Jones, LRE, Chap. 13, note 52 (p. 1178).

34. Joshua Stylites, 31, records a quinquennial payment of 140 lb. gold by Edessa and Zon XIV, 3, 11 that one νόμισμα ἀργουροῦν was levied for each man, horse, mule, or ox and 6 folles for each ass and dog. Both these writers are late which weakens the belief one can have in their accuracy.

35. Seeck, PW IV, 375-6; Kent, CSL, 86ff.; Karayannopulos, Finanzwesen, 126ff.; Jones, LRE, Chap. 13, note 13, (p. 1176). Unfortunately the early legislation dealing with this tax has been lost and is not in the Theodosian Code (CTh 6, 2, 1-11) which makes it difficult to discuss the early period.

36. Zos II, 38, 4; CTh 6, 2, 15 (10) (393).

37. CTh 6, 4, 21 (372). All senators were considered as clarissimi for tax purposes and sons born after their elevation to the Senate were also liable. See also CJ 12, 1, 11 (377). In 383 Theodosius created a 4th class whose liability was 7 folles (CTh 6, 2, 15 (383). Hesychius FHG, 4, p. 154 states that the assessment was in pounds of gold but on the evidence of Zosimus (note 36 above) and CTh 6, 2, 13 the unit of assessment was folles.

38. Jones, LRE p. 431 equates it with 125 miliarenses or 5 solidi. In JRS, 1959. pp. 34ff. Jones argues that the tax as imposed by Constantine was

levied in silver and cites Epiphanius (Met. Script. Rel. I, 269) who records that a follis was made up of 125 silver coins. Jones' attempts to reconstruct value relationships between gold and silver are problematical What is clear is that the relationship between gold and silver would have been much more stable than that between gold and the argentiferous bronze coinage.

39. CTh 6, 2, 13 (383); 2, 17 (397); Symm. Ep 5, 55; Not. Dig., Occ. 4, 8, 31; Seeck, censuales, PW 3, 1911; Sinnigen, The Officium of the Urban Prefecture. 70ff.

40. Symm. rel, 46.

41. CTh 6, 2, 13 (383); 26 (428); 23 (414); 26, 14 (407); 23, 1 (415); 4 (427); 24, 7 (414); 8, 9 (416); 10 (427); 11 (432); 25, 1 (416); 27, 6 (390); 22 (428); 13, 3, 15 (393); 16 (414); 19 (428).

42. Kent, CSL, 90ff.; Karayannopulos, Finanzwesen, 141ff.; Jones, LRE, 430ff. and note 50.

43. Dio, 78, 9, 3; CTh 6, 2, 25 (425); Symm. Rel, 13.

44. Them. Or, 3.

45. Symm. Ep, 2, 57.

46. ibid.

47. CTh 6, 2, 16 (395); 20 (397).

48. Karayannopulos, Finanzwesen, 137ff.; CTh 7, 24, 1.

49. Kent. CSL, 92ff.; Karayannopulos, Finanzwesen, 144ff.; Jones, LRE, 430 and note 49.

50. P Oxy 1413. See also Bowman, BASP, 4, 1967, 59ff for a history of the aurum coronarium in Egypt from Augustus to Diocletian.

51. P Oxy 3121.

52. Lallemand, l'administration, 205. In the principate it was annual; see Bowman, op.cit., 59ff. P Lond 966 supports its having been quinquennial although P Lond 1297 (4th century) and O Strasb 289 (314/5 ?) seem to refer to an annual tax. Perhaps as in the case of the oblatio senatoria some sort of double system operated.

53. Eunapius, Fr, 15, 29; CTh 12, 13, 4 (379); Them., Or, 14 D.

54. Kent, CSL, 93.

55. CTh 12, 13, 4.

56. Kent, CSL, 102ff.; Karayannopulos, Finanzwesen, 119ff.; Jones, LRE, 432 and note 54.

57. Amm., 31, 4, 6; Soc. HE, 4, 34; Soz., HE, 6, 36; CTh 7, 13, 3 (370).

58. Soc., HE, 4, 34 (80 solidi); CTh 13, 2, 13 (397) (25 solidi); 20 (410) (30 solidi).

59. Kent, CSL 79ff.; Karayannopulos, Finanzwesen, 112ff. Jones, LRE, 433 and note 56; Boak, JRS, 1947, 30ff.; Persson, Staat und Manufaktur, 97ff.; Segre, Byzantion, 1942/3, 418ff.

60. CTh 7, 6, 4 (396). The standard of quality required to is referred to in Diocletian's Price Edict as χλαμοῦς στρατιωτικὴ ἰνδικτιονάλια (19, 1a) and στίχη ἰνδικτιωνάλια (19, 2).

61. See note 33. The anabolicum was originally a tax in kind on the principal products of industry, later commuted to cash payments. For compulsory purchase see P Cair Isid 54; P Antinop 39, P Lond 1659. The anabolicae species was probably established by Aurelian and meant a return to the original system of payments in kind. At a time when the coin in which the tax was paid was heavily debased, it was a practical measure. See SHA, Aurelian, 45, 1; Wallace, Taxation in Egypt, 214ff.

62. CTh 7, 6, 2 (368) cited by Kent, CSL, 83 refers to a 7 month indiction which makes the normal form of payment impossible.

63. Oriens: CTh 7, 6, 3 (377) where it seems to have been related to a concurrent reduction in the titulus auri comparaticii. This was probably a compulsory purchase of gold and will be discussed below. Egypt: P Oxy, 1905. For assessments in fractions see: P. Lond, 1259; P Oxy, 1448; P Warren 7; P Oslo 119. By the end of the fourth century the tax had been commuted for cash.

64. P Beatty Panop 2, 215ff. where the fact that citizens were selling bullion at a personal loss is deplored but the practice was not abandoned.

65. P Oxy 2106 (early 4th century); PSI 310 (306); SB 9253 (= P Iand Inv. 315). Rea in CE, 1974, 163ff. furnishes an extremely useful re-assessment of the texts, problems arising from them and argues convincingly that this levy was by definition collected in gold and silver bullion and not commuted to payments in bronze as Johnson and West thought, Currency, 161. see also Bowman, in this volume 27, 31ff.

66. P Cair Isid, 69 (307); P Oxy 1524 (early 4th cent.); P Thead 33 (312); P Oxy 1653; (306); P Merton 31 (307); P Ryl 616 (312); P Strasb 262. The alternatives which have been suggested postulated that these documents represent payments of aurum tironicum or aurum coronarium.

67. Rea, CE, 1974, 168. The phrasing in the other papyri which state that the assessment was on land is compatible with this explanation. (P Cair Isid, 69; 127; P Thead 33; P Merton 31.

68. Lallemand, l'administration, 302; Jones, LRE, 432.

69. Youtie, Hagedorn, and Youtie, ZPE, 8, 1971, 208-9; 214ff.

70. Rea, CE, 1974, 168-9.

71. One of the receipts mentions the term ἐπικεφάλιον which again implies the tax was based on capitatio.

72. CTh 7, 6, 3 (377); 11, 9, 2 (337); conceivably as an oblique reference to the same relationship between militaris vestis and a money tax (...vel etiam ob vestium auri argentique debitum quae annua exactione solvuntur...)

73. Kent, CSL, 95ff.

74. Gold: CTh 11, 16, 1 (319); 2 (323); 12, 6, 2 (325); 11, 19, 3 (364); 11, 16, 13 (383); silver: CTh 11, 9, 2 (337); Corn; CTh 11, 16, 1 (319).

75. Kent, CSL, 98ff.

76. Liban. Or, 30, 6; 37; 62, 8.

77. The revenue from vectigalia was allocated to the CSL after 364 (CTh 11, 19, 3 (364); 5, 15, 20 (366); for the confiscation of civic lands see CTh 15, 1, 18 (374); 4, 13, 7 (374).

78. Kent, CSL, 103ff.

79. Tomb robbery: CTh 9, 17, 2 (349); unauthorized exactions by the prefect: CTh 11, 16, 7-8 (356); neglected appeals: CTh 11, 30, 25 (355); 33 (364); 58 (399); diverting public income; CTh 15, 7, 6 (381).

80. Kent, CSL, 106ff.; Jones, LRE, 429ff. and note 47; Karayannopulos, Finanzwesen, 149ff.

81. CTh, 10, 19, 1 (320); 3 (370); 4 (367); 10 (382); 12 (392);

82. CTh, 1, 32, 5 (386) = CJ 11, 7, 6.

83. CTh 10, 19, 4 (367) = CJ 11, 7, 2.

84. CTh 10, 19, 8 (376).

85. CTh 10, 19, 3 (370) = CJ 11, 7, 1; CTh 10, 19, 2 (392) = CJ 11, 7, 5.

86. CTh 10, 19, 15 (424).

87. Kent, CSL, 108ff.

88. CTh 9, 23, 1 (356).

89. CTh 11, 28, 3 (401). They are also referred to as praepositi vectigalium in the fourth century: CTh 13, 5, 5 (329); 1, 32, 3 (377); 13, 5, 17 (386).

90. CTh 4, 13, 3 (381) = CJ 4, 61, 8; CTh 4, 13, 6 (368) = CJ 4, 61, 7.

91. CTh 4, 13, 2-3 (321).

92. CTh 7, 20, 2 (320/6) = CJ 12, 46, 1; CTh 7, 20, 9 (366).

93a. Symm., Ep, 5, 62 and 65. Jones, LRE, 429.

93b. Crawford, ANRW, II, 2, 560ff.

94. M. Fulford, Arch J., 135, 1978, 67ff.

95. ibid, 81.

96. ibid, 72; see also C. E. King, in Studien zu Fundmünzen der Antike, I, FMRD Colloquium, 1976 Berlin, 1978, 79ff. for a discussion of the kinds of information hoards and site finds can reasonably be expected to yield.

97. Cf. this volume 41ff. and 175ff.

98. ibid, 175ff.

99. ibid, 187ff.

100. ibid, 47ff.

101. ibid, 48ff.

102. ibid, 183.

103. Fulford, Arch J, 135, 1978, 91ff.

104. Callu, this volume, 46ff.

105. Fulford, Arch J., 1978, 91ff.

106. ibid, 102ff

107. Callu, this volume, 44ff.

108. Fulford, Arch J., 135, 1978, 106ff.

109. Callu, this volume, 42ff.

110. Hendy, JRS 1972, 75ff; Univ. of Birmingham Historical Journal, 1971, 129ff; NC 1972, 117ff.

111. Not. Dig. Or XIII, 10-20; Oc XI, 21ff.

112. JRS 1972, 75ff.

113. Not. Dig. Oc XI, 21ff. It should also be remembered that Milan had had a mint for a brief period in the 3rd century and it is by no means impossible that regional treasuries had begun to be established on an ad hoc basis even before Diocletian's reforms.

114. A theory emphatically denied by M. Fulford Arch J., 135, 1978, 69.

115. The hoarding pattern for silver (324-392) and bronze (348-392) discussed by Callu in this volume, 175ff. and 41ff. supports this supposition since silver was buried along the length of the frontier (in the vicinity of garrisons), and tended to be issued intensively during periods of Civil conflict. The bronze while important as a trading medium also played a significant role in the empire's defense, particularly in the 360s and 370s.

116. Univ. of Birmingham Historical Journal, 1971, 137ff.

117. NC 1972, 126ff.

118. See Kent, Essays in Roman Coinage Presented to Harold Mattingly, 199ff. He believes the reform probably applied to silver as well on the basis of silver coins marked P(u)S(ulatum).

119. Hendy, NC 1972, 126ff.

120. See LRBC Pt. 2 Siscia, nos. 1269ff. which records a staggeringly large number of mintmarks for Siscia between 364-378. It is not altogether safe to equate the number of marks with absolute output since individual issues at any mint could at times be small but the overall impression is one of feverish activity. See also Callu, this volume, 41 ff.

121. Callu, "Transformation et Conflits au IVe siecle Ap. J-C," (Bordeaux 1970), Antiquitas 29, 1, Bonn 1978 103ff. has pointed out this phenomenon.

122. I cannot agree with Callu that the weight standard was c. 2.6 g ibid. 110, note 34. Interestingly the San Genesio hoard has a higher average (2.15g) than is normal for British hoards (1.9g) but it is possible that the British averages have been depressed by the presence of subtly and unrecognized clipped coins. For a discussion of the metrology of clipped and unclipped siliquae see C. E. King, "Late Roman Silver Hoards in Britain and the Problem of Clipped Siliquae," RN (forthcoming).

123. Callu, ibid. 112ff. seems to suggest this; cf. 187ff. in this volume where he comments on this problem.

124. Amm. xx, 4, 18.

125. Univ. of Birmingham Historical Journal 1971, 138. Tax payments were demanded in gold and if the amount of the levy fell between 2 denominations, payment in the higher was demanded and the difference refunded in copper.

126. See for example Bastien and Metzger, Le trésor de Beaurains. (dit Arras) Wettern 1978; which has gold, silver, plate and jewellery; H. Cahn, CENB, 1969, 42ff. on the Kaiseraugst hoard (mid 4th century) which had silver coin and plate. For the composition of British hoards see C. E. King "Late Roman Silver Hoards in Britain and the Problem of Clipped Siliquae," RN (forthcoming); and Callu, this volume 175ff. and especially 187-8 (and notes) who has an excellent bibliography of 4th century 'bullion' hoards.

127. CSL Or XIII; Oc.XI.

128. See for example, B. Overbeck, Argentum Romanum, Hypnobank, Munich 1973, 9ff; Archeologija, 3, 1961, 47ff; Bull. de l'institut archeologique, 19, 1952, 32ff; Folia Archeologica, 7, 1955, 104; Situla 3, 1958; Archeologije 15, 1973, BSFN 1971, 115ff, Germania, 1974, 221ff.; R. Noll, vom Altertum zum Mittelalter, 1958, 15ff; Latomus, 21, 1962, 159ff, Bonner Jahrbucher, 1976, 183ff. and supra note 110 for reference to Callu's discussion of this problem.

129. The silver bowls discussed by Overbeck were produced in weights which were an obvious fraction of the Roman pound, or a pound itself, or a multiple. Argententum Romanorum, 53.

130. Simply looking at the number of types, mintmarks, or officinae in which coins were produced cannot give an accurate estimate of relative or absolute quantities since certain officinae often produced more coins than others and issue size varies greatly as well.

131. Examination of siliquae in the British Museum and Ashmolean collections and the Fleetwood hoard suggest that coins of Valens, Valentinian I, and Theodosius are difficult to die link, those of Valentinian II and Eugenius much easier.

FRAPPES ET TRÉSORS D'ARGENT DE 324 à 392

J.-P. Callu

A la suite d'A. Evans, de J. W. E. Pearce et de tant d'autres numismates britanniques, mais en situant notre enquête dans le cadre de l'Empire romain tout entier, nous souhaiterions placer en parallèle sur quelque sept décennies deux types de données, d'une part, la séquence des émissions,[1] de l'autre la succession des dépôts. Ainsi pourrait-on, du moins, nous l'espérons, parvenir à une courbe évolutive mettant en lumière les temps forts du monnayage de l'argent au IVe s.

Nous distinguerons sept périodes: 1) 324-337; 2) 337-350; 3) 350-358; 4) 358-364; 5) 364-375; 6) 375-383; 7) 383-392. Chaque fois, les tendances principales seront dégagées, avec, dans les limites de notre documentation, le témoignage des trésors contemporains.

I. 324-337

La Tétrarchie, lors de la Réforme de 294/295, avait renoué avec les traditions du Haut-Empire en gravant un argenteus au 1/96e de la livre.[2] L'expérience, tôt arrêtée, sauf dans les Balkans, reçut après la mort de Constance Chlore un prolongement qui ne fut durable que dans la zone maxentienne, à Rome de 306 à 310, à Ostie, de 308 à 309, à Carthage, de 306 à 307, à Aquilée aux alentours de 307.[3] Au contraire, Antioche et Serdica n'émirent que peu de mois en 305/307[4] et à Trèves, il en fut de même, dans la seconde moitié de 307.[5]

Cet argenteus de Dioclétien, qui est rapidement accaparé - à la célèbre trouvaille de Sisak, ajoutons une autre moins connue, faite en Italie, ainsi que celles de Krempelstein et de Brigetio[6]—continue néanmoins (et parfois même hors du limes)[7] à figurer avec de plus modestes contingents dans des ensembles autres que tétrarchiques: 2 ex à Rouvroy-les-Merles en 303 mais aussi 5 à Imsbach en 313, 10 à Betteldorf, dans le Barbaricum, ante 324, 11 à Kaiseraugst en 350, 1 à Southsea en 361.[8] Les espèces de Maxence sont plus rares: on en compte 4 à Kellmünz en 308 et deux à Arras en 317.[9]

L'Orient cessait donc toute frappe d'AR jusqu'en 326. En Gaule, Constantin maintenait un temps, en 308, puis en 310, une fabrication de ces quinaires que l'épargnant d'Arras a thésaurisés.[10] Ainsi partout, depuis deux ans, les officines de l'argent étaient fermées, quand l'Auguste de Trèves s'empara de l'Italie.

Cet accroissement de territoire modifia la politique monétaire de Constantin mais sans que se produisent encore des changements décisifs. Une bonne preuve en est fournie par l'émission d'un 1/96e à Trèves en 313, avec seulement 25% d'AR.[11] Cette hésitation à revenir au métal pur se manifestera encore jusqu'en 326 à Sirmium, Thessalonique et Constantinople.[12] Autrement, en Italie (Ticinum, Aquilée, Rome) et à Siscia entre 315 et 321, on se borne à essayer des pieds lourds au 1/48e et au 1/60e.[13]

Le véritable recommencement—et ceci justifie notre terminus post quem—date de la conquête de la Pars Orientis. C'est alors que non seulement fut reprise la gravure de l'argenteus mais encore que l'on créa le miliarensis au 1/72e de la livre.[14]

A vrai dire, la chronologie des espèces d'argent entre 324 et 337 est extrêmement malaisée à établir. Certes plusieurs revers plutôt exceptionnels ne font pas apparemment problème: multiples de la dédicace de la Nouvelle Rome ou des Vicennalia de Constantin II César, miliarenses célébrant la Gloire et la Vertu de l'Armée à Thessalonique et Constantinople en 333-337.[15] Mais pour les plus communs, la fourchette s'élargit.

Il y a, en fait, 4 séries importantes, 2 d'argentei, 2 de miliarenses: La première des 1/96es se caractérise par 3 palmes. Plaident pour une datation haute les émissions de Ticinum fermé après 325 comme un Crispus d'Antioche antérieur à l'été 326.[16] En revanche deux indices sont favorables—mais non contraignants—pour descendre vers la fin du règne: le type réapparaît après 337[17] et une pièce aux 3 palmes de Rome provient du trésor de Mitrovica.[18]

Le second argenteus à l'image de la Victoire pourrait si on se fonde sur l'activité de Constantinople, remonter aux années 326-330. Il existe certainement après les nominations de Constant, puis de Delmace[19] et continue, Constantin une fois disparu.[20]

Quant aux miliarenses, ils représentent ou bien 3 ou 4 Empereurs sous un arc, ou bien 4 étendards. Le premier type, Felicitas Romanorum, a pu débuter en 326, avec 3 Empereurs, à Trèves, Sirmium et Thessalonique, ce dernier atelier frappant pour Crispus. On manque par contre d'un témoignage indubitable attestant une continuation au delà de 330.[21]

Enfin le 1/72e[22] aux 4 étendards est connu aussi bien au début de la période, à Ticinum qu'à son terme, à Trèves, Arles et Constantinople.[23] Les Constantinides en maintiennent la fabrication.[24]

On a donc l'impression qu'autour de 326 l'argenteus aux 3 palmes va de pair avec le miliarensis Felicitas Romanorum, tandis que sur plus de dix ans, mais sans doute avec des coupures, sont émis le 1/96e à la Victoire et le type des étendards, une concentration pouvant être postulée dans l'ultime lustre de Constantin. Pour l'ensemble de ce monnayage de base, une prépondérance de l'Orient n'est pas niable.[25]

La part tenue par les espèces constantiniennes dans la thésaurisation est incroyablement faible: de l'unique dépôt de Mitrovica, 8 pièces ont été conservées: selon la chronologie de P. Bruun, elles se regroupent toutes entre 330 et 337.[26] Les trésors plus tardifs, de même, ne contiennent que très peu d'exemplaires: 10 à Kaiseraugst en 350, 3 à Enns en 351, 4 à Southsea en 361, 1 à East Harptree vers 377.[27] Une refonte est probable,[28] dès les années qui suivirent la mort de Constantin. Elle oblitère notre vision en nous masquant la mise en place d'un système qui va durer.

II. 337-350

La première phase de cette période—celle qui couvre les années 337-340—pour être brève, n'en est pas moins fort intéressante.

En effet, entre les trois frères, les différences s'affirment. A l'Ouest, hormis l'ouverture d'une seconde officine à Trèves, Constantin II innove peu.[29] A l'Est, Constance se cantonne dans la frappe de l'argenteus.[30] Au contraire, Constant, pour secouer son état d'infériorité, pratique ostensiblement une politique monétaire de prestige: les types constantiniens des étendards,[31] des palmes,[32] de la Virtus Exercitus[33] sont complétés en priorité[34] par la série Gaudium Populi Romani[35] qui, utilisant systématiquement quatre pieds dans l'atelier pilote de Siscia inscrit, comme Constance, mais avec plus d'éclat, la succession des Vota et tend ainsi à spécialiser le métal blanc dans la célébration des anniversaires impériaux.

Quand le pouvoir se limite à une dyarchie et que Constant dispose de l'Occident,[36] l'effort, d'abord, ne se ralentit pas. Gaudium Populi Romani, lors des Décennales, est refrappé sur les quatre modules[37] et l'épaulent deux nouvelles séries, aussi complètes ou presque, Victoriae DDNN Augg[38] et Triumfator Gentium Barbararum.[39] Comme précédemment, Siscia joue un rôle moteur,[40] suivi de Thessalonique et d'Aquilée,[41] mais Trèves participe activement avec même des émissions particulières pour le 1/72e et la 1/96.[42] L'opposition demeure ainsi avec un Orient voué seulement à l'argenteus.[43]

Le chronologie interne de la décennie 340-350 reste à déterminer. Il paraît toutefois qu'après 344, quand Vota Decennalia et Vicennalia des deux Augustes Augustes eurent été aussi richement illustrés, une modification intervint. Les multiples au 1/24e cessèrent; les miliarenses légers—les lourds n'existent pratiquement qu'à Trèves[44]—reçurent de façon systématique des légendes propres à chaque atelier: Victoria Augustorum à Siscia,[45] Felicitas Perpetua à Aquilée,[46] Virtus DDNN Augg à Trèves.[47] Des hôtels monétaires fermés rouvrirent à Lyon, Arles, Rome[48] et se joignirent à Trèves, Thessalonique, Siscia et—avec une variante—Aquilée pour des émissions sur grande échelle du 1/96e à la Victoire,[49] doublé à Trèves par Pax Augustorum.[50] A Rome enfin, qui grave aussi quelques miliarenses tardifs,[51] la légende Fel Temp Reparatio, en 348, ne se lit que sur des argentei.[52] La Pars Occidentis en cette fin de règne de Constant, s'alignait de la sorte peu à peu sur Nicomédie et Antioche restés fidèles au 1/96e.[53] La "main", pourrait-on dire, passait au bronze argenté et une nouvelle politique "misait" sur l'aes 2 rétabli.[54]

A la différence de la période précédente, les années 337-350 ont laissé leur empreinte dans la circulation. Et tout d'abord par deux trésors contemporains. L'un, de Trèves, se réduit maintenant à 4 multiples qui nous rappellent la position dominante de Siscia et de Thessalonique.[55] De l'autre, nous saurons beaucoup plus, quanf il sera publié. Les informations recueillies cependant sur l'ensemble de Kaiseraugst confirment pleinement nos précédentes analyses, puisqu'on y dénombre 52 ex de 337-340 et 112 de 240-348, les 17 médaillons mentionnés sur un total de 185 monnaies appartenant vraisemblablement au règne de Constant.[56]

Un troisième dépôt, celui d'Enns,[57] enfoui en 351, est quasiment synchrone: il est lui aussi, même s'il ne comporte pas de 1/24e, très représentatif de l'effort déployé par le dernier fils de Constantin. Un classement provisoire assigne, en effet, au condominium des trois princes 10 1/60es de Siscia et de Thessalonique, 9 au 1/72e des mêmes ateliers et de Trèves, 8 argentei au minimum de Trèves et de Siscia, soit donc quelque 27 espèces d'AR. Après 340, Aquilée entre dans le circuit et se partage avec Siscia les miliarenses lourds et légers, ceux-ci l'emportant nettement (c. 12 contre c. 3). La masse des 1/96es s'élève à sans doute 28 ex répartis comme suit: 20 Gaudium Populi Romani de Siscia, 5 Victoires (Siscia et Thessalonique), 1 Pax Augustorum de Trèves, 2 Vota d'Antioche. On parvient ainsi pour la décennie antérieure à 350 à un total de 43 ex.

Plus avant, en 361, à Southsea, les pièces lourdes sont loin d'avoir toutes disparu: dans ce trésor d'environ 450 ex, Constant et Constance, durant leur règne commun, n'ont que 2 miliarenses lourds et 8 légers mais, il y a encore, semble-t-il, 32 1/96es (pour la plupart des Victoires de Trèves).[58] Sans même parler de dépôt mixte comme Oldcroft,[59] East Harptree, d'une quinzaine d'années postérieur, offrirait avec un 1/72e et 5 argentei,[60] le dernier exemple de cette singulière poussée, si de la pièce de 4.48 g, on ne trouvait un ou deux spécimens à San Genesio, voire à Holwel et à North-Mendip.[61]

III. 350-358

Initialement, la courbe ne fléchit pas et la raison fondamentale en est l'usurpation de Magnence qui imprime sa marque à la fois sur le régime des ateliers et le faciès des trésors.

Quand l'empereur gaulois abandonne l'Italie en 352, les séries d'Aquilée—son seul atelier extérieur à frapper l'argent—sont, à l'exception des plus lourdes,[62] transférées sur Lyon.[63] A ce moment là du règne fonctionnent par conséquent l'officine trévire, très active depuis 350, la lyonnaise et deux d'Arles héritées de Constant. A côté des miliarenses lourds[64] et légers[65] est gravé en abondance l'argenteus, surtout celui de Trèves à la légende Virtus Exerciti.[66]

La contre-offensive de Constance est particulièrement suggestive pour l'analyste. D'une part, pour mieux souligner sa légitimité, l'Auguste oriental choisit de restaurer des revers constantiniens: Empereurs sous un arc, Étendards, images de la Gloire ou de la Vertu de l'Armée. De l'autre, le monopole de l'argenteus à l'Est est rompu, pour la première fois depuis 337 et l'artisan de la reconquête sera le 1/72e: Felicitas Romanorum et son doublet Victoria Romanorum à Sirmium, Nicomédie, Antioche, Aquilée,[67] puis, les émissions se prolongeant dans les Gaules récupérées, types aux étendards à Constantinople et Arles,[68] et, plus encore, dans cette seconde phase, Virtus Exercitus à Constantinople, Cyzique, Thessalonique, Siscia[69]—dans ces deux ateliers, Vétranion avait été éphémère—[70] Rome, Arles et Lyon.[71] Entre Magnence et Constance le conflit avait donc pris un aspect monétaire, puisqu'avec des Virtus Exercitus au 1/72e, l'orthodoxie manifestait sa supériorité sur les Virtus Exerciti du tyran au 1/96e.

Parallèlement au miliarensis léger (il existe aussi quelques lourds à Constantinople, Nicomédie, Cyzique ainsi qu'en Arles après Novembre 353,[72]) se développe une très large production d'argentei pour Gallus et Constance. Les Votis V Multis X et le revers à étoile, propres au César, commencent dès 351 à Sirmium,[73] ensuite une répartition paraît s'opérer: Constantinople,

Thessalonique, Siscia, Aquilée frappent les Vota,[74] Antioche, Rome, Arles—avant et après le passage de PAR à TCON—Lyon enfin, la deuxième figure.[75]

Constance, pour sa part, a droit à des Votis XXX Multis XXXX: sauf, aux deux extrémités, Antioche et Trèves, tout l'arc monétaire est concerné: à l'Est, Nicomédie, Cyzique et Constantinople,[76] dans les Balkans, Thessalonique, Sirmium, et Siscia,[77] en Italie, Aquilée et Rome,[78] dans les Gaules, Arles et Lyon.[79] Concomitantes à celles de Gallus, les émissions constantiennes ont pu, en Arles, durer jusqu'en 358.[80] A cette époque, Julien était déjà César depuis trois ans et le rythme s'était alors assoupi à l'intérieur de l'empire. De fait, peu d'ateliers orientaux frappèrent pour le cousin de l'Auguste: Thessalonique fut le principal qui émit 1/60es, 1/72es et 1/96es avec des types empruntés à Gallus.[81] En Gaule, Trèves, emporté dans la tourmente, n'a laissé que de rares quinaires[82] et pour les trois modules précités tout s'était concentré sur Arles où, exception faite des miliarenses légers, Virtus Exercitus, la troisième officine restait affectée au titulaire du Césarat.[83]

Cet épuisement du Trésor n'avait rien d'imaginaire. Quand Constance doit fêter ses adventus à Rome et Sirmium en 357[84] ou le début de ses 35 années de règne,[85] des monnaies exceptionnelles sont émises mais leur volume, à en juger par nos collections, apparaît tout à fait restreint. Rien de comparable avec la masse d'argentei produits les années précédentes à Constantinople, Sirmium et Arles, poussée que soulignerait encore—pour qui en douterait—le phénomène des imitations.[86] Ainsi en vue cavalière et si on tourne particulièrement ses regards sur les pièces de 4.48et 3.36 g, il semble bien que l'ampleur des actions monétaires des années 350 ait essoufflé l'Empire. La guerre civile et ses séquelles—notamment en Gaule—ont coûté cher à Constance.

L'analyse de la circulation ne dément pas une telle conclusion. Trois sortes de faits sont, au premier chef, à remarquer: disons d'abord que les dépôts se multiplient, 3 à 4 en zone rhénane, 6 dans les parages danubiens.[87] Cette seconde catégorie, connue grâce aux numismates roumains, russes et polonais, a l'intérêt de recentrer la carte des dépôts, en relevant un facteur de thésaurisation presqu'aussi notable que celui de la Reconquête, à savoir les campagnes contre les Sarmates sur le Bas-Danube en 357/358. Que des argentei de Cyzique soient repérables dans deux de ces six trésors laisse présumer une datation antérieure à 358.[88] On aimerait toutefois être mieux renseigné sur ces trouvailles jusqu'à présent un peu négligées par les historiens.

Les deux autres données nous ramènent à Magnence: A Kaiseraugst, dans l'ensemble déjà évoqué, à Ljubljana, en contiguité avec des solidi et d'autres barres de ce métal, ont été découverts trois et deux lingots à l'empreinte de l'usurpateur. Le deuxième groupe mentionne l'atelier d'Aquilée.[89] Nous sommes donc mené à penser que des refontes importantes, à la fois de monnaies et de vaisselle,[90] ont eu lieu au début du dominat de Magnence, ceci afin de financer l'effort de guerre contre Constance.

D'autres dépôts nous introduisent à une considération connexe. La décennie commençant en 350 présente plusieurs cas de résurgence qui ne sont pas sans analogue dans la période précédente et qui se perpétueront par la suite,[91] nous entendons les complexes situés dans le Barbaricum ou à proximité et qui à des deniers du Haut-Empire ajoutent "en queue" quelques argentei du milieu du IVe s. Le dépôt de Laatzen est légèrement postérieur[92] mais rentrent dans la catégorie Famars,[93] peut-être en partie, Tournai,[94] à coup sûr Lengerich où une soixantaine d'argentei de Magnence, des Virtus Exerciti de Trèves, complètent 1220 1/96es de Trajan à Alexandre Sévère.[95] Les peuples barbares étaient donc restés attachés aux frappes d'argent[96] et le poids dont ils pèsent à l'époque, soit comme adversaires, soit comme auxiliaires, est une composante qui a pu jouer dans la renaissance à ce moment du métal blanc.

Reste à dire un mot sur le sort ultérieur des séries de la période. Bien entendu, les espèces de Magnence et de Vétranion furent en général démonétisées, quoique les épargnants aient été séduits par leurs espèces lourdes:[97] à Southsea cela s'est passé ainsi et, pour les années 350-358, on totalise, usurpateurs compris, 8 miliarenses lourds, 43 légers—les Virtus Exercitus de la Reconquête, 29 argentei.[98] En regard d'un seul argenteus, East Harptree recueille encore 7 1/72es[99] et San Genesio 3.[100] Il y avait 3 1/96es dans le petit dépôt Ciani, peut-être d'époque valentinienne, et sans doute à Kecel un certain nombre de la même unité, puisqu'elles ont donné lieu à des imitations de bon poids;[101] une fois de plus, à l'extrémité du siècle, l'ensemble thésaurisant de North Mendip, avec 7 pièces de 4,48 g, est l'exception qui confirme la règle.[102] Car, nous allons le voir, l'invention de la "silique" détermine dans les circuits monétaires un fondamental terminus a quo.

IV. 358-364

Dans l'histoire du monnayage d'argent, 358 est effectivement une date-charnière. En même temps que l'aes 4, Spes Reipublice prenait le relais de l'aes 3, Fel Temp Reparatio, l'Etat renonçait au pied néronien restauré par Dioclétien.[103] Il le faisait au profit d'une unité plus légère et dans sa définition même valant plus que son contenu intrinsèque. Cette monnaie, dans la pensée des Anciens, se présentait comme un nouvel argenteus, mais de la dénommer "silique", selon la terminologie des Modernes n'est pas une aberration, car il est métrologiquement vraisemblable qu'elle était la contrepartie d'un vingt-quatrième de solidus.[104]

Trois revers se partagent la production: Victoria DDNN Aug et Votis XXX Multis XXXX pour Constance II, Votis V Multis X pour Julien César. Ce troisième type n'est connu qu'en Arles, dans l'officine T.[105] Le premier, quasiment propre à Lyon, se développant beaucoup par la suite,[106] c'est en priorité le deuxième qui est l'artisan de la réforme: gravé aussi bien à l'Est (Antioche, Nicomédie, Constantinople)[107] qu'au Centre (Thessalonique, Sirmium, Siscia, Rome)[108] et à l'Ouest (Arles, Lyon, Trèves),[109] il paraît toutefois diffusé davantage par 4 hôtels, deux du ressort de Constance: Constantinople et Sirmium, deux dans celui de Julien: Arles et Lyon. Sur ce point, la concorde régnait dans le collège impérial.

Ainsi s'écoula 359. Mais au début de l'année suivante éclate le pronunciamento de Lutèce. Julien Auguste, à Lyon et Arles, pratique de longs mois le compromis: dans l'un des ateliers, les Victoria DDNN Aug sont frappés pour les deux princes maintenant Augustes et avec cette nouvelle légende les Vot V équilibrent les Vot XXX;[110] dans l'autre—il s'agit des Vota d'Arles—l'empereur gaulois utilise toujours de préférence la troisième officine.[111] La rupture se décidant malgré tout, Julien récupère alors l'ensemble des équipes arlésiennes, double les effectifs à Lyon où les avers se multiplient, enfin promeut Trèves.[112] Sans nul doute, dans les trois grands centres des Gaules, la production qui privilègie la silique—il y a cependant des miliarenses légers à Lyon et Arles[113]—tourne à plein régime. En est-il de même dans les zones sous le contrôle de Constance? On peut en douter, car le quarantième anniversaire du souverain n'est fêté qu'à Constantinople.[114]

Lorsque Julien quitte l'Occident, les ateliers centraux,[115] Rome, Sirmium, Siscia, Thessalonique le reconnaissent mais les frappes sont peu abondantes, sauf à Sirmium où se met en place une fabrication du 1/72e: série Virtus Exercitus en 362, parallèle à celle d'Arles, série Victoria Romanorum en 363, de concert avec Antioche. La dernière partie du règne, en effet, où Julien anticipe sur ses Décennales voit s'effectuer un glissement vers l'Est où, à nouveau, Constantinople et, plus encore, Antioche[116] viennent contrebalancer l'importance toujours forte de Lyon et d'Arles. Ce réveil de l'Est, dû aux circonstances, se confirme sous Jovien, Arles étant le seul atelier occidental à émettre pour l'éphémère empereur.[117]

Au total, les quatre ou cinq années postérieures à la création de la silique ont changé tout le panorama monétaire. Il est regrettable que faute de trésors on ne puisse s'en assurer pour le Centre et l'Orient. Pour l'Ouest, heureusement, les documents sont assez nombreux pour qu'on parvienne à apprécier le caractère décisif de cette étape.

Comme on l'a fait précédemment, nous distinguerons dépôts contemporains et dépôts postérieurs. Mis à part deux ensembles mixtes,[118] sont pour le premier groupe à recenser trois trouvailles seulement: Laatzen, Southsea, Willersey, Laatzen rentre dans une problématique déjà évoquée, celle de la survie dans le Barbaricum de deniers du Haut Empire, la différence étant qu'ici ont été ajoutés deux siliques, dont une imitation, et deux miliarenses, un Constance II et un Julien Auguste de Lyon de c. 361.[119] Southsea et Willersey nous retiennent davantage, car, avec eux, entrent en jeu les trésors britanniques auxquels souvent on réserve le monople de l'épargne de l'argent.

Southsea est un riche ensemble découvert près de Portsmouth. Enfoui en 361, il aide à mieux comprendre le jeu des ateliers gaulois à partir de 358 et, malgré une tendance thésaurisante, comporte 79.8% de siliques.[120] Moins important, le trésor de Willersey (Glos), s'arrête c. 362/363 et lui aussi, à deux exceptions près, ne contient que des siliques, soit 96.4%.[121]

Au fur et à mesure qu'on descend l'échelle des années, le contingent des années 358-364 diminue, mais longtemps il reste d'une ampleur notable. A East Harptree qui confirme les enseignements de Southsea, le pourcentage est de 70.38%.[122] Sur le Continent, les ensembles valentiniens du Danube atteignent plus exceptionnellement des proportions comparables: 85.18% à Redea c. 371,[123] mais 24.81% (?) à Sucidava p. 367,[124] 22.2% à Dranic c. 376.[125] La collection achetée par Ciani, si elle provient de Kecel, pourrait en revanche indiquer une belle survie de la silique de Constance et Julien vers 370.[126] Quoiqu'il en soit, ce faciès n'est pas sans alternative. D'autres découvertes continentales sont constituées d'argent frais et le plus bel exemple en est la caisse militaire de San Genesio qui ne contient que deux Votis XXX Multis XXXX de 358-361.[127]

Dans la dernière partie de notre enquête—après 388—où la documentation est à peu de choses près totalement britannique, les chiffres résultant de 4 dépôts sont assez dissemblables, la moyenne arithmétique se dégageant autour de 10%.

Mr. Wood's Hoard :	17,09%[128]	Shapwick II :	8,80%[130]
Springhead :	9,39%[129]	Honiton :	6,25%[131]

Il est curieux de constater que, loin de diminuer ultérieurement, le contingent, dans une vingtaine de trouvailles postérieures à 393, s'équilibrerait vers le huitième de la masse:

	%		%
North Mendip :	32.19[132]	Colerne II :	8.75[144]
Mildenhall :	30.76[133]	Icklingham II :	8.57[145]
Cleeve Prior :	25.88[134]	Groveley Wood :	8.36[146]
Sproxton :	25.00[135]	Edington :	8.06[147]
Ramshill :	22.22[136]	Manton Downs :	7.69[148]
Holwel :	20.12[137]	Tuddenham :	7.01[149]
South Ferriby :	19.73[138]	Sturmer :	6.66[150]
Dorchester :	16.98[139]	Coleraine :	6.50[151]
Fincham :	14.28[140]	Shapwick I :	5.83[152]
Great Allington :	12.96[141]	Icklingham III :	4.34[153]
Terling :	10.46[142]	Colerne I :	4.00[154]
Fleetwood :	10.05[143]	Icklingham I :	3.85[155]

Ainsi, les siliques de 358-364 qui forment la première couche des trésors bretons n'ont jamais été éliminées du circuit et dans la circulation particulière qui est devenue celle de l'île au début du Ve siècle, elles restent une partie intégrante d'un monnayage qui procède d'elles.

V. 364-375

Non seulement par son catalogue du RIC IX, mais aussi par son commentaire synthétique du trésor de Terling, Pearce ici sera notre guide.[156]

Un contraste éclairant sépare les trois premières années du reste de la période. De 364 à 367 une grande richesse typologique caractérise *miliarenses* lourds et légers,[157] encore que s'esquissent les spécialisations à venir: *Vota* pour les 1/60es, *Gloria Romanorum* pour les 1/72es orientaux, ceux de l'Ouest maintenant la légende traditionnelle de *Virtus Exercitus*. Un rôle intermédiaire est tenu à Constantinople par l'*argenteus* restauré. Cette frappe, commencée au lendemain de l'insurrection de Procope, est une singularité malaisée à interpréter.[158] Elle invite cependant à deux inductions: 1) Si on a gravé à nouveau des 1/96es, il faut croire que c'est parce que la demande du public n'était pas satisfaite et, à son tour, cette carence laisse supposer que les *argentei* antérieurs à 358 avaient été démonétisés; 2) L'utilisation parallèle des deux dénominations—l'*argenteus* et la silique—dissuade de penser, comme le font certains métrologues,[159] que la seconde avait pris la valeur du premier.

A l'Est comme à l'Ouest, enfin, en ces commencements de la dynastie valentinienne, le rythme de production de la silique semble s'être maintenu sur la lancée du précédent lustre. Le type majeur, Restitutor Reipublicae, est quasi commun à la totalité de l'Empire; dans la Pars Occidentis, Lyon semble l'avoir émis en abondance.[160] Un second groupe est consacré aux voeux impériaux: Votis V Multis X, dans le domaine de Valentinien, à Trèves, Lyon, Aquilée, Sirmium, Thessalonique, Rome surtout qui gravait peu de Restitutor Reipublicae,[161] Vota V dans les trois ateliers d'Orient, le plus actif étant celui de Constantinople:[162] les siliques réparties entre les deux Empereurs accusent à partir de l'usurpation de Procope une disproportion favorable à Valens[163] et les officines constantinopolitaines, accrues en nombre, sont les artisans de cette progression qui touche aussi, nous l'avons vu, l'argenteus dédié également aux Vot V.

Troisième type de silique, celui-là promis à un très bel avenir: Vrbs Roma que gravent les hôtels de Lyon et de Rome avec l'image de la Ville Reine assise sur un trône.[164] A en croire East Harptree, les officines romaines sont là prépondérantes.[165] Il s'avère donc que Valentinien, en distribuant les séries de ses siliques, a privilégié les deux cités du Rhône et du Tibre—en 364/365, il a résidé à Milan, mais est-ce pour des raisons politiques, il a préféré recourir aux équipes de l'Vrbs.

Après l'avénement de Gratien, la politique monétaire changea du tout au tout. Jusqu'alors l'héritage de Constance et de Julien avait été assumé; on vivait dans l'esprit de la réforme de 358. Peu à peu des choix nouveaux sont operes. On recherche une situation claire et pour ce faire chaque métal monnayé est purifié: l'or sera obryzum, l'argent pusulatum, quant au numéraire de base il est désormais sans traces d'AR.[166] A l'Ouest, l'Aes 3 devient le support des principales dépenses de l'Etat, celles de la réfection du limes.[167] En contrepartie, la frappe des espèces blanches subit un coup d'arrêt: après Sirmum, Rome est fermée, Arles et Aquilée n'émettent plus de siliques.[168]

Reste le problème des Urbs Roma trévires. Avec acuité, Pearce a noté une anomalie caractéristique: A Terling, mais l'observation vaut également pour East Harptree, San Genesio, Springhead, Grovely Wood, Icklingham I, North Mendip, etc., même en tenant compte de la différence de durée des règnes, le contingent de Valentinien est considérablement inférieur à celui de Valens.[169] Ce phénomène n'appelle qu'une conclusion: à Trèves l'émission d'Vrbs Roma a occupé seulement une fraction des années 367-375: ou bien, elle s'accroche à celle de la phase précédente à Lyon et Rome et après une longue suspension est recommencée après la mort de Valentinien, ou bien plutôt, elle débute tardivement vers la fin de son dominat. De toute façon, il se produit une césure dans le monnayage de la silique, alors que, liées à des occasions plus rares, les Virtus Exercitus au 1/72e paraissent, toutes proportions gardées, avoir été moins touchées.[170]

A l'Est, Constantinople, Nicomédie et Antioche sont ouverts avec, en théorie, une panoplie assez complète de modules, l'argenteus continuant sa carrière dans les deux premiers ateliers.[171] De courts indices dans la circulation[172] et, davantage encore, le nombre des officines et des différents font penser que les siliques Vot X Mult XX d'Antioche—cette résidence de Valens—tranchent sur une production plutôt, semble-t-il, restreinte. Pour étayer cette impression, il y aurait à interroger les catalogues de collections locales.[173] On saurait alors si la récession de l'argent touche l'Orient dès ces années-là. La suite de l'évolution ferait pencher pour une réponse positive.

Indirectement, nous avons déjà abordé la thésaurisation de la période. A vrai dire, celle qui est strictement concomitante se laisse mal cerner, car la documentation est rare et difficile d'accès. Une douzaine de trésors est repertoriable, la très grande majorité appartient aux provinces danubiennes:

c. 366	:	Gura Jalomiţei, Dobroudja, Viespeşti[174]
p. 367	:	Sucidava (3 lots)[175]
c. 370	:	Kecel (et peut-être le dépôt Ciani si les ensembles sont différents)[176]
c. 371	:	Redea[177]
364-378	:	Osica de Sus[178]
367-383	:	Valea Strimba, Stobi[179]

Comme le trésor d'East Harptree est daté par Pearce de 376-377, n'entrent en considération pour la Bretagne que trois dépôts réputés valentiniens et sur lesquels nous ne sommes à peu près pas renseignés: Chaddlesworth, Uphill, Wookey Hole.[180] Pour l'historien, il vaut la peine de remarquer que pas plus que celles de Constant Auguste, les campagnes insulaires de Théodose l'Ancien n'ont entraîné des enfoussements systématiques.[181] L'argent est arrivé après sur les sites bretons. Au demeurant, comme le montre East Harptree, qu'aurait-on pu enterrer de la production de 367-375, sinon, en petite quantité, des Virtus Exercitus et des Vrbs Roma de Trèves?[182]

VI. 375-383

La mort de Valentinien détermine une coupure profonde. Elle rompt l'unité monétaire de l'Empire. A l'Est, Valens accentue la politique de son frère. En même temps que, par un jeu de balance, il restaure un aes 3 qui précisément en Occident disparaît ou peu s'en faut, il arrête les frappes de l'argent à Nicomédie et Antioche. De 375 à 388 ne subsisteront que les siliques aux Vota de Constantinople.[183]

Gratien à l'Ouest agit tout différemment. Ayant donc stoppé les émissions de bronze—la volonté de dégonfler la masse en circulation en la débarrassant des imitations est invoquée par Symmaque[184]—l'élève d'Ausone opère une véritable conversion et transfère sur l'argent le poids majeur de ses fabrications. On aimerait connaître les raisons d'une décision qui prend le contre-pied de ce qu'avait fait Valentinien, de ce que fait maintenant Valens. Gratien a certes souhaité innover. Mais dans le climat de "restauration" qui est alors celui de l'Occident,[185] une pression des milieux sénatoriaux ne s'est-elle pas manifestée pour en revenir au système de Julien et faire un pivot de la circulation de la pièce d'argent traditionnellement liée à l'histoire de Rome? Autre hypothèse plus réaliste, le pouvoir a du céder devant les exigences d'une armée, où les éléments germanique ont de l'ascendant. Après la monnaie de bronze distribuée par Valentinien, on verrait assez bien un gouvernement plus faible se concilier les soldats par des espèces d'un plus fort pouvoir d'achat et qui aux yeux de certains jouissait d'un prestige ancestral.

Quoiqu'on puisse supposer, après les coups d'éclat de Constant, après la crise de la Reconquête, pour la troisième fois—du moins au vu du spectre de la thésaurisation, les émissions d'argent haussent fortement leur volume. L'effort, sensible pour les grands modules à Trèves et Siscia, mais aussi à Aquilée, ensuite à Rome, quand à partir de 378 cet hôtel est remis en fonction,[186a] s'exerce toutefois, de préférence, par l'entremise de la silique.[186b] Deux séries se distinguent. La première est à la légende, déjà évoquée d'Vrbs Roma. De même que, selon une chronologie encore incertaine, elle anticipe 375, elle déborde largement, avec la variété à la cuirasse, la mise en place, en 378, de la triarchie Gratien, Valentinien II, Théodose. Le témoignage des trésors, aussi bien celui de San Genesio que ceux de Bretagne, de Springhead à North Mendip, le prouve éloquemment: elle est représentative du règne de Gratien.[187] A une date intermédiaire sans doute entre 378 et 383 est installée en doublet une seconde structure qui attribue à chaque souverain un revers propre, Virtus Romanorum à Gratien, Concordia Auggg à Théodose, Victoria Auggg à Valentinien II. Ce modèle trévire est appliqué à Lyon, à nouveau en activité après une phase d'éclipse, ainsi qu'à Aquilée.[188] Pour ce deuxième groupement, les proportions de San Genesio diffèrent de celles des trésors bretons: dans la découverte italienne, la contribution d'Aquilée fait pencher la balance en faveur de la triade Virtus, Concordia, Victoria.[189] En Bretagne, au contraire, où Trèves domine, la grande série est celle d'Vrbs Roma.[190]

Mise à part la petite trouvaille de Dranic,[191] fragile témoignage sur Antioche, deux découvertes seulement sont à citer pour les huit ans qui séparent la mort de Valentinien de celle de Gratien: East Harptree près de Bristol vers 376-377, San Genesio (Pavie) en 383: deux ensembles de large ampleur mais d'un style dissemblable: une accumulation qui remonte jusqu'à Constantin n'a rien à voir avec un matériel à 90% postérieur à 375.[192] Les deux faciès ne sont donc pas superposables, mais heureusement nous disposons de l'ensemble des dépôts ultérieurs de Bretagne. Même en s'en tenant à une approximation grossière—un calcul des pourcentages de Valens et de Gratien—on obtient des chiffres qui ne traduisent aucune ambiguité sur la renaissance entreprise en 375 et pour suivie après Andrinople.

Voici quelques unes de ces données:

1) p. 388:

Springhead	: 66.40%	Mr. Wood's Hoard	: 48.70%
Shapwick II	: 56.00%	Honiton	: 25.00%

2) p. 392: Une moyenne arithmétique supérieure à 20% est encore enregistrable:

	%		%
Groveley Wood	: 39.70	Holwel	: 21.06
Icklingham I	: 32.90	Fleetwood	: 20.61
Cleeve Prior	: 31.76	Manton Downs	: 19.23
Colerne II	: 28.75	Colerne I	: 19.00
Sproxton	: 27.00	Great Allington	: 18.51
North Mendip	: 26.41	Tuddenham:	: 17.54
Terling	: 24.60	Edington	: 16.12
Icklingham II	: 24.20	Dorchester	: 13.20
South Ferriby	: 24.12	Icklingham III	: 11.30
Shapwick I	: 23.30	Ramshill	: 11.10
Mildenhall	: 23.07	Coleraine	: 10.35

VII. 383-392

L'usurpation de Maxime divise naturellement la dernière période soumise à notre examen en deux phases: avant et après 388, date de la reconquête de l'Occident par Théodose.

Il est symptomatique qu'à la différence des temps de Constance II, la campagne contre le tyran de l'Ouest n'ait pas été financée par des frappes massives et de fort module en argent, Constantinople se bornant à émettre comme auparavant des siliques à Vota.[193]

Valentinien II, au contraire, affichait sa fidélité à la politique de son frère: non seulement il récupère Thessalonique mais encore ouvre pour l'AR un troisième atelier italien à Milan. Si les multiples paraissent guère nombreux, les siliques ont dû être plus communes, Vrbs Roma dans la vieille capitale, Virtus Romanorum à Milan et Aquilée, Vota peut-être partout.[194]

Le fait majeur toutefois nous semble constitué par la politique inflationniste de Maxime. Plusieurs auteurs parlent de son avaritia: les uns, comme Sulpice Sevère pour l'excuser par la pénurie du Trésor, les autres, comme le Pseudo Aurélius Victor et surtout Pacatus pour l'accabler, le représentant au pied des balances, l'oeil fixé sur les masses d'or et d'argent ravies à ses malheureux sujets.[195]

Les trésors bretons corroborent ces assertions. Le pourcentage de 17.13% dans 4 dépôts postérieurs à 388,[196] se maintient au dessus de 11% dans ceux qui sont contemporains d'Honorius.[197] En effet, la démonétisation, si elle a été ordonnée après la mort de Maxime, a dû être contrariée par l'insécurité monétaire qui s'accentue alors, si bien que la thésaurisation reflète sensiblement la production massive pratiquée par l'Empereur de l'Ouest pour subvenir à sa guerre contre Théodose et Valentinien II.

De là, un choix au détriment des espèces lourdes: aucun 1/24e; une série de Votis V Multis X au 1/60e;[198] quelques Virtus Exercitus trévires et lyonnais.[199] La silique—essentiellement Virtus Romanorum—sort par contre en grande quantité de l'atelier de Trèves et fait significatif, même si les pièces retrouvées sont rarissimes, Londres émet de l'argent avec les marques AVG et AVGPS.[200]

Dès que Maxime s'empare de l'Italie, à leur tour Milan et Aquilée gravent des Virtus Romanorum: une hémorragie de métal blanc accompagne l'usurpateur. La conséquence est inévitable: comme à aucun prix, on ne veut revenir à l'altération du titre, c'est, encore limitée à la péninsule, la chute du poids: la silique passe de 2 g à Trèves à 1.5 g à Milan et Aquilée, ceci en poids médian.[201]

Effets de la répression politique ou prudence de l'épargne devant la dépression pondérale, de l'après-Maxime date la première vague des enfouissements[202] en Bretagne: Springhead, Bath, Honiton, Norwich, Shapwick II, Causeway Lane et le Mr. Wood's Hoard. A l'exception de l'hypothétique trouvaille de Cazères sur Adour,[203] le continent ne peut citer que celle, encore inédite, d'Aquila dans les Abruzzes:[204] cette dizaine de siliques perdues au milieu de dix fois plus de solidi offre matière à reflexion. Sans qu'il se voie accusé d'extrapoler, l'observateur peut en déduire que l'hégémonie de l'or, évidente depuis à peine un lustre, est en train de chasser l'argent de ses positions.[205] Séparée par la géographie, la politique, le niveau de vie, la Bretagne subit un retard qui ne sera pas comblé. L'idée, croyons-nous, n'est pas à rejeter et il faudra y revenir.

Dans notre liste de trésors bretons qui maintenant va s'allonger, la prochaine étape se situe avec la nouvelle crise de 392-393. L'entre-deux qui sépare Eugène de Maxime—au demeurant les dernières années visées par notre recherche—se signale par une tentative organisée pour ralentir le mouvement déclenché en 387-388. Théodose emploie les grands moyens: arrêt de la silique à Constantinople, Thessalonique, Aquilée, Rome—il n'y a, en 392, des Vota hélas! allégés qu'à Milan;[205b] concentration à Constantinople, Milan et Aquilée du miliarensis léger à la légende Gloria Romanorum des temps valentiniens.[206] De même, en Gaule, à Trèves et Lyon, Valentinien II s'efforce de recréer la confiance en faisant regraver Vrbs Roma sur les siliques maintenues à bon poids. Le type Virtus Romanorum, inventé par Gratien, n'a pas disparu de Trèves, mais déjà Vrbs Roma le contamine, puisque sur les deux revers Rome est désormais assise sur la cuirasse.[207] Trèves et surtout Lyon—avec cinq séries et finalement deux officines—sortent donc cette nouvelle silique qui se diffuse immédiatement en Bretagne.[208]

Ainsi en 392—au seuil de l'ultime secousse du IVe s., pouvait-on avoir l'impression que l'essentiel était sauvegardé: Permanence du 1/72e dont la légende traditionnelle, Virtus Exercitus, se perpétue à Trèves et Lyon,[209] solidité ou, à tout le moins, encadrement de la silique. Pourtant, il va suffire de quelques mois pour que l'édifice soit définitivement ébranlé. La guerre civile fait craquer la digue et désormais sans complexes, l'Etat lâche sa monnaie d'argent et, cédant à la pression de la demande, fonde sur l'or son système monétaire.

Conclusions

Arrêtant en ce point l'aperçu général de la dynamique des frappes, nous voudrions poser quelques conclusions:

1) Les 3/4 des trésors bretons—disons près d'une quarantaine,[210] se situent hors des limites de notre enquête: postérieurs à 393, ils témoignent d'un faciès qui, assurément n'est pas totalement étranger au continent: songeons, sinon au trésor de Dortmund, du moins à celui de Wiesbaden qui révèle, sous Honorius et Arcadius, d'énormes envois de siliques à partir de Milan (et de Rome).[211] La différence vient cependant de ce qu'en Bretagne la retraite romaine a pétrifié une situation qui ailleurs a continué de bouger. S'il y avait eu on ne sait quelle singularité bretonne, elle aurait pu se manifester avant 393, or, jusqu'à cette date, le nombre des dépôts publiés fait honneur au zèle de l'Ecole Anglaise mais se situe environ au tiers du total recensé: les découvertes du Rhin et davantage celles du Danube les concurrencent[212] et on pourrait même sans paradoxe parler d'une spécificité dacique, en réalité pas plus réelle que celle supposée pour la Bretagne.

Encore conviendrait-il de modifier cette première approximation: 14 dépôts en Bretagne, 6 sur le Rhin, 18 en zone danubienne, 3 ailleurs, en tenant compte de ces multiples naturels que sont les lingots, les disques et les plats d'anniversaire. On ajouterait alors à la liste précédente les noms de

Numansdorp,[213] Šabac, Červenbreg, Svirkovo, Niš,[214] Kertch,[215] Genève,[216] Gross Bodungen,[217] Almendralejo, Toulouse[218] toutes découvertes qui infirment l'idée d'une primauté bretonne pour la quasi totalité du IVe s.

2) En revanche, l'évidence saute aux yeux, l'argent a été enfoui le long du limes, là où il y avait des garnisons. Ce métal a pu avoir des destinations civiles, le cas échéant: ainsi, lors de la dédicace de Constantinople. Mais sa principle fonction est de nourrir la guerre, Guerres contre les peuplades barbares de Bretagne, du Rhin, du Danube. Guerres aussi civiles, conflits de Constant et de Constantin II peut-être, certainement campagnes de Constance II contre Magnence et de Maxime contre Théodose.

Ne croyons pas toutefois que ce soit toujours la règle: il n'y a pas de traces visibles des activitiés militaires de Constant en Bretagne; le passage dans l'île est commémoré par le bronze, non par les 1/96es. Même attitude de la part de Constance II: la lutte contre les Sassanides trouve son illustration dans les Fel Temp Reparatio. Les espèces blanches étaient réservées à de rares donativa.[219] Certains empereurs, comme Valentinien, choisissent même de limiter systématiquement les émissions. Ils se recontrent par là avec une norme suivie en Orient. Il est en effet caractéristique que la partie asiatique de l'Empire participe peu ou pas à la frappe de l'argent. Sauf dans deux occasions, à la fin du règne de Constantin, puis au moment de la Reconquête sous Constance II, elle limite sa participation à du numéraire courant et, en 375, au lieu de redonner dynamisme au monnayage d'AR, elle décide, alors que pourtant elle dispose de régions métallifères et que ses traditions antérieures et ultérieures[220] y ont été ou y seront favorables, de fermer ses ateliers. On parle toujours du problème breton, celui de l'Asie n'est pas moins intéressant et les solutions ne sont pas aisées à découvrir: volonté politique face aux Sassanides champions de la drachme ou bien décalage de niveau de vie? Les très hautes fortunes, certes sont à l'Ouest, mais le palier moyen des échanges ne serait-il pas plus élevé à l'Est, je serais très tenté de le croire.[221]

3) En effet—et nous souhaiterions terminer par ce point, quoiqu'il échappe en partie au cadre que nous nous sommes fixé—il a été beaucoup discuté sur les raisons de la dégradation, puis de la disparition de la silique. P. Grierson croit en des cours parallèles qui auraient rendu la frappe ruineuse pour l'Etat.[222] Notre point de vue est différent et il se fonde sur une mutation qu'on pourrait ainsi formuler: la vaisselle est thésaurisée en proportion inverse de la monnaie. Par suite de la hausse des prix, une silique dépréciée avait perdu sa dynamis. Que pouvait-on acheter avec un gramme d'argent? Au contraire, pris au poids, plateaux, bols et plats conservaient une valeur d'échange. Lors de ces conférences faites en Mai dernier et que nous évoquions à l'instant, le Baron Chaurand fit circuler un fragment d'argenterie découvert dans l'Isère: il pesait 128.8 g. Autant dire qu'il équivalait à 2 sous.[223] A cet échelon là, l'argent était utile. Cela l'Orient le comprendra aussi bien que l'Occident.[224]

Nos deux exposés ont tenté de jeter un peu de lumière sur l'évolution du IVe siècle, en menant parallèlement nos enquêtes sur les numéraires d'AR et d'AE. Cette méthode a pu révéler des convergences (sous Constance II et Julien, jumelage de la silique et de l'Aes 4) comme aussi des divergences (sous Valentinien I, l'aes 3 à l'Ouest occupe le terrain entre deux phases intenses de production de l'argent). Au lieu d'être simplement linéaire, l'histoire de la monnaie a, grâce à la confrontation avec les trésors, dessiné la courbe de son tracé. Il resterait, pour mieux cerner les politiques qui se suivent ou alternent, à introduire l'or en troisième paramètre. On verrait ainsi le poids des interférences. Plusieurs indications ont déjà été fournies ailleurs[225] mais aujourd'hui nous reculons devant une synthèse qui exige de nous davantage de temps et de réflexion. En ce domaine, comme dans celui, si obscur de la métrologie,[226] la coopération de tous les numismates est encore nécessaire pour que nous laissions à nos successeurs au moins quelques bonnes hypothèses de travail.

J. P. Callu

NOTES

1. Les RIC VII et IX couvrent les années 324-337 et 364-392. Pour l'intervalle 337-364, outre J. P. C. Kent, "An introduction to the Coinage of Julian the Apostate," NC, 6, 9, 1959, 109-117, nous avons recouru à notre mémoire inédit, Le monnayage de l'argent au IVe s. p. Chr. Essai sur le bimétallisme du Bas Empire, Rome, 1959; travail conduit, pour une bonne part, d'après les collections d'Italie du Nord.

2. RIC, VI, Trèves, no. 100-133 (294-301), quinaires, no. 134-236 (303); Ticinum, no. 12-22 (294-300); Aquilée, no. 16-17 (300); Rome, no. 10-44 (294-299); Carthage, no. 10-16 (296-300); Siscia, no. 32-73 (294-300 et 303); Serdica, no. 1-2 (303-305); Thessalonique, no. 6-18 (298-c. 302); Héraclée, no. 1-11 (294-296); Nicomédie, no. 18-26 (295-296); Cyzique, no. 4-6 (294-295); Antioche, no. 31-43 (294-298); Alexandrie, no. 7-13 (295-296).

3. Ibid., Rome no. 153-157 et 187-193; Ostie, no. 11-13; Carthage, no. 49; Aquilée, no. 75 (Plusieurs ex. de Constantin César seraient peut-être à ajouter, mais il n'est pas facile, à l'exergue, de distinguer entre AQ et RQ).

4. Ibid. Serdica, no. 11 et 21-22; Antioche, p. 623, no. 1. Peut-être aussi Siscia, p. 473, no. 1.

5. Ibid. no. 635-638, quinaires, no. 639-641.

6. A. Jeločnik, "The Sisak Hoard of Argentei of the Early Tetrarchy," Situla, 3, Ljubljana, 1964: 1415 deniers (en 296); RIN, 9, 1896, 144: c. 200 deniers; K. Pink, "Der Münzfund von Krempelstein," Mitt. Gesell. in Wien, 1929, 106-108: lot de 52 deniers et 4 aurei (c. 302); K. Bíró-Sey, Coins from Identified Sites of Brigetio and the Question of Local Currency, Budapest, 1977, 135-136: aurei, médaillons d'AV et 46 deniers; il y avait un argenteus de Dioclétien dans la trouvaille de Thibouville, en 298 (Gallia, 19, 1961, 71-104 et 20, 1962, 255-315).

7. K. Regling, Römischer Denarfund von Frondenberg, ZFN, 29, 1912, 230: en plus de plusieurs trouvailles isolées jusqu'en "Prusse Orientale", cite le dépôt de Betteldorf dans l'Eifel: 43 deniers et 577 PB enfouis en 324; S. Bolin, "Die Funde römische und byzantinischer Münzen in freien Germanien," DAI, 19, 1930, 86-146.

8. supra n. 7; BSFN, 27, 1972, 299-301; FMRD, IV, 2, no. 2299; H. A. Cahn, "Trésor d'argenterie et de monnaies en argent à Kaiseraugst," Bull. Cercle d'Et. Num., 3, 1, 1964, 42-45 = BSFN, 26, 1971, 115-120; H. R. Grueber, "The Southsea Find of Fourth-Century Silver Coins," NC, 5, 16, 1936, 292-303 (Add., NC, 6, 19, 1959, 89-91). Ajouter encore 1 argenteus à St. Vincent de Mercuze I, en 313 (Bull. Soc. de Statistique de l'Isère, 1870, 3-16), peut-être des ex. à Famars (Gallia, 19, 1961, 151-190) et en Commagène (Istanbuler Forschungen, 23, 1964, 282-288).

9. H. J. Kellner, "Ein Fund spätrömischen Münzen von Kellmünz," Bayer. Vorgeschichtsblätter, 20, 1954, 119-128; P. Bastien et C. Metzger, Le trésor de Beaurains (dit d'Arras), Wetteren, 1978, 189-190 (Les auteurs, p. 24, signalent également 2 argentei de Maximien Hercule).

10. RIC, VI, Trèves, no. 756-765 et 827-828; P. Bastien et C. Metzger, op. cit., 24: c. 63 quinaires; voir infra n. 95 (Lengerich).

11. J. N. Barrandon, J. P. Callu, C. Brenot, "The Analysis of Constantinian Coins (A.D. 313-340) by Non-destructive Californium 252 Activation" Analysis, Archaeometry, 19, 1977, 173-186.

12. RIC, VII, Sirmium, no. 14 (Bruun 320); Thessalonique, p. 570, no. 1; Constantinople, no. 6 (Bruun 326). Autre hypothèse, bloquer simultanément en 326 la frappe dans les 3 ateliers.

13. ibid.: 315, Ticinum, no. 36; 319, Aquilée, no. 32; 320/321, Aquilée, no. 80-84; Rome, p. 714, no. 224 A; Siscia, p. 716, no. 158B.

14. La première mention du miliarensis date de 392 dans le traité de mensuris et ponderibus, 69 b, d'Epiphane, de Salamine de Chypre. Comme Mommsen, nous attribuons ce nom à la pièce de 1/72e, plus courante que celle au 1/60e car 1) Cosmas Indicopleuste, XI, PG, 88, cols. 448-449, l'assimile à la drachme sassanide de c. 4g; 2) la Novelle CV, 2, 1 de Justinien en fait état à une époque où le 1/60e n'est plus frappé. J'ajoute que dans la version géorgienne d'Epiphane, encore inédite (doc. et trad. R. P. M. van Esbroeck) il est écrit: "miliarision ce qui est la drachme selon les Romains". Voir aussi infra n. 104.

15. 1/18es constantinopolitains au type de la Tyché, MCONSB, Γ, Δ, ς, Z, I RIC, VII, no. 53 et Paris, Cassel et Trèves; 1/24es Augustus/Caesar et Caesar/XX, à Trèves, Lyon, Arles, Rome, Aquilée, Siscia, Thessalonique, Constantinople, Nicomédie (cf. RN, 5, 11, 1949, 35-48 et BSFN, 5, 4, 1950, 3-4). (Malgré nos réserves exprimées in Gnomon, 50, 1978, 295, nous indiquons ici la date proposée par J. Lafaurie et adoptée par P. Bruun, parce que l'ex. à la marque de Lyon provient du trésor de Kaiseraugst. Une autre hypothèse serait de placer la série en 337 et de l'attribuer à un seul prince, Constantin II devenu, de

César, Auguste, cette année là); 1/72es Gloria Exercitus, Virtus Exercitus, Thessalonique, RIC, VII, no. 196-197 et 219; Constantinople, no. 57-58A, 129-131, 133-135 et p. 719. Add. quelques séries: Genium PR de 7.62 g, ibid., 326, Rome, no. 276; Constantinus Aug, Empereur au labarum, 6.6 et 6.1 g, ibid., 337, Rome, no. 399; Felicitas Publica, d'Hannibalien, 3.02 g, ibid., 335, Constantinople, no. 100; Vrbs Roma/Louve, SMTSE, 0.35 g, Reggio Emilia.

16. RIC, VII, Ticinum, no. 184; Rome, no. 379-380; Thessalonique, no. 195; Nicomédie, no. 187; Antioche, p. 689, no. 70 A.

17. Rome: Constance Auguste, R (Mus. Naz.); Siscia: Constant et Constance Augustes, SIS, .SIS., SIS∽, plusieurs ex. dans le trésor d'Enns-d'Enns-Lauriacum cf. infra n. 32.

18. F. Kenner, "Denare der Cäsaren Constantinus und Constantius aus einem Funde in Mitrovic", Wiener Num. Monatshefte, 2, 1866, 32-36, F. S. Kupido, "Inedirte Denare und Medaillons Constantin's d. Gr. und Constantius als Beitrag dem Funde von Mitrovic," ibid., 4, 1868, 145-151, cf. infra n. 26.

19. RIC VII, Rome, no. 377-378; Aquilée, p. 716, no. 130A; Siscia, no. 210, 212-213, 229-230, et 233-234; Thessalonique, no. 152, 181-182, 194 et 214-217; Héraclée, no. 145-147; Constantinople, no. 5, 54, 126-128, 136 et p. 719 (M/CONSA-I); Nicomédie, no. 117, 140-141, 186 et p. 720, no. 186A; Antioche no. 105-107.

20. Type de la Victoire pour Constantin II Auguste à Trèves, TRP (1 ex à Enns-Lauriacum cf. infra n. 27) et Aquilée, SMAQ (Londres) cf. infra n. 29.

21. La légende incline à placer après la guerre civile la série qui ainsi serait contemporaine des dernières expériences de billon cf. supra n. 12—On a successivement 3 Empereurs à Sirmium, Trèves et Thessalonique, puis 4 à Rome, Cyzique et Nicomédie, enfin, à nouveau, 3, à Héraclée et Nicomédie. La 3ème phase est postérieure à la mort de Crispus, mais, durant la première, où pourtant régnaient un Auguste et trois Césars: Crispus, Constantin II et Constance, le revers n'avait pas été adapté à la réalité cf. RIC, VII, Sirmium, no. 15 (Bruun 320-4), Trèves, p. 714, no. 474B (Bruun 324-5), Thessalonique, p. 718, no. 140A-C (Bruun 325); Rome, no. 275 (Bruun 326); Cyzique, no. 42-43 (Bruun 325); Nicomédie, no. 88-89, 142-143 et pp. 628-629 (Bruun 324-5 et 326-7); Héraclée, no. 105 (Bruun 329). Add. P. Bruun, "Felicitas Romanorum," Numismatica, 7, 1966, 1-11 (date corrigée pour Trèves: 328-9).

22. La dispersion pondérale est grande, mais pour 34 ex. la moyenne arithmétique est à 4.46 g.

23. RIC, VII, Ticinum, no. 185; Arles, no. 409 et p. 714; Siscia, no. 198-199, 211 et 231-232; Thessalonique, no. 150-151 et 218; Héraclée, no. 103-104 et 148-149; Constantinople, no. 99 et p. 718, no. 99A, 55-56 et 122-125; Antioche, p. 696, no. 106. Add Rome, tête nue/Constantinus Iun NobC, 4 enseignes, PR, 5.13 g, Karlovy. Une courte série lourde

avec 3 étendards existe à Rome (RIC, VII, no. 376, Fidis Militum, 6.04 g) et à Siscia (5.73 g, d'après Tanini).

24. Constantin II à Trèves (4 étendards), Constant à Siscia (4 étendards) et Thessalonique (4 et 3 étendards) cf. infra n. 29 et 31.

25. A s'en tenir aux 4 types majeurs, Trèves en frappe 1, Arles 1, Ticinum 2, Rome 4, Aquilée 1, Siscia 2, Sirmium 1, Thessalonique 4, Héraclée 3, Constantinople 2, Nicomédie 4, Cyzique 1, Antioche 3.

26. 8 ex sont conservés: 5 miliarenses (2 à 4 enseignes, 2 Gloria Exercitus, 1 Virtus Exercitus), 3 argentei (2 au type de la Victoire, 1 à celui des 3 palmes). Ateliers de Trèves (2), Rome (1), Aquilée (1), Siscia (1), Thessalonique (2), Constantinople (1).

27. Kaiseraugst cf. supra n. 8: dont 7 1/96e à la Victoire; Enns-Lauriacum: F. Kenner, Der römische Limes in Osterreich, IX, Vienne, 1908, 137; 3 1/96es à la Victoire; Southsea cf. supra n. 8: 2 1/72es, 4 Empereurs, 3 étendards, 2 1/96es à la Victoire; J. Evans, "On a Hoard of Roman Coins found at East Harptree near Bristol", NC, 3, 8, 1888, 22-46: 1 1/96e à la Victoire.

28. Exemple plus tardif, j'ai noté au Museo Nazionale un Vot V de Valens surgravé sur un revers constantinien (un autre exemple sera publié par M. Amandry).

29. A. Trèves, les 4 étendards figurent sur des 1/72es au nom des trois frères (5 ex. ? à Enns-Lauriacum, 1 à Southsea, SMTR), les 1/96es se répartissent entre le type de la Victoire et celui de Principi Iuventutis, à l'exergue TRP/S (6 ex. à Enns-Lauriacum). Si l'Italie a été un temps après 337 du ressort de Constantin II, il est probable que l'argenteus de Londres, Victoria DDNN Augg, SMAQ soit dû à son initiative cf. supra n. 20 et infra n. 32.

30. Trois séries de 1/96es: 1) Constantinus Augustus, Constantius Augustus, Constans Augustus à Constantinople (11 officines), Nicomédie, Antioche, Alexandrie (la seule frappe pour cet atelier), type de la Victoire; 2) Felicitas Reipublice, Vot XV Mult XX, Constantinople et Nicomédie, Vot XX Mult XXX, Antioche; 3) Votis XV Multis XX, Votis XX Multis XXX, Antioche.

31. 4 étendards: 1/60e à Siscia, ·SIS· et Thessalonique, TS (2 ex à Enns-Lauriacum); ce deuxième atelier frappe également des revers avec 3 étendards: curieusement, les ex. de Constant, l'Empereur de l'Illiricum, sont au 1/60e, ceux de ses frères au 1/72.

32. Constant partage avec Constance ce revers à Siscia dans trois émissions SIS, ·SIS·, SIS◡, exergues qui se lisent déjà du vivant de Constantin II cf. infra n. 35. La pièce est connue aussi pour Rome (cf. supra n. 17). Elle témoignerait du passage de l'Italie sous le contrôle de Constant. De l'héritage constantinien, Constantin II ainsi aurait retenu le type de la Victoire, Constant, celui des 3 palmes cf. supra n. 29. Un ex. pour Constant à Enns-Lauriacum.

33. A Thessalonique, mais le pied passe du 1/72e au 1/60 e (5 ex. à Enns-Lauriacum).

34. Autres revers, Pax Aeterna, ·SIS·, SIS✧, 1/60e, pour Constantin II (à Enns-Lauriacum); Felicitas Perpetua, Vot V, SIS, quaternion pour Constant (trésor de Trèves).

35. 1) 1/24e: Gaudium Populi Romani, Sic V Sic X, Siscia, SIS, ·SIS·, SIS✧ (Constant); Thessalonique, TSE, TES (Constant, Constance dans le trésor de Trèves); Vot V Mult X, Aquilée, AQ (Constant). 2) 1/60e: Gaudium Populi Romani, Sic V Sic X, Siscia, SIS✧, SISℛ (Constant à Enns-Lauriacum), Sic XX Sic XXX, SIS, SIS✧, SIS✱ (Constantin II à Enns-Lauriacum); 3) 1/72e; Gaudium Populi Romani, Sic V Sic X, Siscia, SIS, SIS✧ (Constant à Enns-Lauriacum et à Holwel cf. infra n. 36); Thessalonique, TSE (Constant, 3 ex à Enns-Lauriacum); 4) 1/96e: Gaudium Populi Romani, Sic V Sic X, Siscia, SIS✧ (Constant à Enns-Lauriacum), Sic XX Sic XXX, Siscia, SIS✧ (Constantin II). L'association de Constance II à cette série est-elle antérieure à 340? Une négation catégorique est à exclure, il nous semble toutefois que la formule Sic X Sic XX employée avec des avers de ce Prince date plutot des Décennales de Constant, car celles de Constance II étaient déjà lointaines cf. infra n. 37. L'importance de Siscia en ces années là pourrait être confirmée, croyons nous, par le coffret de Pecs (cf. D. Gaspar, "Spätrömische Kästchenbeschläge in Pannonia," Acta Antiqua et Archaeologica, 15, 1, 1971, 23-24, pl. LIX): représentation de Rome entourée, porteuses de couronnes, de Carthage et Constantinople à gauche, de Nicomédie et Siscia à droite.

36. Série de transition à Trèves, Gaudium Romanorum, Vot V Mult X, 2 captifs, 1/72e, TR (Constance à Southsea); dans le trésor d'Holwel (Proc. R. Num. Soc., 23 Dec., NC, 1843, 9), il y aurait eu de Constant un Gaudium Populi Romani, Sic V Sic X, 2 captifs, 1/72e, TRP.

37. 1) 1/24e: Gaudiam Populi Romani, Sic X Sic XX, Siscia, .SIS (Constance), Sic XX Sic XXX, Siscia, SIS✧; Sic XX Sic XXX, Thessalonique, TES (Constant et Constance); 2) 1/60e: Gaudium Populi Romani, Sic X Sic XX (sans, puis encadré de palmes), Siscia, SIS, ·SIS·, SIS✧, SISℛ (Constant et Constance à Enns-Lauriacum); Sic XX Sic XXX (avec palmes), SIS✧, SISℛ (Constance); 3) 1/72: Gaudium Populi Romani, Sic X Sic XX (avec palmes), Siscia, SIS, SISℛ (Constant, à Enns-Lauriacum); 4) 1/96e: Gaudium Populi Romani, Sic X Sic XX, Siscia, SIS (Constance, 20 ex. à Enns-Lauriacum dont 1 à 1.48 g seulement "dünner Schrötling mit kleinem Sprung": quinaire?).

38. 1) 1/24e: Victoriae DDNN Augg, Vot X Mult XX, Siscia, ·SIS· (Constant); 2) 1/60e: Victoriae DDNN Augg, Vot X Mult XV, Aquilée, ✱AQ (Constant, 2 ex à Enns-Lauriacum), Vot X Mult XX (à l'avers, la titulature commence par DN), Aquilée, LXAQ (1ère marque explicite du soixantième); 3) 1/72e: Victoriae DDNN Augg, Vot X Mult XV, Aquilée, ✱AQ (Constant, 5 ex à Enns-Lauriacum), Vot X Mult XX (ex. avec DN), Aquilée, ✱AQ (Constant, à Southsea); 4) 1/96e: Victoriae DN Aug (sic, 2 Victoires au lieu d'une), Vot X Mult XV, Trèves, TR (Constant, à Southsea), Vot X Mult XX, Trèves, TR (Constant); Vot X Mult XV (ex. avec DN), Aquilée, AQ, ✱AQ (Constant, à Southsea).

39. 1) 1/24e: Triumfator Gentium Barbararum, Trèves, TR (Constant et Constance); Aquilée, ✳AQ (Constant et Constance); Siscia, SIS, ·SIS· (Constant, dans le trésor de Trèves et Constance); Thessalonique, TES (Constant, et Constance, dans le trésor de Trèves); 2) 1/60e: Triumfator Gentium Barbararum, Trèves, TR (Constance); Thessalonique, TES (Constant et Constance); 3) 1/72e: Triumfator Gentium Barbararum, Thessalonique, TES (Constant et Constance), 4 ex à Southsea, 1 à East Harptree, 1 à North Mendip cf. Sir A. Evans, "Notes on the Coinage and Silver Currency in Roman Britain from Valentinian I to Constantine III, " NC, 4, 15, 1915, 433-478, 1 à San Genesio cf. O. Ulrich-Bansa, "Ripostiglio di monete d'argento del IVe secolo d. Cr.", Atti Acc. Naz. Lincei, NSA, VIII, ser. VIII, 7, 12, 1954, 166-184.

40. Cohen cite un Constant, Votis X Multis XX, SIRM, de Sirmium, no. 198, Rollin. Même si cette pièce existe réellement, l'activité de l'atelier a dû être très réduite.

41. Aquilée possède une série propre de miliarenses légers, Felicitas Perpetua, Vot X Mult XX, ✳AQ (Constance, 3 ex. à Enns-Lauriacum), Vot XX Mult XXX, AQ (Constant).

42. 1) 1/72e: Gaudium Romanorum (2 captifs, cf. supra n. 36), Vot X Mult XV, TR (Constant et Constance), Vot X Mult XX, TR (Constant, à Southsea), Vot XX Mult XXX, TR (Constance); 2) 1/96e: Gaudium Romanorum (2 captifs), Vot X Mult XV, TR (Constant), Vot X Mult XX, TR (Constant et Constance).

43. 1) Felicitas Republice, Vot XX Mult XXX, Constantinople, C.A/B/Γ (Constance); 2): Vot(is) XX Mult(is) XXX, Constantinople, C.B/Γ (Constance); Antioche, ANT, SMANT (?, Constance). Toutes les titulatures commencent par DN.

44. Virtus DDNN Augg, Trèves, TR (Constant, à Southsea, et Constance); on connaît aussi, à Southsea, un ex. du même type, frappé à Lyon, PLG (Constant): ce fait indique une frappe tardive.

45. Ex. avec DN; SIS◡, SIS◡ et palme, SISQ et palme (Constant, 3 ex à Enns-Lauriacum et Constance).

46. Cf. supra n. 41; avec Vot XX Mult XXX, AQS (Constance). Pour l'exergue voir aussi infra n. 52.

47. TR (Constance).

48. Lyon: cf. supra n. 44. L'atelier étant fermé pour l'AR depuis les Vicénnales de Constantin I cf. supra n. 15—Arles: situation identique —Rome cf. supra n. 17 et 32.

49. Victoria DDNN Augg: Lyon, LVG (Constant); Arles, P/SARL (avec DN, Constant et Constance, à Southsea); Rome, R (Victoire avec prisonnier tiré par les cheveux, Constant et Constance, 2 ex. à Southsea, variante Victoria Augustorum); Trèves, TR (Constant et Constance, 23 ex. à Southsea, 4 ex. à East Harptree, variante Victoria Augustorum), TRP (avec DN Constance à Holwel et imitation à Southsea); Thessalonique, TES (Victoire avec couronne, Constant et Constance, 4 ex. à Enns-

Lauriacum; avec trophée, Constant, 2 ex. à Southsea et Constance); Victoria Augustorum: Siscia (Victoire avec couronne, SIS◡, SISQ, Constant— variante Victoria Constantis Aug et Constance—ex. avec DN à Enns-Lauriacum; avec trophée, SIS, SIS◡; Constant, à Southsea, et Constance); Felicitas Perpetua: Aquilée (Victoire avec couronne, AQ✱AQ, Constance, ex. avec DN—à Southsea; avec trophée, AQ, AQ·, Constant et Constance, toujours avec DN). Le type avec trophée, à Thessalonique, Siscia et Aquilée, paraît parallèle à celui à la couronne.

50. TR, TRP/S, à Enns-Lauriacum, Southsea, Willersey (cf. NC, 7, 11, 1971, 203-206), East Harptree et Oldcroft (cf. NC, 7, 14, 1974, 65-74). 74).

51. Virtus Exercitum, 4 enseignes, R (Constant avec DN).

52. Fel Temp Reparatio, Vot XX, prisonnier, R (Constant, à East Harptree et Constance). Add., avec prudence, sinon Fel Temp Reparatio, AQT Phénix, Constant avec DN, (Borghesi, 1881, no. 3005) du moins Felic. Temp. Reparatio, TRP, 1.87 g (Constance avec DN, à Holwel).

53. 1) Votis XXV Multis XXX: Nicomédie, SMN (Constant et Constance avec DN); Antioche, ANT (Constance avec DN, 2 ex. à Enns-Lauriacum; 2) Felicitas Reipublice, Votis XXV Multis XXX: Nicomédie, SMN (Constance); Antioche, ANT (Constance).

54. Le freinage de l'argent au moment de la Réforme de 348 traduisait la volonté de redonner un rôle dominant au "bronze". Pour une attitude analogue de Valentinien 1er cf. infra. Il faudrait aussi examiner de ce point de vue les orientations prises par Magnence et Julien à la fin de leur règne. [Rappelons que pour l'Ecole Anglaise l'Aes n'est pas êmis entre 341 et 347]

55. J. J. Chiflet, Anastasis Childerici Francorum Regis, Anvers, 284: cette découverte, faite le 5 Juin 1635, contenait des monnaies d'AV et d'AR dont 4 multiples cf. supra n. 34, 35 et 39.

56. Cf. supra n. 8: ce trésor devrait permettre de préciser et de rectifier, le cas échéant, le schéma que nous envisageons ici. Répartition des ateliers: 108 Trèves, 1 Lyon, 6 Arles, 3 Rome, 3 Ticinum, 8 Aquilée, 30 Siscia, 20 Thessalonique, 4 Constantinople, 1 Nicomédie, 1 Antioche —voir supra n. 15.

57. Cf. supra n. 27, 29, 31-35, 37, 38, 41, 45, 49, 50 et 53; infra n. 69 et 74. Au total, 9 Constantin II, 28 Constant, 37 Constance II, 1 Gallus. Ateliers: 12 Trèves, 34 Siscia, 15 Thessalonique, 10 Aquilée, 1 Héraclée, 1 Nicomédie, 1 Antioche.

58. Cf. supra n. 8, 36, 38, 39, 42, 44, 49 et 50. Add. un 1/72e aux 4 étendards de Constantin II cf. supra n. 29.

59. Cf. supra n. 50: dans ce dépôt de "bronzes", il y avait 2 argentei, Pax Augustorum, TR, et Victoria Augustorum SIS◡et 4 petites barres d'AR (9.68; 7.86; 3,04 et 2,25 g).

60. Cf. supra n. 27, 39, 49, 50, 52.

61. Cf. supra n. 35, 36 et 39; voir aussi n. 52.

62. 1) 1/24e: Triumfator Gentium Barbararum, TAQ· (à Trèves il convient d'ajouter les Securitas Reipublicae, TR); 2) 1/60e: Felicitas Perpetua, Vot V Mult X, LXAQ, à Southsea.

63. 1) 1/72e: Victoriae DDNN Augg, Vot V Mult X, Aquilée, AQ, ✱AQ, ✱AQ· (à Southsea); Lyon, PLG; 2) 1/96e: Felicitas Perpetua, Aquilée, AQ•, AQ✱, AQ; Lyon, LVG.

64. Cf. supra n. 62; Trèves: AequitasAug Nostri, TR, Principi Iuventutis, TR; Arles, Victoriae DDNN Augg, Vot V Mult X, PAR, Victoriae DDNN Aug et Caes, /IS/SAR (à Southsea).

65. Cf. supra n. 63; Trèves, Virtus Aug Nostri (avec IM, TR à Southsea), Principi iuventutis (avec DN), TR à East Harptree; Arles, Victoriae DDNN Aug et Caes, Vot V Mult X, PAR, Felicitas Perpetua, PAR (à Southsea).

66. Cf. supra n. 63; Trèves; Virtus Exerciti, sic (avec IM, puis avec DN), TR, 3 ex à Southsea; Pour l'ensemble de ces émissions, se référer á l'ouvrage classique de P. Bastien, Le monnayage de Magnence (350-353), Wetteren, 1964, qui, arrêtant les séries d'AR en août 352, préfère postuler un travail parallèle à Lyon, Arles, Aquilée et, bien sûr, Trèves à partir de 351.

67. Felicitas Romanorum (2 Empereurs sous un arc, Constance II et Gallus); Sirmium (rouvert pour l'argent après 25 ans, voir cependant supra n. 40), SIRM, ✱SIRM✱ , 4 ex. à Southsea, 2 à North Mendip, 1 à San Genesio); Nicomédie, SMN; Antioche, SMAN; Aquilée, AQ—Victoria Romanorum (Empereur et Victoire), Antioche, SMAN.

68. 4 étendards; Constantinople, C. A/B; Arles, SCON (après Novembre 353). On ignore le poids de DN Constantius Max Aug/Constantius Aug, 4 étendards, ✱R✱, Khell.

69. Virtus Exercitus, Constantinople, C. A/B/Γ/H/Z (4 ex. à Southsea, 1 à East Harptree, 2 à San Genesio, 2 à North Mendip); Cyzique (même exemple de réouverture que Sirmium), SMK; Thessalonique, TES (14 ex. à Southsea, 3 à East Harptree, 1 à North Mendip); Siscia, SIS (à Enns-Lauriacum).

70. Vétranion avait frappé trois modules: 1) 1/60e: Siscia, Gaudium Populi Romani, Vot V Mul X, SIS et deux palmes; Thessalonique, Virtus Exercitum, TSA; 2) 1/72e: Siscia, Victoria Augustorum, chaque fois avec palme, SIS, SISQ, SIS✱; 3) 1/96e: Siscia, Victoria Augustorum (Victoire avec couronne, SIS—avec trophée, SIS, SIS·).

71. Virtus Exercitus/tum, Rome, R, ✱R✱ (11 ex. à Southsea, 1 à East Harptree et à North Mendip); Arles, P/SCON (après Novembre 353, 7 ex. à Southsea, 1 à East Harptree et à North Mendip); Lyon, LVG (3 ex. à Southsea)—Indéterminés à Southsea: 3.

72. 1/60e: 4 étendards, Constantinople, C. A/B à Southsea); Arles, P/SCON (3 ex. à Southsea); Virtus Exercitus, 3 étendards, Cyzique, SMKΔ Arles, KONSAV; Virtus Exercitus, SCON; Gloria Exercitus, Nicomédie, SMN.

73. SIRM, . SIRM; SIRM.

74. Constantinople, C • Є• ; Thessalonique, TES (à Enns-Lauriacum et à Southsea); Siscia, SIS; Aquilée, AQ.

75. Antioche, ANT; Rome, R; Arles, PAR, CON?, TCON; Lyon, LVG.

76. Nicomédie, SMN (à Southsea); Cyzique, SMK; Constantinople, C. A/B/ Δ/S/Z/H/IA, avec palme: H/ Θ/IA (à Southsea et dans le trésor L. Ciani, 1925)—voir aussi infra n. 86.

77. Thessalonique, TES; Sirmium, SIRM, • SIRM, • SIRM • (2 ex. à Southsea, 2 dans le trésor L. Ciani, 1925); Siscia, SIS—voir aussi infra n. 86.

78. Aquilée, AQ; Rome, R.

79. Arles, PARL (à Southsea, un second ex. de poids faible à 1.94 g)—après Novembre 353, P/S/TCON (19 ex. à Southsea); Lyon, LVG (3 ex. à Southsea)—Indéterminé à Southsea: 1.

80. En parallèle avec les argentei à l'étoile frappés pour Julien César cf. infra n. 83. La légende Votis XXX Multis XXXX passe inchangée sur les"siliques".

81. Thessalonique: 1) 1/60e, Virtus Exercitus, 3 enseignes, TES; 2) 1/72e Virtus Exercitus,. TES (à Southsea); 3) 1/96e, Votis V Multis X, TES; Antioche, 1/96e à l'étoile, ANT, • ANT • (à North Mendip); Constantinople ? DN Iulianus Caes, 3 étendards, CONA, collection Longuet.

82. Vot V Multis X, TR (pour Constance II, hybride Votis V Multis X, Paris et Votis XXX Multis XXXX) peut-être un exemple à Southsea.

83. 1/60e, DN Iulianus (Nob) Caes, 3 étendards, CON, TCON (2 ex. à Southsea); 1/72e, Virtus Exercitus, SCON, P/S/TCONST; 1/96e, étoile, CON, TCON (3 ex. à Southsea et 1 à East Harptree).

84. Rome, Gloria Romanorum, Vot XXX Mult XXXX, multiples de 12/13 g, et de 61.27 g (Tanini); Sirmium, Gaudium Populi Romani, Votis XXX XXXX (• SIRM •), Gloria Reipublicae, Vot XXX Mult XXXX, SIRM (Tanini).

85. Aquilée, Votis XXXV Multis XXXX, AQ, 3.2 g. Windischgraetz. Cette pièce, taillée au 1/96e, pourrait avoir été préparée pour les fêtes du 8 Novembre 358.

86. Exemple des copies du trésor de Kecel cf. A. Alföldi, "Barbarische Nachahmungen römischer Siliquae aus dem 4. Jahrh. n. Chr.," Blätter f. Münzfr., 58, 1923, 393-396: sur 10, 6 ont la légende Votis XXX Multis XXXX et imitent des exergues de Constantinople ou de Sirmium. Les poids sont ceux de l'argenteus. Voir infra n. 176.

87. Kaiseraugst, Lengerich, Famars, Tournai (?) (Le trésor de "bronzes" de Metternich, enfoui en 350, contenait un argenteus de Magnence cf. BJ, 145, 1940, 180-226)—Zamosc, Padea, Unguraşi, Oltenia, Orhei, Chişinau.

88. Zamosc, cf. A. Kunisz, Materialy do prahistorii ziem polskich, 5, 5, Varsovie, 1973, 134, no. 192; 16 ex. dont 15 Votis XXX Multis XXXX,

ateliers repérés: 5 Cyzique (cet hôtel ne frappe pas la "silique"), 2 Nicomédie, 1 Thessalonique, 1 Sirmium; Padea, cf. SCN, 6, 1975, 231: Constance II; Ungurași, cf. D. Protase, Problema continuității in Dacia in lumina arheologiei și numismaticii, Bucarest, 1966, 170-171, no. 65: "vase d'argile plein de monnaies d'argent de Constance II"; Oltenia, ibid., 181, no. 143: " trésor de monnaies d'argent de Constance II"; Orhei, cf. V. V. Kropotkin, Kladi rimskih monet na territorii SSSR, Moscou, 1961, 94: 128 ex. de Constance II, 87 de Cyzique, 27 de Sirmium, 7 d'Antioche, 1 imitation et 6 indéterminés; Chișinau cf. B. Mitrea, "Un tezaur monetar restituit Sucidavei", S. C. Istorie Veche și Arheologie, 30, 1979, 63-77 (se référer à cet important travail de synthèse pour la localisation des trésors danubiens).

89. Kaiseraugst, cf. supra n. 8: 3 lingots d'AR estampillés IM CAE MAGNENTIVS AVG, chacun d'un poids de 3 livres (947/951 g, en pointillé PIII), marques LVGVBRIO et GRONOPI; Ljubljana cf. W. Schmid, "Emona... Ein Fund von Goldmünzen und Silberbarren," Jahrb. f. Altertumskunde, 7, 1913, 171-180: 2 barres de 319 et 640 g (1 et 2 livres), la première a l'empreinte d'un avers de Magnence: DN Magnentius PF Aug et dans un rectangle l'estampille CAQPF ou PS.· Les inscriptions de la seconde barre sont lacunaires: on déchiffre (Ma)gnentius PF Aug et en dessous... FLA. Un deuxième dépôt contenait 50 pièces d'or, dont la plus récente est un Constance II frappé à Antioche, Victoria Augustorum, Vot XXX, SMANT, ainsi que 9 barres d'AR (376.1; 356,82; 357.89; 390.24; 308.53; 303.75; 208.9; 187.78 et 77.23 g). Voir aussi A. Jeločnik, "Les multiples d'or de Magnence découverts à Emona," RN, 6, 9, 1967, 209-235 et K. S. Painter, "A Late Roman Silver Ingot from Kent," The Antiquaries Journal, 52, 1972, 84-92.

90. Cf. infra n. 214-218.

91. Antérieurement le trésor d'Arras; postérieurement ceux de Kecel et de Valea Strimbà, cf. infra n. 176 et 179.

92. V. Zedelius, Spätkaiserzeitlich-Völkerwanderungszeitliche Keramik und Römische Münzen von Laatzen, Ldkr. Hannover, Hildesheim, 1974, cf. infra n. 119.

93. Gallia, 19, 1961, 189-190: le trésor A contenait 9955 AR d'Auguste à Constance [II] (deniers ou siliques, on ne sait). Voir aussi notre étude, "Cachettes monétaires multiples (IIIe-IVe S.)", in Studien zu Fundmünzen der Antike, 1, 1979, 5-16, no. 24.

94. J. J. Chiflet, op. cit. supra n. 55, 270, V. Zedelius, op. cit., 23-26: sur 200 pièces d'AR, on ne connaît que 42 ex. 1 consulaire, 30 deniers jusqu'à Julia Domna et Caracalla, 1 argenteus de Constance II, Votis XXX Multis XXXX. Voir encore F. Dumas, "Le tombeau de Childéric," Centenaire de la mort de l'Abbé Cochet, Rouen, 1975. Le dépôt de Tournai, dans son ensemble est évidemment postérieur, puisque Childéric est mort en 482. Il est cependant plausible de supposer que le contingent d'argent a été rassemblé aux alentours de 358.

95. A. v. Werlhof, "Ueber einen Fund römischen Münzen bei Freren im Königreiche Hannover, Numismatische Zeitung, 3, 1849, 16; Fr. Hahn, Der Fund von Lengerich im Königreiche Hannover, Goldschmuck und römischer Münzen, Hannover, 1854; V. Zedelius, op. cit. 28-30: a) 1 monnaie d'AV d'Auguste et 1220 deniers de Trajan à Alexandre Sévère, dont une imitation d'Antonin; b) c. 10 monnaies d'or de Constantin et de ses fils dont 1 Constantin II (cf. Cohen, 66) et 2 Constance II (dont RIC, VII, Thessalonique, no. 148), c. 200 g d'AV (boutons, anneaux, bracelets, fibule, collier), patère d'AR, "4 petites monnaies d'argent de Constantin" (cf. supra n. 10); c) c. 70 argentei, Im Cae Magnentius Aug/Virtus Exerciti, TR, et un "médaillon d'argent de Constance II". Metternich voir supra n. 87.

96. V. Zedelius, op. cit., 35-40 (dépôts de Lashorst, Görlitz, Kecel II, Frauenbur Frauenburg. (Celui-ci, déterré en "Prusse Orientale" contenait 27 deniers de Titus à Commode et 1 solidus de Théodose II). Cette longue habitude de l'argent explique en partie la résurgence d'un monnayage du métal blanc dans les royaumes barbares dès le Ve s. (Pour toute cette période et plus avant, consulter les travaux fondamentaux de J. Lafaurie, sans oublier la monographie de G. Mickwitz, Die Systeme des römisches Silbergeldes im IV. Jhdt. n. Chr., Helsingfors, 1933 et celle de S. Bolin Fynden av romerska mynt i det fria Germanien, Diss. Lund, 1926).

97. A Southsea de Magnence et Décence 2 1/60es, 3 1/72es, 3 1/96 es, à East Harptree 1 1/72e.

98. Cf. supra n. 97 et n. 67, 69, 71, 72, 74, 76, 77, 79, 81-83. Ajouter aux 31 argentei peut-être un quinaire cf. supra n. 82.

99. Cf. supra n. 97 et n. 69, 71 et 83.

100. Cf. supra n. 67 et 69.

101. Trésor acheté par L. Ciani en 1925, cf. supra, n. 76 et 77; Kecel I cf. supra n. 86 et V. Zedelius, op. cit., 41: poids moyen de 10 imitations à 3.26 g; voir infra n. 176.

102. Cf. supra n. 67, 69 et 71.

103. La simultanéité entre réformes du bronze et de l'argent n'est peut-être pas absolue, si le Spes Republice, TES, de Constance II, figurant dans le trésor d'East Harptree est un quinaire et non une silique: poids indiqué de 1.81 g. (Autre ex., marqué SMPL, Lyon? pour Julien César, cf. Cohen 40). Quant à la date de la mutation pondérale du 1/96e au 1/144e, elle serait pour qui prend en considération les argentei d'Aquilée Votis XXXV Multis XXXX, cf. supra n. 85, postérieure à Novembre 358. Ce terminus nous paraît le plus bas envisageable, car il faut laisser aux siliques de Julien César un temps suffisant de fabrication, avant la proclamation de Lutèce en Février 360. On ne saurait par conséquent accepter la datation tardive (360) proposée par A. Missong, art. cit. infra n. 175, qui se fondait sur un rapport de 4 à 1 entre espèces lourdes et légères à la légende Votis XXX Multis XXXX. L'environnement historique, campagne contre les Sarmates, invasion perse, serait à préciser; cf. infra n. 215.

104. Au IVe. s. la silique est un poids égal au sixième d'un scrupule d'or (ainsi dans la célèbre inscription de Feltre, ILS, 9420, en 323). Sous bénéfice de recherches ultérieures, nous admettons le système de Mommsen qui s'appuie sur des textes métrologiques de VIe s., c'est-à-dire à une époque où la silique est une "monnaie" intermédiaire entre le sou et le follis (cf. notre article à paraître, " Le tarif d'Abydos et la réforme monétaire d'Anastase"): "silique" d'un poids réel de 2.24 g, d'un poids théoretique de 2.56 g (surévaluation de 12.50%), le miliarensis de 4.48 g étant tout à la fois le millième de la livre d'or, le 1/14e du solidus et les 7/4e de la "silique". Pour sa part, Ammien Marcellin appelle la nouvelle dénomination "argenteus nummus", (XXIV, 3, 3), mais le terme est sans valeur technique, puisque dans les mêmes années le Code Théodosien, XV, 9, 1 (en 384) l'emploie pour désigner le 1/60e. Dans le sens de l'hypothèse formulée par Mommsen, on notera que dans les trésors tardifs de Bretagne, la silique est très généralement rognée, le miliarensis, jamais. On avait donc le sentiment que la première de ces deux espèces était fiduciaire et qu'on pouvait jouer sur la valeur ajoutée.

105. TCON, 75 ex. à Southsea, 61 à East Harptree, 4 à Willersey cf. supra n. 50, exergue CON, à Honiton cf. infra n. 131.

106. A Southsea, il y a un Victoria DDNN Aug pour Constance II à Thessalonique (TES) et un autre à Trèves (TR); à Lyon, le type a été continué après l'Augustat de Julien au début de 360 et il semble que cette seconde phase soit beaucoup plus active cf. infra n. 110.

107. Antioche: ANT (2 ex. à East Harptree et à Sucidava, cf. infra n. 175, 1 dans le trésor Ciani); Nicomédie: SMN (à East Harptree et dans le trésor Ciani); Constantinople: C.A./B/Γ/Δ/E/Z/H/Θ/IA (9 ex. à Sucidava, 4 dans le trésor Ciani, 1 à Redea, cf. infra n. 177): Cyzique ne frappe pas la "silique".

108. Sirmium: SIRM (c. 60 ex. dans le trésor Ciani, 21 à Redea, 7 à Sucidava, 2 à East Harptree et San Genesio); Siscia: SIS (2 ex à Sucidava, 1 à Redea); Rome: R (à Southsea); Thessalonique grave le type à la Victoire cf. supra n. 106 mais a dû avoir des Votis XXX Multis XXXX (à Southsea); Aquilée ne frappe pas la "silique".

109. Arles: CON, P/SCON—par erreur avec T—(158 ex. à Southsea, 156 à East Harptree, 14 à Willersey); Lyon: LVG (130 ex. à Southsea, 114 à East Harptree, 1 à Willersey); Trèves: Gloria Reipublice, Vot XXX Mult XXXX, TR, Mus. Naz. Il faut insister sur l'unanimitas qui inspirait la Réforme et compte tenu du rapport des forces politiques, Constance II, soucieux de la situation sur le Danube et l'Euphrate, en fut le promoteur, Julien eut simplement à la mettre en oeuvre dans les Gaules.

110. Lyon: Victoria DDNN Aug, LVG, Constance II (27 ex. à Southsea, 49 à East Harptree), Julien Auguste (42 ex. à Southsea, 26 à East Harptree); Vot XXX, LVG, Constance II (130 ex. à Southsea, 114 à East Harptree); Vot V, LVG, Julien Auguste (134 ex. à Southsea, 125 à East Harptree); Arles: à Southsea, Constance: 78 PCON, 74 SCON, Julien César: 65 TCON, à East Harptree, 78, 78 et 61 ex.

111. DN Cl Iulianus Aug/Votis V Multis X, PCON (2 à Southsea, 2 à East Harptree), SCON (2 à Southsea, 3 à East Harptree), TCON (28 à Southsea, 16 à East Harptree).

112. Arles: DN Iulianus PF Aug/Votis V Multis X, pour les mêmes trésors PCON (5 et 24), SCON (11 et 26), TCON (18 et 39); Lyon: Fl Cl Iulianus PP Aug/Votis V Multis X, PLVG (10 et 28), SLVG (7 et 36)—pour les Vota V/X, exprimés ou non sous forme abrégée, on compte 7 variantes de titulature. Trèves: Votis V Multis X, TR, 106 ex. à Southsea, 36 à East Harptree; sans parallèle pour Constance II, cette série est postérieure à la rupture. Revers plus rares: Restitutor Reip, SCON (à Holwel); Victoria Perpetu, TR, Paris.

113. Virtus Exercitus, Lyon, LVG (à Southsea); Arles, CON, S/TCON (à Southsea avec Exercitum).

114. Multiple au 1/60e: Victoria Augusti, Vot XXXX, 2 prisonniers, CH; silique, Vot XXXX, C. A/B/Δ/E (à East Harptree).

115a. Rome: Votis V Multis X, R (2 ex. à Southsea), Victoria Augusti N, R (Paris); Sirmium: Votis V Multis X, SIRM; Siscia: VICTONIA ONVM, SIS, imitation (à Southsea); Thessalonique (au 1/60e): Votis V Multis X, TES, 5. 22 g (coll. part).

115b. Virtus Exercitus, aigle, Arles P/S/TCONST (3ex. à Southsea, 1 à East Harptree, 1 à North Mendip); Sirmium, SIRM, ·SIRM · (à Holwel). Victoria Romanorum, Sirmium, SIRM, ✱SIRM (à Willersey et Holwel); Antioche, ANT.

116. Vot(is) X Mult(is) XX, Trèves, TR et palme, TRP (à Holwel et Tuddenham cf. infra n. 149); Lyon (5 avers), LVG, P/SLVG, SLVGD et avec aigle (22 ex. à North Mendip); Arles (6 avers), P/S/TCON puis CONST, ·CONST, CONST·, P/S/TCONST, et avec aigle (158 ex. à North Mendip); Rome, R; Constantinople, CP. A/B/Δ, cf. infra n. 163; Antioche (5 avers), ANT (à Holwel et Shapwick I cf. infra n. 152).

117. 1) 1/60e: Antioche, Gloria Romanorum, ANT, Empereur sous arc; 2) 1/72e: Antioche, Gloria Romanorum, ANT, id. (à East Harptree), Votis V Multis X, ANT; Arles, Restitutor Reip, PCONST; 3) silique: Vot(is) V Mult(is) X, Antioche, ANT; Nicomédie, SMN; Constantinople, CP· A/B/Γ/Δ (à Grovely Wood cf. infra n. 146); Sirmium, SIRM; Arles, P/S/TCONST (à Holwel et Terling cf. infra n. 142); Restitutor Reip, Arles, PCONST.

118. Kaiseraugst, SMB, 18, 66, 1967, 50-57 (il n'est pas assuré que la silique de Julien fasse partie du trésor); Merelbeke, Thirion no. 194, dont une silique de Julien Auguste.

119. Cf. supra n. 92.

120. Cf. supra n. 8, 27, 29, 36, 38, 39, 42, 49, 50, 58, 62-67, 69, 71, 72, 74, 76, 77, 79, 81-83, 97, 98, 106, 108-113, 115, 115 a et b; 781 ex. sur un total de 978. Au total 2 Trajan, 2 Antonin, 1 Faustine, 1 Marc Aurèle, 1 Dioclétien, 2 Constantin I, 1 Crispus, 2 Constantin II, 36 Constant, 422 Constance II, 5 Magnence, 3 Décence, 5 Galle, 495

Julien. Ateliers: 143 Trèves, 358 Lyon, 380 Arles, 5 Aquilée, 16 Rome, 2 Siscia, 7 Sirmium, 24 Thessalonique, 7 Constantinople, 2 Nicomédie. Southsea est dans le Hampshire.

121. Cf. supra n. 50, 105, 109, 115b. Au total 21 Constance II, 35 Julien. Ateliers: 6 Trèves, 17 Lyon, 29 Arles, 2 Rome, 2 Sirmium. Willersey est dans le Gloucestershire.

122. Cf. supra n. 27, 39, 49, 50, 52, 60, 65, 69, 71, 83, 97, 99, 105, 107-112, 114, 115b, 117; 1053 ex. sur un total de 1496. Il y avait 1 Constantin I, 4 Constant, 340 Constance II, 1 Décence, 718 Julien, 8 Jovien, 165 Valentinien I, 199 Valens, 60 Gratien, Ateliers: 207 Trèves, 574 Lyon, 553 Arles, 1 Aquilée, 99 Rome, 1 Siscia, 6 Sirmium, 12 Thessalonique, 4 Constantinople, 4 Nicomédie, 22 Antioche. East Harptree est dans le Somerset. Voir infra n. 160, 169-170 et 192.

123. Cf. infra n. 177: 23 ex. sur 27.

124. Cf. infra n. 175: 133 ex. sur 536.

125. Cf. infra n. 191: 2 ex. sur 9.

126. Cf. supra n. 76, 86 et 101. Homogénéité du trésor Ciani et de Kecel: pour: 1) Kecel a été signalé en 1922/1923 et Ciani a acheté en 1925; 2) le pourcentage important de Sirmium dans les deux trouvailles; contre: 1) Kecel semble constitué d'argentei, le dépôt Ciani privilégie au contraire les siliques; 2) Constantinople est inégalement représenté: Le lot Ciani ne comprend que des Votis XXX Multis XXXX de Constance II (3 argentei et c. 67 siliques); à Kecel, les Tricennalia de ce même Empereur sont aussi largement évoquées (y compris sur les imitations) mais on comptait en outre, d'une part, un certain nombre de deniers du Haut-Empire (un deuxième trésor découvert à Kecel en 1934 contenait 2816 deniers de Néron à Septime Sévère), de l'autre, des frappes de Valentinien I et de Valens. Voir infra n. 176.

127. Cf. supra n. 39, no. 100-101, siliques de Sirmium Votis XXX Multis XXXX.

128. NC, 6, 14, 1954, 209-211, 20 ex. sur 117.

129. ibid., 7, 5, 1965, 177-182, 42 ex. sur 447.

130. ibid., 5, 18, 1938, 53-58, 11 ex. sur 125.

131. ibid., 5, 5, 1925, 396-397, 1 ex. sur 16.

132. ibid., 4, 15, 1915, 433-478, 658 ex. sur 2044.

133. ibid., 6, 2, 1942, 105-106, 4 ex. sur 13.

134. ibid., 5, 16, 1936, 314-316, 22 ex. sur 85.

135. ibid., 5, 14, 1934, 61-73, 25 ex. sur 100.

136. Antiquaries Journal, 1940, 481, 2 ex. sur 9.

137. Cf. supra n. 36, 64 ex. sur 318.

138. NC, 5, 15, 1935, 254-274, 45 ex. sur 228.

139. ibid., 5, 2, 1922, 134-139, 7 ex. sur 53.

140. ibid., 5, 15, 1935, 67-68, 1 ex. sur 7.

141. ibid., 2, 9, 1869, 372, 7 ex. sur 54.

142. ibid., 5, 13, 1933, 144-181, 34 ex. sur 325.

143. ibid., 6, 8, 1948, 205-214, 39 ex. sur 388.

144. ibid., 6, 2, 1942, 101-104, 7 ex. sur 80.

145. ibid., 5, 9, 1929, 319-327, 6 ex. sur 70.

146. ibid., 4, 6, 1906, 329-347, 25 ex. sur 299.

147. ibid., 6, 8, 1948, 82-85, 5 ex. sur 62.

148. ibid., 3, 4, 1884, 348, 2 ex. sur 26.

149. ibid., 6, 8, 1948, 169-173, 8 ex. sur 114.

150. Archeologia, XIV, 71, 2 ex. sur 30.

151. NC, 1, 17, 1855, 101-115, 98 ex. sur 1506.

152. ibid., 5, 16, 1936, 245-250, 7 ex. sur 120.

153. ibid., 5, 16, 1936, 257-261, 10 ex. sur 230.

154. ibid., 6, 2, 1942, 97-104, 8 ex. sur 200.

155. ibid., 4, 8, 1908, 215-217, 13 ex. sur 337.

156. RIC, IX, 1951; J. W. E. Pearce, "Notes on the Terling and other Silver Hoards found in Britain," NC, 5, 13, 1933, 170-181.

157. 1) 1/60e: Salus Reipublicae, RIC, IX, Lyon, no. 3, Arles, no. 3; Victoria Augustorum, Rome, no. 6; Securitas Reip, Constantinople, no. 8; Vota, Lyon, no. 4, Aquilée, no. 3, Thessalonique, no. 9. 2) 1/72e: Restitutor Reip(ublicae), Lyon, no. 5, Arles, no. 4, Rome, no. 7, Antioche, no. 6 (Par une systématisation unique au Bas-Empire la légende appartient aussi au solidus, à la silique et à l'Aes 3); Victoria Augustorum (2 variantes), Rome, no. 8, Constantinople, no. 10; Securitas Reipublic(ae) (2 variantes), Nicomédie, no. 3, Siscia, SM·SISC, Gloria Romanorum (3 variantes), Siscia, no. 3-4, Constantinople, no. 9, Antioche, no. 4-5; Virtus Exercitus (3 variantes), Arles, no. 5, Thessalonique, no. 10-11, Siscia (coll. part.). Add. multiples au 1/24e, Virtus Romani Exercitus, Virtus Exercitus, Arles, no. 2, Thessalonique, no. 7-8.

158. Constantinople, no. 11; peut-être à Rome, no. 9.

159. G. Mickwitz, op. cit. n. 96, p. 9; J. W. E. Pearce, RIC, IX, XXVIII. Voir infra n. 176.

160. Trèves, no. 2; Lyon, no. 6; Arles, no. 6; Aquilée, no. 4; Siscia, p. 145 (imitation, à East Harptree); Thessalonique, no. 12; Constantinople, no. 12; Nicomédie, no. 4-5; Antioche, no. 7. Il n'y a pas de frappe à Sirmium, mais pour Rome, nous connaissons un ex. pour

Valentinien, RB, 2.46 g (coll. part.). A East Harptree, sur 169 Restitutor Reip, 125 proviennent de Lyon, 20 seulement d'Arles où Pearce note au moins 6 émissions.

161. Trèves, no. 3-4; Lyon, no. 8; Aquilée, no. 5; Rome, no. 10; Sirmium, no. 2; Thessalonique, no. 14. A East Harptree, sur 54 Vota occidentaux, 49 proviennent de Rome.

162. Constantinople, no. 13, séquence des 8 émissions englobant celles de Procope cf. ibid., p. 200 (dans la série C·A, il y a à Milan, coll. Gerin, une silique C·Θ); Antioche, no. 8; Nicomédie, SMNE, 2.03 g, Muz. Naz.

163. 1) CP·A et assimilés, avant Procope: Valentinien I, 15 à Gura Ialomiţei (cf. infra n. 174), 10 en Dobroudja (cf. infra ibid.), 10 à Sucidava (cf. infra n. 175); Valens, 21 à Gura Ialomiţei, 10 en Dobroudja, 8 à Sucidava; 2) C·A· avant et pendant Procope; Valentinien I, 7 à Gura Ialomiţei, 4 en Dobroudja, 5 à Sucidava; Valens, 0 à Gura Ialomiţei, 8 en Dobroudja, 19 à Sucidava; Procope, 8 en Dobroudja, 5 à Sucidava (+ 4 ·C·A) 3) *C·A, après Procope: Valentinien I, 1 à Sucidava, Valens 6 ibid.; 4) CONSA et assimilé, après Procope: Valentinien I, 1 en Dobroudja, Valens, 2 ibid. Outre les 3 trésors mentionnés, Viespesti (cf. infra n.174) où toutes les monnaies postérieures à 364 sont émises par l'atelier du Bosphore, témoigne de la vitalité de Constantinople où sous Julien et Jovien 4 officines et non pas 8/9 travaillaient sur le métal blanc—Procope à Héraclée, Cohen 14, Nicomédie, RIC, IX, no. 6, Cyzique, ibid., no. 3.

164. Lyon, no. 9, Rome, no. 11.

165. 22 Valentinien I, 24 Valens; cf. supra n. 160 et 161.

166. Les textes législatifs pour l'or, C. Th., XII, 6, 12, 13 et 7, 3, sont de 366-367; cf. J. P. C. Kent, "Gold Coinage in the Late Roman Empire", Essays in Roman Coinage Presented to Harold Mattingly, (ed. R. A. G. Carson, C. H. V. Sutherland), Oxford, 1956, 190-204. Cependant, sur les monnaies, les marques OB et PS ne se lisent pas avant l'avènement de Gratien: OB à Trèves, Thessalonique, Constantinople et Antioche, PS à Trèves et—sous forme abrégée—P à Lyon, Arles et Siscia. Par la suite, de 375 à 395, la marque PS est régulière à Trèves et relativement fréquente à Lyon, Aquilée et Siscia.

167. Voir notre rapport sur le Rôle et la Distribution des espèces de bronze de 348 à 392, supra p. 41ff. A l'Est, fortifications en Scythie cf. Themist, Or., X, 136-138.

168. Hormis Trèves, cf. infra. la silique, avec des Vota, demeure gravée à Lyon, no. 19, Siscia, no. 11-13 et Thessalonique, no. 25. La diffusion semble restreinte, 2 ex., de Lyon et de Siscia, à North-Mendip.

169. Cf. supra n. 156; Terling: 2 Valentinien I, 29 Valens; East Harptree: 7 Valentinien I, 79 Valens; San Genesio: 3 Valentinien I, 32 Valens; Springhead: 12 Valentinien I, 89 Valens; Grovely Wood: 3 Valentinien I, 52 Valens; Icklingham I: 2 Valentinien I, 63 Valens; North Mendip: 12 Valentinien I, 214 Valens. Par la communication faite au présent

colloque par C. E. King,"The Sacrae Largitiones: Revenues, Expenditures and the Production of Coin, 141ff. nous savons maintenant que la division lustrale jouait dans les ateliers et qu'en conséquence l'arrêt de la silique à Trèves a dû se prolonger cinq années de 367/8 à 372/3; à noter que l'argent n'est pas mentionné dans le de rebus bellicis rédigé peut-être c. 368-369, cf. BAR, S 63, 1979.

170. 1) 1/72e: Vota, Arles, no. 14; Victoria Augustorum, Trèves, no. 24 (2 ex. à North Mendip), Lyon, no. 18, Arles, no. 13; Virtus Exercitus, Trèves, no. 26, SMTR (à East Harptree et North Mendip), TRPS. (2 ex. à East Harptree, 1 à San Genesio, à North Mendip et dans le Mr. Wood's Hoard), Aquilée, no. 10, Siscia, no. 10 (à San Genesio, North Mendip et Grovely Wood). A Trèves, il est impossible de distinguer les Valens d'avant et d'après 375 (no. 26, b, 2 et 42, a, 1); 2) 1/60e: Vota, Trèves, no. 23, Lyon, no. 16-17, Arles, no. 11-12 (à North Mendip), Siscia, no. 9; 3) 1/24e: Triumfator Gent Barb (rappel des Constantinides), Trèves, no. 22 (2 ex. à San Genesio), Siscia, no. 8.

171. 1) 1/60e: Victoria DN Aug, Constantinople, no. 31, Vota, Antioche, no. 27-28; 2) 1/72e: Victoria DN Aug, Constantinople, no. 32, Virtus Ex-serciti, Constantinople, no. 33, Gloria Romanorum (3 variantes), Antioche, no. 29-31; 3) 1/96e: Vota, Constantinople, no. 34-35, Nicomédie, no. 19, Virtus Exercitus (3 étendards), Nicomédie, no. 18; 4) siliques: Vota, Constantinople, no. 36-39 (11 ex. à Sucidava, dont 7 de Valens), Nicomédie, no. 20-22 (7 ex. à Sucidava, 1 à Redea), Antioche, no. 32-34 (cf. note suivante).

172. San Genesio contient 16 siliques d'Antioche en regard d'une seule de Constantinople. A Dranic et Redea (cf. infra n. 191 et 177), il y a 5 et 3 ex. antiochènes. Par ailleurs, on relève dans le RIC, IX, pp. 279-281, pour Antioche, 12 combinaisons d'exergue et, dans la série ANTA, 10 officines sont au travail.

173. On sait que les catalogues de monnaies de fouilles sont par nature pauvres en espèces d'argent, mais, même réduits à quelques exemplaires, ils sont significatifs (cf. infra n. 203).

174. Gura Ialomiţei, SCN, 1, 1957, 146-147: 46 siliques de Valentinien I et Valens frappées à Constantinople; Dobroudja cf. L. Ruzicka, "Siliquenfund in der Dobrogea (Rümanien)", Blätter f. Münzfr., 15, 1920-1923, 345-351: 44 siliques de Constantinople au nom de Jovien (I), Valentinien 1 (15), Valens (20) et Procope (8); Viespesti, cf. B. Mitrea, art. cit. supra n. 88 qui se réfère à C. Stirbu, Muzeul National, 3, 1976, 193-204 (non vidimus): 30 ex. dont 2 Constance II (Sirmium et Nicomédie), 3 Jovien (1 Constantinople et 2 Nicomédie), 2 Procope (Constantinople), 9 Valentinien Ier et 13 Valens (tous de Constantinople). Voir aussi supra n. 163.

175. B. Mitrea, art. cit. supra n. 88: on dispose d'informations sur 3 lots: 1) 105 ex. publiés par A. Missong, "Fund römischer Siliquen aus den Jahren 360-367", Wiener Num. Monatshefte, 4, 1868, 248-267: 11 Constance II (1 Lyon, 2 Siscia, 6 Sirmium, 1 Constantinople, 1 Antioche), 3 Julien (2 Constantinople, 1 Antioche), 7 Jovien (5 Constantinople,

2 Nicomédie), 24 Valentinien Ier (19 Constantinople, 5 Nicomédie), 50 Valens (40 Constantinople, 10 Nicomédie), 9 Procope (Constantinople), 1 Gratien (Constantinople); 2) un lot de 31 siliques acheté en 1926: 11 Constance II (1 Sirmium, 8 Constantinople, 2 Antioche), 9 Valentinien Ier et 11 Valens (8 Constantinople, 3 Nicomédie, 9 Antioche). 3) 300 ex. déposés à l'Institut d'Archéologie de Bucarest: 67 Constance II, 21 Julien, 13 Jovien, 95 Valentinien Ier, 96 Valens, 16 Gratien, 92 indéterminées. Le trésor originel s'élevait à c. 6000 monnaies. Voir aussi supra n. 107, 108, 124, 163 et 171.

176. Kecel cf. Arch. Ert., 39, 1920-1922, 99-102: au moins 62 siliques peut-être le double, de Constance II à Valentinien Ier—Valens: 3 d'Arles et d'Aquilée, 2 Siscia, 21 Sirmium, 1 Thessalonique, 27 Constantinople, 4 Nicomédie, 4 Antioche, 10 ex. sont des imitations de Sirmium et de Constantinople (argentei de Constance II et de Valens), en outre des deniers des 1er et 2e s. Trésor Ciani: c. 70 ex. de Constance II, 3 argentei (2 Sirmium, 1 Constantinople), 67 siliques (1 Arles, c. 60 Sirmium, 4 Constantinople, 1 Nicomédie, 1 Antioche). Voir aussi supra n. 76, 77, 86, 91, 101, 107, 108 et 126.

177. Creştera Coleçtiilor Caiet Selectiv de Informare, 6, 1962, 304-305: 27 siliques de Constance II et Valens (1 Siscia, 21 Sirmium, 1 Constantinople, 1 Nicomédie, 3 Antioche); au Cabinet de Numismatique de Bucarest 3 Constance II (Siscia, Sirmium, Constantinople) et 4 Valens (1 Nicomédie et 3 Antioche). Voir aussi supra n. 107, 108, 123, 171.

178. B. Mitrea, art. cit., 72, dont une silique: Valens (Nicomédie, 367-375).

179. ibid. et Folia Arch., 5, 1945, 95-99. Trésor mixte: deniers du IIe s., 10 monnaies d'AR de Constant et 3 solidi de Gratien; Journal of Field Archaeology, 1, 1974, 117-148: 69 AR, 4 AV, 10 fragments, Valentinien Ier, Valens et Gratien.

180. Chaddlesworth (Berks), NC, 3, 20, 1900, 337: 800 AR de Constance II, Valentinien Ier, Valens et Gratien; Uphill, VCH, Somerset, I, 1906, 355: 129 AR et AE, surtout Valentinien Ier et Gratien; Wookey Hole, ibid.: AR, Constance II, Julien, Valens, Gratien; AE, Constantin, Valentinien, Valens et Gratien.

181. Add. dans le trésor de bronzes de Wroxeter, NC, 1, 20, 1857, 79-83, enfoui après 364, une silique fourrée de Julien.

182. Cf. supra n. 169 et 170.

183. Constantinople, no. 42, 375-378, (5 ex. à San Genesio et 1 dans le Mr. Wood's Hoard); no. 51, 378-383. Le catalogue MM6, no. 2069 signale une silique de 1.97g, DN Gratianus PF Aug/Vot XX Mult XXX, ANT, qui serait la trace d'une rare émission antiochène postérieure à 375 et donc parallèle au no. 42 de Constantinople.

184. Symm, Ep., X, 2, 4 (376): pari vigilia prospectum videmus ut... flandae monetae nequitiam decoquat larga purgatio.

185. ibid., Ep., I, 13 et A. Alföldi, A Conflict of Ideas in the Late Roman Empire: The Clash between Valentinian and the Senatorial Aristocracy, Oxford, 1952.

186a. 1) 1/24e: Triumfator Gent Barb, 375-378, Aquilée (2 ex. à San Genesio, no. 6-7), Siscia (2 ex. à San Genesio, no. 5 et 8); 378-383, Rome, no. 32 (et pour Théodose, à San Genesio, no. 9); 2) 1/60e: Vota, 375-378, Trèves, no. 41, Siscia, no. 16; 378-383, Trèves, no. 52, Aquilée (2 ex. à San Genesio no. 85 et 99); Victoria Augustorum, 378-383, Rome, no. 33 (à San Genesio, Holwel et North Mendip); 3) 1/72e: Virtus Exercitus, 375-378, Trèves, no. 42 (à Holwel et North Mendip); 378-383, Trèves, no. 53 (difficilement discernable du précédent, à San Genesio, Holwel, North Mendip et dans le Mr. Wood's Hoard), Aquilée, no. 23 (4 ex. à San Genesio, dont 1 à 5.26 g, 2 à North Mendip et 1 dans le Mr. Wood's Hoard), Rome, no. 34 (à Holwel), Siscia, no. 23, (42 ex. à San Genesio, 1 à Holwel et North Mendip).

186b. Add. des fractions de la silique à Trèves, no. 56 et Rome, no. 36. Argentei à Aquilée, no. 24 et peut-être à Trèves, no. 54.

187. Trône: ante 375, Trèves, no. 27; 375-378, Trèves, no. 45, Siscia, no. 20; 378-383, Rome, no. 35. Cuirasse: 375-378, Trèves, no. 46, Aquilée, no. 15; 378-383, Trèves, no. 64, Lyon, no. 27, Aquilée (Paris), Siscia (Mus. Naz.).

188. Virtus Romanorum (trône), 378-383, Trèves, no. 58, Lyon, no. 26, Aquilée, no. 28, Arles (Paris); Concordia Auggg, 378-383, Trèves, no. 55, Lyon, no. 24, Aquilée, no. 25; Victoria Auggg, 375-378, Trèves, no. 43, Siscia, no. 17; 378-383, Trèves, no. 57, Lyon, no. 25, Aquilée, no. 26-27. Il faut ajouter une troisième série de siliques, celle des Vota: 1) 375-378: Trèves, no. 44 (dans le Mr. Wood's Hoard). Aquilée, no. 13-14, Siscia, no. 18-19 (7 ex. à San Genesio), Thessalonique, no. 29-30 (à San Genesio; 2) 378-383, Trèves, no. 59-63, Siscia no. 24-25, Thessalonique, no. 36 (à San Genesio).

189. 150 Vrbs Roma: 41 au trône (35 Trèves, 4 Siscia, 2 Rome), 109 à la cuirasse (62 Trèves, 37 Aquilée, 10 Lyon); 88 Virtus Romanorum (51 Trèves, 37 Aquilée); 75 Victoria Auggg (39 Trèves, 27 Aquilée, 9 Lyon); 36 Concordia Auggg (25 Trèves, 11 Aquilée) = 199 ex.

190. Springhead: 223 Vrbs Roma dont 158 au trône (156 Trèves, 2 Rome) et 65 à la cuirasse (53 Trèves, 11 Aquilée, 1 Lyon); 64 Virtus Romanorum (57 Trèves, 7 Aquilée), 25 Victoria Auggg (23 Trèves, 2 Aquilée), 5 Concordia Auggg (4 Trèves, 1 Lyon) = 94 ex; Mr. Wood's Hoard: 44 Vrbs Roma dont 30 au trône (29 Trèves, 1 Rome) et 14 à la cuirasse (10 Trèves, 4 Aquilée); 9 Virtus Romanorum (6 Trèves, 3 Aquilée); 4 Victoria Auggg (3 Trèves, 1 Aquilée); 1 Concordia Auggg (Trèves) = 14 ex; Shapwick II: 67 Vrbs Roma dont 44 au trône (42 Trèves, 2 Rome) et 23 à la cuirasse (17 Trèves, 5 Aquilée, 1 Lyon); 13 Virtus Romanorum (Trèves); 2 Victoria Auggg (Trèves) =15 ex. Des constatations semblables pourraient être faites sur des trésors bretons postérieurs à 388. Une autre anomalie se fait jour entre San Genesio et les dépôts insulaires: le type d'Vrbs Roma à la cuirasse l'emporte dans la péninsule, celui au trône, en Bretagne. Comme San Genesio s'arrête après 383, Springhead, Shapwick II et le Mr. Wood's Hoard, après 388, mais que Maxime, maître en Extrême Occident, n'a pas frappé d'Vrbs Roma, la différence dans les proportions pour le type, plus tardif, à la cuirasse s'explique par les distances géographiques, sources d'une diffusion plus lente.

191. SCN, 6, 1975, 229-231: 2 Constance II, 1 Gratien (Siscia), 6 Valens (5 Antioche et 1 Trèves post 375: RIC no. 44). Voir aussi supra n. 172.

192. East Harptree cf. supra n. 122, 160, 169-170; San Genesio cf. supra n. 39, 61, 67, 69, 100, 108, 127, 169, 170, 172, 183, 186, 188-190, le trésor s'achève par 6 siliques d'Aquilée, dont 1 Arcadius-postérieures à 383, RIC IX, no. 41. Au total 1 Constant, 5 Constance II, 8 Valentinien Ier, 82 Valens, 286 Gratien, 115 Valentinien II, 46 Théodose, 1 Arcadius. Ateliers: 250 Trèves, 19 Lyon, 126 Aquilée, 6 Rome, 57 Siscia, 3 Sirmium, 9 Thessalonique, 9 Constantinople, 16 Antioche.

193. no. 77. Add. un revers, no. 78, pour Flaccila.

194. O. Ulrich Bansa, Moneta Mediolanensis, Venise, 1949, 72-74. Les multiples paraissent n'être gravés qu'à Rome: Triumf Gent Barb, no. 52 et Thessalonique, Restitutor Reipublice, no. 56, cet atelier émettant aussi un miliarensis léger, Victoria Augustorum, no. 57. Siliques: Vrbs Roma, Rome, no. 53; Virtus Romanorum, Aquilée, no. 41 (cf. supra n. 192), Milan, no. 12 mais p. 73, Pearce ouvre la possibilité que ces frappes milanaises datent de l'invasion de Maxime, O. Ulrich Bansa préférant les dater de 388, op. cit., 118; Vota, Milan, no. 13-14 (32 ex. à Grovely Wood, North Mendip, South Ferriby, Terling, Sproxton, Icklingham I et III cf. O. Ulrich Bansa, op. cit., 74); Thessalonique, no. 58; Rome, cf. no. 62 (A cause de l'importance des Décennales de Valentinien II à Rome, cf. Symm, Rel., 13, nous plaçons en 385 les Vot X Mult XX datés par Pearce de 388, RIC, 113); Aquilée (Paris).

195. Sulp. Sev., Dial., III, 11; Ps. Aurel. Vict., 48, 17; Pacat, Pan., XII, 26.

196. Honiton 25%, Shapwick II 21.6%, Mr. Wood's Hoard 13.67%, Springhead 8.27%.

197. Manton Downs 26.92%, Grovely Wood 22.42%, Sturmer 16.66%, Mildenhall 15.38%, Cleeve Prior 15,29%, Colerne II 15%, Icklingham I 13.94%, Shapwick I 13.33%, North Mendip 12.67%, Tuddenham 12.28%, Terling 12%, Edington 9.67%, Icklingham III 8.26%, Colerne I 8%, Fleetwood c. 7.6%, South Ferriby 7.45%, Holwel 7.23%, Sproxton 7%, Icklingham II 5.71%, Coleraine 3.98%, Great Allington 3.7%, Dorchester 1.88%.

198. Trèves, RIC, IX, no. 80-81.

199. Trèves, no. 82 (2 ex. à Springhead), Lyon no. 31.

200. Londres, no. 3, Victoria Augg (à North Mendip), no. 4, Vot V Mult X (ibid.); Trèves, no. 83, Concordia Auggg (dans le Mr. Wood's Hoard), no. 84, Virtus Romanorum (214 à North Mendip, 59 à Grovely Wood, 41 à Icklingham I, 39 à Coleraine, 34 à Springhead et à Terling, 26 à Shapwick II); Lyon, Votis V Multis X pour Victor, Muz. Naz. (?).

201. Milan, Virtus Romanorum, no. 19; Aquilée, Victoria Augustorum, no. 53, Virtus Romanorum, no. 54. Moyennes arithmétiques sur pièces de collection: 1.53 g, Milan (28), 1.6 g, Aquilée (19).

202. Springhead (Kent), NC, 7, 5, 1965, 177-182: 3 solidi, 12 miliarenses, (dont 2 au 1/60e), 432 siliques; 16 Constance II, 25 Julien, 1 Jovien, 29 Valentinien Ier, 128 Valens, 169 Gratien, 32 Valentinien II, 9 Théodose, 37 Maxime; Ateliers: 343 Trèves, 14 Lyon, 23 Arles, 1 Milan, 33 Rome, 22 Aquilée, 2 Siscia, 1 Sirmium, 1 Nicomédie, 5 Antioche, 1 imitation; la pièce la plus récente est un Virtus Exercitus de Trèves post 388, no. 93 a; voir aussi supra n. 169, 190, 196, 199, 200; Bath (entre Bath et Bristol, Somerset), NC, 1840, 144: 250 dont 150 examinés, Valens, Gratien et Maxime, en proportions égales, types d'Vrbs Roma, Virtus Romanorum, Concordia Auggg (2), Vot V Mult X, Ateliers de Trèves, Rome (2) et d'Aquilée (1); Honiton (Devon), NC, 5, 5, 1925, 396: 16 siliques, 1 Julien, 3 Valens, 1 Gratien, 2 Valentinien II, 1 Théodose, 4 Maxime, 4 Arcadius (les plus récentes); Ateliers de Trèves (13), Lyon (1), Arles (1) et de Constantinople (1); voir supra n. 105 et 196. Norwich (?), Coin Hoards, III, 1977, no. 211: 15 siliques de Constance II à Valens (M. J. Vincenzi, Sales List, Colchester, Essex, Sept. 1975, no. 38-51) et no. 215: 59 siliques de Constance II à Maxime (Irelands, Norwich, Norfolk, Sale Catalogue 20th Oct. 1976 et 25th Jan. 1977, no. 730-759 et 790-819; Shapwick II (Somerset; à noter que ce trésor a été enfoui à 6 ft de Shapwick I, NC, 5, 16, 1936, 245-250, qui s'achève sans Honorius; selon le principe des cachettes multiples que nous avons exposé dans notre article cité supra n. 93, le 2ème dépôt pourrait avoir été mis en terre en même temps que le premier: il serait ainsi un précieux témoignage sur l'attitude du thésaurisateur, conscient de la chute pondérale de 387-388), NC, 5, 18, 1938, 53-58: 4 Constance II, 7 Julien, 2 Valentinien Ier, 34 Valens, 36 Gratien, 10 Valentinien II, 4 Théodose, 26 Maxime, 1 Victor, 1 Arcadius (7 ex. post 388); Ateliers: 101 Trèves, 7 Lyon, 5 Arles, 6 Rome, 6 Aquilée; voir aussi supra n. 190 et 196; Causeway Lane, (Leics.) Trans. Leicestershire Architect. and Archaeol. Soc., 10, 59: 60 AR jusqu'à Théodose; Mr. Wood's Hoard, NC, 6, 14, 1954, 209-211: 6 miliarenses, 111 siliques, 3 Constance II, 16 Julien, 1 Jovien, 10 Valentinien Ier, 26 Valens, 31 Gratien, 9 Valentinien II, 5 Théodose, 15 Maxime, 1 Victor; Ateliers: 72 Trèves, 4 Lyon, 13 Arles, 13 Rome, 9 Aquilée, 1 Siscia, 1 Constantinople, 2 Antioche. Les pièces les plus récentes sont un miliarensis de Lyon, no. 40 et 2 siliques de Trèves, no. 94, post 388; voir aussi supra n. 183, 186, 188, 190, 196 et 200. Add. St-Martory, Revue de Comminges, 90, 1977, 159-171: 1 silique de Maxime et Wiveliscombe, NC, 6, 6, 1946, 163-165: 1 silique de Julien. [Kempston I (Beds.), British Museum Occasional Papers, 5, 1979, (103-104 et C. E. King, "Late Roman Silver Hoards in Britain and the Problem of Clipped Siliquae" (à paraître): 53 ex. de Constance II à Maxime].

203. Blanchet 610, Landes: une douzaine de monnaies en argent de Valentinien Ier, de Gratien et de Théodose Ier; 6 siliques trouvées dans le fanum de Loubers, Tarn, cf. Gallia, 36, 1, 1978, 213-218, pourraient être considérées comme un trésor: 367-378, 2 Vrbs Roma de Trèves; 378-383, id. à Rome (1); 383-388, 3 Virtus Romanorum de Trèves.

204. Doc. inédite P. Bastien, dont 3 Vrbs Roma: 375-378, Aquilée, no. 15b; 378-383, Rome, no. 35a et c. (add. 3 solidi: 378-383, Trèves no. 49b et c, 383-388, Trèves, no. 77b). Voir aussi MM, 35, 16-17 Juin 1967, no. 159, 160, 163-166, 168, 170, 172-176, 178-182, tous des solidi dont 2 postérieurs à 388: Trèves, no. 90c et Milan, no. 20a. Total originel de 116 pièces.

205a. J. P. Callu, "Le centenarium et l'enrichissement monétaire au Bas Empire," Ktema,3, 1978, 301-316.

205b. Milan no. 27a (la série se poursuit pour Honorius); voir aussi supra n. 194. Ajouter de rares demi-siliques à Aquilée, no. 57. A cause d'un Théodose (ou Honorius?)au revers XV, AQ, on pourrait envisager de placer en 392, les piécettes X ou XV de Trèves, no. 109-110 cf. NC, 4, 15, 1915, 472-473.

206. Gloria Romanorum (globe), Constantinople, no. 85, Aquilée, no. 56, Milan, no. 25. Add. pour le 1/60e, Constantinople, Gloria Romanorum (sceptre), no. 84 et Milan, Vota, no. 24.

207. Virtus Romanorum, Trèves, no. 94, Vrbs Roma, Trèves, no. 95, Lyon, no. 43. Add. à Lyon un argenteus, no. 42.

208. A Shapwick II et dans le Mr. Wood's Hoard cf. supra n. 202. Très gros contingent trévire ultérieurement à North Mendip.

209. Trèves, no. 93, Lyon, no. 41 (un ex. avec la marque LVG.. sera publié par R. Delmaire). Add. à Lyon, Gloria Romanorum (étendard), no. 40, cf. supra n. 202 et à Trèves, pour Valentinien II, Vot XV Mult XX, Saint Germain (en 389).

210. Aux trésors mentionnés supra n. 132-155, ajouter ceux de Whorlton, Reading, Cornwall, Holyoke, Carletone, Bristol, Milverton, Taunton, Wiltshire, Traprain Law, Shanklin, North Cury, Charlton Mackrel, Chotham, Long's farm, Bentley, Guisborough, Richmond. Il appartiendra à C. King et à J. Casey de préciser cette première liste fondée sur les informations recueillies par A. Evans, S. Bolin, C. H. V. Sutherland, A. S. Robertson, R. A. G. Carson. Add. de ce dernier, The British Museum Yearbook, 1, 1976, pp. 74-75.

211. Dortmund: K. Regling. Der Dortmunder Fund römischer Goldmünzen, Dortmund, 1908, et Nachtrag zum Dortmunder Fund römischer Goldmünzen, ibid., 1910: 16 monnaies d'AR, imitations de style barbare, c. 407 (?). Wiesbaden, M. R. Alföldi, "Le trésor de Wiesbaden Kastel IV-V. siècle," Bull. Cercle d'Et. Num., 5, 4, 1968, 95-102, 16 solidi et c. 650 siliques post 408. On note, pour Honorius, 131 ex. de Milan et 122 de Rome.

212. L'argent de Bretagne a suscité l'intérêt des historiens et numismates anglais. En dernier lieu, voir les suggestives mises au point de R. A. G. Carson dans le Bull. Cercle d'Et. Num., 12, 4, 1975, 61-64 et surtout dans le British Museum Yearbook, 1, 1976, 68-82. Déjà en 1933, JRS, 23, 217, parlant des espèces d'AR, F. S. Salisbury écrivait: "It looks as if the areas where they were found were cut off at an early date from the process of withdrawal which went on elsewhere".

213. Votis XX Augg NN, Oudheidkundige Mededelingen, XLII, 1961, 63-77: Vicennalia de la Première Tétrarchie, 2 lingots de 305, 89 et 300. 43 g.

214. Šabac: 6 lingots, 628.4; 626.17; 627.37; 623.5; 232.73 g (avec référence probable à SIRM) cf. Sirmium, VIII, 1978, 110-111; Červenbreg: 2 plats marqués Licinius Invict Aug ob diem X suorum; Svirkovo: 2 lingots 635 et 631 g (avec référence—en pointillé—à SIRMIS), 3 vases marqués Licinius Invictus Augustus ob diem Decennalium suorum (Sic X Sic XX sur un seul vase); Niš: 5 plats marqués Licini Auguste semper vincas, Sic X Sic XX. Ajouter la trouvaille conservée à Munich: 3 plats pour les Quinquennales de Licinius II avec poincoins d'Antioche et de Nicomédie, un quatrième plat pour les Décennales du même prince, un cinquième, enfin, pour les Quinquennales de Crispus et Constantin II avec, en pointillé, NAIS. Pour toute cette question, voir Sirmium, VIII, 1978, 101-105 et 2 et Journal des Savants, 1975, 193ff.

215. 3 plats conservés à Léningrad dont 2 portent l'inscription DN Constanti Augusti Votis XX c. 343 cf. W. Grünhagen, Der Schatzfund von Gross Bodungen, Berlin, 1954, 18. (Add. J. Jurukova, "ingots en argent et une phiale en argent de Constance II," Archeologica, 1973, 50: deux lingots avec référence à Naissus et Constantinopolis en Bulgarie).

216. Plat marqué Largitas DN Valentiniani Augusti, 369 ou 374, ibid.

217. Missorium de Maxime ? c. 388, ibid. 15-38.

218. Missorium de Théodose I, Valentinien II et Arcadius, trouvé près de Badajoz, datable de 388, légende DN Theodosius Perpet Aug ob diem felicissimum X, ibid., 22. On connaît moins les patères de Toulouse cf. Magasin pittoresque, 1857, 95 et Vente Hoffmann, 1899, no. 138-139: un de ces deux objets en AR a au centre un petit médaillon en AV, buste impérial entouré de la titulature DN Theodosius PF Aug, d. de 185 cm.

219. Amm., XXIV, 3, 3, promesse par Julien de 100 argenteos nummos pendant la campagne de Perse (cf. infra n. 221); Zosim., III, 13, 130 pièces d'argent.

220. Songeons au tétradrachme séleucide, à l'héxagramme d'Héraclius.

221. Il est curieux qu'en 384 à Héraclée l'Empereur fasse allusion au 1/60e, appelé, sans spécification (cf. supra n. 219), argenteus, alors que ce multiple n'est plus frappé dans la Pars Orientis depuis 375; de même, Epiphane, évêque dans l'île de Chypre, définit en 392 un miliarensis (léger) qui de 375 à cette date n'est connu que par une frappe de Constantinople cf. supra n. 206. Faut-il croire alors que, malgré tout, l'Orient continuait à s'intéresser à l'argent monnayé? La loi du Code Théodosien VIII, 5, 48, donnée à Constantinople en 386 traite du transport du métal blanc, mais, avec des chargements de 1000 livres, on est passé à une autre échelle, cf. infra n. 223. Autres indices à verser au dossier: en 372, le chrysargyre à Beyrouth est qualifié de pensitatio auri (C. Th., XIII, 1, 8); en Egypte, SB, 6086, une somme mixte (AR + 10% AV) voit la moitié de l'argent ultérieurement exigée en or.

222. Pour Grierson, la valeur de l'argent aurait augmenté sur le marché libre. A la base de cette opinion, il y a en partie la croyance que pendant la première moitié du IVe s. l'argenteus est une silique du 1/24e du sou (cf. supra n. 159). A notre sens, la ratio, de 12 en 301, se maintient autour de 14.4, au moins du point de vue officiel, jusqu'à la fin du IVe s., le barême de 18, attesté en Egypte par SB, 6086 (cf. supra n. 221) étant un accident plus ou moins local datable du dernier quart du siècle. Voir notre article où nous avions présenté une première esquisse du monnayage d'argent: "Problèmes monétaires du Quatrième Siècle (311-395)", Antiquitas, I, 29, Bonn, 1978, 103-126.

223. Trouvaille effectuée entre St Quentin S/Isère et la Rivière avec 3000 monnaies du Bas Empire: 128.8: 14.4 = 8,94:2 = 4.47 g. La vaste enquête menée par F. Baratte révèlera encore mieux avec quelle ampleur la vaisselle d'argent a été communément thésaurisée au Bas Empire.

224. Estampille d'Abalatos avec la Tyché de Constantinople cf. Sirmium, VIII, 1978, 108-109; E. Cruickshank Dodd, Byzantine Silver Stamps, Dumbarton Oaks Studies, 7 Washington, 1961.

225. Cf. supra n. 205; l'étude de la circulation de l'or sera particulièrement difficile, car, un solidus représentant un véritable trésor, il faudra repertorier les trouvailles isolées pour mieux déterminer les différentes phases de diffusion. Importance des témoignages d'Ammien Marcellin, XVI, 8, 12 et de Symmaque, Rel., 13, 2.

226. Nous avons dessiné quelques prolégomènes dans trois articles à paraître, "Pensa et follis dans une inscription d'Afrique," Mélanges J. Lassus, "Le tarif d'Abydos et la réforme d'Anastase," Actes du 9ème Congrès Int. de Num., "Une constante arithmétique dans la métrologie du Bas Empire," Pact, 3, 1979.

Nous remercions C. E. King, M. R. Alföldi, et P. Bastien de leur amical concours.

SILVER HOARDS AND EMISSIONS FROM 324 TO 392

J. P. Callu

In the tradition of A. Evans, J. W. E. Pearce and many other British numismatists I shall try in this study to discuss two parallel phenomena for some seven decades, not just for the province of Britain, but for the empire as a whole. They are: 1) firstly, the sequence of silver emissions,[1] and 2) secondly, the hoarding pattern. In this way one ought at least to see how the minting of silver issues evolved and this, considered in conjunction with the pattern of hoard burial, should shed some light on those periods during the fourth century when government decisions led to important innovations in the silver coinage.

The period under investigation can be divided into 7 subgroups: . 1) 324-337; 2) 337-350; 3) 350-358; 4) 358-364; 5) 364-375; 6) 375-383; 7) 383-392. In each, the chief characteristics of the silver coinage will be examined in the context of the evidence which is available to us, i.e. the contemporary hoards.

I. 324-337

In the coinage reform of 294-295, the tetrarchy had returned to the practice and tradition of the earlier empire by issuing an argenteus at 1/96th of the Roman pound.[2] The issue of silver coins of high quality soon ceased except in the Balkans and was restricted in the West after the death of Constantius I to those territories controlled by Maxentius, i.e. Rome from 306-310, Ostia in 308-309, Carthage in 306-307, and Aquileia c. 307.[3] By contrast Antioch and Serdica minted silver for only a few months sometime in 305/307,[4] as did Trier in the second half of 307.[5]

The argenteus of Diocletian which was minted for so brief a time quickly found its way into hoards (as is attested by the often cited Sisak hoard, and a less well known one from Italy, as well as those from Krempelstein and Brigetio).[6] Nonetheless the argenteus continued to form a modest proportion in later finds and are sometimes found even beyond the limes:[7] there were 2 pieces in the Rouvroy-les-Merles deposit of 303; 5 in the Imsbach hoard of 313; 10 from Betteldorf (pre 324) in the Barbaricum; 11 in the Kaiseraugst find of 350; and 1 in the Southsea hoard of 361.[8] Silver coins of Maxentius are much more rare; there were 6 in the Kellmünz hoard of 308, and 2 from Arras in 317.[9]

The East struck no more silver until 326. In Gaul Constantine minted silver quinarii for a time in 308 and again in 310 which were included in the Arras hoard.[10] After 310 all of the workshops producing silver coins were closed when Constantine left Gaul for Italy.

The increase of territory in 312 resulting from the defeat of Maxentius led to a modification of Constantine's policy but did not yet result in any decisive changes. A good example of this is provided by the issue in 313 at Trier of a silver coin at 1/96th of the pound but containing only 25% silver.[11] This reluctance to revert to minting pure silver can be seen again as late as 326 at Sirmium, Thessalonica and Constantinople.[12] On the other hand in Italy (Ticinum, Aquileia, Rome) and at Siscia between 315 and 321 silver coins were issued on a heavier standard (1/48th and 1/60th of the Roman pound).[13]

The date when silver coinage was again minted in earnest occurred after the recovery of the Eastern half of the empire, and this explains the terminus post quem of this study. At this time not only was the argenteus again minted but the creation of the miliarensis at 1/72nd of the pound also took place.[14]

It must be admitted that the chronology of the silver issues between 324 and 337 is extremely difficult to establish. The group of coins with rather unusual reverse types apparently poses no real problem. These consist of: 1) multiples commemorating the foundation of Constantinople or the vicennalia of Constantine II Caesar, and 2) miliarenses celebrating the 'glory' and the 'courage' of the army at Thessalonica and Constantinople minted between 333 and 337.[15] However, for the more common types, the difficulties increase.

In fact there are four important series, 2 of argentei and 2 of miliarenses. The former, minted on a standard of 1/96th of the pound, has the 3 palms as its reverse type. An early date for its issue is suggested by the fact that this type was minted at Ticinum which was closed after 325, and the representation at Antioch of Crispus who was put to death in the summer of 326.[16] The reappearance of the type after 337[17] and the existence of a 3 palms reverse from Rome in the Mitrovica hoard[18] however could suggest a date later in Constantine's reign for the appearance of this issue.

The second argenteus with the Victory reverse could, on the basis of the involvement of the Constantinople mint, be dated to the years 326-330. Certainly pieces exist for Constans and later for Delmatius[19] and these continue once Constantine I has disappeared.[20]

The miliarenses represent either 3 or 4 emperors under an arch, or 4 standards. The first type Felicitas Romanorum could have begun with 3 emperors in 326 at Trier. The reverse is also known at Sirmium and Thessalonica and the latter mint also struck pieces for Crispus. There is no clear evidence, however, that the issue continued after 330.[21]

In conclusion, the miliarensis[22] with the 4 standards reverse is also attested at the beginning of the period at Ticinum and at Trier, Arles and Constantinople in turn.[23] The house of Constantine clearly continued to mint the type.[24]

One is left with the impression that about 326 the argenteus with the 3 palms reverse formed a pair with the Felicitas Romanorum, while for more than 10 years, no doubt with interruptions, the Victory type (at 1/96th of a pound) and the 4 standards reverse continued to be minted. Their production could have been concentrated in the final lustrum of Constantine I. The dominance of the Eastern mints in the production of these coins is undeniable.[25]

The role played by Constantinian silver pieces in 4th century hoards is incredibly small: 8 examples were recovered from the unique Mitrovica hoard; according to P. Bruun's chronology they all fall into the years 330 and 337.[26] Later hoards contain very few specimens, 10 in the Kaiseraugst hoard of 350, 3 in the Enns hoard of 351, 4 in the Southsea deposit in 361, and 1 in the East Harptree find c. 377.[27] It is likely that these coins were melted down and reminted in the years which followed the death of Constantine.[28] If this occurred then the view we have of this coinage is obscured as is the way in which a system was introduced which was by necessity to last for so many years.

II. 337-350

The first phase of this period which includes the years 337-340 is brief but particularly interesting.

In fact, differences in practice between the 3 brothers can be distinguished. In the West Constantine II instituted little that was new except to open a second silver officina at Trier.[29] Constantius busied himself in minting only *argentei*.[30] By contrast, Constans, as if to overcome his position of inferiority, visibly followed a monetary policy designed to enhance his prestige: issues of the Constantinian type with the standards,[31] the palms,[32] and *Virtvs Exercitvs*,[33] were complemented[34] by the *Gaudium Populi Romani* type[35] systematically produced on four different weight standards in the pilot mint at Siscia which also produced a series of Vota types, as Constantius did, but with considerably more flare and tended to specialize in minting silver on imperial anniversaries.

After power was divided between only 2 rulers, so long as Constans was in control of the West[36] activity did not slacken. *Gaudium Populi Romani* had been struck on 4 standards[37] at the time of the *decennalia* and was accompanied by 2 new series, which were as comprehensive or nearly so: *Victoriae DDNN Augg*[38] and *Triumfator Gentium Barbararum*.[39] As before Siscia[40] played the dominant role followed by Thessalonica and Aquileia.[41] Trier however participated actively with special emissions at 1/72nd and 1/96th of the pound.[42] Constantius, in the Eastern half of the empire, continued with a system concentrated entirely on the production of the *argenteus*.[43]

The internal chronology of the years 340-350 has yet to be determined. It would appear that some kind of change took place sometime after 344 when the *vota decennalia* and *vicennalia* of the two Augusti had been lavishly celebrated. Multiples at 1/24th of the pound were no longer struck, light *miliarenses* (heavy ones existed only at Trier) were minted in a systematic fashion with different legends assigned to each mint:[44] *Victoria Augustorum* at Siscia,[45] *Felicitas Perpetua* at Aquileia,[46] and *Virtus DDNN Avgg* at Trier.[47] The mints of Lyons, Arles, and Rome[48] were reopened and joined Trier, Thessalonica, Siscia and Aquileia (which produced a variant) in minting on a large scale the denomination at 1/96th of a pound with the Victory reverse,[49] paired at Trier by *Pax Augustorum*.[50] At Rome, also, a few late *miliarenses* were produced,[51] while the legend *Fel Temp Reparatio* in 348 appeared only on *argentei*.[52] The Western half of the empire at the end of the reign of Constans began to fall slowly into line with the minting practice at Nicomedia and Antioch remained faithful to the denomination 1/96th of a pound.[53] Monetary policy was now concerned with silvered bronze coins and the introduction of an *aes* 2 denomination reflected the change of emphasis.[54]

Unlike the preceding period, the silver issues of the years 337-350 left their mark on the circulation pattern and particularly in 2 contemporary hoards. One, from Trier, contained at least 4 multiples which underlines the dominance of Siscia and Thessalonica at this time.[55] We will know a great deal more about the other when it is finally published. However, current information about the composition of the Kaiseraugst hoard supports the theories outlined above. There are 52 coins of 337-40; 112 of 340-348, and 17 medallions out of a total of 185 pieces presumably datable to the reign of Constans.[56]

A third deposit, the Enns hoard buried in 351,[57] is almost identical and even if it does not contain any examples struck at 1/24th of the pound, it is entirely typical of the silver output of Constantine's youngest son. A provisional classification, in effect, assigns to the 3 Augusti 10 pieces at 1/60th of a pound from Siscia and Thessalonica, 9 at 1/72nd of a pound from Siscia, Thessalonica and Trier, at least 8 argentei from Trier and Siscia, i.e. some 27 silver coins altogether. After 340 Aquileia entered the picture and shared with Siscia the minting of heavy and light miliarenses although the latter were clearly dominant (c. 12 pieces vs. c. 3). The 28 coins struck at 1/96th of the pound are distributed by mint as follows: 20 Gaudium Populi Romani from Siscia, 5 Victories (Siscia and Thessalonica), 1 Pax Augustorum of Trier, 2 Vota from Antioch. Thus altogether there were 43 coins datable to 340-350.

Later, in 361 in the Southsea find, the heavy pieces have far from completely disappeared. In this hoard of approximately 450 coins, Constans and Constantius are represented by only 2 heavy miliarenses and 8 light ones but there are still 32 argentei struck at 1/96th of the pound (largely Victory types from Trier).[58] In addition to a mixed hoard like Oldcroft,[59] the East Harptree find about 15 years later still contained 1 coin at 1/72nd of the pound and 5 argentei.[60] The extraordinary persistence of this piece weighing 4.48g. is attested by the survival of 1 or 2 specimens in the San Genesio hoard and indeed even in the Holwell (Holway) and North Mendip finds.[61]

III. 350-358

Initially there was no change in the curve manifested by the emission pattern during these years and the fundamental reason for this was the usurpation of Magnentius which left its mark on both mint operation and the composition of hoards in this period.

When the Gallic emperor abandoned Italy in 352 silver production at Aquileia, the only mint outside Gaul to strike this metal, was transferred to Lyons[62] with the exception of the heaviest pieces.[63] From this time onwards the workshop at Trier, extremely active after 350, continued to work simultaneously with the single officina at Lyons and the two at Arles inherited from Constans. In addition to heavy[64] and light[65] miliarenses, argentei were produced in abundance, above all the Virtus Exerciti type from Trier.[66]

The counteroffensive mounted by Constantius is particularly interesting for anyone investigating this coinage. On the one hand, the Eastern emperor chose to re-issue the reverse types of Constantine I (the emperors standing under an arch, the standards, the Gloria and Virtus Exercitus types) in order to stress his legitimacy more openly. On the other hand the monopoly in the East of the argenteus was destroyed and its successor used to pay the army, was the silver piece struck at 1/72nd of the pound with the Felicitas Romanorum reverse paired with Victoria Romanorum at Sirmium, Nicomedia, Antioch and Aquileia.[67] Minting continued in Gaul after its recovery with the standards type which was also produced at Constantinople and Arles,[68] and output increased during the second phase with the Virtus Exercitus type (minted at Constantinople, Cyzicus, Thessalonica and Siscia[69] (obverses of Vetranio appeared briefly at the latter 2 mints),[70] Rome, Arles and Lyons.[71] The conflict between Magnentius and Constantius therefore had also had a monetary aspect since the issue of the Virtus Exercitus reverse struck at 1/72nd of the pound established the superiority of the 'orthodox' silver denomination over that of the usurper's Virtus Exerciti reverse struck at 1/96th of the pound.

A large output of argentei was produced for Gallus and Constantius which paralleled the production of light miliarenses (some heavy miliarenses were also minted at Constantinople, Nicomedia, Cyzicus, and Arles after November 353).[72] The Votis V Multis X and the "star" reverse, appropriate to the Caesar began at Sirmium in 351.[73] Then the types were redistributed: Constantinople, Thessalonica, Siscia and Aquileia struck the Vota reverses,[74] while Antioch, Rome, Arles, (before and after the progression from the PAR mark to TCON) and Lyons struck the second type.[75]

Constantius minted the Votis XXX Multis XXXX type for himself at every mint except Trier in the extreme West and Antioch in the East. It was therefore produced at the following mints: Nicomedia, Cyzicus and Constantinople in the East,[76] Thessalonica, Sirmium and Siscia in the Balkans,[77] Aquileia and Rome in Italy[78] and Arles and Lyons in Gaul.[79] The Constantian emissions, which were concurrent with those of Gallus must have lasted at Arles until 358.[80] By this time Julian had been Caesar for 3 years and the rate at which new emissions were produced had been slowing down in the interior parts of the empire. In fact very few Eastern mints struck for the emperor's cousin: Thessalonica was the principal mint to do so and put out the denominations weighing 1/60th, 1/72nd and 1/96th of the Roman pound with reverse types previously used for Gallus.[81] In Gaul, Trier embroiled in revolution issued only rare quinarii[82] and production of the denominations noted above was concentrated at Arles where, with the exception of the light miliarenses with the Virtus Exercitus reverse, the output of the 3rd workshop was concerned exclusively with the production of coins for the Caesar Julian.[83]

The exhaustion of the silver available to be coined, became a reality. When Constantius celebrated the occasion of his adventus at Rome and later at Sirmium in 357[84] and the beginning of his 35th anniversary as emperor special silver coins were minted[85] but, to judge by their comparative rarity in modern collections, their numbers were small. The issues were nothing like so large as the comparable mass of argentei minted in earlier years at Constantinople, Sirmium and Arles; a vast output, whose size, if anyone were to doubt its volume, is emphasized by the incidence of contemporary imitations.[86]

Thus if one sketches a somewhat general outline, especially in considering the pieces weighing 4.48g. and 3.36g., it would seem that the liberal issues of silver during the 350s had exhausted the empire's resources. The civil war and its aftermath, especially in Gaul, had cost Constantius a very great deal.

The circulation pattern during these years supports this conclusion. There are three sorts of evidence which should be mentioned: 1) the number of hoards increased: there are 3 to 4 on the Rhine frontier and 6 in the Danubian area.[87] This second group, of which we are aware thanks to the works by Roumanian, Russian and Polish numismatists is of interest because it shifts the geographic focus of these finds and in so doing reveals an aspect of the hoarding pattern nearly as significant as that relating to the reconquest, i.e. that the burial of the Danubian hoards was linked to the Sarmatian campaigns of 357-358. The existence of argentei of Cyzicus in 2 of the 6 hoards suggests they were concealed before 358.[88] However, one would like to have more information about these finds which up to now have been somewhat neglected by historians.

The other two categories of evidence lead one back to Magnentius; 3 ingots were found at Kaiseraugst noted above, and in conjunction with solidi and bullion bars, 2 were found at Ljubljana which bore the usurper's stamp. At least one from Ljubljana was related to Aquileia.[89] This evidence suggests that significant numbers of coins and plate were remelted at the beginning of the usurpation of Magnentius and that this occurred in order to finance his wars against Constantius.[90]

Other hoards give rise to similar considerations: during the decade which began in 350 there was a recurrence in several instances of a hoarding practice which was analogous to that of the preceding period and which would continue into the next.[91] These hoards are found either in settlements within the Barbaricum or near it and are composed of denarii of the earlier empire to which several argentei of the mid-fourth century have been added as a "tail". The Laatzen find is slightly later in date but still falls within the category.[92] Famars[93] perhaps in part, Tournai[94] and certainly Lengerich in which there are about 60 argentei of Magnentius from the Trier mint with the Virtus Exerciti reverse together with 1220 denarii ranging in date from Trajan to Alexander Severus[95] are prime examples of this sort of hoard. It is clear, then, that in the 4th century the barbarians continued to esteem and collect silver coins and that the importance of these "non-Romans" in this period either as adversaries, or auxiliaries could well have been a significant factor in the reappearance of large silver issues at precisely this time.[96]

It is now necessary to discuss briefly what ultimately happened to the emissions of this period. Clearly, the coinage of Magnentius and of Vetranio were, in general, demonetized although hoarders were tempted by the heavier denominations and kept them:[97] the number of silver multiples in the Southsea find for the years 350-358 including usurpers consists of 8 heavy miliarenses and 43 light ones (with the Virtus Exercitus reverse issued during the reconquest) and 29 argentei.[98] East Harptree which had only one argenteus nonetheless contained seven multiples struck at 1/72nd of the pound[99] and the San Genesio find had three.[100] There were three pieces struck at 1/96th of the pound in the small Ciani hoard, perhaps datable to the Valentinianic period and there is no doubt that there were a number of coins in the Kecel find on the same standard since it also contains several imitations at 1/96th of the pound.[101] The North Mendip savings hoard which dates to the end of the century has 7 coins weighing c.4.48g. and is the exception which proves the rule.[102] Because, as will be seen, the creation of the siliqua marked a fundamental terminus a quo of the silver circulation.

IV. 358-364

The year 358 is a pivotal date in the history of the silver coinage. At the same moment as the aes 4 Spes Reipvblice reverses superseded the aes 3 Fel Temp Reparatio type, the government abandoned the Neronian weight standard reinstated by Diocletian.[103] From this measure they realised a profit both from the lighter weight of the new denomination and the fact that it was tariffed at a rate higher than its intrinsic value. This coin was considered as a new argenteus by contemporaries but the term siliqua applied to it in modern times is not in fact a misnomer since it is probable that it was the metrological equivalent of a 1/24th of the solidus.[104]

Three types were minted: Victoria DDNN Aug and Votis XXX Multis XXXX for Constantius II, and Votis V Multis X for Julian as Caesar. This last type is known only from Lyons in officina T.[105] The first type, almost exclusive to Arles initially, was later much more widely produced.[106] The Votis XXX Multis XXXX took priority as the major reverse of the reformed coinage: it was minted in the East at Antioch, Nicomedia and Constantinople,[107] in the central empire at Thessalonica, Sirmium, Siscia and Rome,[108] and in the West at Arles, Lyons and Trier.[109] The bulk of the production was shared among four mints, two for Constantius (Constantinople and Sirmium) and two for Julian (Arles and Lyons). On this point at least there was agreement between the two emperors.

The year 359 passed in this manner. However, the proclamation of Lutetia occurred the following year. Julian, now Augustus, spent several long months trying to compromise; at one of his mints the Victoria DDNN Aug type was struck for both Augusti and the Vot V reverses now balanced the Vot XXX.[110] At the other mint, Arles, the Gallic emperor continued to show a preference for the 3rd officina which produced most of his Vota types.[111] Once there was a decisive break between the 2 emperors, Julian recovered control of the whole of the Arles mint, doubled the number of workmen at Lyons (where the number of different obverse legends was increasing), and Trier was pressed into service.[112] There is no doubt whatever, that the 3 major Gallic mints concentrated on producing siliquae although a few light miliarenses were minted at Lyons and Arles.[113] Was the picture the same at the territories under the control of Constantius? It seems unlikely since his fortieth anniversary was celebrated only at Constantinople.[114]

When Julian left the West, the central mints formally recognized him (Rome, Sirmium, Siscia, and Thessalonica)[115] but the issues were small except at Sirmium where a series was produced in 362 at 1/72nd of the pound with the Virtus Exercitus reverse which paralleled that of Arles, and a Victoria Romanorum issue in 363 also minted at Antioch. In the later part of his reign when Julian was beginning to anticipate the demand imposed by his decennalia celebrations the output at the Eastern mints grew more important, and production at Constantinople and especially at Antioch began to counterbalance that of Lyons and Arles which remained large.[116] The resurgence of the Eastern mints was continued under Jovian and Arles was the only Western mint to produce coins for this ephemeral emperor.[117]

In conclusion, the 4 or 5 years following the creation of the siliqua had completely altered the monetary scene. It is unfortunate that the Central and Eastern empire have yielded so few hoards that one cannot be certain of the pattern which prevailed there. Happily, the evidence is sufficiently abundant from the Western part of the empire to see the decisive character of developments.

As was stated above contemporary hoards can be distinguished from later deposits. Excluding two mixed hoards,[118] only three finds belong in the first category: Laatzen, Southsea and Willersey. Laatzen belongs in a somewhat problematical context mentioned above, that of the survival of *denarii* of the earlier empire in the *Barbaricum* but differs from them since two *siliquae* were added to the find (1 of which was an imitation) and two *miliarenses*, 1 of Constantius and 1 of Julian Augustus from the Lyons mint *c*. 361.[119] Southsea and Willersey require some explanation because they mark the beginning of the numerous British hoards from the latter half of the 4th century, composed almost exclusively of silver.

Southsea was a large hoard found near Portsmouth. Buried in 361 it is useful in illustrating how the Gallic mints functioned after 358, for despite the inclusion of many earlier pieces there was an overwhelming preference for *siliquae* (79.8%).[120] The Willersey find from Gloucestershire buried *c*. 362/363 is less important and it too is almost entirely composed of *siliquae* (96.4%) with only two exceptions.[121]

Output gradually diminished thereafter but for a time it was still significantly large. The composition of the East Harptree find is very similar to the Southsea hoard and demonstrates the same tendencies; it had 70.38% *siliquae* in it.[122] On the continent the Valentinianic hoards from the Danube reached comparable proportions of *siliquae* less frequently; 85.18% at Redea *c*. 371[123] but only 24.81% (?) at Sucidava which was buried after 367.[124] and 22.2% at Dranic *c*. A.D. 376.[125] The find purchased by Ciani, if it actually did come from Kecel, could demonstrate a healthy survival of *siliquae* of Constantius and Julian about 370.[126] However there are alternatives to this picture. Some continental finds were composed of newly minted silver of which the best example is the military pay chest from San Genesio which had only 2 *Votis XXX Multis XXXX* of 358-361.[127]

The survival of the *Vota* types into the final period of this study, i.e. the years after 388, for which the documentation is almost entirely British, suggest that from 4 rather dissimilar hoards, the percentage of these earlier pieces nonetheless is still *c*. 10%.

Mr. Wood's Hoard	17.09[128]	Shapwick II	8.80[130]
Springhead	9.39[129]	Honiton	6.25[131]

Oddly enough, the number of these pieces, which might have been expected to dwindle in later hoards, tended to compose about 1/8th of the total in approximately 20 hoards buried after 393:

	%		%		%
North Mendip	: 32.19[132]	Fincham	: 14.28[140]	Manton Downs	: 7.69[148]
Mildenhall	: 30.76[133]	Great Allington	: 12.96[141]	Tuddenham	: 7.01[149]
Cleeve Prior	: 25.88[134]	Terling	: 10.46[142]	Sturmer	: 6.66[150]
Sproxton	: 25.00[135]	Fleetwood	: 10.05[143]	Coleraine	: 6.50[151]
Ramshill	: 22.22[136]	Colerne II	: 8.75[144]	Shapwick I	: 5.83[152]
Holwel (Holway)	: 20.12[137]	Icklingham II	: 8.57[145]	Icklingham III	: 4.34[153]
South Ferriby	: 19.73[138]	Grovely Wood	: 8.36[146]	Colerne I	: 4.00[154]
Dorchester	: 16.98[139]	Edington	: 8.06[147]	Icklingham I	: 3.85[155]

From this evidence it can be seen that the siliquae which formed the earliest chronological group in British hoards never entirely disappeared from the highly individual circulation characteristic of Britain by the early fifth century, and in fact that they remained an integral part of the silver coinage of this period.

V. 364-375

For this period, I shall follow the theories advanced by Pearce since he not only produced RIC IX, but also provided in his comments on the Terling hoard a synthesis of the emission pattern and circulation of the silver coinage during these years.[156]

The first three years present a striking contrast with the remainder of the period. Between 364 and 367 the heavy and light miliarenses demonstrated great typological variety[157] which hint at the course of future developments: Vota types were minted on the standard of 1/60th of the pound, and Gloria Romanorum on the standard at 1/72nd of the pound in the East. Their Western counterparts continued to appear with the traditional Virtus Exercitus reverse. Constantinople played an intermediate role with the reissue of the argenteus. This series which was begun after the insurrection of Procopius has a singularity which is difficult to explain.[158] It nonetheless suggests two hypotheses: 1) if silver coins at 1/96th of the pound were again being minted, the reason for this must have been that public demand had not been satisfied and, as a consequence, that argentei produced before 358 had been demonetized; 2) the parallel use of 2 denominations, the argenteus and the siliqua, suggests that the theory held by some students must be abandoned, i.e. that the latter had taken the value away from the former.[159]

Finally the pulse of the production of siliquae seems to have been maintained in the East as in the West during the initial phase of the Valentinianic dynasty at the same rate as had existed in the preceding lustrum. The main type Restitutor Reipublicae was common to almost the whole of the empire; in the Pars Occidentis, Lyons seems to have minted them in abundance.[160] A second series was reserved for the imperial Vota: in the territory controlled by Valentinian the Votis V Multis X reverse appeared at Trier, Lyons, Aquileia, Sirmium, Thessalonica, and above all at Rome which issued few Restitutor Reipublicae;[161] the Vota V type also appeared at the three Eastern mints of which the most active was Constantinople.[162] The division of obverses between the two emperors began to show a bias towards Valens after the beginning of the usurpation of Procopius[163] while the number of officinae in use at at Constantinople increased and these helped to produce the vota siliquae and, as noted above, the argenteus as well with a Vot V reverse.

There was a third siliqua reverse type which gave promise of having a very fruitful future: Vrbs Roma which the Lyons and Rome mints produced with the image of the goddess of the city seated on a throne.[164] If the evidence of the East Harptree hoard is to be believed, the Rome workshops dominated.[165] It is thus clear that Valentinian in distributing his siliquae series had particularly favoured two cities; one on the Rhone and the other on the Tiber. In 364-365 he was in residence at Milan but probably for political reasons he chose to coin money at Rome.

After the accession of Gratian, monetary policy changed almost completely. Up to this point the tradition established by Constantius and Julian had been unquestioningly accepted; the empire was still living in the aftermath of the reform of 358. Little by little, however, new decisions were put into effect. The emperors sought to clarify the situation and in order to do so, the precious metals were ordered to be purified: gold was to be obryzum and silver pusulatum while all silver was now removed from the base metal coinage.[166] In the West the aes 3 pieces were to underwrite the principal expenditures of the state, those undertaken in the strengthening of the limes.[167] By contrast, the minting of silver ceased abruptly; Sirmium was closed and then Rome while Arles and Aquileia issued no more siliquae.[168]

A problem remains in explaining the Vrbs Roma siliquae issued by Trier. With his customary acuity Pearce noted a typical anomaly. In the Terling hoard the number of specimens for Valentinian I was considerably lower than those of Valens and the observation also holds true for the East Harptree, San Genesio, Grovely Wood, Icklingham I, and North Mendip finds et al. Even taking into account the different length of their reigns the number of siliquae existing for Valentinian is considerably less than that of Valens.[169] This fact can lead us to only one conclusion; at Trier the Vrbs Roma reverse was issued for only a brief period during the years 367-375. Either its issue at Trier cohered with that of the preceding phase at Lyons and Rome and after a long gap it was reminted after the death of Valentinian, or a second explanation is possible, and perhaps more likely; the Vrbs Roma type began at Trier very late in Valentinian's reign. In any case there was a break in the production of siliquae while the Virtvs Exercitus reverse minted on the standard of 1/72nd of the pound and produced for special occasions continued to be minted in the same proportions as before.[170]

In the East, Constantinople, Nicomedia and Antioch had opened with what in theory represented a full range of denominations and the argenteus continued to be produced by the first two mints.[171] The hoards give some indication which is supported by the large number of officinae and mintmarks in use at Antioch that the issue of Vot X Mult X siliquae at Antioch (Valens' residence) was somewhat bigger than anywhere else.[172] Catalogues and lists of local collections from the East should be consulted in order to support this conclusion.[173] On the basis of this evidence one would also know whether the East, like the West experienced a diminution in the production of silver during these years. The subsequent evolution of the silver coinage suggests that this was probably what happened.

The hoarding pattern of this period has already been touched on indirectly. However, the sparseness of the evidence and its inaccessibility make it difficult to establish precisely what the contemporary picture was. There are a dozen hoards published which can be used in such a study, most of which were found in the Danubian provinces.

c.366: Gura Jalomitei, Dobroudja, Viespeşti.[174]
c.367: Sucidava (3 lots)[175]
c.370: Kecel (and possibly the Ciani hoard as well if the two finds are in fact different.)[176]
c.371: Redea[177]
364-378: Osica de Sus[178]
367-383: Valea Strimba Stobi[179]

Since the East Harptree find was dated by Pearce to 376-377, only 3 British hoards of assumed Valentinianic date (Chaddleworth, Uphill and Wookey Hole) are suitable for inclusion in this discussion and the information published about all three is meagre.[180] It is worth mentioning for the benefit of historians that as in the military campaigns of Constans, the British campaigns of Theodosius I did not result in any systematic wave of hoard burials.[181] British silver hoards were buried later than this. In any case, as the East Harptree find demonstrates, was there anything that could have been buried from issues of the years 367-375 except a small number of Virtus Exercitus and Vrbs Roma reverses from Trier?[182]

VI. 375-383

The death of Valentinian had led to a profound division within the empire and destroyed its monetary unity. In the East Valens vigorously continued his brother's policy. In what appears to have been a careful balancing act, he reminted an aes 3 denomination which was disappearing in the West at the same moment that he was stopping silver production at Nicomedia and Antioch. Between 375 and 388 Vota siliquae alone were minted and only at Constantinople.[183]

Gratian's actions in the West were completely different. He ceased minting bronze for which Symmachus has perhaps supplied the motives: the desire to lower the amount of circulating coin and rid it of imitations.[184] Ausonius' pupil underwent a virtual conversion and chose to mint the bulk of his issues in silver. One would like to know the reasons which prompted this decision, which was the opposite of that which had been taken by Valentinian I and which Valens continued to maintain.

Gratian clearly wished to innovate a new policy. However, within the context prevailing in the West, i.e. an atmosphere of restoration, pressure from Senatorial circles would have manifested itself in a return to Julian's system and given pride of place to the circulation of the silver coinage traditionally linked to the history of Rome.[185] Another more plausible hypothesis is that Gratian was forced to institute his new policy because of pressure by his army in which the German elements were in the ascendant. Following the issue of bronze coinage by Valentinian, a strong emperor, it is easy to see how a weaker government would be forced to conciliate the soldiers by issuing coins with a higher purchasing power which in some peoples' view would also have enjoyed an hereditary prestige.

Thus it can be assumed that after the burst of silver production by Constans, and the crisis of the reconquest in the West, the size of silver issues had increased for the third time at least if the evidence of the hoards is to be trusted. The increased output which is obvious for the larger denominations at Trier and Siscia but also took place at Aquileia and then in Rome since the latter again opened after 378,[186] seems to have produced siliquae in preference to heavier pieces.[186b] Two series can be distinguished. The first has the Vrbs Roma legend discussed above. Although it probably began to be minted before 375, according to the chronological arrangement of these coins (which is rather uncertain), the fact that most reverses were of the cuirass type places the issue after 378 as well when Gratian, Valentinian II and Theodosius were joint rulers. The hoard evidence, which includes the San Genesio find as well as the British ones ranging in date from Springhead to North Mendip, demonstrates this drastically; the coinage of Gratian is heavily represented.[187] At some date no doubt midway between 378 and 383 a second range of types was introduced in which each ruler had his own reverse: Virtus Romanorum for Gratian, Concordia Avggg for Theodosius and Victoria Avggg for Valentinian II. This range of types, invented at Trier, was also minted at Lyons, once again in operation after a period during which it had been closed, as well as at Aquileia.[188] The numerical proportions in the San Genesio hoard for this second group of types differ from those in British hoards; in the Italian find the coins from Aquileia tipped the balance in favour of the Virtus, Concordia, and Victoria triad.[189] In Britain, on the other hand, where coins from Trier were dominant, the large series was that with the Vrbs Roma reverse.[190]

Excluding the small Dranic find[191] and its sparse evidence concerning the Antioch mint, only two hoards can be cited for the eight years which separate the death of Valentinian I from that of Gratian: East Harptree (near Bristol) c. 376-377 and San Genesio (Pavia) in 383 both of which are large hoards but of very different composition; a deposit which has coins as early as Constantine has very little in common with one composed almost entirely (90%) of coins minted after 375.[192] The 2 finds therefore cannot be compared but fortunately there are a number of other late British hoards. Even if only a general estimate of their contents is made, i.e. a calculation on the percentage of coins of Valens and Gratian, the resulting figures leave no doubt that there was an upsurge of silver production in 375 which continued after the Battle of Adrianople.

The evidence can be summarized as follows:

			%		%
1.	p. 388:	Springhead	66.40	Mr. Wood's Hoard	48.70
		Shapwick II	56.00	Honiton	25.00

2. p. 392: an average higher than 20% can still be discerned:

	%		%		%
Grovely Wood:	39.70	South Ferriby :	24.12	Great Allington:	18.51
Icklingham :	32.90	Shapwick I :	23.30	Tuddenham :	17.54
Cleeve Prior :	31.76	Mildenhall :	23.07	Edington :	16.12
Colerne II :	28.75	Holwel :	21.06	Dorchester :	13.20
Sproxton :	27.00	Fleetwood :	20.61	Icklingham III :	11.30
North Mendip :	26.41	Manton Downs:	19.23	Ramshill :	11.10
Terling :	24.60	Colerne I :	19.00	Coleraine :	10.35
Icklingham II :	24.20				

VII. 383-392

The usurpation of Magnus Maximus permits a natural division to be made into two parts in the final period of this study: the years before and after 388, the date of the reconquest of the West by Theodosius.

It is symptomatic of how different this era was from that of Constantius II that the campaign against Maximus was not financed by large silver issues and a wide variety of denominations. Constantinople was occupied in minting Vota siliquae as it had been previously.[193]

Valentinian II, however, placed his faith in the policy of his brother. Not only did he reopen Thessalonica but he also opened a third Italian workshop at Milan to produce silver. If the silver multiples seem to have been scarce, the siliquae must have become more common: Vrbs Roma was minted at Rome, Virtus Romanorum at Milan and Aquileia and the Vota reverses were probably universal.[194]

The major factor in this period would seem to be the inflationary policy pursued by Magnus Maximus. Several authors mention his avaritia: some like Sulpicius Severus in order to excuse the poverty of the treasury, others like the pseudo-Aurelius Victor and Pacatus in particular in order to present Maximus in the worst possible light by depicting him standing before the scales with his gaze fixed on the large mass of gold and silver seized from his unhappy subjects.[195]

The British hoards support these assumptions. The 17.13 percentage of coins of Maximus in 4 hoards buried after 388[196] was maintained at a level of c. 11% in finds contemporaneous with Honorius.[197]

The effect of a demonetization, if there was one, after the death of Maximus would have been negated by the prevailing monetary insecurity which was acute and the large issues produced by the Western Emperor to pay for his wars against Theodosius and Valentinian are clearly reflected in the hoards.

For this reason the heavier denominations were discriminated against: none of the pieces on the 1/24th of the pound was minted; there was an issue of Votis V Multis X at 1/60th of the pound[198] and a few Virtus Exercitus reverses produced at Trier and Lyons.[199] The siliqua, almost always with the Virtus Romanorum type, on the other hand, was minted in great quantities at Trier and significantly, although the pieces are extremely rare, at London in the AVG and AVGPS marks.[200]

Once Maximus controlled Italy, Milan and Aquileia in turn minted the Virtus Romanorum type: a veritable flood of silver accompanied the usurper. The result of this policy was inevitable: since it was not possible in any sense to alter the fineness of the metal, it was decided instead to lower the weight of the coins minted in Italy: thus the siliqua dropped from c. 2g. at Trier to c. 1.5g. at Milan and Aquileia on average.[201]

The first wave of hoard burials after 388 (and the fall of Maximus) in Britain may have resulted from the ensuing political repression or caution on the part of hoarders in view of the lower weight standard. They include: Springhead, Bath, Honiton, Norwich, Shapwick II, Causeway Lane and Mr. Wood's hoard.[202] With the exception of the hypothetical find at Cazères sur Adour[203] there is only one continental hoard, as yet unpublished, at Aquila in the Abruzzi:[204] This group of 10 siliquae immersed in a quantity of solidi ten times its size offers food for thought. Without meaning to give the appearance of extrapolating, this period marks the obvious beginning of the large scale production of gold which was in due course to replace silver as the major coinage metal, and this change took place virtually within 5 years (i.e. the period of a single lustrum).[205] Britain, which was separated from the continent geographically, politically, and by its standard of living evinced a backwardness from which she never recovered. This theory held by many scholars is not to be dismissed lightly and will be discussed more fully below.

The list of British silver hoards now begins to lengthen, and the next stage of concealment resulted from the crises of 392-393. The years between the fall of Maximus and the usurpation of Eugenius (which mark the virtual end of this study) are characterized by a tentative attempt to slow down the inflation set in motion by the events of 387-388. Theodosius chose to do this in two significant ways: 1) He stopped minting the siliqua at Constantinople, Thessalonica, Aquileia and Rome. Lighter Vota reverses of 392 are attested only at Milan.[205b] 2) The production of light miliarenses with the Gloria Romanorum reverse dating to the time of Valentinian was concentrated at Constantinople, Milan and Aquileia.[206] Nonetheless, in Gaul Valentinian II endeavoured to restore confidence in the silver coinage by issuing the Vrbs Roma siliqua at Lyons and Trier on a maintained 2g. standard. The Virtus Romanorum type, an invention of Gratian's, had not disappeared at Trier but had been modified by the Vrbs Roma reverse; on both types Rome is now found seated on a cuirass.[207] Trier and above all Lyons, with its 5 issues and later its second workshop, minted this new siliqua type which was immediately circulated in Britain.[208]

Thus in 392, on the verge of the final crisis of the 4th century one has the impression that the essence of the monetary system had been preserved. The permanence of the denomination struck at 1/72nd of the Roman pound with the traditional legend, Virtus Exercitus was assured and continued to be issued at Trier and Lyons,[209] while the siliqua had not been fully restored in the public's confidence, at least its decline had been checked.

However, it was only a few months before the structure was completely destroyed. The civil war opened the floodgates and the government quite simply ceased to concern itself with the production of silver, acceded to public pressure, and based its monetary system on the gold coinage.

Conclusions

At this point the survey of the 4th century silver coinage and its effect on the economic life of the empire with which this paper has been concerned ends and a number of conclusions emerge.

1) Three quarters of the British hoards, i.e. c. 40 fall outside the limits of this study;[210] datable to after 393 they present a picture not totally unlike that found on the continent. If the Dortmund hoard does not belong in this context, the Wiesbaden find certainly does with its enormous quantity of siliquae minted under Honorius and Arcadius at Milan and Rome and which were sent to Germany.[211]

The different pattern in Britain arises from the fact that the Roman retreat had allowed a situation to ossify which elsewhere in the empire was still evolving. If there had been any other factor which had occasioned the singularity of the hoarding pattern, it would have become manifest before 393. However before 393, although the number of British hoards published by British scholars is a tribute to their energy,they nevertheless form only a third of the received total.[212] There are parallel groups of finds from the Rhine and the Danube and one could, in fact, speak of the individual picture presented by the Dacian hoarding pattern without any sense of paradox, since this is more real than that commonly supposed to exist for Britain.

This initial enumeration needs some amplification and modification. There are 14 hoards from Britain, 6 from the Rhine, 18 from the Danubian region and 3 elsewhere, but if one takes ingots, plate and anniversary gifts into account which functioned as natural multiples of the coins, then one can add to the list previously cited the Numansdorp,[213] Šabac, Červenbreg, Svirkovo,Niš,[214] Kertch,[215] Geneva,[216] Gross Bodungen,[217] Almendralejo and Toulouse[218] finds, all of which serve to weaken the notion that finds of silver coins in Britain predominated for virtually the whole of the century.

2) Upon re-examination the evidence leaves no doubt as to how it should be interpreted; silver was buried along the length of the frontier wherever there were garrisons. Silver could be produced in non-military contexts if the need arose as for example the dedication of Constantinople. But its principal function was to finance the wars of the 4th century—wars undertaken both against the barbarians in Britain, on the Rhine and the Danube, and civil wars possibly including the conflict between Constans and Constantine II and certainly those of Constantius II against Magnentius and Maximus against Theodosius.

It must not be thought that this pattern always operated; there are no visible traces of military activity by Constans in Britain and the coinage from this period found in Britain is bronze not argentei, Constantius shared a similar attitude; the struggle against the Sassanians found its expression in the minting of the Fel Temp Reparatio bronzes. Silver coins were restricted to rare donativa.[219] Certain emperors like Valentinian chose to limit output systematically. They thus tried to reconcile the size of Western silver emissions with the norm for the East. Characteristically the Eastern half of the empire took very little part in the minting of silver. Except for two instances (the end of Constantine I's reign and the occasion of the reconquest by Constantius II) output was limited and in 375 rather than permit the stimulation of silver production it was decided to shut down the workshops minting silver in the East even though the East had control of areas which contained silver mines and earlier and later traditions favoured the minting of silver.[220] The problem of Britain is a constant source of discussion but that posed by Asia is no less interesting, nor are answers to it easy to discover. Was it a policy decision made in response to the fact that the Sassanians were championing the silver drachm, or did it result from a change in the standard of living? The largest personal fortunes certainly existed in the Western half of the empire but it is tempting to suggest that the average level of monetary exchange was higher in the East.[221]

3) This study will close by considering a fact which although slightly outside its chronological framework is nonetheless significant; the reasons for the debasement and disappearance of the siliqua have been discussed at length. P. Grierson believes that difference between the official tariff and the open market value of silver would have made it ruinous for the government to produce.[222] In my view the situation was somewhat different and can be formulated as follows: plate was hoarded in inverse proportion to coin. As a result of the rise in prices the siliqua would have depreciated in value and lost its 'dynamis' as a medium of circulation. What after all could one have bought with a gramme of silver? On the other hand, plates, bowls and dishes would have retained their value since they were exchanged by weight. Baron Chaurand,

at a conference held last May, circulated a fragment of worked silver found at Isère. It weighed 128.8g. which is to say it was equivalent to two solidi.[223] At this level silver was useful, a fact of which the East was as fully aware as the West.[224]

My two papers in this volume have attempted to throw some light on the evolution of the coinage in the 4th century by investigating the behaviour of the silver and aes coins in parallel contexts. By this means the times when policy and production in regard to both metals converged can be isolated (as for example the simultaneous introduction of the siliqua and the aes 4 pieces under Constantius II and Julian) as can the instances when the two diverged (i.e. when Valentinian I aes 3 issues in the West were minted in a period between two intense phases of silver production). Rather than being a simple linear phenomenon, the development of the coinage in the 4th century can be seen in outline form through the interrelationship of the hoarding and emission pattern.

In order to perceive more clearly the successive or alternating monetary policies followed by fourth century emperors the third parameter of the system, the gold coinage, should also be investigated in the same manner as the aes and the silver. One could thus see how modifications altered the balance among the three metals. Several theories have been suggested[225] elsewhere but it is not possible in this paper to put forward an overall view of the interrelationship of the three metals since its formulation requires much more time and reflection. Here, as in that other very complicated area, metrology,[226] close cooperation among numismatists remains essential if we are to endow our successors at the very least with some good working hypotheses.

NOTES

1. RIC volumes VII and IX cover the years 324-337 and 364-392. For the intervening years 337-364 see J. P. C. Kent, "An Introduction to the Coinage of Julian the Apostate", NC, 6, 9, 1959, 109ff. I have also made use of my unpublished study: Le monnayage de l'argent au IVe s. p. Chr. Essai sur le bimetallisme du Bas Empire, Rome, 1959, a work primarily based on the collections of Northern Italy.

2. RIC VI, Trier, nos. 100-133 (294-301), quinarii, nos. 134-136 (303); Ticinum, nos. 12-22 (294-300); Aquileia, nos. 16-17 (300); Rome, nos. 10-44 (294-299); Carthage, nos. 10-16 (296-300); Siscia, nos. 32-73 (294-300 and 303); Serdica, nos. 1-2 (303-305); Thessalonica, nos. 6-18 (298-c. 302); Heraclea, nos. 1-11 (294-296); Nicomedia, nos. 18-26 (295-296); Cyzicus, nos. 4-6 (294-295); Antioch, nos. 31-43 (294-298); Alexandria, nos. 7-13 (295-296).

3. Ibid. Rome nos. 153-157 and 187-193; Ostia, nos. 11-13; Carthage, no. 49; Aquileia, no. 75. (Several examples of Constantine I Caesar should perhaps be added but it is difficult to distinguish between AQ and RQ in the exergue.)

4. Ibid. Serdica, nos. 11 and 21-22; Antioch, p. 623, no. 1. Perhaps also Siscia, p. 473, no. 1.

5. Ibid. nos. 635-638, quinarii, nos. 639-641.

6. A. Jeločnik, "The Sisak Hoard of Argentei of the Early Tetrarchy," Situla, 3, Ljubljana, 1964: 1415 denarii (in 296); RIN, 9, 1896, 144: c. 200 denarii; K. Pink, Der Münzfund von Krempelstein," Mitt. Num. Gesell. in Wien, 1929, 106ff.: a group of 52 denarii and 4 aurei (c. 302); K. Bîró-Sey, Coins from Identified Sites of Brigetio and the Question of Local Currency, Budapest, 1977, 135ff.: aurei, gold medallions, and 46 denarii; there was an argenteus of Diocletian in the Thibouville find of 298; (Gallia, 19, 1961, 71ff. and 20, 1962, 255ff.).

7. K. Regling, "Römischer Denarfund von Frondenberg", ZFN, 29, 1912, 230: in addition to several isolated hoards found in eastern Prussia, the Betteldorf find (in Eifel) should be cited: 43 denarii and 577 small bronzes buried in 324; S. Bolin, "Die Funde römischer und byzantinischer Münzen in freien Germanien," DAI, 19, 1930, 86ff.

8. supra n. 7; BSFN, 27, 1972, 299ff.; FMRD, IV, 2, no. 2299; H. A. Cahn, "Trésor d'argenterie et de monnaies en argent à Kaiseraugst, Bull. Cercle d'Ét. Num., 3, 1, 1964, 42ff. = BSFN, 26, 1971, 115ff; H. R. Grueber, "The Southsea Find of Fourth-Century Silver Coins," NC, 5, 16, 1936, 292ff. (Add., NC, 6, 19, 1959, 89ff). To these can be added the single argenteus from the St. Vincent de Mercuze I find of 313 (Bull. Soc. de Statistique de l'Isère, 1870, 3ff.); and possibly some pieces from Famars (Gallia, 19, 1961, 151ff.) and from Commagene (Istanbuler Forschungen, 23, 1964, 282ff.).

9. H. J. Kellner, "Ein Fund spätrömischen Münzen von Kellmünz", Bayer. Vorgeschichtsblätter, 20, 1954, 119ff.; P. Bastien and C. Metzger, Le trésor de Beaurains (dit d'Arras), Wetteren, 1978, 189ff. (The authors also mention two argentei of Maximianus Herculius on p. 24).

10. RIC VI, Trier nos. 756-765 and 827-828; P. Bastien and C. Metzger, op. cit., 24: c. 63 quinarii; see infra note 95 (Lengerich).

11. J. N. Barrandon, J. P. Callu, C. Brenot, "The Analysis of Constantinian Coins (A.D. 313-340) by Non-destructive Californium 252 Activation Analysis", Archaeometry, 19, 1977, 173ff.

12. RIC VII, Sirmium, no. 14 (Bruun 320); Thessalonica, p. 570, no. 1; Constantinople, no. 6 (Bruun 326). Another possibility is that the three mints minted simultaneously in 326.

13. Ibid.: 315, Ticinum, no. 36; 319, Aquileia, no. 32; 320/321, Aquileia, nos. 80-84; Rome, p. 714, no. 224A; Siscia, p. 716, no. 158B.

14. The first mention of the miliarensis dates from 392 and is found in the treatise de mensuris et ponderibus (69 b) of Epiphanius. Following Mommsen, I would apply this name to the piece minted at 1/72nd of the pound, which was more commonly minted and circulated than that at 1/60th of the pound because 1) Cosmas Indicopleustes, XI, PG, 88,

cols. 448-449 equates it with the Sassanian drachm of c. 4 g.; 2) Justinian's Novel, CV 2, 1 in fact dates to a period when the piece at 1/60th of the pound was no longer struck. I should add that in the Georgian versian of Epiphanius, as yet unpublished (translated by R. P. M. van Esbroeck) it is described as follows: the miliarision which is called a drachma by the Romans." See also infra note 104.

15. Constantinople issued pieces at 1/18th of the pound with the Tyche type: MCONSB, Γ, Δ, S, Z, I; RIC VII, no. 53 and Paris, Cassel, and Trier; pieces at 1/24th of the pound with the Augustus/Caesar and Caesar/XX were issued at Trier, Lyons, Arles, Rome, Aquileia, Siscia, Thessalonica, Constantinople and Nicomedia (cf. RN, 5, 11, 1949, 35ff. and BSFN, 5, 4, 1950, 3ff. Despite the reservations which I expressed in Gnomon, 50, 1978, 295, I am following in this study the date suggested by J. Lafaurie and adopted by P. Bruun because of the example with the Lyons mark from the Kaiseraugst hoard. Another theory would be to date the series to 337 and to attribute it to Constantine II only (who rose to the rank of Augustus from that of Caesar in that year); Pieces at 1/72nd of the pound with the Gloria Exercitus and Virtus Exercitus reverses were issued at Thessalonica, RIC VII, nos. 196-197 and 219; Constantinople, nos. 57-58A, 129-131, 133-135 and p. 719. The following series can also be added to this list: Genium PR at 7.62 g., 326, Rome, no. 276; Constantinus Aug, (emperor with the labarum) 6.6 g, 6.1 g, ibid., 337, Rome, no. 399; Felicitas Publica, of Hannibalianus, 3.02 g, ibid., 335, Constantinople, no. 100; Vrbs Roma/Wolf, SMTSE, 0.35 g, Reggio Emilia.

16. RIC VII, Ticinum, no. 184; Rome, no. 379-380; Thessalonica no. 195; Nicomedia, no. 187; Antioch, 689, no. 70A.

17. Rome: Constantius Augustus, (R), (Mus. Naz.); Siscia: Constans and Constantius Augusti, (SIS, ·SIS·, SIS☾); there are several examples of which one was in the Enns-Lauriacum find, cf. infra note 32.

18. F. Kenner, "Denare der Cäseren Constantinus and Constantius aus einem Funde in Mitrovic", Wiener Num. Monatshefte, 2, 1866, 32ff.; F. S. Kupido, "Inedirte Denare und Medaillons Constantin's d. Gr. und Constantius als Beitrag dem Funde von Mitrovic," ibid., 4, 1868, 145ff.; cf. infra note 26.

19. RIC VII, Rome, nos. 377-378; Aquileia, p. 716, no. 130A; Siscia, nos. 210, 212-213, 229-230, and 233-234; Thessalonica, nos. 152, 181-182, 194 and 214-217; Heraclea, nos. 145-147; Constantinople, nos. 5, 54, 126-128, 136 and p. 719 (M/CONSA-I); Nicomedia, nos. 117, 140-141, 186 and p. 720, no. 186A; Antioch, nos. 105-107.

20. The Victory type is found for Constantine II Augustus at Trier, TRP, (1 example from the Enns-Lauriacum find, cf. infra note 27) and Aquileia, SMAQ (London), cf. infra note 29.

21. The legend suggests that the series should be dated to after the civil war which would thus make it contemporary with the final issues of billon. cf. supra note 12. There were in turn three emperors represented at Sirmium, Trier and Thessalonica, then four at Rome, Cyzicus

and Nicomedia, and finally three once more at Heraclea and Nicomedia. The third phase followed the death of Crispus but during the first when one Augustus and three Caesars ruled (Crispus, Constantine II, and Constantius) the reverse type did not express the reality of the situation. Cf. RIC VII, Sirmium, no. 15 (Bruun 320-4); Trier, p. 714, no. 474B (Bruun 324-5); Thessalonica, p. 718, nos. 140A-C (Bruun 325); Rome, no. 275 (Bruun 326); Cyzicus, nos. 42-3 (Bruun 325); Nicomedia, nos. 88-89, 142-143, and pp. 628-629 (Bruun 324-5 and 326-7); Heraclea, no. 105 (Bruun 329). To these should be added: P. Bruun, "Felicitas Romanorum", Numismatica, 7, 1966, 1ff. (the corrected date for Trier is 328-9).

22. The range of weights is large but the mean for 34 pieces is 4.46 g.

23. RIC VII, Ticinum, no. 185; Arles, no. 409 and p. 714; Siscia, nos. 198-199, 211, and 231-232; Thessalonica, nos. 150-151 and 218; Heraclea, nos. 103-104 and 148-149; Constantinople, no. 99 and p. 718, no. 99A, 55-56, and 122-125; Antioch, 696, no. 106. To which should be added: Rome, head bare Constantinus Iun Nob C, 4 standards, (PR), 5.13 g Karlovy. A brief emission of heavy pieces with the three standards reverse is known to exist for Rome (RIC VII, no. 376, Fidis Militum, 6.04 g) and at Siscia (5.73 g according to Tanini).

24. Constantine II at Trier (four standards), Constans at Siscia (four standards) and Thessalonica (four and three standards), cf. infra notes 29 and 31.

25. In the context of the four major types, Trier struck one, Arles one, Ticinum two, Rome four, Aquileia one, Siscia two, Sirmium one, Thessalonica four, Heraclea three, Constantinople two, Nicomedia four, Cyzicus one, and Antioch three.

26. Eight pieces have survived: 5 miliarenses (two with the four standards reverse, two Gloria Exercitus and 1 Virtus Exercitus), and 3 argentei (2 with the Victory type and one with the three palms). The mint distribution is as follows: Trier (2), Rome (1), Aquileia (1), Siscia (1), Thessalonica (2), and Constantinople (1).

27. For the Kaiseraugst hoard cf. supra note 8: 7 are on the standard of 1/96 th of the pound with the Victory reverse; for Enns-Lauriacum see: F. Kenner, Der römische Limes in Osterreich, IX, Vienna, 1908, 137; there were 3 Victory reverses on the 1/96th of the pound standard; Southsea cf. supra note 8: there were two pieces on the 1/72nd of a pound standard with four emperors and one with three standards; 2 at 1/96th of the pound with the Victory reverse; J. Evans "On a Hoard of Roman Coins found at East Harptree near Bristol", NC, 3, 8, 1888, 22ff.: there is 1 1/96th of the pound piece with the Victory reverse.

28. As a later example of this I have noted in the Museo Nazionale (Rome) a Vot V piece of Valens overstruck on a Constantinian reverse. (Another example will be published by M. Amandry).

29. At Trier the four standards type was minted on the 1/72nd of the pound standard in the name of the three brothers (5 pieces? from Enns-Lauriacum,

and one from Southsea, SMTR). The Victory reverse and Principi Iuventutis were produced on the 1/96th of the pound standard, with the TRP/S mintmark (6 specimens were found in the Enns-Lauriacum find). If Italy had been under the control of Constantine II for a time after 337 it is possible that the British Museum argenteus, Victoria DDNN Augg piece with the SMAQ mark was minted by his authority, cf. supra note 20 and infra note 32.

30. There were three series of the 1/96th of the pound denomination: 1) Constantinus Augustus; Constantius Augustus, Constans Augustus at Constantinople (11 officinae), Nicomedia, Antioch, and Alexandria (the only issue from this mint) with the Victory reverse; 2) Felicitas Reipublice, Vot XV Mult XX at Constantinople and Nicomedia, Vot XX Mult XXX at Antioch; 3) Votis XV Multis XX, Votis XX Multis XXX, at Antioch.

31. Four standards: 1/60th of the pound at Siscia (·SIS·) and at Thessalonica (TS) of which there were two specimens in the Enns-Lauriacum find. Thessalonica also struck the reverse with three standards: oddly enough the pieces known for Constans who was emperor in Illyricum are on the 1/60th of the pound standard, those of his brothers on the 1/72nd.

32. Constans shared this reverse at Siscia with Constantius in three issues: SIS, ·SIS·, SIS⌣ mintmarks which had already been used during the lifetime of Constantine II cf. infra note 35. The type is also known for Rome (cf. supra note 17) and is a mute witness to the fact that the control of Italy had passed into the hands of Constans. From his father's tradition, Constantine II thus retained the type with the Victory, Constans that of the three palms, cf. supra note 29. There is one piece of Constantius in the Enns-Lauriacum find.

33. At Thessalonica, but the weight changed from the 1/72nd of the pound standard to 1/60th. (There are 5 specimens in the Enns-Lauriacum find).

34. Other reverses include: Pax Aeterna (·SIS·, SIS⌣) at 1/60th for Constantine II (in the Enns-Lauriacum find); Felicitas Perpetua, Vot V (SIS) a quaternio for Constans (Trier hoard).

35. 1) 1/24th: Gaudium Populi Romani, Sic V Sic X for Constans at Siscia (SIS, ·SIS·, SIS⌣); Thessalonica for Constans, and Constantius (TSE, TES) in the Trier hoard; Vot V Mult X at Aquileia (AQ) for Constans; 2) 1/60th: Gaudium Populi Romani, Sic V Sic X at Siscia (SIS⌣; SISQ) for Constans in the Enns-Lauriacum hoard); Sic XX Sic XXX (SIS, SIS⌣, SIS*) for Constantine II in the Enns-Lauriacum find; 3) 1/72nd: Gaudium Populi Romani, Sic V Sic X, at Siscia (SIS, SIS⌣, for Constans in the Enns-Lauriacum and Holwel(=Holway) finds, cf. infra note 36; Thessalonica (TSE); there are three pieces of Constans in the Enns-Lauriacum find; 4) 1/96th: Gaudium Populi Romani, Sic V Sic X at Siscia (SIS⌣) for Constans in the Enns-Lauriacum find; Sic XX Sic XXX at Siscia (SIS⌣) for Constantine II.
Can the inclusion of Constantius II in this series be supposed to give a date before 340? Although the possibility cannot be entirely ruled out, it seems to me that the use of the Sic X Sic reverse with obverses of

Constantius should date to the *decennalia* of Constans since those of Constantius were long finished, *cf. infra* note 37. The importance of Siscia in these years is corroborated by the small chest from Pecs (*cf.* D. Gaspar, "Spätromische Kästchenbeschläge in Pannonia", *Acta Antiqua et Archaeologica*, 15, 1, 1971, 23ff., pl. LIX): on it Rome is represented as surrounded by Carthage and Constantinople on the left and Nicomedia and Siscia on the right, all offering crowns.

36. A transitional series at Trier: *Gaudium Romanorum*, *Vot V Mult X*, two captives, at 1/72nd of the pound (TR) for Constantius in the Southsea find; in the Holwel (Holway) find (Proc. of the Royal Num. Soc. 23 Dec., *NC*, 1843, 9) there was a *Gaudium Populi Romani*, *Sic V Sic X*, two captives on the 1/72nd of the pound standard (TRP).

37. 1) 1/24th: *Gaudium Populi Romani*, *Sic X Sic XX* for Constantius at Siscia (·SIS·); *Sic XX Sic XXX*; at Thessalonica for Constans and Constantius (TES); 2) 1/60th: *Gaudium Populi Romani*, *Sic X Sic XX* (without and then framed with palms) at Siscia for Constans and Constantius, in the Enns-Lauriacum find (SIS, ·SIS·, SIS~, SISQ); *Sic XX Sic XXX* (with palms) for Constantius at Siscia (SIS~, SISQ); 4) 1/96th: *Gaudium Populi Romani*, *Sic X Sic XX*, at Siscia for Constantius (SIS), there are two pieces in the Enns-Lauriacum hoard of which one at 1.48 g is described as "dünner Schröttling mit kleinem Sprung": is it a quinarius?

38. 1) 1/24th: *Victoriae DDNN Augg*, *Vot X Mult XX* at Siscia for Constans (·SIS·); 2) 1/60th: *Victoriae DDNN Augg*, *Vot X Mult XV*, at Aquileia for Constans (*AQ) of which there are two examples in the Enns-Lauriacum find), *Vot X Mult XX* (with the obverse titulature beginning with DN) at Aquileia (LXAQ) with the LX meant to express 1/60th of the pound (the first explicit reference to 1/60th); 3) 1/72nd: *Victoriae DDNN Augg*, *Vot X Mult XV* at Aquileia (*AQ) for Constans of which there are five examples in the Enns-Lauriacum find, Vot X Mult XX (sometimes with the obverse legend beginning with DN) at Aquileia (*AQ) for Constans known from the Southsea hoard; 4) 1/96th: *Victoriae DN Aug* (*sic* - two victories instead of one), *Vot X Mult XV*, Trier (TR) known for Constans in the Southsea hoard, *Vot X Mult XX*, Trier, (TR), for Constans; *Vot X Mult XV* (sometimes with the obverse legend beginning with DN) at Aquileia (AQ, *AQ) for Constans in the Southsea find.

39. 1) 1/24th: *Triumfator Gentium Barbararum*, Trier, (TR), for Constans and Constantius; Aquileia (*AQ) for Constans and Constantius; Siscia (SIS, ·SIS·) for Constans (in the Trier hoard) and Constantius; Thessalonica, (TES) for Constans and Constantius in the Trier hoard; 2) 1/60th: *Triumfator Gentium Barbararum*, Trier (TR) for Constantius; Thessalonica, (TES) for Constans and Constantius; 3) 1/72nd: *Triumfator Gentium Barbararum*, Thessalonica (TES) for Constans and Constantius. There are four pieces in the Southsea hoard, and one each in the East Harptree and North Mendip finds; *cf.* Sir A. Evans, "Notes on the Coinage and Silver Currency in Roman Britain from Valentinian I to Constantine III", *NC*, 1915, 433ff. There is one example in the San Genesio find, *cf.* O. Ulrich-Bansa, "Ripostiglio di monete d'argento del IVe secolo d. Cr.", *Atti Acc. Naz. Lincei, NSA*, VIII, ser. VIII, 7, 12, 1954, 166ff.

40. Cohen lists a Votis X Multis XX of Constans from Sirmium (SIRM), no. 198, Rollin. Even if this piece does in fact exist, the activity of the mint must have been much reduced.

41. Aquileia had its own series of light miliarenses: Felicitas Perpetua, Vot X Mult XX (*AQ) for Constantius (there are three pieces in the Enns-Lauriacum find) and Vot XX Mult XXX (AQ) for Constans.

42. 1) 1/72nd: Gaudium Romanorum (two captives, cf. supra note 36), Vot X Mult XV (TR) for Constans and Constantius, Vot X Mult XX (TR) for Constans, in the Southsea hoard, Vot XX Mult XXX (TR) for Constantius; 2) 1/96th: Gaudium Romanorum (two captives), Vot X Mult XV (TR) for Constans, Vot X Mult XX (TR) for Constans and Constantius.

43. 1) Felicitas Republice, Vot XX Mult XXX, Constantinople, (C·A/BΓ) for Constantius; 2) Vot(is) XX Mult(is) XXX, Constantinople, (C·B/Γ) for Constantius; Antioch (ANT, SMANT?) for Constans and Constantius. All of the obverse legends begin with DN.

44. Virtus DDNN Augg, Trier (TR) for Constans (in the Southsea find) and Constantius; there was also a specimen with the same type struck at Lyons (PLG) for Constans in the Southsea find: this suggests it was a late issue.

45. There are specimens with the DN obverse, SIS, SIS, and SISQ marks for Constans (3 pieces in the Enns-Lauriacum find) and Constantius.

46. Cf. supra note 41; with Vot XX Mult XXX (AQS) for Constantius. For the mintmark see also infra note 52.

47. (TR) for Constantius.

48. Lyons; cf. supra note 44. The mint had been closed since the vicennalia of Constantine II at the end of Constantine I's reign, cf. supra note 15; at Arles the situation was identical; for Rome cf. supra notes 17 and 32.

49. Victoria DDNN Augg: Lyons (LVG) for Constans; Arles (P/SARL) with the DN obverse for Constans and Constantius, in the Southsea find; Rome, (R), and the type is a Victory dragging a captive by the hair for Constans and Constantius (two pieces in the Southsea find; there is the variant legend Victoria Augustorum); Trier, (TR), for Constans and Constantius, (there are 23 pieces in the Southsea find, and four in the East Harptree hoard; in addition the variant Victoria Augustorum); (TRP) for DN Constantius in the Holwel (Holway) find and an imitation from the Southsea hoard; Thessalonica, (TES) with the Victory holding a crown, for Constans and Constantius (4 pieces in the Enns-Lauriacum find); with Victory holding a trophy, for Constans and Constantius (2 pieces in the Southsea hoard); Victoria Augustorum: Siscia, (SIS, SISQ) with the Victory and crown reverse for Constans, (there is a variant: Victoria Constantis Aug, and for Constantius, a piece with the DN obverse legend), in the Enns-Lauriacum find; the Victory and trophy reverse (SIS, SIS) is known for Constans (in the Southsea find) and for Constantius; Felicitas Perpetua: Aquileia (AQ, *AQ) with the Victory and crown reverse for Constantius (pieces exist with the DN obverse

legend, in the Southsea find; Victory with trophy (AQ AQ·) for Constans and Constans which always have the DN obverse legend. The reverse type of Victory holding a trophy at Thessalonica, Siscia and Aquileia seems to have been contemporaneous to that with the crown.

50. TR, TRP/S in the Enns-Lauriacum, Southsea, and Willersey finds (cf. NC, 7, 11, 1971, 203ff.) as well as East Harptree and Oldcroft (cf. NC, 7, 14, 1974, 65ff.).

51. Virtus Exercitum: 4 standards (R) for Constans with the DN legend.

52. Fel Temp Reparatio, Vot XX, captive (R) for Constans in the East Harptree hoard and for Constantius. To these can be added but with caution if not Fel Temp Reparatio, (AQT) with the phoenix reverse and the DN obverse of Constans (Borghesi, 1881, no. 3005) the Felic. Temp. Reparatio piece (TRP), 1.87 g for Constantius with the DN obverse in the Holwel (Holway) find.

53. 1) Votis XXV Multis XXX: Nicomedia (SMN) for Constans and Constantius with the DN obverse; Antioch (ANT) for Constantius with the DN obverse (of which there are two examples in the Enns-Lauriacum find); 2) Felicitas Reipublice, Votis XXV Multis XXX: Nicomedia (SMN) for Constantius; Antioch (ANT) for Constantius.

54. The decision to reduce the number and size of silver issues at the time of the reform of 348 is an expression of the desire to restore the bronze coinage to a dominant position. For a similar attitude on the part of Valentinian I cf. infra. With regard to this problem it would be appropriate to examine the attitudes taken by Magnentius and Julian at the end of their reigns. (It should be noted here that in the view of the British numismatists there was no aes minted between 341 and 347).

55. J. J. Chiflet, Anastasis Childerici Francorum Regis, Anvers, 284; this find which was discovered on 5 June 1635 contained gold and silver coins and four silver multiples, cf. supra note 34, 35, and 39.

56. Cf. supra note 8: this hoard should help to make the arrangement suggested here more precise or, if necessary, to modify it. The mint distribution is as follows: 108 Trier, 1 Lyons, 6 Arles, 3 Rome, 3 Ticinum, 8 Aquileia, 30 Siscia, 20 Thessalonica, 4 Constantinople, 1 Nicomedia, and 1 Antioch. Cf. supra note 15.

57. Cf. supra notes 27, 29, 31-35, 37, 38, 41, 45, 49, 50 and 53; infra notes 69 and 74. The ruler distribution is as follows: 9 Constantine II, 28 Constans, 37 Constantius II, and 1 Gallus. The coins are distributed among mints as follows: 12 Trier, 34 Siscia, 15 Thessalonica, 10 Aquileia, 1 Heraclea, 1 Nicomedia, and 1 Antioch.

58. Cf. supra notes 8, 36, 38, 39, 42, 44, 49 and 50. To these can be added a piece struck at 1/72nd of the pound with the four standards reverse of Constantine II, cf. supra note 29.

59. Cf. supra note 50: in this bronze hoard there were two argentei: Pax Augustorum (TR) and Victoria Augustorum (SIS⌣) and four small silver ingots (9.68, 7.86, 3.04 and 2.25 g).

60. Cf. supra notes 27, 39, 49, 50, 52.

61. Cf. supra notes 35, 36, and 39; see also note 52.

62. 1) 1/72nd: Victoriae DDNN Augg, Vot V Mult X, Aquileia (AQ, *AQ, *AQ·) in the Southsea find; Lyons (PLG); 2) 1/96th: Felicitas Perpetua, Aquileia, (AQ·, AQ*, AQ); Lyons (LVG).

63. 1) 1/24th: Triumfator Gentium Barbararum (TAQ·); for Trier the Securitas Republicae (TR) piece should be included; 2) 1/60th: Felicitas Perpetua, Vot V Mult X (LXAQ·), in the Southsea find.

64. Cf. supra note 62; Trier: Aequitas Aug Nostri, (TR), Principi Iuventutis, (TR); Arles, Victoriae DDNN Augg, Vot V Mult X, (PAR), Victoriae DDNN Aug et Caes, (E/IS/SAR), in the Southsea find.

65. Cf. supra note 62; Trier, Virtus Aug Nostri, with IM (TR) in the Southsea find; Principi Iuventutis (with DN) (TR) in the East Harptree find; Arles Victoriae DDNN Aug et Caes, Vot V Mult X (PAR), Felicitas Perpetua (PAR) in the Southsea find.

66. Cf. supra note 62; Trier, Virtus Exerciti, sic, with IM and later DN in the obverse (TR), of which there are three examples in the Southsea find. For a complete study of these issues the standard work of P. Bastien, Le monnayage de Magnence (350-353), Wetteren, 1964 should be consulted. In it he thinks that the silver issues ended in August 352 and that Lyons, Arles, Aquileia, and Trier, of course, put out parallel series from 351.

67. Felicitas Romanorum (reverse: two emperors under an arch) for Constantius II and Gallus; Sirmium (reminting silver after a 25 year gap, cf. supra note 40) in the SIRM and *SIRM* marks of which there are four specimens in the Southsea find, two in the North Mendip hoard, and one in the San Genesio find; Nicomedia (SMN); Antioch (SMAN); Aquileia (AQ); Victoria Romanorum (emperor and Victory reverse), Antioch (SMAN).

68. 4 standards: Constantinople, (C·A/B); Arles (SCON) after November 353. The weight of the DN Constantius Max Aug/Constantius Aug, with the four standards reverse (*R*), Khell, is unknown.

69. Virtus Exercitus, Constantinople, (C·A/B/Γ/H/Z) of which there are four examples in the Southsea find, one in the East Harptree hoard, 2 from San Genesio and two from North Mendip); Cyzicus (which like Sirmium had been reopened), (SMK); Thessalonica, (TES), 14 examples from the Southsea find, 3 from East Harptree, and one from North Mendip); Siscia (SIS) in the Enns-Lauriacum find.

70. Virtus Exercitus/tum, Rome, (R, *R*), of which there are 11 examples in the Southsea find, one from East Harptree and one from North Mendip); Arles, (P/SCON) post November 353, of which 7 examples are from Southsea, and one each from East Harptree and North Mendip; Lyons (LVG), of which are from Southsea. There are also 3 pieces from Southsea of indeterminate mark.

71. Vetranio had struck three denominations: 1) 1/60th: Siscia, Gaudium Populi Romani, Vot V Mul X (*SIS*); Thessalonica, Virtus Exercitum, (TSA); 2) 1/72nd: Siscia, Victoria Augustorum (SIS, SISQ, SIS*, each mark also had a palm); 3) 1/96th: Siscia, Victoria Augustorum, Victory with crown reverse, (SIS); Victory with trophy reverse (SIS, SIS~).

72. 1/60th: 4 standards, Constantinople, (C·A/B), in the Southsea find; Arles, (P/SCON), of which there are 3 examples in the Southsea find; Virtus Exercitus, 3 standards, Cyzicus (SMKΔ); Arles, (KONSAV); Virtus Exercitus, (SCON); Gloria Exercitus, Nicomedia, (SMN).

73. SIRM, ·SIRM; SIRM.

74. Constantinople (C·Ɛ·); Thessalonica (TES) known from Enns-Lauriacum and Southsea; Siscia (SIS); Aquileia (AQ).

75. Antioch (ANT); Rome (R); Arles (PAR, CON ?, TCON); Lyons (LVG).

76. Nicomedia (SMN) in the Southsea find; Cyzicus (SMK); Constantinople (C·A/B/Δ/S/Z/H/IA; with palm; H/Θ/IA) known from the Southsea find and from the L. Ciani hoard, 1925; see also infra note 86.

77. Thessalonica (TES); Sirmium (SIRM, ·SIRM, ·SIRM·); there are two examples from Southsea and two in the L. Ciani hoard of 1925; Siscia (SIS); see also infra note 86.

78. Aquileia (AQ); Rome (R).

79. Arles (PARL), in the Southsea find there is a second piece of low weight (1.94 g.); post November 353 (P/S/TCON) of which there are 19 examples from Southsea; Lyons (LVG) of which there are 3 pieces in the Southsea hoard; there is one piece of uncertain mintmark in the Southsea find.

80. These were minted as a parallel series with the argentei with the star reverse struck for Julian as Caesar, cf. infra note 83. The legend Votis XXX Multis XXXX was transferred unchanged to the siliquae.

81. Thessalonica: 1) 1/60th: Virtus Exercitus, 3 standards, (TES); 2) 1/72nd: Virtus Exercitus (TES) in the Southsea find; 3) 1/96th: Votis V Multis X (TES); Antioch, star reverse, (ANT, ·ANT·) known from the North Mendip hoard; Constantinople ? DN Iulianus Caes, 3 standards (CONA), in the Longuet collection.

82. Vot V Multis X (TR); for Constantius II there is a hybrid Votis V Multis X in Paris and Votis XXX Multis XXXX of which there may be an example from Southsea.

83. 1/60th: DN Iulianus (Nob) Caes, 3 standards (CON, TCON) of which two examples are known from Southsea; 1/72nd: Virtus Exercitus (SCON, P/S/TCONST); 1/96th: star (CON, TCON) of which there are three examples from Southsea and one from East Harptree.

84. Rome: Gloria Romanorum, Vot XXX Mult XXXX, multiples of 12-13g. and 61.27g. (Tanini); Sirmium: Gaudium Populi Romani, Votis XXX Multis XXXX (·SIRM·), Gloria Reipublicae, Vot XXX Mult XXXX (SIRM), Tanini.

85. Aquileia: Votis XXXV Multis XXXX (AQ), 3.2g., Windishgraetz. These pieces struck on the 1/96th of the pound standard could have been prepared for the celebrations of 8 November 358.

86. For the occurrence of imitations in the Kecel hoard cf. A. Alföldi, "Barbarische Nachahmungen römischer Siliquae aus dem 4 Jahrh. n. Chr.," Blätter f. Münzfr., 58, 1923, 393ff.: 6 out of 10 have the Votis XXX Multis XXXX legend and copy the mintmarks of Constantinople or Sirmium. The weight is on the standard of the argenteus. See infra note 176.

87. Kaiseraugst, Lengerich, Famars, Tournai (?), (the Metternich hoard of bronze coins buried in 350 contained an argenteus of Magnentius, cf. BJ, 145, 1940, 180ff.), Zamosc, Padea, Unguraşi, Oltenia, Orhei, and Chişinau.

88. Zamosc, cf. A. Kunisz, Materialy do prahistorii ziem polskich, 5, 5, Varsovie, 1973, 134, no. 192: there are 16 specimens, 15 of which are Votis XXX Multis XXXX; mints: 5 are from Cyzicus (this mint never struck siliquae), 2 of Nicomedia, 1 of Thessalonica, and 1 from Sirmium; Padea, cf. SCN, 6, 1975, 231: Constantius II, Unguraşi cf. D Protase, Problema continuitătii in Dacia in lumina arheologiei şi numismaticii, Bucarest, 1966, 170ff. no. 65: "a clay pot full of silver coins of Constantius II; Oltenia, ibid., 181, no. 143: "a hoard of silver coins of Constantius II"; Orhei: cf. V.V. Kropotkin, Kladi rim skih monet na territorii SSSR, Moscow, 1961, 94: 128 coins of Constantius II: 87 from Cyzicus, 27 from Sirmium, 7 from Antioch, 1 imitation, and 6 with illegible mintmarks; Chişinau, cf. B. Mitrea, "Un tezaur monetar restituit Sucidavei," S.C. Istorie Veche si Arheologie, 30, 1979, 63ff. (this study is extremely valuable for its discussion of the find pattern of Danubian hoards).

89. Kauseraugst, cf. supra note 8: There 3 silver ingots stamped IM CAE MAGNENTIVS AVG, each weighing 3 pounds (947-951g. with PIII inscribed on it in dotted letters and the marks LVGVBRIO and GRONOPI, for Ljubljana cf. W. Schmid, "Emona...Ein Fund von Goldmünzen und Silberbarren", Jahrb. f. Altertumskunde, 7, 1913, 171ff.: 2 bars weighing 319 and 640 g. (i.e. one and two pounds), the first bears an imprint of an obverse legend of Magnentius: DN MAGNENTIUS PF AVG and the stamp CAQPF or PS in a rectangle. The inscriptions on the second have gaps: (MA)GNENTIVS PF AVG can be deciphered and below it ...FLA. A second deposit contained 50 gold pieces of which the latest was of Constantius and struck at Antioch, Victoria Augustorum Vot XXX (SMANT), as well as 9 silver bars (376.1g., 356.82g., 357.89g., 390.24g., 308.53g., 303.75g., 208.9g., 187.78g., and 77.23g.). See also A. Jeločnik, "Les multiples d'or de Magnence découverts à Emona", RN, 6, 9, 1967, 209ff. and K. S. Painter, "A Late Roman Silver Ingot from Kent", The Antiquaries Journal, 52, 1972, 84ff.

90. Cf. infra notes 214-218.

91. Preceding the Arras hoard and following those from Kecel and Valea Strimbà, cf. infra notes 176 and 179.

92. V. Zedelius, Spätkaiserzeitlich-Völkerwanderungeszeitliche Keramik und Römische Münzen von Laatzen, Ldkr., Hannover, 1974; cf. infra note 119.

93. Gallia, 19, 1961, 189ff.: hoard A contained 9,955 silver coins from Augustus to Constantius II (whether denarii or siliquae is uncertain). See also my study, "Cachettes monétaries multiples (IIIe-IVe S.)", in Studien zu Fündmunzen der Antike, (ed. M. R. Alföldi) 1, 1979, 5ff., no. 24.

94. J. J. Chiflet, op. cit. supra note 55, p. 270; V. Zedelius, op cit., 23ff.: only 42 coins are now known out of the original 200: 1 consular, 40 denarii ending with Julia Domna and Caracalla, 1 argenteus of Constantius II (Votis XXX Multis XXXX). See also F. Dumas, "Le tombeau de Childéric", Centenaire de la mort de l'Abbé Cochet, Rouen, 1975. The Tournai deposit is obviously later since Childeric died in 482. It is however reasonable to suppose that the silver coins were assembled as a group about 358.

95. A. v. Werlhof, "Ueber einen Fund römischen Münzen bei Freren im Königreiche Hannover", Numismatische Zeitung, 3, 1849, 16; Fr. Hahn, Der Fund von Lengerich im Königreiche Hannover, Goldschmuck und römische Münzen, Hannover, 1854; V. Zedelius, op. cit., 28ff.: a) one gold coin of Augustus and 1220 denarii from Trajan to Alexander Severus including an imitation of Antoninus Pius; b) c. 10 gold coins of Constantine and his sons including one of Constantine II (cf. Cohen 66) and two of Constantius II (of which one cf. RIC VII, Thessalonica, no. 148), c. 200g. of gold (in the form of buttons, rings, bracelets, a fibula, and a collar), a silver patera, and 4 small coins of Constantine (cf. supra note 10). c) c. 70 argentei, Im Cae Magnentius Aug/Virtus Exerciti (TR), and a silver 'medallion' of Constantius II. Metternich, see above note 87.

96. V. Zedelius, op. cit., 35ff. (the Lashorst, Görlitz, Kecel II, and Frauenburg hoards, the latter buried in Eastern Prussia contained 27 denarii dating from Titus to Commodus and 1 solidus of Theodosius II). The persistence of silver hoarding can explain in part the resurgence of a silver coinage in the barbarian kingdoms from the 5th century A.D. (For this period and the years following it, see the fundamental works of J. Lafaurie as well as G. Mickwitz, Die Systeme des römisches Silbergeldes im IV. Jhdt. n. Chr., Helsingfors, 1933, and that of S. Bolin, Fynden av romerska mynt i det fria Germanien, Diss. Lund, 1926).

97. Southsea coins of Magnentius and Decentius: 2 1/60ths, 3 1/72nds, 3 1/96ths; East Harptree had 1 1/72nd.

98. Cf. supra note 97 and notes 67, 69, 71, 72, 74, 76, 77, 79, and 81-83. In addition to 31 argentei there is also possibly 1 quinarius, cf. supra note 82.

99. Cf. supra notes 97, 69, 71 and 83.

100. Cf. supra notes 67 and 69.

101. For the hoard bought by L. Ciani in 1925, cf. supra notes 76 and 77; Kecel I, cf. supra note 86 and V. Zedelius, op. cit., 41: the average weight of the 10 imitations was 3.26g. see infra, note 176.

102. Cf. supra notes 67, 69 and 71.

103. The reform of the bronze and silver was not perhaps completely simultaneous if the Spes Republice (TES) of Constantius II which forms part of the East Harptree find is a quinarius and not a siliqua (its weight was 1.81g.). There may be another example marked SMPL (Lyons?) for Julian Caesar (cf. Cohen 40). As to the date of the weight change from 1/96th to 1/144th of the pound, the argentei from Aquileia with the Votis XXXV Multis XXXX reverse must be taken into account since they are after November 358. This seems to me to be the latest possible terminus because some time must be allowed for the manufacture of siliquae for Julian as Caesar before the proclamation at Lutetia in February 360. It is not therefore possible to accept the late date proposed by A. Missong (360), art. cit. infra note 175, which was based on a 4 to 1 relationship between heavy and light pieces with the Votis XXX Multis XXXX type. The precise historical context, i.e. whether it was related to the campaign against the Sarmatians or an invasion by the Persians, has yet to be established. See also infra note 215.

104. In the 4th century the siliqua had a weight equal to 1/6th of a scruple of gold (as attested in the renowned Feltre inscription, ILS, 9420, of A.D. 323). In the light of more recent research we can now admit that the system proposed by Mommsen was based on metrological documents from a period when the siliqua was an intermediate denomination between the solidus and the follis (cf. my unpublished article, "Le tarif d'Abydos et la réforme monétaire d'Anastase): the siliqua had a real weight of 2.24g. and a theoretical weight of 2.56g. (i.e. an overvaluation of 12.5%); the miliarensis of 4.48g. was equal to a thousandth of a pound of gold, 1/14th of a solidus and 7/4ths of the siliqua. Ammianus calls the new denomination argenteus nummus (XXIV, 3, 3) but the term has no technical value since during the same years the Theodosian Code (XV, 9, 1, A.D. 384) uses the same term to designate the denomination at 1/60th. In the context of the theory formulated by Mommsen it is worth noting that in the late silver hoards from Britain the siliqua was often clipped, the miliarensis, never so. This suggests that the former was fiduciary and that one could modify the amount of overvaluation.

105. TCON: 75 pieces in the Southsea find, 61 in the East Harptree hoard, and 4 from Willersey, cf. supra note 50. For the CON mintmark in the Honiton find, cf. infra note 131.

106. In the Southsea find there was a Victoria DDNN Aug for Constantius II from Thessalonica (TES) and another from Trier (TR); at Lyons the type had been continued after Julian became Augustus in 360 and it seems that the second phase of its production was much more active; cf. infra note 110.

107. Antioch: ANT (two specimens from the East Harptree and the Sucidava finds, cf. infra note 175, one in the Ciani hoard); Nicomedia: SMN (in the East Harptree and Ciani finds); Constantinople: C·A/B/Γ/Δ/Ɛ/Z/H Θ/IA (there are 9 pieces in the Sucidava find, 4 in the Ciani hoard, and 1 from Redea, cf. infra note 177); Cyzicus did not strike the siliqua. x

108. Sirmium: (SIRM), there are c. 60 pieces in the Ciani hoard, 21 from Redea, 7 from Sucidava, 2 from East Harptree and 2 from San Genesio; Siscia: (SIS) 2 pieces from the Sucidava find, 1 from Redea; Rome (R), in the Southsea hoard; Thessalonica minted the Victory type, cf. supra note 106 but must have also minted Votis XXX Multis XXXX (cf. the Southsea hoard); Aquileia didn't strike siliquae.

109. Arles: (CON, P/SCON, and T in error), there are 158 specimens in the Southsea find, 156 from East Harptree, and 14 from Willersey; Lyons: (LVG), there are 130 pieces in the Southsea hoard, 114 from East Harptree, and 1 from Willersey; Trier: Gloria Reipublice, Vot XXX Mult XXXX (TR), Mus. Naz. (Rome). The unanimitas of the reform must be emphasized and the role played by political considerations. Constantius II who was concerned about the situation on the Danube and the Euphrates was the instigator and Julian's role was to implement the reform in Gaul.

110. Lyons: Victoria DDNN Aug (LVG), for Constantius II,there are 27 pieces in the Southsea find, and 49 from East Harptree, for Julian as Augustus there are 42 pieces from Southsea and 26 from East Harptree; Vot XXX (LVG), Constantius II: 130 pieces from Southsea, 114 from East Harptree; Vot V (LVG), Julian Augustus: 134 pieces from Southsea, 125 from East Harptree; Arles: in the Southsea find there are 78 PCON and 74 SCON for Constantius and 65 TCON for Julian as Caesar; in the East Harptree hoard the numbers are: 78 PCON, 78 SCON (for Constantius) and 61 TCON (for Julian Caesar).

111. DN Cl Iulianus Aug/Votis V Multis X (PCON) of which there are two from Southsea and two from East Harptree, (SCON) of which there are 2 from Southsea and 3 from East Harptree, (TCON) of which there are 28 from Southsea and 16 from East Harptree.

112. Arles: DN Iulianus PF Aug/Votis V Multis X (PCON) of which there were 5 from Southsea and 24 from East Harptree, (SCON) of which there were 11 from Southsea and 26 from East Harptree, and (TCON) for which the numbers are 18 and 39 respectively; Lyons: Fl Cl Iulianus PP Aug/ Votis V Multis X (PLVG) for which the numbers are Southsea: 10, East Harptree 28, (SLVG) Southsea: 7, East Harptree 36. There are 7 variants in obverse titulature. Trier: Votis V Multis X (TR) of which there are 106 from Southsea and 36 from East Harptree. There is no comparable series for Constantius since this issue was after the break. Rarer reverses include: Restitutor Reip (SCON) in the Holwel (Holway) find; Victoria Perpetu (TR) in Paris.

113. Virtus Exercitus, for Lyons (LVG) in the Southsea find; and for Arles (CON, S/TCON) in the Southsea find but with the variant Exercitum.

114. Multiple at 1/60th of the pound: Victoria Augusti, Vot XXXX, with the two prisoners type (CH); siliqua: Vot XXXX (C·A/B/Δ/Ɛ)in the East Harptree find.

115a. Rome: Votis V Multis X (R), 2 pieces from Southsea, Victoria Augusti N (R) in Paris; Sirmium: Votis V Multis X (SIRM); Siscia: VICTONIA ONVM (SIS), imitation in the Southsea find; Thessalonica (at 1/60th of the pound): Votis V Multis X (TES) 522 g.in a private collection.

115b. Virtus Exercitus (eagle), Arles: (P/S/TCONST) of which there are 3 pieces in the Southsea find, 1 from East Harptree and 1 from North Mendip; Sirmium (SIRM, ·SIRM·) in the Holwel (Holway) hoard; Victoria Romanorum, Sirmium (SIRM, *SIRM) in the Willersey and Holwel (Holway) finds; Antioch (ANT).

116. Vot(is) X Multi(is) XX, Trier (TR✱, and TRP) in the Holwel (Holway) and Tuddenham hoards, cf. infra note 149; Lyons: with 5 obverses, (LVG, P/SLVG, SLVGD, and with eagle), 22 pieces from North Mendip; Arles: with six obverses, (P/S/TCON, CONST, ·CONST, CONST·, P/S/CONST, and with eagle), 158 pieces from North Mendip; Rome (R); Constantinople (CP·A/B/Δ), cf. infra note 163; Antioch: with 5.obverses, (ANT) in the Holwel and Shapwick I finds, cf. infra note 152.

117. 1) 1/60th of a pound: Antioch: (ANT) Gloria Romanorum, emperor under an arch; 2) 1/72nd of a pound: Antioch: (ANT) Gloria Romanorum, id. (in the East Harptree find), Votis V Multis X; Arles: (PCONST) Restitutor Reip; 3) siliqua: Vot(is) V Multi(is) X: Antioch (ANT); Nicomedia (SMN), Constantinople: (CP·A/B/Γ/Δ) in the Grovely Wood find, cf. infra note 146; Sirmium (SIRM); Arles (P/CONST) in the Holwel (Holway) and Terling hoards, cf. infra note 142; Restitutor Reip, Arles (PCONST).

118. Kaiseraugst, SMB, 18, 66, 1967, 50ff. (it is uncertain whether the siliqua of Julian forms part of the hoard); Merelbeke, Thirion no. 194 in which there is a siliqua of Julian Augustus.

119. Cf. supra note 92.

120. Cf. supra notes 8, 27, 29, 36, 38, 39, 42, 44, 49, 50, 58, 62-67, 69, 71, 72, 74, 76, 77, 79, 81-3, 97, 98, 106, 108-113, 115a-b; there are 781 pieces out of a total of 978. The distribution is as follows: 2 Trajan, 2 Antoninus, 1 Faustina, 1 Marcus Aurelius, 1 Diocletian, 2 Constantine I, 1 Crispus, 2 Constantine II, 36 Constans, 422 Constantius II, 5 Magnentius, 3 Decentius, 5 Gallus, 495 Julian. The mints are: 143 Trier, 358 Lyons, 380 Arles, 5 Aquileia, 16 Rome, 2 Siscia, 7 Sirmium, 24 Thessalonica, 7 Constantinople, 2 Nicomedia. Southsea is in Hampshire.

121. Cf. supra notes 50, 105, 109, 115b. There were 21 coins of Constantius II, 35 of Julian. Mints: 6 Trier, 17 Lyons, 29 Arles, 2 Rome and 2 of Sirmium. Willersey is in Gloucestershire.

122. Cf. supra notes 27, 39, 49, 50, 52, 60, 65, 69, 71, 83, 97, 99, 105, 107-112, 114, 115b, 117; there were 1,053 pieces out of a total of 1,496. The ruler distribution is as follows: 1 Constantine I, 4 Constans, 340 Constantius II, 1 Decentius, 718 Julian, 8 Jovian, 165 Valentinian I,

199 Valens, 60 Gratian. Mints: 207 Trier, 574 Lyons, 553 Arles, 1 Aquileia, 99 Rome, 1 Siscia, 6 Sirmium, 12 Thessalonica, 4 Constantinople, 4 Nicomedia, 22 Antioch. East Harptree is in Somerset. Cf. infra notes 160, 169-170 and 192.

123. Cf. infra note 177: 23 pieces out of a total of 27.

124. Cf. infra note 175: 133 pieces out of 536.

125. Cf. infra note 191: 2 pieces out of 9.

126. Cf. supra notes 76, 86 and 101. Regarding the homogeneity of the Ciani and Kecel hoards: For: 1) Kecel was discovered in 1922/23 and Ciani was bought in 1925; 2) the significant percentage of Sirmium coins in both hoards; Against: Kecel seems to have been composed of argentei while the Ciani hoard favoured siliquae; 2) Constantinople is unevenly represented in the two finds—the Ciani find had only Votis XXX Multis XXXX pieces of Constantius II 3) argentei and c. 67 siliquae); in the Kecel hoard the tricennalia pieces of this emperor are also heavily represented (including imitations) but there are also a fair number of denarii of the early empire and issues of Valentinian I and Valens. A second hoard discovered at Kecel in 1934 had 2,816 denarii ranging from Nero to Septimius Severus in date. See infra note 176.

127. Cf. supra notes 39, nos. 100-101; Siliquae of Sirmium with the Votis XXX Multis XXXX.

128. NC, 6, 14, 1954, 209ff.; 20 examples out of 117.

129. Ibid., 7, 5, 1965, 177ff.; 42 pieces out of 447.

130. Ibid., 5, 18, 1938, 53ff.; 11 pieces out of 125.

131. Ibid., 5, 5, 1925, 396ff.; 1 piece out of 16.

132. Ibid., 4, 15, 1915, 433ff.; 658 pieces out of 2,044.

133. Ibid., 6, 2, 1942, 105ff.; 4 pieces out of 13.

134. Ibid., 5, 16, 1936, 314ff.; 22 pieces out of 85.

135. Ibid., 5, 14, 1934, 61ff.; 25 pieces out of 100.

136. Antiquaries Journal, 1940, 481; 2 pieces out of 9.

137. Cf. supra note 36; 64 pieces out of 318.

138. NC, 5, 15, 1935, 254ff.; 45 pieces out of 228.

139. Ibid., 5, 2, 1922, 1934ff.; 7 pieces out of 53.

140. Ibid., 5, 15, 1935, 67ff.; 1 piece out of 7.

141. Ibid., 2, 9, 1869, 372; 7 pieces out of 54.

142. Ibid., 5, 13, 1933, 144ff.; 34 pieces out of 325.

143. Ibid., 6, 8, 1948, 205ff.; 39 examples out of 388.

144. Ibid., 6, 2, 1942, 101ff.; 7 pieces out of 80.

145. Ibid., 5, 9, 1929, 319ff.; 6 pieces out of 70.

146. Ibid., 4, 6, 1906, 329ff.; 25 pieces out of 299.

147. Ibid., 6, 8, 1948, 82ff.; 5 pieces out of 62.

148. Ibid., 3, 4, 1884, 348; 2 pieces out of 26.

149. Ibid., 6, 8, 1948, 169ff.; 8 pieces out of 114.

150. Archeologia XIV, 71; 2 pieces out of 30.

151. NC, 1, 17, 1855, 101ff.; 98 pieces out of 1,506.

152. Ibid., 5, 16, 1936, 245ff.; 7 pieces out of 120.

153. Ibid., 5, 16, 1936, 257; 10 pieces out of 230.

154. Ibid., 6, 2, 1942, 97ff.; 8 pieces out of 200.

155. Ibid., 4, 8, 1908, 215ff.; 13 pieces out of 337.

156. RIC IX, 1951; J. W. E. Pearce "Notes on the Terling and other Silver Hoards found in Britain", NC, 5, 13, 1933, 170ff.

157. 1) 1/60th of a pound: Salus Reipublicae, RIC IX, Lyons, no. 3, Arles, no. 3; Victoria Augustorum, Rome, no. 6; Securitas Reip, Constantinople, no. 8; Vota, Lyons, no. 4, Aquileia, no. 3, Thessalonica, no. 9; 2) 1/72nd of a pound: Restitutor Reip(ublicae), Lyons, no. 5, Arles no. 4, Rome, no. 7, Antioch, no. 6. (As a result of a systemization which was unique in the late empire, the legend appeared on the solidus, siliqua, and aes (3) Victoria Augustorum (2 variants), Rome, no. 8, Constantinople, no. 10; Securitas Reipublic(ae) (2 variants), Nicomedia no. 3, Siscia (SM·SISC); Gloria Romanorum (3 variants), Siscia, nos. 3-4, Constantinople, no. 9, Antioch nos. 4-5; Virtus Exercitus (3 variants), Arles, no. 5, Thessalonica, nos. 10-11, Siscia (private collection). There are also multiples at 1/24th of the pound with the Virtus Romani Exercitus, and Virtus Exercitus reverses, Arles no. 2, Thessalonica, nos. 7-8.

158. Constantinople, no. 11; and perhaps at Rome, no. 9.

159. G. Mickwitz, op. cit., note 96, p. 9; J. W. E. Pearce, RIC IX, p. xxviii. See infra note 176.

160. Trier, no. 2; Lyons, no. 6; Arles, no. 6; Aquileia, no. 4; Siscia, p. 145 (there is an imitation in the East Harptree find); Thessalonica, no. 12; Constantinople, no. 12; Nicomedia, nos. 4-5; Antioch, no. 7. There are no issues from Sirmium but at Rome a piece is known for Valentinian from a private collection (RB, 2.46 g). In the East Harptree find out of 169 Restitutor Reip pieces, 125 were minted at Lyons and only 20 at Arles where Pearce noted at least 6 issues.

161. Trier, nos. 3-4; Lyons, no. 8; Aquileia, no. 5; Rome, no. 10; Sirmium, no. 2; Thessalonica, no. 14. In the East Harptree find, out of 54 Vota coins from Western mints, 49 came from Rome.

162. Constantinople: no. 13; Constantinople put out a series of 8 issues which include those of Procopius, cf. ibid., p. 200. In the C·A issue there is a siliqua in the Gerin collection in Milan with the mark C·Θ. Antioch, no. 8; Nicomedia: (SMNE), 2.03 g, Mus. Naz. (Rome).

163. CP·A and related marks were minted before Procopius: Valentinian I: 15 in the Gura Ialomiţei find, cf. infra note 174, 10 in the Dobroudja hoard, cf. infra ibidem, 10 from Sucidava, cf. infra note 175; Valens: 21 from Gura Ialomiţei, 10 from Dobroudja, and 8 from Sucidava; 2) C·A was minted before and during the reign of Procopius: Valentinian I: 7 from Gura Ialomiţei, 4 from Dobroudja, 5 from Sucidava; Valens: none from Gura Ialomiţei, 8 from Dobroudja, 19 from Sucidava; Procopius: 8 from Dobroudja, 5 from Sucidava, and 4 with the mark ·C·A; 3) *C·A was minted after Procopius: Valentinian I: 1 from Sucidava; Valens: 6 ibid.; 4) CONSA and related marks were minted after Procopius: Valentinian I: 1 from Dobroudja, Valens: 2 ibid. In addition to the 3 hoards cited, Viespesti, cf. infra note 174, in which all the coins that postdate 364 were minted at Constantinople a fact which testifies to the vitality of that mint which during the reigns of Julian and Jovian had worked in only 4 officinae and not in 8/9 for silver. For coins of Procopius at Heraclea see Cohen 14; Nicomedia, RIC IX, no. 6; Cyzicus, ibid., no. 3.

164. Lyons, no. 9; Rome, no. 11.

165. 22 Valentinian I, 24 Valens; cf. supra notes 160 and 161.

166. The legal texts related to the gold are C. Th. XII, 6, 12, 13, and 7, 3 and date from 366-7; cf. J. P. C. Kent, "Gold Coinage in the Late Roman Empire", "Essays in Roman Coinage Presented to Harold Mattingly (ed. R. A. G. Carson, C. H. V. Sutherland), Oxford, 1956, 190ff. However the marks OB and PS are not found on coins until the accession of Gratian: OB is found at Trier, Thessalonica, Constantinople, and Antioch; PS at Trier and, in an abbreviated form P, at Lyons, Arles and Siscia. Subsequently (from 375-395) the PS mark is regularly found at Trier and relatively frequently at Lyons, Aquileia, and Siscia.

167. See my study on "The Role and Distribution of the Bronze Coinage from 348 to 392", pp.41ff. in this volume. cf. Themist. Or., X, 136-138 for fortifications in Scythia.

168. With the exception of Trier, cf. infra, the siliqua with the Vota type continued to be minted at Lyons, no. 19, Siscia, nos. 11-13, and Thessalonica, no. 25. The distribution seems to have been somewhat restricted; there are two coins of Lyons and of Siscia in the North Mendip hoard.

169. Cf. supra note 156; Terling: 2 Valentinian I, 29 Valens; East Harptree: 7 Valentinian I, 79 Valens; San Genesio: 3 Valentinian I, 32 Valens; Springhead: 12 Valentinian I, 89 Valens; Grovely Wood: 3 Valentinian I, 52 Valens; Icklingham I: 2 Valentinian I, 63 Valens; North Mendip: 12 Valentinian I, 214 Valens. From the paper presented by C. E. King, "The Sacrae Largitiones: Revenues, Expenditures, and the Production of Coin," p. 141ff., in this volume we now know that the lustral cycle affected the emission pattern mints. As a result the period when the siliqua was not produced at Trier must have lasted for five years i.e. from 367/8 to 372/3. It is worth noting that silver was not mentioned in the de rebus bellicis which may have been written c. 368-369; cf. M. W. E.

Hassell and R. Ireland (eds.) De Rebus Bellicis Papers Presented to Professor E. A. Thompson, British Archaeological Reports, S63, 1979.

170. 1) 1/72nd: Vota: Arles, no. 14; Victoria Augustorum: Trier, no. 24, 2 pieces in the North Mendip find; Lyons: no. 18, Arles, no. 13; Virtus Exercitus: Trier, no. 26 (SMTR) in the East Harptree and North Mendip finds, and (TRPS·); 2 pieces in the East Harptree find, 1 from San Genesio, North Mendip and Mr. Wood's hoard; Aquileia: no. 10, Siscia: no. 10 (examples exist in the San Genesio, North Mendip and Grovely Wood hoards. At Trier it is impossible to distinguish coins of Valens minted before 375 from those produced after (nos. 26b, 2, and 42a, 1); 2) 1/60th: Vota: Trier, no. 23, Lyons, nos. 16-17, Arles, nos. 11-12 (in the North Mendip find) and Siscia, no. 9; 3) 1/24th: Triumfator Gent Barb, echoing a type of the house of Constantine, Trier, no. 22, of which there are two coins in the San Genesio hoard, Siscia, no. 8.

171. 1) 1/60th: Victoria DN Aug, Constantinople: no. 31; Vota: Antioch, nos. 27-28; 2) 1/72nd: Victoria DN Aug, Constantinople, no. 32; Virtus Ex-serciti, Constantinople, no. 33, Gloria Romanorum (3 variants), Antioch, nos. 29-31; 3) 1/96th: Vota: Constantinople, nos. 34-35, Nicomedia, no. 19, Virtus Exercitus (3 standards): Nicomedia, no. 18; 4) siliquae: Vota: Constantinople, nos. 36-39, 11 pieces from Sucidava 7 of which are of Valens, Nicomedia, nos. 20-22, 7 pieces from Sucidava, 1 from Redea, Antioch, nos. 32-34, cf. the next note.

172. San Genesio contained 16 siliquae of Antioch and by comparison only 1 of Constantinople. In the Dranic and Redea finds, cf. infra notes 191 and 177, there were 5 and 3 Antioch pieces respectively. RIC XI, 279ff. records 12 mintmarks for Antioch and in the ·ANTA issue there were 10 officinae working.

173. Lists of coins found on sites are by definition likely to have few silver coins but even if there are only a few examples, they are nonetheless significant, cf. infra note 203.

174. Gura Ialomiței, SCN, 1, 1957, 146ff.; 46 siliquae of Valentinian I and Valens struck at Constantinople; Dobroudja, cf. L. Ruzicka, "Siliquenfund in der Dobrogea (Rümanien", Blätter fur Münzfr., 15, 1920-1923, 345ff. 44 siliquae from Constantinople: 1 Jovian, 15 Valentinian I, 20 Valens, 8 Procopius; Viespesti, cf. B. Mitrea, art cit. supra note 88 which refers to C. Stirbu, Muzeul National, 3, 1976, 193ff. (non vidimus): 30 coins with the following distribution: 2 Constantius II (Sirmium and Nicomedia), 3 Jovian (1 Constantinople and 2 Nicomedia), 2 Procopius (Constantinople), 9 Valentinian I and 13 Valens (all of Constantinople). See also note 163 supra.

175. B. Mitrea art cit. supra note 88: there is information on three lots: 1) 105 coins published by A. Missong, "Fund römischer Siliquen aus den Jahren 360-367", Wiener Num. Monatshefte, 4, 1868, 248ff: 11 Constantius II (1 Lyons, 2 Siscia, 6 Sirmium, 1 Constantinople, 1 Antioch); 3 Julian (2 Constantinople, 1 Antioch); 7 Jovian (5 Constantinople, 2 Nicomedia); 24 Valentinian I (19 Constantinople, 5 Nicomedia);

50 Valens (40 Constantinople, 10 Nicomedia); 9 Procopius (Constantinople); 1 Gratian (Constantinople); 2) a group of 31 siliquae bought in 1926: 11 Constantius II (1 Sirmium, 8 Constantinople, 2 Antioch), 9 Valentinian I and 11 Valens (8 Constantinople, 3 Nicomedia, 9 Antioch); 3) 400 coins in the Archaeological Institute in Bucarest: 67 Constantius II, 21 Julian, 13 Jovian, 95 Valentinian, 96 Valens, 16 Gratian, and 92 unidentifiable. The original hoard must have had as many as c. 6,000 pieces. See also supra notes 107, 108, 124, 163, and 171.

176. Kecel, cf. Arch. Ert., 39, 1920-1922, 99ff: at least 62 siliquae and perhaps double that number from Constantius II to Valentinian I and Valens: 3 of Arles and Aquileia, 2 Siscia, 21 Sirmium, 1 Thessalonica, 27 Constantinople, 4 Nicomedia, 4 Antioch, and 10 imitations of Constantinople and Sirmium coins (argentei of Constantius II and of Valens) in addition to 1st and 2nd century denarii. Ciani hoard: c. 70 coins of Constantius II: 3 argentei (2 Sirmium, 1 Constantinople), 67 siliquae (1 Arles, c. 60 Sirmium, 4 Constantinople, 1 Nicomedia, 1 Antioch). See also supra notes 76, 77, 86, 91, 101, 107, 108, and 126.

177. Crestera, Coleçitiilor Caiet Selectiv de Informare, 6, 1962, 304ff: 27 siliquae of Constantius II and Valens (1 Siscia, 21 Sirmium, 1 Constantinople, 1 Nicomedia, 3 Antioch); at Bucharest, 3 Constantius II (Siscia, Sirmium, Constantinople) and 4 Valens (1 Nicomedia, 3 Antioch); see also supra notes 107, 108, 123, 171.

178. B. Mitrea, art. cit., 72 (total number unknown) of which one is a siliqua: Valens (Nicomedia, 367-375).

179. ibid., and Folia Arch., 5, 1945, 95ff. Mixed hoard: 2nd century denarii, 10 silver coins of Constans and 3 solidi of Gratian—Journal of Field Archaeology, 1, 1974, 117ff.: 69 silver coins, 4 gold, 10 fragments of Valentinian I, Valens and Gratian.

180. Chaddleworth (Berks), NC, 3, 20, 1900, 337; 800 silver coins of Constantius II, Valentinian I, Valens and Gratian; Uphill, VCH, Somerset, I, 1906, 355: 129 silver and bronze coins mainly of Valentinian I and Gratian; Wookey Hole, ibid., silver coins of Constantius II, Julian, Valens and Gratian; bronze of Constantine, Valentinian, Valens, and Gratian.

181. Add. in the Wroxeter hoard of bronze coins, NC, 1, 20, 1857, 79ff. which was buried after 364, there was a plated siliqua of Julian.

182. Cf. supra notes 169 and 170.

183. Constantinople, no. 42, 375-378, (5 pieces in the San Genesio find and 1 in Mr. Wood's hoard); no. 51, 378-383. The MM6 catalogue no. 2069 lists a siliqua of 1.97 g. DN Gratianus PF Aug/Vot XX Mult XXX, (ANT), which is an indication of a very rare issue at Antioch after 375 and therefore parallels no. 42 at Constantinople.

184. Symm., Ep., X, 2,4 (376): pari vigilia prospectum videmus ut... monetae nequitiam decoquat largo purgatio.

185. ibid., Ep. I, 13 and A. Alföldi, A Conflict of Ideas in the Late Roman Empire: The Clash between Valentinian and the Senatorial Aristocracy, Oxford, 1952.

186a. 1) 1/24th: Triumfator Gent Barb, 375-378: Aquileia (2 from San Genesio, nos. 6-7); Siscia: (2 from the San Genesio hoard, nos. 5 and 8); 378-383: Rome, no. 32 (and for Theodosius in the San Genesio hoard, no. 9); 2) 1/60th: Vota: 375-378, Trier, no. 41, Siscia, no. 16; 378-383: Trier, no. 52, Aquileia (2 pieces in the San Genesio hoard, nos. 85 and 99); Victoria Augustorum: 378-383, Rome no. 33 (pieces in the San Genesio, Holwel, and North Mendip finds); 3) 1/72nd: Virtus Exercitus: 375-378, Trier, no. 42 (pieces in the Holwel (Holway) and North Mendip hoards); 378-383: Trier, no. 53 (distinguishable with difficulty from the preceding issue but examples exist in San Genesio, Holwel (Holway), North Mendip, and Mr. Wood's hoard); Aquileia, no. 23 (4 coins in the San Genesio hoard one of which weighs 5.26 g., 2 in the North Mendip find and 1 in Mr. Wood's hoard); Rome, no. 34 (in the Holwel find); Siscia, no. 23 (42 pieces from San Genesio, 1 from Holwel and the North Mendip hoards).

186b. To which should be added the fractions of the siliqua minted at Trier, no. 56, and at Rome, no. 36. There were argentei at Aquileia, no. 24 and possibly at Trier, no. 54.

187. Throne: ante 375: Trier, no. 27; 375-378: Trier, no. 45, Siscia, no. 20; 378-383: Rome, no. 35; Cuirass: 375-378: Trier, no. 46, Aquileia, no. 15; 378-383: Trier, no. 64, Lyons, no. 27, Aquileia (there is a specimen in Paris); Siscia (Mus. Naz. in Rome).

188. Virtus Romanorum (throne): 378-383: Trier, no. 58, Lyons, no. 26, Aquileia, no. 28, Arles (there is a coin in Paris); Concordia Auggg: 378-383: Trier, no. 55, Lyons, no. 24, Aquileia, no. 25; Victoria Auggg: 375-378: Trier, no. 43, Siscia, no. 17; 378-383: Trier, no. 57, Lyons, no. 25, Aquileia, nos. 26-7. To these a third series of siliquae issues should be added, those with Vota reverses: 1) 375-378: Trier, no. 44 (in Mr. Wood's hoard), Aquileia, nos. 13-14; Siscia, nos. 18-19 (7 pieces in the San Genesio find), Thessalonica, nos. 29-30 (in the San Genesio hoard); 2) 378-383: Trier, nos. 59-63, Siscia nos. 24-25, Thessalonica, no. 36 (in the San Genesio hoard).

189. 150 Vrbs Roma: 41 with the throne reverse (35 Trier, 4 Siscia, and 2 Rome), 109 with the cuirass (62 Trier, 37 Aquileia, 10 Lyons); 88 Virtus Romanorum: (51 Trier, 37 Aquileia); 75 Victoria Auggg: (39 Trier, 27 Aquileia, 9 Lyons); 36 Concordia Auggg: (25 Trier, 11 Aquileia); total: 199 coins.

190. Springhead: 223 Vrbs Roma, of which 158 have the throne reverse (156 Trier, 2 Rome) and 65 have the cuirass (53 Trier, 11 Aquileia, 1 Lyons); 64 Virtus Romanorum: (57 Trier, 7 Aquileia); 25 Victoria Auggg: (23 Trier, 2 Aquileia); 5 Concordia Auggg: (4 Trier, 1 Lyons); Total: 94 coins; Mr. Wood's hoard: 44 Vrbs Roma, 30 with the throne reverse: (29 Trier, 1 Rome) and 14 with the cuirass: (10 Trier, 4 Aquileia); 9 Virtus Romanorum: (6 Trier, 3 Aquileia); 4 Victoria Auggg: (3 Trier,

1 Aquileia); 1 *Concordia Auggg*: (Trier); Total: 14 coins; Shapwick II: 67 *Vrbs Roma*, 44 with the throne reverse (42 Trier, 2 Rome) and 23 with the cuirass (17 Trier, 5 Aquileia, 1 Lyons); 13 *Virtus Romanorum*: (Trier); 2 *Victoria Auggg*: (Trier); Total: 15 coins. A similar distribution occurs in British hoards buried after 388. Another anomaly emerges between the San Genesio and British hoards: the *Vrbs Roma* type with the later cuirass reverse is widely found in Italy, that with the throne in Britain. Since the San Genesio hoard postdates 383, and Springhead, Shapwick II and Mr. Wood's hoard were buried after 388, but since Magnus Maximus had not struck the *Vrbs Roma* type, the difference between the proportions for the throne and cuirass type could be explained by the distances involved which would have meant their diffusion was slower the further away they were from the issuing mint.

191. *SCN*, 6, 1975, 229ff.: 2 Constantius II, 1 Gratian (Siscia), 6 Valens (5 Antioch and 1 Trier *post* 375, *RIC* no. 44). See also *supra* note 172.

192. East Harptree: *cf*. *supra* notes 122, 160, 169-170; San Genesio *cf*. *supra* notes 39, 61, 67, 69, 100, 108, 127, 169, 170, 172, 183, 186, 188-190; the hoard ends with 6 *siliquae* from Aquileia of which 1 is of Arcadius and minted after 383, (*RIC* IX, no. 41). The ruler distribution is as follows: 1 Constans, 5 Constantius II, 8 Valentinian I, 82 Valens, 286 Gratian, 115 Valentinian II, 46 Theodosius, 1 Arcadius. Mints: 250 Trier, 19 Lyons, 126 Aquileia, 6 Rome, 57 Siscia, 3 Sirmium, 9 Thessalonica, 9 Constantinople, 16 Antioch.

193. No. 77. *Add*.: a reverse, no. 78, for Flaccilla.

194. O. Ulrich Bansa, *Moneta Mediolanensis*, Venice, 1949, 72ff. Multiples seem to have been minted only at Rome: *Triumf Gent Barb*, no. 52, and at Thessalonica, *Restitutor Reipublice*, no. 56. Thessalonica also minted a light *miliarensis*, *Victoria Augustorum*, no. 57. *Siliquae*: *Vrbs Roma*, Rome, no. 53; *Virtus Romanorum*, Aquileia, no. 41 (*cf*. *supra* note 192); Milan, no. 12, on p. 73 Pearce suggests that these issues from Milan date from the invasion of Maximus but Ulrich Bansa prefers to date them to 388, *op*. *cit*., 118. *Vota*: Milan, nos. 13-14 (32 coins from Grovely Wood, North Mendip, South Ferriby, Terling, Sproxton, Icklingham I and III; *cf*. O. Ulrich Bansa, *op*. *cit*., 74); Thessalonica, no. 58; Rome, *cf*. note 62 (owing to the importance of the *decennalia* celebrations of Valentinian II at Rome, *cf*. Symm., *Rel*., 13, I have dated the *Vot X Mult XX* type to 385 rather than 388 as Pearce did, *RIC* IX, p. 113); Aquileia (there is a coin in Paris).

195. Sulp. Sev., *Dial*., III, 11; Ps. Aurel. Vict., 48, 17; Pacat, *Pan*. XII, 26.

196. Honiton 25%, Shapwick II 21.6%, Mr. Wood's hoard 13.67%, Springhead 8.27%.

197. Manton Downs 26.92%, Grovely Wood 22.42%, Sturmer 16.66%, Mildenhall 15.38%, Cleeve Prior 15.29%, Colerne II 15%, Icklingham I 13.94%, Shapwick I 13.33%, North Mendip 12.67%, Tuddenham 12.28%, Terling 12%, Edington 9.67%, Icklingham III 8.26%, Colerne I 8%, Fleetwood *c*. 7.6%, South Ferriby 7.45%, Holwel 7.23%, Sproxton 7%, Icklingham II 5.71%, Coleraine 3.98%, Great Allington 3.7%, Dorchester 1.88%.

198. Trier RIC IX, nos. 80-81.

199. Trier, no. 82 (two pieces in the Springhead find); Lyons no. 31.

200. London, no. 3 Victoria Augg (in the North Mendip find); no. 4 Vot V Mult X (ibid.); Trier, no. 83, Concordia Auggg, (in Mr. Wood's hoard), no. 84, Virtus Romanorum (214 in the North Mendip find, 59 from Grovely Wood, 41 from Icklingham I, 39 from Coleraine, 34 from Springhead and Terling, 26 from Shapwick II); Lyons, Votis V Multis X for Victor (Mus. Naz. Rome?).

201. Milan, Virtus Romanorum, no. 19; Aquileia, Victoria Augustorum, no. 53, Virtus Romanorum, no. 54. The average weight of coins in public collections is: 1.53 g. Milan (28 coins), 1.6 g. Aquileia (19).

202. Springhead (Kent), NC, 7, 5, 1965, 177ff.: 3 solidi, 12 miliarenses (2 of which were minted on the 1/60th of the pound standard), and 432 siliquae: 16 Constantius II, 25 Julian, 1 Jovian, 29 Valentinian I, 128 Valens, 169 Gratian, 32 Valentinian II, 9 Theodosius, 37 Magnus Maximus; Mints: 343 Trier, 14 Lyons, 23 Arles, 1 Milan, 33 Rome, 22 Aquileia, 2 Siscia, 1 Sirmium, 1 Nicomedia, 5 Antioch, 1 imitation; the latest piece is a Virtus Exercitus from Trier which was minted after 388 (no. 93a); see also supra notes 169, 190, 196, 199, 200; Bath (between Bath and Bristol, Somerset), NC, 1840, 144: 250 coins of which 150 were seen; Valens, Gratian, and Maximus were equally represented. Reverse types consisted of Virtus Romanorum, Vrbs Roma, Concordia Auggg (2), Vot V Mult X. Mints: Trier, Rome (2), and Aquileia (1); Honiton (Devon), NC, 5, 5, 1925, 396: 16 siliquae: 1 Julian, 3 Valens, 1 Gratian, 2 Valentinian II, 1 Theodosius, 4 Maximus, 4 Arcadius (which are the latest in date); Mints: Trier (13), Lyons (1), Arles (1), and Constantinople (1); see supra notes 105 and 196; Norwich (?) Coin Hoards, III, 1977, no. 211: 15 siliquae of Constantius II to Valens (M. J. Vincenzi, Sales List, Colchester, Essex, Sept. 1975, nos. 38-51) and no. 215: 59 siliquae of Constantius II to Magnus Maximus (Irelands, Norwich, Norfolk, Sale Catalogue, 20th Oct. 1976 and 25th Jan. 1977, nos. 730-759 and 790-819; Shapwick II (Somerset); it is worth noting that this hoard was buried 6 feet from Shapwick I (NC, 5, 16, 1936, 245ff.) which had no coins of Honorius; according to the theory regarding multiple deposits which I put forward in my article cited supra in note 93, the second hoard could have been buried at the same time as the first: it would thus provide valuable evidence as to the state of mind of the hoarder who would have been aware of the drop in the weight of the siliqua in 387-388; NC, 5, 18, 1938, 53ff.: 4 Constantius II, 7 Julian, 2 Valentinian I, 34 Valens, 36 Gratian, 10 Valentinian II, 4 Theodosius, 26 Magnus Maximus, 1 Victor, 1 Arcadius (7 coins are post 388); Mints: 101 Trier, 7 Lyons, 5 Arles, 6 Rome, 6 Aquileia; see also supra notes 190 and 196; Causeway Lane (Leics.), Trans. of the Leicestershire Architect. and Archaeol. Soc. 10, 59: 60 silver coins ending with Theodosius; Mr. Wood's Hoard (?), NC, 6, 14, 1954, 209ff.: 6 miliarenses, 111 siliquae; 3 Constantius II, 16 Julian, 1 Jovian, 10 Valentinian I, 26 Valens, 31 Gratian, 9 Valentinian II, 5 Theodosius, 15 Maximus, 1 Victor. Mints: 72 Trier, 4 Lyons, 13 Arles, 13 Rome, 9 Aquileia, 1

Siscia, 1 Constantinople, 2 Antioch. The latest pieces are a miliarensis of Lyons (no. 40) and 2 siliquae from Trier (no. 94) which are after 388; see also supra notes 183, 186, 188, 190, 196, and 200. Add. St.-Martory, Revue de Comminges, 90, 1977, 159ff.: 1 siliqua of Maximus, and Wiveliscombe, NC, 6, 6, 1946, 163ff.: 1 siliqua of Julian; Kempston I (Beds.), British Museum Occasional Papers, 5, 1979, 103ff. and C. E. King, "Late Roman Silver Hoards in Britain and the Problem of Clipped Siliquae", (forthcoming): there were 53 coins ranging in date from Constantius II to Magnus Maximus.

203. Blanchet 610. Landes: a dozen silver coins of Valentinian I, Gratian and Theodosius; 6 siliquae were found in the fanum at Loubers, Tarn, cf. Gallia, 36, 1, 1978, 213ff. which could be considered as a hoard: 367-378: 2 Vrbs Roma of Trier; 378-383: id., Rome (1); 383-388: 3 Virtus Romanorum from Trier.

204. Unpublished study by P. Bastien in which there were 3 Vrbs Roma: 375-378: Aquileia (no. 15b); 378-383: Rome, (nos. 35a and 35c); to which should be added 3 solidi: 378-383: Trier (nos. 49b and 49c); 383-388: Trier (no. 77b). See also MM, 35, 16-17, June 1967, no. 159, 160, 163-166, 168, 170, 172-176, 178-182 all of which are solidi and two are after 388: Trier (no. 90c) and Milan (no. 20a). The total originally consisted of 116 pieces.

205a. J. P. Callu, "Le centenarium et l'enrichissement monétaire au Bas Empire", Ktema, 3, 1978, 301ff.

205b. Milan no. 27a (this series continued under Honorius); see also supra note 194. To these should be added the rare half siliqua from Aquileia (no. 57). Since there is a coin of Theodosius (or Honorius?) from Aquileia (AQ), one could date the X and XV coins of Trier (nos. 109-110) to 392; cf. NC, 4, 15, 1915, 472ff.

206. Gloria Romanorum (globe): Constantinople (no. 85), Aquileia, (no. 56), Milan, (no. 25). Add. for the 1/60th: Constantinople, Gloria Romanorum (sceptre) no. 84 and Milan, Vota, (no. 24).

207. Virtus Romanorum: Trier (no. 94); Vrbs Roma: Trier, (no. 95), Lyons (no. 43). Add. an argenteus of Lyons (no. 42).

208. In the Shapwick II and Mr. Wood's hoard; cf. supra note 202. There is a very large group of coins from Trier in the later North Mendip find.

209. Trier (no. 93), Lyons (no. 41); there is a coin with the LVG·· mark which will be published by R. Delmaire. Add. for Lyons: Gloria Romanorum (standard), no. 40; cf. supra note 202; Trier: Vot XV Mult XX of 389 for Valentinian II (Saint Germain).

210. To the hoards already mentioned supra notes 132-155 the Whorlton, Reading, Cornwall, Holyoke, Carleton, Bristol, Milverton, Taunton, Wiltshire, Traprain Law, Shanklin, North Curry, Charlton Mackrel, Chobham, Long's Farm, Bentley, Guisborough, and Richmond finds should be added. C. E. King and J. Casey in their forthcoming studies of British siliqua hoards should provide refinements to this list which is

based on information drawn from A. Evans, S. Bolin, C. H. V. Sutherland, A. S. Robertson, and R. A. G. Carson. Add. R. A. G. Carson, The British Museum Yearbook, 1, 1976, 74ff. gives an extensive bibliography of silver hoards.

211. Dortmund: K. Regling, Der Dortmunder Fund römischer Goldmünzen, Dortmund, 1908, and Nachtrag zum Dortmunder Fund römischer Goldmünzen, ibid., 1910: 16 silver imitations of barbarous style of c. 407. Wiesbaden, M. R. Alföldi, "Le trésor de Wiesbaden Kastel IV-V siècle", Bull. Cercle d'Et. Num., 5,4, 1968, 95ff.: 16 solidi and c. 650 siliquae post 408. For Honorius there were 131 coins from Milan and 122 from Rome.

212. The problem of silver in Britain has aroused the interest of English historians and numismatists. For current opinion on this topic see the remarks of R. A. G. Carson in Bull. Cercle d'Et. Num. 12, 4, 1974, 61ff. and above all in The British Museum Yearbook, 1, 1976, 68ff. As early as 1933 F. S. Salisbury writing in JRS, 23, 217 commented that "It looks as if the areas where they were found were cut off at an early date from the process of withdrawal which went on elsewhere".

213. Votis XX Augg NN, Oudheidkundige Mededelingen, XLII, 1961, 63ff.: celebrating the vicennalia of the first tetrarchy: 2 ingots weighing 305.89 g. and 300.43 g. respectively.

214. Šabac: 6 ingots: 628.4; 626.17; 627.38; 623.5; 232.73 g. (with a likely reference to SIRM) cf. Sirmium, VIII, 1978, 110ff.; Červenbreg: 2 plates inscribed in dotted letters with Licinius Invict Aug ob diem X suorum; Svirkovo: 2 ingots of 635 and 631 g. (with SIRMIS engraved on them), 3 vases engraved Licinius Invictus Augustus ob diem Decennalium suorum (Sic X Sic XX appears on one of them); Niš: 5 plates marked Licini Auguste semper vincas, Sic X Sic XX and stamped NAISS. To these should be added the find now preserved in Munich: 3 plates mentioning the quinquennalia of Licinius II stamped with marks of Antioch and Nicomedia, a fourth plate celebrating his decennalia, and a fifth in honour of the quinquennalia of Crispus and Constantine II stamped NAIS. For a full discussion of this problem see Sirmium, VIII, 1978, 101ff. and 2. and Journal des Savants, 1975, 193ff.

215. 3 plates exist in Leningrad two of which have the inscription DN Constanti Augusti Votis XX c. A.D. 343, cf. W. Grünhagen, Der Schatzfund von Gross Bodungen, Berlin, 1954, 18. Add. J. Jurukova, "Lingots en argent et une phiale en argent de Constance II", Archeologica, 1973, 50: two ingots of 358 related to Naissus and Constantinopolis found in Bulgaria.

216. Plate inscribed Largitas DN Valentiniani Augusti, 369 or 374, ibid.

217. Missorium of Maximus ? c. 388, ibid., 15ff.

218. Missorium of Theodosius I, Valentinian II, and Arcadius found near Badajoz and datable to 388. The legend reads DN Theodosius Perpet Aug ob diem felicissimum X, ibid., 22. Much less is known about the plates from Toulouse, cf. Magasin pittoresque, 1857, 95 and Vente Hoffman, 1889, nos. 138-139: one of these two silver objects had a small gold medallion in the centre which consisted of the imperial bust surrounded by the title DN Theodosius PF Aug with a diameter of 185 cm.

219. Amm. XXIV, 3, 3 records the promise made by Julian during the Persian campaign of 100 argenteos nummos (cf. infra note 221); Zosim., III, 13, mentions 130 pieces of silver.

220. Referring in this context to the Seleucid tetradrachm and the hexagram of Heraclius.

221. It is odd that in 384 at Heraclea the emperor makes reference to the coin struck at 1/60th of the pound and called argenteus in a non-specific sense when this multiple had not been struck in the Pars Orientis since 375; moreover, Epiphanius, Bishop of Cypress, defined the miliarensis (light) in 392 when from 375 to 392 only one issue had been produced (at Constantinople), cf. supra note 206. Can one assume then on this evidence that the East continued to be concerned with a silver coinage? CTh VIII, 5, 48 issued at Constantinople in 386 dealt with the transport of silver but with cargos of 1,000 pounds one is operating on an entirely different level, cf. infra note 223. Other evidence to add to the record: in 372 the chrysargyrion at Beirut was described as pensitatio auri (CTh, XIII, 1, 8) in Egypt, SB 6086 payment of a sum composed of silver with a supplement of gold (10%) was ultimately demanded in gold (for the silver portion).

222. In Grierson's view the value of the silver would have increased on the open market. This view is based in part on the belief that a siliqua was worth 1/24th of a solidus (cf. supra note 159) in the first half of the fourth century. In my view the ratio of 12 which existed in 301 was maintained at about 14.4, at least from the official point of view, until the end of the fourth century. The figure of 18 attested for Egypt by SB 6086 (cf. supra note 221) was a more-or-less local phenomenon occuring in the last quarter of the century. See my article in which I have included a preliminary investigation of the silver coinage, "Problèmes monétaires du Quatrième Siècle (311-385)", Antiquitas, I, 29, Bonn, 1978 103ff.

223. A find discovered between St. Quentin S/Isère and la Rivière with 3,000 coins of the late empire: 128.8: 14.4 = 4.47 g = 8.94 ÷ 2. The detailed investigation undertaken by F. Baratte should reveal the scale on which silver plate was normally hoarded in the late empire.

224. Stamped Abalatos with the Tyche of Constantinople, cf. Sirmium, VIII, 1978, 108ff; E. Cruikshank Dodd, Byzantine Silver Stamps, Dumbarton Oaks Studies 7, Washington, 1961.

225. Cf. supra note 205; an examination of the circulation of gold will be particularly difficult because a single solidus is in fact a real hoard. It will be necessary to list isolated finds in order to determine more precisely the different stages of the diffusion of gold. Ammianus, XVI, 8, 12 and Symmachus. Rel., 13, 2 contribute valuable evidence about gold.

226. I have discussed this problem and suggested some preliminary solutions in three forthcoming articles, "Pensa et follis dans une inscription d'Afrique", Mélanges, J. Lassus, "La tarif d'Abydos et la réforme d'Anastase", Actes du 9ème Congrès Int. de Num., "Une constante arithmétique dans la métrologie du Bas Empire", Pact, 3, 1979.

I should like to thank C. E. King, M. R. Alfoldi and P. Bastien for their kind cooperation.

FAIRY GOLD: MONETARY HISTORY IN THE AUGUSTAN HISTORY

R. S. O. Tomlin

When the Sicilian historian Flavius Vopiscus was discussing whether the usurper Firmus had been an 'emperor' or a 'brigand', the question was settled by Severus Archontius, who quoted published edicts of that emperor, and even produced coins which gave him the title of Augustus. This caused Vopiscus to change his mind.[1] Unfortunately the coins—like the two historians—are attested only by the Augustan history.

At this late season—as Sir Ronald Syme would say—no one will take the Augustan History for gospel. Even the computer has acclaimed his championship of Dessau's thesis. This collection of biographies of second- and third-century emperors and usurpers is ostensibly the work of six historians, Vopiscus included, in the reigns of Diocletian or Constantine, but its uniformity of style (if 'style' is the word) and a wealth of fiction sustained by fictive documents and 'sources' suggest that it was composed later, by one man. The date is still a matter for controversy, but may have been the last decade of the fourth century.[2] Mommsen tried to escape this conclusion by arguing that genuine biographies had been fraudulently 'edited', but he was refuted by Menadier, who observed that numismatic fiction permeates both text and 'documents' of the third-century lives.[3] Menadier's lucid and convincing paper has not always received due attention, which is why I venture to restate it in English, with the aid of a glossary of the Augustan History's numismatic terms (to include finance and economics).

By 'Fairy Gold' I mean the sort of numismatics that melts in the sun, numismatic fiction and anachronism over the centuries, from the golden armour of Glaucus (worth 100 oxen and foolishly swapped for an Achaean suit worth 9) to the 45,000 lbs of gold accumulated for charitable purposes by St. Melania and her husband. When the Saint entered her dining room, the heap of bullion seemed to light up the whole house.[4] Anachronism is also beguiling. Think of the Seven Sleepers of Ephesus, walled up in their cave during the Decian persecution. They fell asleep, and woke next morning (or so they thought) after some farmworkers had unblocked the entrance. One of them went into Ephesus to buy breakfast, where he was surprised to find a Cross over the gates, and to see churches and clergy in the streets. When he produced mid-third century coins to pay for his food, he was arrested on suspicion of having found a buried treasure. It happened to be the reign of Theodosius II. However, the story ended happily. The Sleepers were interviewed by Theodosius himself, and were able to reassure him on the subject of the resurrection of the dead, before falling asleep once more—this time for good.[5]

An Egyptian cave was the refuge of another fugitive from the Decian persecution, St. Paul the first hermit. Inside, he found rusty anvils and hammers, which had been used for striking money. According to Egyptian sources, it had been a secret mint in the time of Antony and Cleopatra.[6] This survival may be hard to credit, but the inspired anachronism of the Decian coins in the fifth century almost guarantees the bona fides of the Seven Sleepers. The Augustan History is a treasury of such stories: let me begin with the hardiest of numismatic misnomers, the antoninianus. This term is used, with appropriate misgiving, for the (?) double denarius first struck by M. Aurelius Antoninus Augustus, the emperor Caracalla. The adjective antoninianus ('of Antoninus') appears four times in the Augustan History, three times in letters of Valerian to qualify 'gold pieces' (aurei), and once in a letter of Aurelian to qualify 'silver pieces' (argentei). Its usage is precisely comparable with that of the other imperial adjectives applied to coins, Aurelianus, Philippeus, Saloninianus and Valerianus. Philippeus is used once as a substantive (apparently equivalent to aureus), but on other occasions, like antoninianus and the rest, it is an adjective. Thus the antoninianus of the Augustan History is not a specific coin, nor one minted exclusively in silver, nor one first minted by Caracalla. His innovation is in fact never mentioned, despite the History's fondness for new coins and novel nomenclature; the Life of Caracalla is actually one of the few third-century lives not to furnish material for my glossary. The later history of the double denarius is implied by a passage from a letter of Valerian: 'Antonine gold pieces...Philippic small silver pieces... denarii of bronze'.[7] During the sole reign of Gallienus, the antoninianus had indeed become a nasty bronze disc with traces of silver and a silver coating; but someone who could write 'denarii of bronze' can hardly have seen a 'real' denarius (or, for that matter, be using a source which had), but was writing at a time when the coinage consisted of gold, silver, and bronze. He was not familiar with a mass coinage in copper, 'brass', or probably even silvered-bronze, but he presumably knew the denarius as a unit of account.

This, I am afraid, is to labour the obvious. The Augustan History, notoriously, is obsessed with the name Antoninus. Thus among the acclamations by the Senate which greet the accession of Alexander Severus is: "Let the name 'Antoninus' return to the coinage".[8] The truth is, of course, that the name 'Antoninus' had never left the coinage. It was virtually the title of the late emperor, M. Aurelius Antoninus, the alleged son of Caracalla; it only disappeared now, with the accession of M. Aurelius Severus Alexander, who also (as it happens) suspended the striking of the double denarius. It is difficult, therefore, to reconcile the evidence of the Augustan History with the numismatic history of the antoninianus; and easier to retrace what seem to have been the steps of its invention. Only the Philippeus of these imperial adjectives is attested outside the Augustan History. Unlike them, it has a respectable pedigree. Philip II of Macedon gained control of gold and silver mines; the resulting coins were named after him, and not only formed an international medium of exchange, but became the model for the currency of less sophisticated states. Livy often speaks of 'Philippei nummi aurei' in the proper sense of Macedonian (or at least hellenistic) gold coins, but the term was already current in the time of Plautus for gold coins in general. When the jurist Ulpian discussed whether bequests of 'gold' or 'silver' included coin, he concluded that gold or silver plate was meant: coins were 'struck' gold or silver in some form, such as 'Philippi' and other currencies. The word perhaps had an exotic, archaic ring. In Varro's version of the story of King Tarquin and the Sibyl, the asking price for the Sibylline Books was 'trecentos Philippeos'; the price paid (which was of course identical) was 'trecentis aureis'. They must have been among the coins distributed by Augustus at the Saturnalia, which were of all types, including ancient royal and foreign ones.[9] They were also literary currency: Horace speaks of 'regale nomisma, Philippos', a phrase twice reproduced by an alert late-Roman litterateur, the poet and politician Ausonius, to express sums of 6 solidi (an imperial New Year's gift to a teacher of literature) and 14 solidi (a bad debt).[10] It seems a reasonable guess, therefore, that the well-read author of the Augustan History developed the genuine old Philippus into a new gold module, the Philippeus, presumably first struck by the emperor Philip, whose Life is conveniently missing. A substantive at its first appearance, it becomes an adjective applied indiscriminately to gold, silver and bronze coins, and inspires Aureliani and the rest, in an orgy of numismatic invention.

The History of Apollonius Prince of Tyre, a Latin romance of probably the third century A.D., also invents its own currency, but without the verve of the Augustan History.[11] Apollonius was forced to flee for his life when he paid court to King Antiochus' incestuous daughter, with a price on his head of 'one hundred talents of gold, two hundred if dead'. He was cast ashore, ship-wrecked and naked, on the shore of Cyrenaica, where a king's daughter fell in love with him and presented him with 'two hundred talents of gold, forty weights of silver, twenty slaves, and [a necessary detail] a great quantity of clothing'. The catalogue is a miniature salary in kind as in the Augustan History; it even came by courtesy of her father, "indulgentia patris", the regular word for imperial generosity. Apollonius and the princess were duly married and set sail for home, but she died on the voyage, after giving birth to a baby girl. The body (she was not really dead, but that is another story) was sealed up in a special floating coffin and cast adrift, with twenty thousand "gold sesterces" to pay for funeral expenses. Apollonius left his baby daughter with foster-parents at Tarsus, where at the age of fourteen she was opportunely carried off by pirates when her jealous foster-mother was on the point of murdering her. The pirates put her on the market at Mytilene, where there was keen competition between the local prince, who wanted her to himself, and the owner of the local brothel, who was more public-spirited. The bidding rose by ten thousand "gold sesterces" a time until it reached one hundred thousand, when the brothel-keeper announced he would top any bid by ten thousand more, and the prince decided it would be cheaper to become her first customer instead. For this the fee was half a pound of gold. There is a distant parallel with the Life of Elagabalus: that emperor bought the most beautiful whore in Rome for one hundred thousand sesterces, it is said, and kept her as if she were virgo intacta.[12] The prince of Mytilene, too, was so touched by the girl's sad story that he gave her forty aurei and refrained from ravishing her. The next customer, a friend of his, gave her a whole pound of gold. Subsequent customers gave her an aureus each, and went away in tears at her story. So the girl became an opera singer instead, and was even reunited with her father, who in gratitude gave Mytilene a hundred talents of gold to restore public buildings, the baths, walls and towers—an authentic late-Roman touch: a second-century benefactor would have built another gymnasium.

The romance of Apollonius, with a rambling plot that makes the Augustan History a prodigy of tight-knit construction by comparison, displays the same numismatic idiosyncrasies: an eccentric currency loosely based upon the real thing, some spuriously precise figures (like the two aurei the prince of Mytilene tipped a sailor for an introduction to Apollonius), and even a characteristically 'late' detail, the circulation of gold and silver bullion by weight. Just as there was allegedly an eighteenth-century clergyman who said of Gulliver's Travels that he did not believe a word of it, so can one feel some scepticism about the Prince of Tyre; but it would be unfair to dismiss the motif of shipwreck. When St. Melania sailed from Sicily after the sack of Rome, she was carried by a storm to an island besieged by barbarians (how they got the boats is not stated); they were demanding a ransom "in gold, cash down", and the local bishop explained that they were still 2,500 solidi short. These the good lady provided, and a thousand more, and even provisions—just as Apollonius was honoured with a bronze statue on an inscribed base for selling corn cheaply in a time of famine.[13]

Exact sums of money are an important 'novelistic' device. The Augustan History, despite its obsessive interest in such data, provides few which are demonstrably true, or even plausible. These occur in second-century Lives, and will be found in the glossary under denarius, nummus and sestertius. The second-century Lives contain no numismatic innovations, not even a sesterce with a Britannia reverse, and their data amount to little more than the figures of the accession donatives given by Hadrian, Marcus Aurelius, Pertinax and Didius Julianus. Septimius Severus simply gave his soldiers "more thousands of sesterces than any previous emperor".[14] One numismatic item of the third century is also, as it happens, authentic: the revolt of the moneyers at Rome in the reign of Aurelian.[15] This exception, however, is promptly camouflaged by Aurelian's own account of his casualties: seven thousand soldiers were killed, lembarii, riparienses, castriani and Dacisci, categories of troops which are decidedly fourth-century.[16] As a rule, in the third-century Lives we enter a happier world of lies, damned lies, and statistics. Or it might be fairer to divide the numismatic data into statements which are implausible but not demonstrably untrue, statements which are demonstrably untrue, and statements which are demonstrably and purposely untrue, for which a kinder and more appropriate word is "fiction". (I will ignore the question of whether this is "historical fiction", or "fictional history"). No less significant are the statements which the Augustan History does not make.

The third century, as contemporaries knew perfectly well, was a period of severe inflation.[17] The Augustan History, however, is unaware of this numismatic Rake's Progress. It ignores, as I have said, the introduction by Caracalla of a lightweight double denarius. It also ignores Alexander Severus' return to the denarius. The gold coinage of the sole reign of Gallienus defies classification, but the Augustan History implies that there was a standard module with neat subdivisions: the emperor's gifts to the future emperor Claudius conclude with "150 aurei of Valerian, and 300 third-aurei of Saloninus".[18] The Augustan History says nothing of the progressive debasement of the silver coinage, though perhaps it implies it by those "denarii of bronze". It ignores Aurelian's attempt to reform the silvered-bronze coinage, which is known to Zosimus. Did this reform have anything to do with the moneyers' revolt, who according to other sources (of the mid-fourth century) were privately debasing the currency?[19] Of course the Augustan History contains incidental details which attest inflation: salaries are paid in kind, and commutation for cash is forbidden; sesterces as well as denarii are "bronze"; there is an obsession with hard cash, gold and silver, not necessarily in coin, but in plate or bullion. Tacitus even forbids the debasement of the coinage, whether privately or (an absurdity) "publicly".[20] But all these details are quite as true—perhaps more true—of the fourth century than the third.

These significant silences are obscured by a clamour of numismatic 'facts', which may be worth summarising. The usurper Macrinus, out of respect for the Senate, struck his first coins in the name of his son Diadumenianus; he struck them for himself only when the Senate had given permission. The logic of this does not bear discussion.[21] Elagabalus never spent less than 100,000 sesterces on dinner, "that is, thirty pounds of silver". It is not clear whether this is intended to be true of Elagabalus' reign (which it is not), or of the writer's own day (whenever that is).[22] Elagabalus also struck multiple gold coins, 'medallions' of double module, triple, quadruple, tenfold, fiftyfold (apparently one pound in weight), and one hundredfold. These 'medallions' were melted down by Alexander Severus, who by implication struck none of his own.[23] Also by implication, Alexander resumed the use of 'Antoninus' on his coins, which had been dropped by Elagabalus. (Both statements are of course untrue).[24] Alexander was the first emperor to strike half-aurei. (They were in fact struck by Augustus and his successors).[25] Alexander also struck third-aurei, as a result of his success in reducing taxes from ten aurei to one-third of an aureus; in the hope of further reduction, he even struck quarter-aurei which, however, were never put into circulation.[26] Three ephemeral figures struck coins: Trebellianus, described by others as an Isaurian pirate-chief; Victoria, mother of the Gallic emperor Tetricus, whose gold, silver and bronze coinage is still extant at Trier; and Firmus, whom I mentioned at the beginning, the usurper who rode on ostriches.[27] Gallienus gave the Palmyrene sheikh Odaenathus the title of Augustus and struck coins in his name depicting him 'dragging Persian captives'.[28] None of these coins has survived. There is no other evidence that Trebellianus or Firmus even existed, or that Odaenathus assumed (or was given) the title of Augustus. The reverse-type attributed to him first appears on 'medallions' of Constantine and his sons, and is a common solidus-reverse of Julian.[29] The coins of gold, silver or bronze, named after Antoninus, Aurelian, Philip, Saloninus and Valerian, have already been discussed. There was also a third-aureus called the triens, as well as the tremis, and a small silver coin called (or known as) the minutulus. A monetary unit called the follis was already current under Elagabalus, and a solidus in the reign of Alexander Severus. These are not the only features of fourth-century economic life which occur somewhat earlier than might have been expected. The imperial treasury is called "The Largesses" on one occasion; and what sounds suspiciously like Constantine's five-yearly levy on commerce, the collatio lustralis, is already attested as "Business Gold" in the reign of Alexander.[30] Denarii and sesterces, as I have said, are 'bronze'; the word pecunia is once used in its fourth-century sense of 'bronze coinage'.[31] Taxation in kind (annona) has become common; soldiers and officials sometimes receive multiple salaries in kind, not just their keep. (The prohibition of commutation for cash, adaeratio, implies that payment in kind has been made before). Salaries are not reckoned in a single denomination (denarii or sesterces), but in gold, silver and bronze, with the addition of silver plate, soldier's jewellery, foodstuffs in profuse and fantastic detail, and even slaves and concubines (the former to be returned on retirement). "These details may seem trivial", Vopiscus remarks at the end of one such catalogue, "but research stops at nothing". Curiositas nihil recusat.[32]

Some of these 'facts' deserve discussion, like the equation of 100,000 sesterces with 30 pounds of silver. This cannot be true of c. A.D. 220, when 12,500 double denarii (45-50% fine, struck at 60 to the pound) would have contained about 100 pounds of silver. Nor is it true of the early fourth century. The official price of silver in A.D. 301 is 6,000 denarii a pound; 100,000 sesterces would thus buy just 4 pounds (and less on the open market).[33] By A.D. 306, 1 oz. silver is equated with 2,776 drachmas, a notional price of 33,312 sesterces a pound; 100,000 sesterces would buy 3 pounds. In A.D. 324, the terminus post quem of the 'Elagabalus', $10\frac{1}{2}$ grammata of gold are equated with 45,720 drachmas; if one assumes a (low) ratio of 1:12 between gold and silver, 100,000 sesterces would buy just one pound of silver.[34] There seems no point in seeking a moment at which the equation may have been true, let alone positing various 'mistakes' which would make it true for this time or that: the Augustan History is not in the habit of giving away genuine statistics. The two figures, 100,000 sesterces and 30 pounds of silver, are arbitrary sums reminiscent of those in one of the biggest groups of Roman fictive prices, the formulaic 'fines' for opening a tomb. Dessau collects about fifty such inscriptions, a fifth of them fourth-century or slightly later (because of nomenclature or Christian formula).[35] All of them are much the same: to disturb the grave (to bury someone else) is prohibited, on pain of a fine payable to the imperial fisc. The wide variety of 'fines' proves that there was no standard; I do not know whether there is any evidence that the prohibition was effective. (The Theodosian Code contains legislation of a slightly different kind, which imposes heavy fines in weight of gold for the demolition of tombs for building materials).[36] Epitaphs until the third century quote the 'fine' in currency, almost always in sesterces, most commonly ten, twenty, thirty, fifty and a hundred thousand. After the third century, the 'fines' are almost always in weight of gold or silver. This can be seen most clearly in the remarkable group of inscribed sarcophagi from the Early Christian cemetery at Concordia in north-eastern Italy: almost every one threatens a 'fine' for being opened, with the usual wide range of figures, but by preference, 5 or 10 pounds of silver, or 1 or 2 pounds of gold.[37]

Perhaps the principal interest of the equation between 100,000 sesterces and 30 pounds of silver is the impression it gives, like the funerary 'fines', of two (successive) monetary systems, though I would rather not discuss the question of when—and to what extent—one yielded to the other.[38] The circulation of precious metals by weight is a feature of the Augustan History, the references being found in my glossary under aurum and argentum or libra and pondo. The future emperor Claudius as a tribune received a bewildering variety of commodities, including silver plate and jewellery of specified weight. On his promotion to 'dux' of Illyricum, his salary included "as much silver as the Superintendent of Mines for Illyricum is paid"; and when Gallienus tried to purchase his good opinion, his letter was a virtual inventory (with weights) of all the silver plate he was sending.[39] These catalogues irresistibly recall the silver bowls and dishes distributed by the generosity (largitas) of Licinius and Constantine, and their successors.[40] The catalogues include gold coins, like the 150 "Philippei nostri vultus" paid to Claudius, but even the solidus in the fourth century circulated by weight, and was 'bought' and 'sold' like other commodities.[41] The catalogues, however, do not recall what little we know of third-century salaries: I am thinking of two famous letters of appointment, that of Claudius Paulinus governor of Lower Britain (A.D. 220) to his client Sennius Sollemnis, and of the Caesar Constantius I to his secretary Eumenius (A.D. 297/8). The letter of Paulinus reads like a page from the Augustan History: "...I hope that you will gladly accept the following: a Canossa cloak, a Laodician tunic, a gold clasp set with jewels, two wraps, a British overcoat, and a sealskin. I will send you the letter for a six-months commission as soon as one falls vacant; the salary of this office, 25,000 sesterces, you are to receive in gold..."[42] The similarities with the Augustan History, the fact that Sollemnis received his salary in gold "and gifts worth much more besides", were thought worth mentioning in the honorific inscription which quotes Paulinus' letter; but it must be emphasised—for here the resemblance ends—that his salary, however paid, is reckoned in one denomination, not two or three. This remains true at the end of the third century. In appointing Eumenius to a professorship at Autun, Constantius doubled the salary of 300,000 sesterces which he had received as magister memoriae; after some generalities about the dignity of a university lecturer's life, the imperial letter briskly concludes: "We wish you to receive from public funds a salary of 600,000 sesterces, so that you may understand that Our Clemency also has recognized your deserts. Farewell, Eumenius, dearest to Us".[43] No one will accuse the Augustan History of lack of invention, but it a pity, perhaps, that it does not provide an overblown academic salary to contrast with this drab statistic of 600,000 sesterces.

The numismatic innovations of Elagabalus and Alexander Severus are also not all they seem to be. Nothing survives of Elagabalus' gold multiples except a unique double aureus. Alexander, who by implication struck no multiples at all, is better represented—by two double aurei, two quadruples, and the octuple from Tarsus. J. M. C. Toynbee, to whose Roman Medallions I owe this information, does not reject the Augustan History, but certainly hedges her bet: "It is another question whether multiples of so large a size would really have been struck as early as the first half of the third century or whether the writer's statement has been coloured by his knowledge of the great gold medallions of the later Empire".[44] The coins struck by Alexander Severus in silver-gold alloy with a portrait of Alexander the Great, needless to say, have not survived. Electrum was never a Roman coinage-metal, but it is a recurrent motif in the Augustan History: Elagabalus, who used gold and silver dust as a cosmetic, regretted that electrum dust was not also available. The Alexander-complex with which Alexander Severus is credited more properly belongs to Caracalla, as indeed the Augustan History is elsewhere aware. The head of Alexander the Great happens to be a favourite obverse of the fourth-century 'contorniates' struck at Rome, but it never occurs on the coins of his namesake.[45] Alexander's reason for melting down Elagabalus' multiples is remarkable: he reckoned that largess would be cheaper if he only gave away one gold piece per coin, rather than ten or more.[46] Something of the same simplicity is inherent in the dream of the golden age which would have followed Probus' abolition of the army: 'No provincial would pay annona, the Treasury would not be asked for pay, the Roman state's resources would be everlasting, the emperor would pay nothing, nor would the landowner'.[47] Such passages, it has often been noted, must belong to a time of high public expenditure—and high taxation. The parallel with the anonymous De Rebus Bellicis, with its denunciation of 'the prodigal liberality of the age of Constantine', is compelling. This too invents its own coins, and comes out with the interesting idea that coinage is struck 'for military donatives and the various commercial transactions of the people'.[48] Even Constantius II pays lip-service to this idea of "money established in public use", admittedly in a law designed to restrict its use.[49] The Augustan History implies that Alexander Severus struck his third-aureus for the taxpayer's convenience, after reducing taxation from 10 aurei to one-third of an aureus; a quarter-aureus was struck, in case taxation was further reduced.[50] This report is interesting on other counts. No example of course survives of the third-aureus, let alone the (unissued) quarter-aureus. The third-solidus or tremis is a rare coin even in the fourth century, until the reign of Theodosius. Judging by the rentals recorded in the Liber Pontificalis (which apparently drew on reliable archives), the third-solidus did not circulate in the way envisaged by the Augustan History for its 'triens'. There are 160 of them, and 300, on their two appearances. But whenever the rents of properties in the fourth-century endowment of the church of Rome include fractions, it is always one tremissius or two, never more.[51] Alexander's reduction of taxation to one-thirtieth is, it needs no saying, a fantasy; but the way in which it is expressed, from ten aurei to one-third, implies a fixed unit of taxation like the Diocletianic capitulum, on which a variable amount was levied year by year. Thus the Caesar Julian, according to Ammianus Marcellinus, reduced taxation in Gaul in the late 350s from 25 aurei per capitulum to 7 aurei.[52]

This cautious paddle through the possible anachronisms in the Augustan History leads to numismatic quicksands—the follis of Elagabalus and the solidus of Alexander Severus. The lottery prizes distributed by Elagabalus include 100 aurei, 1000 argentei, and 100 folles of bronze.[53] Since the total numbers of coins in the Augustan History's characteristic trios of gold, silver and bronze, increase as their intrinsic value decreases— "100 Antonine aurei, 1,000 Aurelian argentei, 10,000 Philippean bronze pieces" for instance—the hundred folles ought to consist of more coins than the 1,000 silver and 100 gold which precede them. So follis ought to mean, not a denomination, but (its primary sense) a 'bag' of coin. This first appears in a famous letter of about 1 March 300, from the file of Aurelius Isidorus, procurator of the Lower Thebaid: "50 pounds of silver and 4 folles of (silver) money, which makes 33 talents and 500 denarii" [50,000 denarii] are to be issued to a legionary detachment stationed in the Panopolite nome. The follis is a specific multiple, apparently 12,500 denarii.[54] Before this letter was published, the late A. H. M. Jones had already noticed that the moneybag prizes in one of the (contemporary?) Piazza Armerina mosaics were labelled" (denarii) XIIS", and suggested that they were folles of 12,500 denarii each.[55] What it was like to handle such a bulky currency is suggested by the interrogation of witnesses at the inquiry into whether Silvanus, the Donatist bishop of Cirta (Constantine), was guilty of simony and other offences. In A.D. 305, apparently, a certain Victor gave twenty folles to be ordained priest. How many folles changed hands? "He handed over a sack, sir," said one of Silvanus' clergy, "but what it contained, I do not know". "I saw basketfuls of money being brought", said another.[56]

A gap remains, however, of three-quarters of a century between the folles of Elagabalus and the Diocletianic follis. While Elagabalus could have carried money in bags like anyone else, it strains belief to see them as a standardised unit in a monetary system.[57] The solidus of Alexander Severus presents a similar problem. The word immediately suggests the famous Constantinian gold coin, struck on a lighter standard than the old aureus, but stable for centuries afterwards. Since 'Lampridius' wrote the Life of Alexander in the reign of Constantine, and presumably after 324 like the Elagabalus, his use of a Constantinian term is anachronistic, but not impossible.[58] But the question is more complex than this. The word solidus makes only two appearances, whereas aureus is common. On its first appearance, solidus could be an adjective: Alexander "melted down the quarters, and struck only thirds and whole pieces". Solidos understands aureos, as in Apuleius' phrase "20 bright new solid gold pieces", solidos aureos.[59] On its second appearance, however, solidus is sandwiched between two adjectives, multos solidos minores, and it is difficult not to see it as a substantive.[60] As a substantive it is securely pre-Constantinian, since it is now attested on the Aezani copy of the Maximum Prices Edict (A.D. 301) as the standard gold coin.[61] The Greek translation is holokottinos, which is already being used in a private letter of A.D. 297/8. In a steward's account of A.D. 306 it is a gold coin of 4 5/6ths grammata, clearly the (Diocletianic) aureus.[62] It then becomes the usual fourth-century Greek term for solidus, even if (rather like nomisma) it retains a sense of 'coin' to judge by a later Greek gloss of the denarius as 'a specific silver coin' (holokottinos).[63] Solidus and holokottinos were thus already current usage before Constantine, though they were applied to a slightly different coin. It is possible that solidus took some time to establish itself. An Italian charitable foundation of A.D. 323 still reckons its income in aurei (and its capital endowment in denarii). The solidus first appears in the Theodosian Code in A.D. 325.[64] As late as the 390s, Ammianus Marcellinus, although he uses the word solidus, seems to prefer aureus or even aureus nummus; but this is no more than a 'classicizing' literary archaism, like Ausonius' Philippos. Five or ten years before, the litterateur Symmachus, in his official correspondence as urban prefect of Rome (A.D. 384), was using solidus freely.[65]

It is hardly strange, therefore, that the Augustan History uses the word solidus, but strange that it uses it so little. This may suggest that it was being avoided like other 'late' terms (follis, largitiones and so forth) which only appear once, but whether this is a delicate way of exposing an anachronism to readers with eyes to see, or no more than a slip like the soda water which does not appear in Vanity Fair, I would not care to say. Nor do I know how much later than the reign of Constantine one can take the Augustan History on numismatic (and related) evidence, even if it is certain that no third-century numismatist can afford to draw on it, since his cheque will bounce. But does this matter? If the iniquity of oblivion had not dealt so hard with its sources, we would not be reading the Augustan History, resentfully, as history; like its first readers, we could enjoy it with a clear conscience as a work of fiction.

NOTES

I am grateful to members of the Symposium who commented on this paper when it was read, in particular Professor J. P. Callu and Dr. A. K. Bowman. I am not a numismatist, and what little I know of the subject is mostly due to conversations with Mr. P. J. Casey and Dr. C. E. King. Among written sources, I acknowledge my particular debt to Menadier (see n. 3) and to a typescript glossary of numismatic references in the Augustan History arranged by Lives, by Mr. R. M. Reece, some of whose ideas I now find (see n. 48) I share. His glossary was made available by Dr. King. Where the reference is obvious, I do not cite my own glossary, but I do include a cross-reference in the notes (of the form '(s.v. denarius)') to where the passage cited is transcribed in the glossary. The Lives are cited by abbreviated title (but note '30 Tyr.' for Tyranni triginta and 'Firm.' for Firmus Saturninus Proculus et Bonosus or Quadriga tyrannorum).

1. Firm. 2.1 (s.v. nummus 1 (iii)).

2. R. Syme, Ammianus and the Historia Augusta, 1968. I. Marriott, 'The authorship of the Historia Augusta: two computer studies', JRS, 69, 1979, 65ff.

3. K. Menadier, 'Die Münzen und das Münzwesen bei den Scriptores Historiae Augustae', ZFN, 31, 1914, 1ff.

4. Iliad VI 234-6. D. Gorce (ed.), Vie de Sainte Mélanie (Sources Chrétiennes 90, 1962, ch. 17. The most implausible of late-Roman lump sums are the two buried treasures, one of them the accumulated loot of Justinian's general Narses, which were unearthed by the emperor Tiberius Constantine as a reward for his lavish almsgiving; they amounted to hundreds of thousands of pounds of gold and silver (Gregory of Tours, Hist. Franc. V, 19). A seventh-century patriarch of Alexandria, St. John the Almsgiver, whose personal estate amounted to one-third of a solidus, claimed in his will to have found 8,000 pounds of gold in the cathedral treasury at his accession. His Life is rich in detailed investment-stories on the theme of St. Matthew XIX, 21: see E. Dawes and N. H. Baynes, Three Byzantine Saints, 1948.

5. Gregory of Tours, Passio VII Dormientium apud Ephesum, ed. B. Krusch in Analecta Bollandiana 12, 1893, 371ff. (8) "dixerunt: "hic homo thesauros repperit antiquos; nam ecce argenteos de temporibus Decii profert"."

6. Jerome, vita S. Pauli, 5, (PL 23, 21), "... in quibus scabrae iam incudes et mallei, quibus pecunia signatur, visebantur. hunc locum Aegyptiorum litterae ferunt furtivum monetae officium fuisse, ea tempestate qua Cleopatrae iunctus est Antonius".

7. Aurel. 9.7 (s.v. denarius).

8. Alex. 8.3 (s.v. antoninianus).

9. Livy XXXIV, 52.7, Philippei nummi aurei distinguished from gold bullion, etc. Plautus, Asin. I, 3.1, etc. Ulpian, Dig. XXXIV, 2.27, "... aurum vel argentum signatum...aliqua forma...veluti quae Filippi sunt, itemque nomismata et similia". Lactantius, Div. Inst. (CSEL 19), I, 6.10-11 (quoting Varro). Suetonius, Div. Aug. 75, "...nummos omnis notae, etiam veteres regios ac peregrinos".

10. Horace, epist. II, 1, 234. Ausonius (ed. Prete), epist, 11.5; ibid. 14, 19, "bis septem rutilos, regale nomisma, Philippos".

11. A. Riese (ed.), Historia Apollonii Regis Tyri, 1893; there is a condensed translation in B. E. Perry, The Ancient Romances, 1967, 294ff. There is an excellent treatment of the question in R. Duncan-Jones, The Economy of the Roman Empire, 1974, ch. 5, "The use of prices in the Latin novel" (esp. 251ff.). Historia Apollonii, 7, "auri talenta centum ... ducenta"; 17, "ducenta talenta auri, argenti pondera XL, servos XX et vestem copiosissimam"; 25, "XX sestertia auri"; 33 "decem sestertia auri" (etc.); ibid., (poster) "qui Tharsiam virginem violare voluerit, dimidiam auri libram dabit; postea vero singulos aureos populo patefit", cf. 34, "XL aureos ... plus quam virginitas tua expostulat" (i.e. this aureus was struck at less than 80 to the pound of gold).

12. Elag. 31.1 (s.v. sestertium).

13. Vie de Sainte Mélanie (see n. 4), 19, phahneron khrusion; solidi are translated as nomismata. Historia Apollonii (see n. 11), 10: he sold 100,000 modii of corn at 8 'aerei' each, when the market price as an aureus.

14. Sept. 5.2 (s.v. sestertium).

15. Aurel. 38.2 (s.v. monetarius). cf. Aurelius Victor, Caes. 35.6 (and ps. Victor, Epit. 35.4); Eutropius, Brev. 9.14.

16. Aurel. 38.4. The casualty figure of 7,000 closely agrees with that of Aurelius Victor (see no. 15), but the Thesaurus Linguae Latinae cites no instance of lembarii and only this instance of castriani. Dacisci is a unit-title in the Notitia Dignitatum (c. A.D. 395, but incorporating earlier material), and riparienses a category of units stationed on river-frontiers; the barcarii (lightermen) may be similar to lembarii. Riparienses and castriciani are coupled as categories of troops in CTh. VII.1.18 (400); there is a variant reading in the Cod. Iust. tradition of the same text (XII.35.14), of castriani. I do not know an earlier instance of this particular category of troops.

17. They had enough sense to hoard coins of higher silver content each time the currency was debased, as coin hoards make clear. Cf. also such well-known documents as P. Oxy. XII, 1411 (A.D. 260, the banks have closed, rather than accept "imperial" money) and P. Rylands IV 607 (Diocletianic, speculator's instructions to spend all 'Italian silver' because the Italian nomisma is being officially reduced to half a nummus).

18. *Claud*. 17.7 (s.v. *Valerianus*).

19. Zosimus I,61.3 (source uncertain). See n. 15.

20. *Tac*. 9.3 (s.v. *miscere*).

21. *Diad*. 2.6 (s.v. *moneta*).

22. *Elag*. 24.3 (s.v. *sestertium*).

23. *Alex*. 39.9 (s.v. *forma*).

24. *Alex*. 8.3 (s.v. *antoninianus*).

25. *Alex*. 39.7 (s.v. *semis*). *BMCRE* I, s.v. *quinarius aureus*, esp. p. lii.

26. *Alex*. 39.6 (s.v. *aureus* 2(ii)).

27. *30 Tyr*. 26.2 (Trebellianus, s.v. *moneta*). *Ibid*. 31.3 (Victoria, s.v. *nummus* 1(iii)). *Firm*. 2.1 (s.v. *nummus* 1(iii)).

28. *Gall*. 12.1 (s.v. *moneta*).

29. J. M. C. Toynbee, *Roman Medallions*, 1941, 181 = *RIC* VII, Trier 356 (A.D. 322-3), double *solidus*. Cohen VIII, Julian 75-80 (*solidi*). The type also appears on Julian's bronze coinage (*ibid*., 81-2), and then in abundance as the GLORIA ROMANORUM *aes* III of Valentinian I.

30. *Prob*. 23.2 (s.v. *largitiones*): the Augustan History's usual term is *aerarium* or *fiscus*. *Alex*. 32.5, "aurum negotiatorium et coronarium Romae remisit": in fact Alexander seems to have remitted only extra-ordinary levies of crown gold, but in Italy and elsewhere (see A. K. Bowman, 'The Crown-Tax in Roman Egypt', *Bulletin of the American Society of Papyrologists* 4, 1967, 59ff.

31. *Alex*. 33.3 (s.v. *pecunia*): cf. *Not. Dig. Or*. 13.31 and *Occ*. 11.97, and *Cod. Iust*. XII 23.7 (A.D. 384), where *pecuniae* are distinguished from gold and silver coin and bullion by the Mint.

32. *Aurel*. 10.1.

33. R. and F. Naumann, *Der Rundbau in Aezani*, 1973, the Aezani copy of Diocletian's Prices Edict, ch. 30.

34. *P.S.I*. 310, with revised text and commentary by J. R. Rea, "P.S.I. 310 and imperial bullion purchases", *Chronique d'Egypte*, 49, 1974, 163ff. Note *Archiv* 15, 1953, 104-5, an official order to a town council to provide silver at 8,000 denarii a pound; and P. Oxy XVII 2106, an order requiring 38 pounds of gold at 100,000 denarii a pound. P. Oxy, XII 1430 (A.D. 324): the *solidus* (struck at 72 to the pound of gold) weighs 4 *grammata*.

35. *ILS* 8209-56.

36. *CTh*. IX, 17 (esp. 2).

37. D. Hoffmann, 'Die spätrömischen Soldatengrabschriften von Concordia', *Museum Helveticum*, 20, 1963, publishes 38 of the inscribed sarcophagi from the Concordia cemetery, almost all of them of late-Roman mobile troops (*comitatenses*) who may have been buried in A.D. 394/5. 36 epitaphs include 'fines', the air of unreality being occasionally heightened

by threats of capital punishment or mutilation. The range of fines, with numbers of instances, is: IN SILVER, 3 lbs (1), 5 lbs (6-7), 10 lbs (4), 12 lbs (1); and IN GOLD, 3 oz. (1), 25 solidi (1), 6 oz. (2), 1 lb (4), 2 lbs (5-6), 3 lbs (1), 5 lbs (1), 6 lbs (2), 8 lbs (1).

38. O. Seeck, 'Die Münzpolitik Diocletians and seiner Nachfolger', ZFN, 17, 1890, 36ff., esp. 52ff. (after A.D. 328).

39. Claud. 14.2ff., 15.4 (s.v. metallarius), 17.5ff. (s.v. argentum (4)). C. E. van Sickle, "The salarium of Claudius Gothicus", L'Antiquité Classique 23, 1974, 47ff., believes that Claud, 14.2ff. is based upon 'a genuine salary-warrant' of a dux of A.D. 296/312.

40. R. MacMullen, "The Emperor's Largesses", Latomus, 21, 1962, 159ff.

41. CTh XII 7.1 (A.D. 325, weight of solidi in gold); IX 22.1 (343, all solidi of the same weight are worth the same, irrespective of the size of their flan); XII 6.3 (367, solidi paid in taxes are to be melted down and accepted at the rate of 72:1 lb gold), etc. As a commodity: IX 22.1, "omnes solidi...uno pretio aestimandi sunt atque vendendi"; Anon. de rebus bell. 3.1, 'ementis eundem solidum...et vendentis'; Augustine, Sermo 389,3 (PL. 39, 1704), "quidam...cum solidum, ut assolet, vendidisset, centum folles ex pretio solidi pauperibus iussit erogari".

42. H. G. Pflaum, Le marbre de Thorigny, 1948, CIL XIII 3162, Left Face, 8ff., 'velim accipas libenter: chlamidem Canusinam, dalmaticam Laodiciam, fibulam auream cum gemmis, rachanas duas, tossiam Britannicam, pellem vituli marini. semestris autem epistulam, ubi propediem vacare coeperit, mittam, cuius militiae salarium, id est (sestertium) XXV n(ummum) in auro suscipe..."

43. Pan. Lat. 4 (9), 14, esp. 5, "denique etiam salarium te in sescenis milibus nummum ex rei publicae viribus consequi volumus, ut intellegas meritis tuis etiam nostram consulere clementiam. vale, Eumeni carissime nobis".

44. op. cit. 23-4, citing also what is apparently the only other literary reference to 'medallions', the description by Gregory of Tours (Hist. Franc. VI 2) of the one-pound aurei presented by the emperor Tiberius Constantine to King Chilperic.

45. Carac. 2.2. A. Alföldi, Die Kontorniaten, 1943, 130ff.

46. Alex. 39.9-10 (s.v. forma and solidus). cf. CTh XV 9.1 (A.D. 384), which forbids the distribution of gold coins or silver multiples at praetorian games: "nec maiorem argenteum nummum fas sit expendere, quam qui formari solet, cum argenti libra una in argenteos sexaginta dividitur".

48. De rebus bell. 2.1, "Constantini temporibus profusa largitio"; 1.9, "aeris autem materia ... ad dona militaria et varia populorum commercia signabatur". See also the next note; and in general, R. M. Reece, "The Anonymus: a numismatic commentary", in M. W. C. Hassall (ed.), Aspects of the De Rebus Bellicis, 1979, 59ff.

49. CTh IX 23.1 (A.D. 356?), "pecunias vero nulli emere omnino fas erit nec vetitas contrectare, quia in usu publico constitutas pretium oportet esse, non mercem. placet denique, ut, si quis forsitan nummus praeter eum, qui in usu publico perseverat, aput aliquem mercatorem fuerit inventus, fisci dominio cum omnibus delinquentis facultatibus vindicetur". The intention is, apparently, to prevent (bronze) coinage being sold for its metal-value; and to withdraw 'forbidden' coinage (that of the usurper Magnentius?) from circulation. The phrases incorporating in usu publico thus mean no more than 'current' (coin). Cf. Symmachus, Rel. 29.1, "vendendis solidis, quos plerumque publicus usus exposcit', where the context (the forced sale of solidi by bankers) does not require publicus usus to be any more than a euphemism for the Sacred Largesses. See also J. P. Callu, this volume, 47 ff. for a discussion of this text.

50. Alex. 39.7 (s.v. quartarius).

51. L. Duchesne (ed.), Liber Pontificalis I, 1886, 202 (Pope Marcus, A.D. 336), for example: the emperor Constantine endowed a new basilica with properties including (15) "fundum Baccanas, via Appia, praest. sol. XL et tremissios II"; and (16) "fundum Orrea, via Ardiatina, praest. sol. LV et tremissium".

52. Amm. Marc. 16.5.14. By aurei he means solidi (see n. 65).

53. Elag. 22.3 (s.v. follis).

54. P. Beatty Panop. 2, 300ff. (with T. C. Skeat's note ad loc.).

55. The bags can be seen in Plate XLI of G. V. Gentili, La villa erculia di Piazza Armerina: i mosaici figurati (c. 1964). A. H. M. Jones, The Origin and Early History of the Follis, JRS 49, 1959, 34ff. To the illustrations of labelled moneybags can be added the insignia of the eastern comes sacrarum largitionum in the Notitia Dignitatum. Among the various glosses of follis collected by F. Hultsch (ed.), Metrologicorum Scriptorum Reliquiae, 1864 is one that defines it as a bag of 125 denarii.

56. Gesta apud Zenophilum consularem (Dec. 320), preserved as Appendix I of Optatus Milevitanus: CSEL 26, p. 195, Zenophilus v.c. consularis Casto dixit: confitere, quot folles dedit Victor, ut presbyter fieret. Castus dixit: optulit, domine, saccellum, et quid habuerrit, nescio. p. 197, Crescentianus dixit: vidi allatos cophinos cum pecunia.

57. Cf. Apuleius, Metam. 4.9, for an example of follis in its broad sense of 'money bag': "aureos folles incubabat". (The action of a miser, not a strange new currency of 'gold folles').

58. Alex. 65.1; Elag. 35.6.

59. Alex. 39.8 (s.v. solidus). Cf. Apuleius, Metam. 9.18, "demonstrat ei novitate nimia candentes solidos aureos, quorum viginti quidem puellae destinasset".

60. Alex. 39.10 (s.v. solidus).

61. See n. 33. Ch. 30,1 "[aurum]obryzae in regulis sive [in] solidis".

62. P. Mich. III 218. For the date see J. D. Thomas, "The date of the revolt of L. Domitius Domitianus", ZPE 22, 1976, 253ff., esp. 266-7 (the Paniskos letters). P. Oxy XIV 1653 (2 oz. 10 grammata of gold = 12 solidi).

63. For example, P. Abinn. 13, 6 (A.D. 342/51); P. Oxy, IX 1223 (350/400); IG XIV 142 (Syracuse). But cf. Suda II 49, 25, s.v. denarion.

64. ILS 9420, with commentary by Dessau ad loc., and W. Kubitschek, "Eine Stiftung aus Feltre", NZ 42, 1909, 47ff. The arithmetic and some of the readings are difficult, but there is clear reference to a capital sum of "(denariorum) quingenta milia" and an annual distribution of 'aureos den(os)'. CTh XII 7.1 (A.D. 325, confirmed by XII 6.2, which is part of the same constitution).

65. Amm. Marc. 28.1.1, "singulis solidis" (a famine price for 10 modii of corn), cf. 25.8.15, "aureis decem" (another famine price, for 1 modius); 16.5.14, "vicenos quinos aureos" (taxes in Gaul); 20.4.18, "quinos aureos argentique singula pondo" (Julian's accession donative); 24.4.26, "e tribus aureis nummis" (valuation of a slave); 26.7.11, "aureos nummos effigiatos in vultum novi principis" (the coinage of the usurper Procopius, who struck nothing heavier than solidi). For the language of 26.7.11, cf. Claud. 14.3, "Philippeos nostri vultus", and CTh XII 7.1 (A.D. 325), "solidos...nostris vultibus figuratos"; IX 22.1 (A.D. 343?), "omnes solidi, in quibus nostri vultus ac veneratio una est". Symmachus, Rel. 15, "sollemnes pateras cum quinis solidis" (gifts for the Emperor, cf. CTh VII 24.1 (A.D. 395), which requires them to be full weight); Rel. 29.1, "vendendis solidis" (see n. 49); Rel. 34.3, "XI milia CCCCXLVI solidos" (missing from the arca vinaria).

GLOSSARY OF NUMISMATIC AND RELATED TERMS IN THE HISTORIA AUGUSTA

based on C. Lessing, Scriptorum historiae Augustae Lexicon (1901-06)

ADAERARE, commute (for cash)

Claud. 14.14, concludes an elaborate salarium in kind with "sed ita ut nihil adaeret".

AERARIUM, treasury

(1) The Treasury: commonly; once aerarium Saturni (Marc. 9.7)
(2) specific: privatum aerarium contrasted with publicum, Avid. Cass. 7.6, Claud. 14.3, cf. Hadr. 7.7, fiscum privatum.
sacrum aerarium, Alex, 24.3
maius aerarium, Diad. 4.1 (Macrinus as procurator aerarii maioris looked after purple clothing)

AES, bronze

(1) metal: Carac. 9.5
(2) coinage metal: Elag. 22.3, centum folles aeris; Aurel. 9.7, aeris denarios centum; 12.1, in aere sestertium quinquagies; Tac. 9.3, si quis argento publice privatimque aes miscuisset ... si quis aeri plumbum (debasement a capital offence); Firm. 15.8, aeris sestertium decies.
(3) money: Alex. 66.4, mancipia aere empta. Cf. aes alienum (debt), Hadr. 2.6 etc.

AEREUS, bronze (adj.)

(1) metallic: Alex. 28.6
(2) of coins: 30 Tyr. 31.1, cusi sunt eius nummi aerei, aurei et argentei; Prob. 4.5, aereos Philippeos decem milia.

ANNONA, food, rations; hence, taxation/payment in kind

(1) food supply of Rome: commonly, e.g. Aurel. 47.1, epistula data ad praefectum annonae urbis
(2) military supplies, esp. food (in sing.): Avid. Cass. 5.12, annona militaris omnis parata est; Alex. 15.5, annonam militum diligenter inspexit; Prob. 10.7 (letter to a praet. prefect), annonam et commeatus et quicquid necessarium est ubique militi pares; etc. In plur. (with similar sense): Alex. 47.1; 30 Tyr. 18.6; Aurel. 33.4.

(3) taxation in kind (implicitly for military consumption): Alex. 53.9, the emperor the soldiers' paymaster, qui acceptam a provincialibus annonam, qui vestem, qui stipendia vobis adtribuit; Aurel. 7.5, order to soldiers, oleum, salem, lignum nemo exigat, annona sua contentus sit; Prob. 20.6, without soldiers orbls terrarum non arma fabricabitur, non annonam praebebit; 23.2, annonam provincialis daret nullus.

(4) payment in kind, for soldiers and officials (ANNONAE, plur.): Macr. 13.2, in annonis tribuendis largissimus fuit, in auro parcissimus; Gord. 28.3, (Timesitheus PPo) nullum senem militare passus est, nullum puerum annonas accipere; Alex. 41.3 (court personnel reduced (ita ut annonas non dignitatem acciperent fullones (etc.) et omnes castrenses ministri, quemadmodum (Elagabalus) instituerat, sed annonas singulas vix binas; 42.3, medicus sub eo unus palatinus salarium accepit, ceterique omnes usque ad sex fuerunt, qui annonas binas aut ternas accipiebant, ita ut mundas singulas consequerentur, alias aliter; 44.5, in provinciis oratoribus forensibus multum detulit, plerisque etiam annonas dedit; 15.3, iure iurando deinde se constrinxit ne quem adscriptum, id est vacantivum, haberet, ne annonis rem publicam gravaret.

ANTONINIANUS, adj. only

(1) of gold: Aurel. 9.7, aureos Antoninianos diurnos binos; 12.1, aureos Antoninianos trecentos; Prob. 4.5, aureos Antoninianos centum.

(2) of silver: Firm. 15.8, argenteos Antoninianos mille.

cf. Alex. 8.3 (acclamation), monetae nomen Antonini reddatur.

ARGENTUM, silver

(1) metal: Elag. 20.4, hic solido argento factos habuit lectos; 31.8, silver-dust; Aurel. 46.1,use in ornament.

(2) coinage metal: Alex. 33.3, scaenicis numquam aurum, numquam argentum, vix pecuniam donavit; Tac. 9.3 (debasement a capital offence), si quis argento publice privatimque aes miscuisset, si quis auro argentum.

(3) by weight, as currency: Elag. 24.3, idem numquam minus centum sestertiis cenavit, hoc est argenti libris triginta; Claud. 15.4 (a general's pay includes) tantum argenti quantum accipit curator Illyrici metallarius; Elag. 21.7, dedit et aureos millenos et centena pondo argenti cf. Aurel. 31.8, the loot of Palmyra includes "trecentas auri libras' and "argenti mille octingenta pondo".

(4) by weight, as tableware: (i) an item of 'salary' (thus virtually category 3), Alex. 42.4, iudices cum promoveret ... et argento et necessariis instruebat, ita ut praesides provinciarum acciperent argenti pondo vicena; Claud. 14.3, argenti in opere annua pondo quinquaginta (followed by gold coin); 17.5, items of silver plate variously 20 lbs, 30 lbs, 23 lbs, 20 lbs, 6 lbs, and (in total) 25 lbs.
(ii) imperial generosity; Alex. 44.9, in templis sane numquam praeter quattuor aut quinque argenti libras ... posuit.
(iii) imperial tableware: 30 Tyr. 32.6, (lanx) centum librarum argenti; Alex. 34.1, 41.4, limited to 200 lbs; Aurel. 49.9, limited to 30 lbs; cf. Claud. 3.5, imp. statue of 1,500 lbs. silver.

(5) coupled with aurum, loosely as 'money': Alex. 14.7, mulier sancta sed avara et auri atque argenti cupida. etc.

ARGENTEUS, silver (adj.), esp. of coins; a silver coin

(1) objects made of, including statues, tableware, jewellery: common, but note Aurel. 46.5, ut fibulas aureas gregarii milites haberent idem primus concessit, cum antea argenteas habuissent; cf. Claud. 14.5 (tribune's salary), fibulas argenteas inauratas duas ... balteum argenteum inauratum unum.
(2) of coins (adj.): Pesc. N. 10.7, idem iussit, ne zona milites ad bellum ituri aureos vel argenteos nummos portarent; Elag. 8.3, nummos vel argenteos vel aureos; 30 Tyr. 31.3, cusi sunt eius nummi aerei, aurei et argentei.
(ii) subst. Elag. 22.3, centum aureos et mille argenteos; Aurel. 9.7 (salary) aureos Antoninianos diurnos binos, argenteos Philippeos minutulos quinquagenos, aeris denarios centum; 12.1, argenteos Philippeos minutulos tria milia (etc.); Prob. 4.5 (salary), aureos Antoninianos centum, argenteos Aurelianos mille, aereos Philippeos decem milia; Firm. 15.8 (gifts), aureos Philippeos centum, argenteos Antoninianos mille, aeris sestertium decies.

AURELIANUS, adj. (of silver coin)

Prob. 4.5, aureos Antoninianos centum, argenteos Aurelianos mille, aereos Philippeos decem milia.

AURUM, gold

(1) metal: in the form of leaf, dust, and manufactured objects (statues, plate).
(2) loosely, as 'money', 'wealth', esp. coupled with argentum; as the proceeds of auctions of imp. furnishings etc., Marc. 17.5, Alex. 41.1, etc.
(3) in coin: Macr. 13.2, in annonis tribuendis largissimus fuit, in auro parcissimus; Alex. 32.4, aurum et argentum raro cuiquam nisi militi divisit; 33.3, scaenicis numquam aurum, numquam argentum, vix pecuniam donavit; Tac. 9.3 (debasement a capital offence), si quis argento publice privatimque aes miscuisset, si quis auro argentum.
(4) by weight; (i): Aurel. 41.11, quindecim milia librarum auri ex eius liberalitate unum tenet templum; 31.8, habes trecentas auri libras de Zenobiae capsulis; Alex. 41.1, a limit on clothing worn by royal women, "quae sex uncias auri plus non haberet".
(ii) as currency: Elag. 22.1-2, lottery tickets including "decem libras auri"; 23.6, his guests promised a phoenix, "vel pro ea libras auri mille"; Aurel. 45.5, "absit ut auro fila pensentur". libra enim auri tunc libra serici fuit. cf. (imperial gifts), Sept. 6.4, septingenos vicenos aureos legatis dedit (10 lbs of gold at 1:72?); Claud. 17.5, scyphos aureos gemmatos trilibres duos.
(5) in taxation: (i) Hadr. 6.5, aurum coronarium Italiae remisit, in provinciis minuit, cf. Ant. P. 4.10; cf. Aurel. 34.3, praeferebantur coronae omnium civitatum aureae.
(ii) Alex. 32.5, aurum negotiatorium et coronarium Romae remisit.

AUREUS, gold (adj.)

(1) objects made of (statues, tableware, military equipment, etc): note Aurel. 46.5, ut fibulas aureas gregarii milites haberent idem primus concessit. And metaphorically, e.g. Elag. 35.4, Diocletianus, aurei parens saeculi.

(2) coins, (i) adj.,: Pesc. N. 10.7, ne zona milites aureos vel argenteos nummos portarent; Alex. 25.9, Alexandri habitu nummos plurimos figuravit, et quidem electros aliquantos, sed plurimos tamen aureos; 30 Tyr. 31.3, cusi sunt eius nummi aerei, aurei et argentei.
(ii) subst.: Hadr. 7.3, ternis iam per singulos aureis se absente divisis; Marc. 11.4 (limits cost of plays), ut quinos aureos scaenici acciperent, ita tamen ut nullus editor decem aureos egrederetur; Ver. 6.5, in huius equi gratiam primum coeperunt equis aurei.... postulari. (6) in tanto autem equus ille honore fuit, ut ei a populo Prasinianorum saepe modius aureorum postularetur; Did. J. 4.6, pollicitationibus aureorum; Sept. 6.4 , septingenos vicenos aureos legatis dedit; Clod. A. 2.4, dandi stipendii usque ad tres aureos liberam potestatem; Diad. 2.1, habete ... pro imperio aureos ternos, pro Antonini nomine aureos quinos; Elag. 8.3, non nummos vel argenteos vel aureos vel bellaria vel minuta animalia; 21.3, exhibuit ... pisum cum aureis; 21.7, dedit et aureos millenos et centena pondo argenti; 22.3 (lottery prizes inc.) centum aureos et mille argenteos et centum folles aeris; 26.5, pronuntiavit iis quasi militibus ternos aureos donativum; 32.9, cum tamen omnibus meretricibus sine effectu libidinis aureos donaret; Alex. 39.6 (taxes reduced), ut qui decem aureos sub Heliogabalo praestiterant tertiam partem aurei praestarent ... tuncque primum semisses aureorum formati sunt, tunc etiam, cum ad tertiam aurei partem vectigal desidisset, tremisses; 23.8, a quodam militari centum aureos acceperat; 4.24 (salary of praeses inc.) aureos centenos; Gall. 15.2, promissis aureis vicenis et acceptis; 16.6, isdemque manum sibi osculantibus quaternos aureos sui nominis dedit; Claud. 17.7, aureos Valerianos centum quinquaginta; Aurel. 9.7, aureos Antoninianos diurnos binos; 12.1, aureos Antoninianos trecentos; Prob. 4.5, aureos Antoninianos centum; 14.2 (head-hunting), ad singulos aureos singula; Firm. 15.8, aureos Philippeos centum.

BINARIUS, double (adj.), of 'medallions'

Alex. 39.9, formas binarias (etc.) resolvi praecipit.

CENTENARIUS, hundred-times (of 'medallions')

Alex. 39.9, formas binarias (etc.) et denarias etiam atque amplius usque ad libriles quoque et centenarias.

DENARIUS, ten-times (of 'medallions'); a silver coin; a bronze coin

(1) Alex. 39.9, formas binarias (etc.) et denarias ... resolvi praecipit

(2) Commod. 16.8, congiarium dedit populo singulis denarios septingenos vicenos quinos; Pert. 15.7, congiarium dedit populo denarios centenos.

(3) Aurel. 9.7, aureos Antoninianos diurnos binos, argenteos Philippeos minutulos quinquagenos, aeris denarios centum.

ELECTRUM, gold alloyed with silver

Elag. 31.8, scobe auri porticum stravit et argenti, dolens quod non posset et electri.

ELECTRUS, ELECTRINUS, of gold-silver alloy

Alex. 25.9, Alexandri habitu nummos plurimos figuravit, et quidem electros aliquantos sed plurimos tamen aureos; 30 Tyr. 14.5, pateram electrinam, quae in medio vultum Alexandri haberet. cf. Tac. 9.3 (a capital offence) si quis auro argentum (miscuisset).

FISCUS, the imperial treasury

Frequent. But note Alex. 43-4 (quaestors' games), arcarios vero instituit, qui de arca fisci ederent munera eademque parciora.

FOLLIS, moneybag

Elag. 22.3 (lottery prizes include) centum aureos et mille argenteos et centum folles aeris.
cf. Elag. 25.2 (its only other occurrence), a kind of air-cushion.

FORMA, module, type (of coins)

Alex. 39.9 (multiple gold pieces), formas binarias, ternarias et quaternarias et denarias etiam atque amplius usque ad libriles quoque et centenarias, quas Heliogabalus invenerat, resolvi praecipit neque in usu cuiusquam versari; 39.10, dans decem vel amplius una forma. cf. 39.6-8, where formari is used of striking sub-divisions of the aureus.
(ii) 30 Tyr. 31.3, cusi sunt eius nummi aerei, aurei et argentei, quorum hodieque forma exstat apud Treviros.

LARGITIONES (plur.), 'treasury'

Also used of Hadrian and Marcus correctly, of 'imperial generosity'. But Prob. 23.2 (if there were no soldiers), annonam provincialis daret nullus, stipendia de largitionibus nulla erogarentur, aeternos thesauros haberet Romana res publica.

LARGITIONALIS, treasury official

Car. 20.2, Diocletiani denique dictum fertur, cum ei quidam largitionalis suus editionem Cari laudaret ....

LIBRA, pound (weight)

(1) Meat: Max. 4.1, constat comedisse et quadraginta libras carnis. etc.
(2) Gold and silver plate: Alex. 34.1 (cf. 41.4), ducentarum librarum argenti pondus ministerium eius numquam transiit; 44.9, in templis sane

numquam praeter quattuor aut quinque libras auri ... posuit; 30 Tyr. 32.6, lancem centum librarum argenti; Claud. 17.5, discum corymbiatum argenteum librarum viginti, etc. (ibid.); cf. 14.3, argenti in opere annua pondo quinquaginta; Aurel. 41.11, quindecim milia librarum auri ex eius liberalitate unum tenet templum; 49.9, vas argenti eius numquam triginta libras transiit.

(3) specie: Elag. 22.1 (lottery prize), decem libras auri; 23.6, fertur et promisisse phoenicem convivis vel pro ea libras auri mille; 24.3, numquam minus centum sestertiis cenavit, hoc est argenti libris triginta; Aurel. 31.8, habes trecentas auri libras de Zenobiae capsulis, habes argenti mille octingenta pondo de Palmyrenorum bonis, habes gemmas regias; 45.5, respondit, "absit ut auro fila pensentur". libra enim auri tunc libra serici fuit. cf. Sept. 6.4, septingenos vicenos aureos legatis dedit (i.e. 10 lbs gold at the 1:72 solidus standard?); Alex. 39.9-10 (gold multiples, or 'medallions'), formas binarias, ternarias et quaternarias et denarias etiam atque amplius usque ad libriles quoque et centenarias ... dans decem vel amplius una forma triginta et quinquaginta et centum dare cogeretur. (Which seems to equate libriles with quinquaginta, implying a standard of 50 gold pieces to the pound of gold: the terms aurei and solidi are both used, however). See also metallarius (below).

LIBRILIS, 1lb in weight

Gold 'medallions': Alex. 39.9 , formas binarias (etc.) usque ad libriles quoque et centenarias ...

METALLARIUS, mining official

Claud. 15.4 (part of a general's salary), tantum argenti quantum accipit curator Illyrici metallarius.

MINUTULUS, minute (adj.), a small coin

(1) of lettering: Tac. 11.8, minutulas litteras, cf. 30 Tyr. 14.5 ('signis').

(2) of coins: Aurel. 9.7, aureos Antoninianos diurnos binos, argenteos Philippeos minutulos quinquagenos, aeris denarios centum; 12.1, aureos Antoninianos trecentos, argenteos Philippeos minutulos tria milia, in aere sestertium quinquagies.

(3) Alex. 22.8 (emended), price of meat falls: ut, cum fuisset octo minutulis libra, ad duos unumque utriusque carnis libra redigeretur.

MISCERE, alloy, i.e. debase

Tac. 9.3, in eadem oratione cavit ut si quis argento publice privatimque aes miscuisset, si quis auro argentum, si quis aeri plumbum, capital esset cum bonorum proscriptione.

MONETA, the mint, coinage

(1) Alex. 39.8 (quarter-aurei), quos quidem iam formatos in moneta detinuit.

(2) Diad. 2.6, apud Antiochiam moneta Antonini Diadumeniani nomine percussa

est; Alex. 8.3 (acclamation), monetae nomen Antonini reddatur; Gall. 12.1, Odaenathum participato imperio Augustum vocavit, eiusque monetam, qua Persas captos traheret, cudi iussit; 30 Tyr. 26.2, monetam etiam cudi iussit; Firm. 2.1, dicentes illum et purpura usum et percussa moneta Augustum esse vocitatum.

MONETARIUS, moneyer

Aurel. 38.2 (cf. 3), fuit sub Aureliano etiam monetariorum bellum Felicissimo rationali auctore. (7,000 soldiers were killed in suppressing them).

NUMMUS, coin, hence 'cash'

(1) Coin, (i) base metal: Ver. 4.7, iaciebat et nummos in popinas maximos, quibus calices frangeret; Elag. 8.3, cum consulatum inisset, in populum non nummos vel argenteos vel aureos vel bellaria (etc.)... abiecit.

(ii) sesterces: Marc. 7.9, vicena milia nummum singulis ... militibus promiserunt; Pert. 15.7, praetorianis promisit duodena milia nummum, sed dedit sena.

(iii) gold and silver: Pesc. N. 10.7, iussit, ne zona milites ad bellum ituri aureos vel argenteos nummos portarent; Alex. 25.9, Alexandri habitu nummos plurimos figuravit, et quidem electros aliquantos, sed plurimos tamen aureos; 30 Tyr. 31.3, cusi sunt eius nummi aerei, aurei et argentei, quorum hodieque forma exstat apud Treviros; Firm. 2.1, dicentes illum et purpura usum et percussa moneta Augustum esse vocitatum, cum etiam nummos eius Severus Archontius protulit.

(2) Cash: Claud. 14.14, cetera ... praestabis, sed ita ut nihil adaeret, et si alicubi aliquid defuerit, non praestetur nec in nummo exigatur; Firm. 8.6, unus illis deus nummus est.

PECUNIA, money, (bronze) coin

(1) Marc. 23.2, in largitionibus pecuniae publicae parcissimus fuit; Tac. 10.1 patrimonium suum publicavit, quod habuit in reditibus, sestertium bis milies octingenties. pecuniam, quam domi collegerat, in stipendium militum vertit. etc. etc. (frequent)

(2) uniquely: Alex. 33.3, scaenicis numquam aurum, numquam argentum, vix pecuniam donavit.

PHILIPPEUS, adj. of gold/silver/bronze coins; a (gold) coin

(1) adj. (i) of gold: Firm. 15.8, ipsi dabis aureos Philippeos centum, argenteos Antoninianos mille, aeris sestertium decies.

(ii) of silver: Aurel. 9.7, aureos Antoninianos diurnos binos, argenteos Philippeos minutulos quinquagenos, aeris denarios centum; 12.1, aureos Antoninianos trecentos, argenteos Philippeos minutulos tria milia, in aere sestertium quinquagies.

(iii) in bronze: Prob. 4.5, aureos Antoninianos centum, argenteos Aurelianos mille, aereos Philippeos decem milia.

(2) a coin: Claud. 14.3, argenti in opere annua pondo quinquaginta, Philippeos nostri vultus annuos centum quinquaginta et in strenis quadraginta septem et trientes centum sexaginta. (apparently = aureus)

PLUMBUM

Tac. 9.3 (debasement a capital offence), si quis aeri plumbum (sc. miscuisset).

PONDO, by weight (librae understood)

Elag. 21.7, dedit et aureos millenos et centena pondo argenti; Alex. 42.4, ita ut praesides provinciarum acciperent argenti pondo vicena (of silver plate).

QUARTARIUS, quarter-aureus

Alex. 39.7, tuncque primum semisses aureorum formati sunt, tunc etiam, cum ad tertiam partem vectigal desidisset, tremisses, dicente Alexandro etiam quartarios futuros, quod minus non posset. quos quidem iam formatos in moneta detinuit ... conflari eos iussit et tremisses tantum solidosque formari.

QUATERNARIUS, quadruple (of 'medallions')

Alex. 39.9, formas binarias, ternarias et quaternarias (etc.) quas Heliogabalus invenerat, resolvi praecipit. cf. Gall. 16.6, isdemque manum sibi osculantibus quaternos aureos sui nominis dedit (4 aurei, not 4-aurei pieces, cf. Elag. 26.5, ternos aureos).

RADIATUS, wearing a radiate crown

Gall. 16.4, radiatus saepe processit.

SALARIUM, (cash) salary, salary in kind

(1) (cash) salary: Ant. P. 11.3, rhetoribus et philosophis per omnes provincias et honores et salaria detulit. etc.
(ii) dist. from annona: Alex. 42.3, medicus sub eo unus palatinus salarium accepit, ceterique omnes ... annonas binas aut ternas accipiebant; 44.4, rhetoribus (etc.) salaria instituit et auditoria decrevit et discipulos cum annonis pauperum filios modo ingenuos dari iussit.
(2) salary in kind: Claud. 14.3, huic salarium de nostro privato aerario dabis annuos frumenti modios tria milia (etc. etc.); Prob. 4.6 (cf. 3) item in salario diurno bubulae pondo ... (etc. etc.); Firm. 15.6 (maintenance of Gothic ladies), decretis salariis, non ut singulae acciperent, sed ut septem simul unum convivium haberent.
(ii) multiple salaria: duplex, Cl. A. 10.8, Prob. 5.8; quinquiplex, Prob. 7.4.

SALONINIANUS, adj. of a (gold) coin

Claud. 17.7, aureos Valerianos centum quinquaginta, trientes Saloninianos trecentos (letter of Gallienus).

SEMIS, half-aureus

Alex. 39.7, tuncque primum semisses aureorum formati sunt.

SESTERTIUS

Ver. 5.5, omne autem convivium aestimatum dicitur sexagies centenis milibus sestertiorum; cf. Did. J. 3.2, sane cum vicena quina milia militibus promisisset, tricena dedit; Sept. 7.6, milites per seditionem dena milia poposcerunt a senatu, exemplo eorum qui Augustum Octavianum Roman deduxerant. cf. nummus (1) (ii).

(2) a bronze coin: Aurel. 12.1, aureos Antoninianos trecentos, argenteos Philippeos minutulos tria milia, in aere sestertium quinquagies; Firm. 15.8, aureos Philippeos centum, argenteos Antoninianos mille, aeris sestertium decies.

SESTERTIUM, 100,000 HS; 1,000 HS

(1) Hadr. 3.8, cum sestertium vicies ad ludos edendos a Traiano accepit; 23.14, perdidimus quater milies sestertium quod populo et militibus pro adoptione Commodi dedimus, cf. Ael. 3.3, 6.3, sestertium ter milies (etc.); Pert. 7.6, cum tantam penuriam aerarii haberet, ut praeter decies sestertium non se invenisse fateretur; Tac. 10.1, patrimonium suum publicavit, quod habuit in reditibus, sestertium bis milies octingenties.

(2) Pert. 2.4, ad ducenum sestertiorum stipendium translatus; Sept. 5.2, qui etiam sestertia, quot nemo umquam principum, militibus dedit; Elag. 31.1, fertur et meretricem notissimam et pulcherrimam redemisse centum sestertiis eamque intactam velut virginem coluisse; 24.3, numquam minus centum sestertiis cenavit, hoc est argenti libris triginta.

SOLIDUS, solid (adj.), a gold coin

(1) Elag. 20.4, hic solido argento factos habuit lectos (etc.).

(2) Alex. 39.8 (quarter-aurei envisaged), conflari eos iussit et tremisses tantum solidosque formari; 39.10 (Elagabalus' gold multiples were melted down), cum diceret plus largiendi hanc esse imperatori causam, si, cum multos solidos minores dare possit, dans decem vel amplius una forma triginta et quinquaginta et centum dare cogeretur. cf. Sept. 6.4, septingenos vicenos aureos legatis dedit (i.e. 10 lbs gold at the 1:72 solidus standard?).

STIPENDIUM, (military) pay

Pert. 2.4, ad ducenum sestertiorum stipendium translatus in Daciam; Alex. 53.9 (the emperor), qui acceptam a provincialibus annonam, qui vestem, qui stipendia vobis adtribuit; Aurel. 7.6, stipendium in balteo, non in popina habeat; Tac. 9.1, stipendium et donativum ex more promisit; but cf. Clod. A. 2.4 (accession donative as Caesar), habebis... dandi stipendii usque ad tres aureos liberam potestatem. etc. etc.

TERNARIUS, triple (adj.), of gold 'medallions'

Alex. 39.9, formas binarias, ternarias et quaternarias (etc.) resolvi praecipit. cf. Elag. 26.5, ternos aureos (3 aurei, not 3-aurei pieces).

TREMIS, third-aureus

Alex. 39.7, cum ad tertiam aurei partem vectigal desidisset, tremisses (sc. formati sunt), dicente Alexandro etiam quartarios futuros, quod minus non posset.

TRIENS, third-aureus(?)

Claud. 14.3, argenti in opere annua pondo quinquaginta, Philippeos nostri vultus annuos centum quinquaginta et in strenis quadraginta septem et trientes centum sexaginta; 17.7, aureos Valerianos centum quinquaginta, trientes Saloninianos trecentos.

VALERIANUS, adj. (of aurei)

Claud. 17.7 (letter of Gallienus), aureos Valerianos centum quinquaginta, trientes Saloninianos trecentos.

PARTICIPANTS

Dr. P. Bastien
R. D. I. Box 80A
Cranbury, N.J. 08512
U.S.A.

R. F. Bland Esq.
Dept. of Coins and Medals
British Museum
London WC1 3DG

Dr. A. K. Bowman
Christ Church
Oxford

Mlle. C. Brenot
Cabinet des Médailles
Bibliothèque Nationale
58 rue de Richelieu
Paris 75084-02
France

Professor Patrick Bruun
Furuvaegen 32 B2
20540 Turku 54
Finland

Professor J. P. Callu
Institut de Latin
Université de Paris X
Nanterre 92001
France

G. L. Duncan Esq.
Dept of Archaeology
31-34 Gordon Square
London WC1H 0PY

Professor K. Hopkins
Dept. of Sociology
Brunel University
Uxbridge,
Middlesex

Dr. C. E. King
Heberden Coin Room
Ashmolean Museum
Oxford

Dr. C. M. Kraay
Keeper
Heberden Coin Room
Ashmolean Museum
Oxford

Dr. J. F. Matthews
Queen's College
Oxford

Professor F. G. B. Millar
Dept. of History,
University College,
London

O. Nicholson, Esq.
Wolfson College
Oxford

Dr. R. S. O. Tomlin
Wolfson College
Oxford

D. R. Walker Esq.
General Editor,
British Archaeological Reports
122 Banbury Road
Oxford

C. R. Whittaker, Esq.
Churchill College
Cambridge

www.ingramcontent.com/pod-product-compliance
Ingram Content Group UK Ltd.
Pitfield, Milton Keynes, MK11 3LW, UK
UKHW061157081026
15591UKWH00034B/930

9 780860 540847